CONTROL AND
DYNAMIC SYSTEMS

*Advances in Theory
and Applications*

Volume 22

CONTRIBUTORS TO THIS VOLUME

BRIAN D. O. ANDERSON
D. BENSOUSSAN
DAVID A. CASTANON
ALBERT B. CHAMMAS
E. J. DAVISON
YOUSRI M. EL-FATTAH
BENJAMIN FRIEDLANDER
P. P. GROUMPOS
FARHAD KIANFAR
JOHN B. MOORE
Ü. ÖZGÜNER
NILS R. SANDELL, JR.
R. E. SKELTON
DEMOSTHENIS TENEKETZIS
A. YOUSUFF
G. ZAMES

CONTROL AND DYNAMIC SYSTEMS

ADVANCES IN THEORY AND APPLICATIONS

Edited by
C. T. LEONDES

School of Engineering and Applied Sciences
University of California
Los Angeles, California

VOLUME 22: DECENTRALIZED/DISTRIBUTED CONTROL AND DYNAMIC SYSTEMS
Part 1 of 3

1985

ACADEMIC PRESS, INC.
(Harcourt Brace Jovanovich, Publishers)

Orlando San Diego New York London
Toronto Montreal Sydney Tokyo

ACADEMIC PRESS RAPID MANUSCRIPT REPRODUCTION

ACADEMIC PRESS, INC.
Orlando, Florida 32887

United Kingdom Edition published by
ACADEMIC PRESS INC. (LONDON) LTD.
24–28 Oval Road, London NW1 7DX

LIBRARY OF CONGRESS CATALOG CARD NUMBER: 64-8027

ISBN: 0-12-012722-9

PRINTED IN THE UNITED STATES OF AMERICA

85 86 87 88 9 8 7 6 5 4 3 2 1

CONTENTS

Learning Automata in Distributed Control Systems

Yousri M. El-Fattah

Covariance Equivalent Realizations with Application to Model Reduction of Large-Scale Systems

A. Yousuff and R. E. Skelton

Decentralized Estimation and Control of One-Way Connected Subsystems

Farhad Kianfar

Multivariable Feedback and Decentralized Control

G. Zames and D. Bensoussan

CONTRIBUTORS

Numbers in parentheses indicate the pages on which the authors' contributions begin.

Brian D. O. Anderson (85), *Department of Systems Engineering, Institute of Advanced Studies, Australian National University, Canberra, Australia*

D. Bensoussan (373), *Department of Electrical Engineering, McGill University, Montreal, Quebec H3A 2A7, Canada*

David A. Castanon (1), *Alphatech, Inc., Burlington, Massachusetts 01803*

Albert B. Chammas (47), *Northrop Corporation, Electro-Mechanical Division, Anaheim, California 92801*

E. J. Davison (195), *Department of Electrical Engineering, University of Toronto, Toronto, Ontario, M5S 1A4, Canada*

Yousri M. El-Fattah (233), *Faculty of Sciences, University of Mohamed V, Rabat, Morocco*

Benjamin Friedlander (165), *Systems Control Technology, Inc., Palo Alto, California 94304*

P. P. Groumpos (117), *Energy Research Center, Department of Electrical Engineering, Cleveland State University, Cleveland, Ohio 44115*

Farhad Kianfar (349), *Industrial and Manufacturing Engineering Department, California State Polytechnic University, Pomona, California 91766*

John B. Moore (85), *Department of Systems Engineering, Institute of Advanced Studies, Australian National University, Canberra, Australia*

Ü. Özgüner (195), *Department of Electrical Engineering, The Ohio State University, Columbus, Ohio 43210*

Nils R. Sandell, Jr. (1), *Alphatech, Inc., Burlington, Massachusetts 01803*

R. E. Skelton (273), *School of Aeronautics and Astronautics, Purdue University, W. Lafayette, Indiana 47907*

Demosthenis Teneketzis (1), *Alphatech, Inc., Burlington, Massachusetts 01803*

A. Yousuff[1] (273), *School of Aeronautics and Astronautics, Purdue University, W. Lafayette, Indiana 47907*

G. Zames (373), *Department of Electrical Engineering, McGill University, Montreal, Quebec H3A 2A7, Canada*

[1]Present address: *Department of Mechanical Engineering and Mechanics, Drexel University, Philadelphia, Pennsylvania 19104.*

PREFACE

The theme for Volume 22 deals with advances in techniques for the analysis and synthesis of decentralized or distributed control and dynamic systems. The subject of decentralized but coordinated systems is emerging as a major issue in industrial and aerospace systems, and so this is a most appropriate theme for this series at this time. As this volume crystallized, there was so much material of basic value that it has grown to three very substantive volumes in this series; this theme, therefore, will be treated in this volume and continued in the next two.

These three volumes thus comprise the most comprehensive treatment of the theory of this broad and complex subject and its many applications to date. It is in the various complex "real world" applications that many practitioners may find these two volumes particularly useful. This includes the chapters on the many computational issues and techniques appearing in the textbook literature for the first time.

The first chapter in this volume, "Distributed Estimation for Large-Scale Event-Driven Systems," by Teneketzis, Castanon, and Sandell constitutes a unique presentation in the textbook literature of the extensive efforts over a number of years of the fundamentally important work conducted by the coauthors and their associates integated with works of others. In Chapter 2, "Decentralized Control of Discrete Time Linear Systems with Incomplete Information," Chammas presents fundamentally important results and techniques which decentralized control systems often face due to the fact that the individual systems in a collection or set of decentralized control systems do not "have the whole picture"; or, in other words, their information is of necessity somewhat incomplete and their performance must be optimal in some sense. In Chapter 3, "Decentralized Control Using Time-Varying Feedback," Anderson and Moore present their virtually unique work on the international scene on several fundamentally important issues in controllability and observability for decentralized control systems and their implications. In Chapter 4, "Structural Dynamic Hierarchical Stabilization and Control of Large-Scale Systems," P. P. Groumpos presents some essential and powerful techniques for stabilization and control of decentralized systems, and in so doing addresses a wide variety of issues including inexact knowledge of the system, system sensitivity, critical parameters, and a host of other fundamental issues. The decentralized design of decentralized controllers is another fundamentally important issue addressed in Chapter 5 by Friedlander. In Chapter 6, "Decentralized Control Using Local Models for Large-Scale Systems," Davison and Özgüner present fundamental techniques for control of decentralized systems when, as is often the case, it is difficult or virtually impossible to have an overall knowledge of the system or system models. The potentially highly useful avenue of learning automata in distributed control systems for treating the decentralized control system problem is treated in the chapter by El-Fattah. Model reduction is often an essential technique in the control of decentralized systems, and is treated in comprehensive manner in Chapter 8, "Covariance Equivalent Realizations with Application to Model Reductions of Large-Scale Systems," by Yousuff and Skelton.

In Chapter 9, "Decentralized Estimation and Control of One-Way Connected Subsystems," Kianfar treats the stochastic filtering and control problem in decentralized systems and presents a number of essential techniques. In the concluding chapter, "Multivariable Feedback and Decentralized Control," Zames and Bensoussan present many fundamental results extending multivariable theory from conventional control systems to the highly challenging problems of decentralized control.

When the theme for this volume was decided upon, there seemed little doubt that it was most timely. However, because of the substantially important contributions of the authors to this and the next two volumes, all volumes promise to be not only timely but of substantial lasting value.

CONTENTS OF PREVIOUS VOLUMES

Volume 4

Volume 5

Volume 6

Volume 7

Volume 8

Volume 9

Volume 10

Volume 14

Volume 15

Volume 19

Volume 20

Volume 21

Distributed Estimation for Large-Scale Event-Driven Systems

DEMOSTHENIS TENEKETZIS
Department of Electrical Engineering and Computer Science
University of Michigan
Ann Arbor, Michigan

DAVID A. CASTANON

NILS R. SANDELL, JR.
ALPHATECH, Inc.
Burlington, Massachusetts

I. INTRODUCTION

Classical statistical estimation theory [1,2] has been developed under the assumption that all observations are available in a central location for computation of estimates. In recent years, however, there has been an increasing interest in distributed estimation systems [3,4,20]. This interest has been sparked by such application areas as power systems and military surveillance systems, where because of considerations such as

ISBN 0-12-012722-9

cost, reliability, survivability, communication bandwidth, compartmentalization, or even problems caused by flooding a central processor with more information than it can process, there is never centralization of information in practice. Thus, extensions are needed to the classical estimation theory if it is to be relevant to the design of distributed estimation systems.

This paper is concerned with distributed estimation theory for dynamic stochastic systems. To bring into mathematical focus the issues arising from the absence of centralized information, we consider the class of event-driven stochastic dynamic systems. These are *hybrid state systems* whose state consists of a discrete component and a continuous component, where the transitions between the discrete components of the state correspond to the occurrence of the events. The evolution of the events in time is modeled by a Markov chain; the states of the Markov chain influence the dynamics of a linear stochastic system which models the evolution of the continuous components of the state. The distributed estimation problem is to estimate the hybrid state using noise corrupted, distributed observations.

The absence of a centralized estimator creates a multitude of conceptual problems and new technical issues that must be addressed. The distributed nature of event estimation necessitates the consideration of the structure or architecture of information flow among the *estimation agents*; in addition, it may require the presence of *coordination agents* who process information obtained from other agents, rather than directly from the system.

In this paper we examine two different structures for distributed event estimation: (1) *hierarchical structures* and (2) *decentralized structures*. Such structures are illustrated in Figs. 1 and 2.

The hierarchical estimation structure that we consider has multiple local estimation agents with different information. Each agent computes local estimates which are communicated in full or in part to a coordinating agent who processes the local estimate to form a final estimate. Since each local estimation agent has different information, their estimates may be conflicting. Various issues arise in such a situation: How does the coordinator combine the received messages? What is the quality of the coordinator's estimate? How does the quality of the coordinator's estimate depend on the amount of information transmitted by the local observation agents?

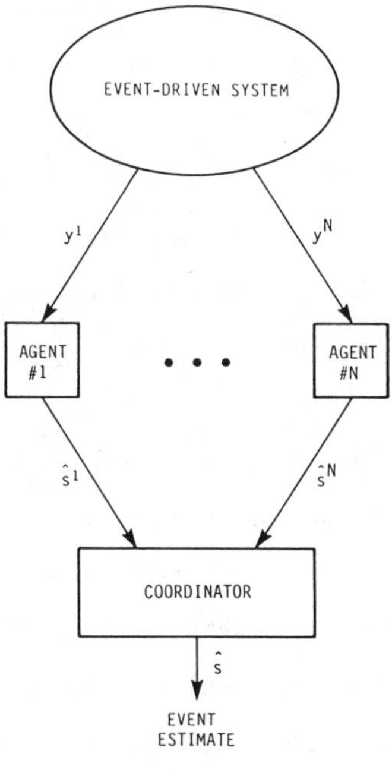

Fig. 1. Hierarchical event-estimation structure.

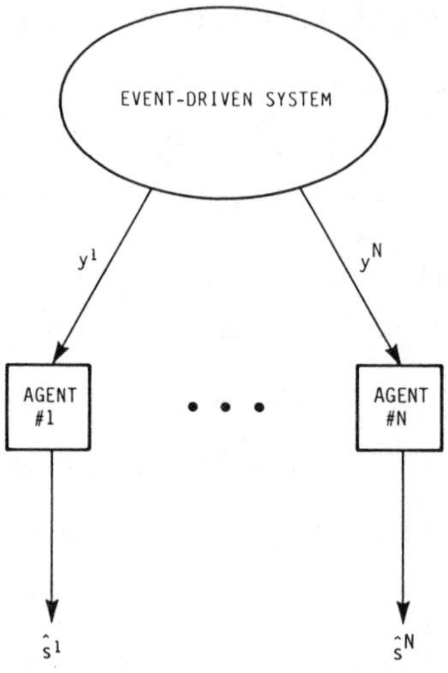

Fig. 2. Decentralized event-estimation structure.

We study these issues by considering two specific patterns of communication between the coordinator and the local observation agents. Under the first pattern of communication the local observation agents transmit full sufficient statistics of their information to the coordinator. Under the second pattern of communication each local observation agent transmits only his discrete state estimate (i.e., his estimate of which event has occurred). These two information patterns represent extreme cases of unlimited and very limited communication and highlight the problems faced by the coordinator in a hierarchical estimation structure.

The decentralized estimation structure that we consider also has local estimation agents with different information. However, these agents do not communicate with each other and there is no coordination agent, so the only interaction among agents is through their common objective. Various issues arise within this structure: What are the agents' optimal estimation rules? How is the interaction through the objective reflected in these rules? How do they relate to the optimal centralized estimation rules?

We investigate these issues by studying two specific problems which are generalizations of classical centralized problems: (1) the decentralized Wald problem and (2) the decentralized quickest detection problem. In the decentralized Wald problem one of two possible events impacts the system and the observation agents attempt to identify the event using costly observations; in the decentralized quickest detection problem there is one transition between the two possible events that impact the system and the observation agents attempt to detect the time of this transition as accurately as possible. Both problems are among the simplest decentralized estimation problems for event-driven systems. However, they highlight all the issues raised above and show that these problems are subtle and complicated.

The rest of the paper is organized as follows. In Section II we define the class of event-driven dynamical systems that we will investigate, and motivate the consideration of these systems. In Section III we develop estimation algorithms for two specific hierarchical estimation structures. In Section IV we formulate and solve two estimation problems under the decentralized information structure. Section V presents a concluding discussion.

II. EVENT-DRIVEN DYNAMICAL SYSTEMS

In this section we present a mathematical model which describes the evolution in time of events that impact a system, the dynamics of this system, and the observations of the system

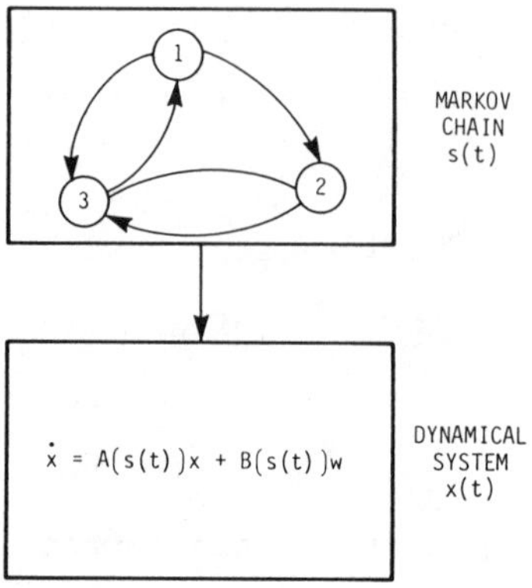

Fig. 3. Event-driven dynamical system.

state made by a set of distributed agents. The basic idea is to model the events that occur in terms of the state transitions of a Markov chain. The model of the system dynamics and observations is then parametrized by the state of this chain (Fig. 3).

The evolution of the events that can occur is modeled by a finite state Markov chain with state s(t) that takes the values 1, 2, ..., K, has initial (prior) probabilities

$$\pi^i = \text{Prob}\{s(0) = i\} \tag{1}$$

and transition probabilities

$$q(i, j) = \text{Prob}\{s(t + 1) = j | s(t) = i\}. \tag{2}$$

The continuous-state dynamic system is described by a vector stochastic difference equation of the form

$$x(t + 1) = A(s(t))x(t) + b(s(t)) + w(t), \tag{3}$$

where

$$x(t), w(t), b(s(t)) \in \mathscr{R}^n, \tag{4}$$

$$A(s(t)) \in \mathscr{R}^n \times \mathscr{R}^n, \tag{5}$$

and w(t) is zero-mean Gaussian random vector with covariance matrix

$$E\{w(t)w^T(s)\} = W\delta(t - s), \tag{6}$$

and where $\delta(t - s)$ denotes the Kronecker delta function.

The observations for the N distributed agents are modeled by equations of the form

$$y^i(t) = C^i(s(t))x(t) + d^i(s(t)) + v^i(t), \tag{7}$$

where the superscript i indicates the ith agent and where

$$y^i(t),\ d^i(t),\ v^i(t) \in \mathscr{R}^{p_i} \tag{8}$$

$$C^i(s(t)) \in \mathscr{R}^{p_i} \times \mathscr{R}^n. \tag{9}$$

The vector $v^i(t)$ is a zero-mean Gaussian vector modeling the observation uncertainty of the ith agent and has covariance matrix

$$E\{v^i(t)(v^i(\tau))^T\} = V^i\delta(t - \tau). \tag{10}$$

The random vectors $v^i(t)$, $v^j(u)$, and $w(s)$ are assumed independent of each other and of $x(0)$, $s(0)$ for all $i \neq j$ and all values of t, u, s.

Equations (3) and (7) show that the impact of an event can occur in two ways: It can affect the system and the observation structure via the system and observation matrices A and C, respectively, or it can affect the input or bias terms via the vectors b and d, respectively. In the latter case, we say that the event has *additive effects* on the system dynamics and the observations. In the former case, we say that the events have *multiplicative effects* on the system dynamics and the observations. Algorithms for hybrid state estimation are considerably simpler in the additive case.

The mathematical model defined by the preceding equations can be readily extended to include discrete-valued measurements and feedback from the continuous to the discrete portion of the system. However, these extensions complicate the solution of the estimation problems that are defined in terms of the model and will not be considered in the sequel.

Event-driven or hybrid-state dynamical systems have been studied explicitly in the context of power system dynamics [5] and military surveillance systems [6,7]. Special simulation languages have been devised to handle combined continuous-discrete state systems [8]. Buslenko [21] has introduced a similar model termed an *aggregat* that has been extensively studied in the Russian literature. These systems are of considerable interest since a wide variety of engineering problems can be mathematically modeled using event-driven dynamical systems, as illustrated by the following examples.

Example 1. Interconnected power systems. The linearized dynamics of an interconnected power system can be represented by equations of the form [5]

$$\dot{x}_j(t) = A_{jj}x_j(t) + \sum_{k\neq j} A_{jk}x_k(t),$$

where $x_j(t)$ is the state vector of the jth generator (including its prime mover) of the system. The matrix A_{jk} depends upon the impedance of the transmission network interconnecting generators j and k. The opening of a circuit breaker protecting one of the lines of the network will change the value of this impedance. Thus, if s(t) denotes the state of these circuit breakers, then

$$A_{jk} = A_{jk}(s(t)).$$

If s(t) is modeled as the state of the Markov chain, then an event-driven dynamical system as defined above (albeit in continuous time) is obtained, in which the events correspond to switching in and out of transmission lines.

Example 2. Multitarget tracking. State space models of the form given by Eqs. (3) through (10) (without the s(t) dependence) are often used for tracking filter design. In a dense target environment, the problem of data association, i.e., of determining from which target a given observation comes, must be solved along with the usual tracking problem of estimating the target state from noise-corrupted observations.

To see how the combined tracking/data association problem can be modeled, consider a simple single observation agent case in which there are two targets from which exactly two observations come every sampling period. The data association process is modeled via a two-state Markov chain with

$$s(t) = \begin{cases} 1 & \text{observation 1 comes from target 1,} \\ 2 & \text{observation 1 comes from target 2,} \end{cases}$$

and with

$$\begin{bmatrix} y_1(t) \\ y_2(t) \end{bmatrix} = C(s(t)) \begin{bmatrix} x_1(t) \\ x_2(t) \end{bmatrix} + v(t),$$

where y_i = observation i, $x_i(t)$ = state vector of target i, and

$$C(s) = \begin{cases} \begin{bmatrix} C_{11} & 0 \\ 0 & C_{22} \end{bmatrix}, & s = 1 \\ \begin{bmatrix} 0 & C_{12} \\ C_{21} & 0 \end{bmatrix}, & s = 2 \end{cases}.$$

If there are not correlations in the data association from sample to sample, we can take

$$\pi^i \equiv \frac{1}{2}, \quad q(i, j) = \frac{1}{2}.$$

In this example, computing the estimate of the discrete state provides the solution of the data association problem, while computing the estimate of the continuous state solves the tracking problem of determining the position and velocity of the various targets.

Our description of event-driven dynamical systems and of the motivation for their study is now complete. In the rest of the paper we shall discuss distributed estimation problems for these systems. We consider two classes of estimation structures: Hierarchical estimation structures and decentralized estimation structures.

III. HIERARCHICAL ESTIMATION STRUCTURES

A. *INTRODUCTION*

A hierarchical structure for distributed estimation is shown in Fig. 1. Each agent has access to uncertain observations of the state and then transmits the result of his processing to the coordinator. The coordinator receives these messages and computes a (full or partial) state estimate.

The quality of the coordinator's estimate depends on the amount and quality of information transmitted to the coordinator by the observation agents. In the following subsections, we develop optimal and suboptimal algorithms for producing the coordinator's estimate for different levels of observation agent communications.

B. *OPTIMAL HIERARCHICAL ESTIMATION STRUCTURE*

Consider the following communication pattern for the hierarchical estimation structure of Fig. 1.

(C.1) At each time t, each local agent communicates sufficient statistics representing the conditional probability distribution of the state at time t, given his information up to time t.

Our objective is to derive the optimal algorithm which the coordinator should use to combine the local sufficient statistics. For a clear exposition, we will consider two cases:

Case 1. Static event structure: $q(i, j) = 0$ for $i \neq j$, that is, $s(t) = s(0)$ for all t.

Case 2. Dynamic event structure: All other cases.

Denote the overall state of the event-driven dynamical system at time t as $(s(t), x(t))$. In case 1, the conditional density of the state at each local observation agent i can be summarized by a fixed-dimension on-line sufficient statistic, which is

$$G^i(t) = \begin{bmatrix} P^{i1}(t) \\ \vdots \\ P^{iK}(t) \\ x^{i1}(t) \\ \vdots \\ x^{iK}(t) \end{bmatrix}, \tag{11}$$

where $P^{ik}(t)$ is the conditional probability that $s(t) = k$ given $Y^i(t)$,

$$Y^i(t) \triangleq \{(y^i(1), y^i(2), \ldots, y^i(t))\}, \tag{12}$$

and

$$x^{ik}(t) = E\{x(t) \mid Y^i(t), s(t) = k\}. \tag{13}$$

The conditional density of the state for agent i given $Y^i(t)$

can be written as

$$p(x(t), k \mid Y^i(t))$$

$$= p^{ik}(t) \frac{1}{(2\pi)^{n/2}|\det \Sigma^{ik}(t)|^{1/2}} \tag{14}$$

$$\times \exp\{-(1/2)(x(t) - x^{ik}(t))^T \Sigma^{ik}(t)^{-1}(x(t) - x^{ik}(t))\},$$

where

$$\Sigma^{ik}(t) = E\{(x(t) - x^{ik}(t))$$

$$\times (x(t) - x^{ik}(t))^T \mid Y^i(t), s(t) = k\} \tag{15}$$

can be computed a priori from the parameters of Eqs. (1) through (10). For each k, the estimate $x^{ik}(t)$ is generated by a Kalman filter with parameters $b(k)$, $C^i(k)$, $d^i(k)$, assuming that $s(t) = k$ for all t. The covariance of this estimate, Σ^{ik}, is derived from these parameters. Thus, the local processing of agent i consists of a bank of K parallel Kalman filters generating $x^{ik}(t)$, whose outputs are used to compute the probabilities $p^{ik}(t)$ as follows [10]: Define the one-step predicted estimate $\overline{x}^{ik}(t)$ and covariance $M^{ik}(t)$ given $s(t) = k$ as

$$\overline{x}^{ik}(t) = A(k)x^{ik}(t - 1) + b(k) \tag{16}$$

$$M^{ik}(t) = A(k)\Sigma^{ik}(t - 1)A^T(k) + W. \tag{17}$$

The weighted square of residuals for agent i when $s(t) = k$ is given by $r^{ik}(t)$, where

$$r^{ik}(t) = (y^i(t) - C^i(k)\overline{x}^{ik}(t) - d^i(k))^T$$

$$\times (C^i(k)M^{ik}(t)C^i(k)^T + V^i)^{-1} \tag{18}$$

$$\times (y^i(t) - C^i(k)\overline{x}^{ik}(t) - d^i(k)).$$

Let

$$B^{ik}(t) = (2\pi^{pi}|\det(C^i(k)M^{ik}(t)C^i(k)^T + V^i)|)^{-1/2}. \tag{19}$$

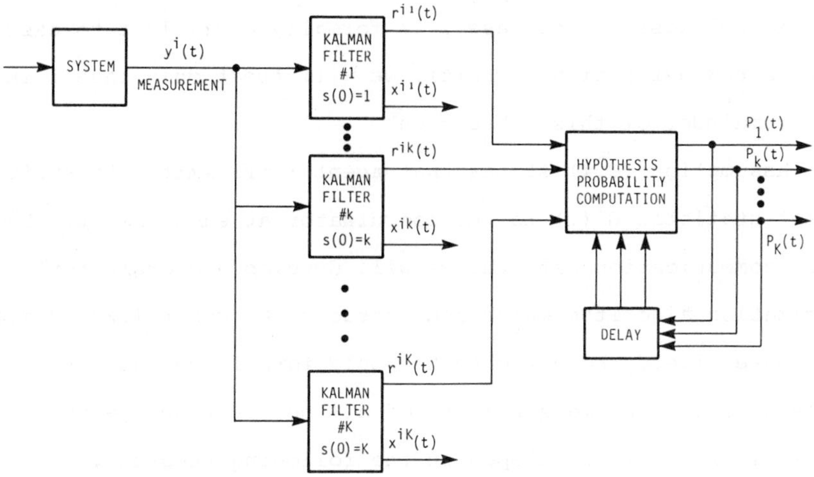

Fig. 4. Local processing algorithm for agent i.

Then, $P^{ik}(t)$ is obtained recursively by agent i using the outputs of the bank of Kalman filters, as

$$P^{ik}(t) = \frac{P^{ik}(t-1)B^{ik}(t)\exp\left(-\frac{1}{2}r^{ik}(t)\right)}{\sum_{l=1}^{K} B^{il}(t)\exp\left(-\frac{1}{2}r^{il}(t)\right)}. \tag{20}$$

The local processing algorithm for agent i is illustrated in Fig. 4.

In case 2, a similar sufficient statistic can be determined. However, this statistic must be based on the history of events S(t), defined as

$$S(t) = \{s(0), s(1), \ldots, s(t)\},$$

with values in $\{1, \ldots, K\}^t$. Equations (11) through (15) apply with this new definition of S(t), with values from 1 to K^t. Note that, in this case, the dimension of the sufficient statistics grows with t, so that suboptimal processing rules are essential to deal with the exponentially growing cardinality of S(t).

Nonetheless, since case 2 is formally equivalent to case 1 with a new definition for s(t), we will treat only case 1 in the remainder of this subsection.

Assumption (C.1) states that agent i transmits its sufficient statistic $G^i(t)$ to the coordinator at each time t. Under this communication pattern, we will develop a coordinator's estimation algorithm which reconstructs the centralized state estimate (i.e., the estimate he would form if he had direct access to all the measurements of all observation agents). This algorithm is developed in the following theorems.

Theorem 1. Let $x^k(t)$ denote the centralized estimate of x(t) given $\{Y^1(t), \ldots, Y^N(t)\}$ assuming that $s(0) = s(t) = k$. Then,

$$x^k(t) = \sum_{i=1}^{N} \Sigma^k(t)(\Sigma^{ik}(t)^{-1}x^{ik}(t) - M^{ik}(t)^{-1}\overline{x}^{ik}(t)) + \Sigma^k(t)M^k(t)^{-1}\overline{x}^k(t), \tag{21}$$

where

$$\overline{x}^k(t + 1) = A(k)x^k(t) + b(k) \tag{22a}$$

$$M^k(t + 1) = A(k)\Sigma^k(t)A^T(k) + W \tag{22b}$$

$$\Sigma^k(t) = \left[\sum_{i=1}^{N} (\Sigma^{ik}(t)^{-1} - M^{ik}(t)^{-1}) + M^k(t)^{-1}\right]^{-1} \tag{22c}$$

$$\overline{x}^{ik}(t + 1) = A(k)x^{ik}(t) + b(k), \tag{22d}$$

and $\Sigma^k(k)$, $M^k(t)$ are the updated and predicted centralized error covariances.

Proof. The proof is adapted from [11]. The equations for optimal estimation in linear Gaussian systems yield

$$\Sigma^k(t)^{-1} = M^k(t)^{-1} + \sum_{i=1}^{N} C^i(k)^T (V^i)^{-1} C^i(k) \tag{23}$$

$$\Sigma^{ik}(t)^{-1} = M^{ik}(t)^{-1} + C^i(k)^T (V^i)^{-1} C^i(k) \tag{24}$$

$$\begin{aligned} x^k(t) &= \bar{x}^k(t) \\ &\quad + \Sigma^k(t) \sum_{i=1}^{N} C^i(k)^T (V^i)^{-1} \\ &\quad \times (y^i(t) - C^i(k)\bar{x}^k(t) - d^i(k)) \end{aligned} \tag{25}$$

$$\begin{aligned} x^{ik}(t) &= \bar{x}^{ik}(t) \\ &\quad + \Sigma^{ik}(t) C^i(k)^T (V^i)^{-1} \\ &\quad \times (y^i(t) - C^i(k)\bar{x}^{ik}(t) - d^i(k)) \end{aligned} \tag{26}$$

using the independence of the random vectors $v^i(t)$, $v^j(t)$, for $i \neq j$. Equations (26) and (24) imply

$$\begin{aligned} \Sigma^{ik}(t)^{-1} x^{ik}(t) &= M^{ik}(t)^{-1} \bar{x}^{ik}(t) \\ &\quad + C^i(k)^T (V^i)^{-1} (y^i(t) - d^i(k)). \end{aligned} \tag{27}$$

A similar combination of Eqs. (23) and (25) yields

$$\begin{aligned} \Sigma^k(t)^{-1} x^k(t) &= M^k(t)^{-1} \bar{x}^k(t) \\ &\quad + \sum_{i=1}^{N} C^i(k)^T (V^i)^{-1} (y^i(t) - d^i(k)). \end{aligned} \tag{28}$$

Equation (21) follows directly from Eqs. (27) and (28).

Theorem 1 establishes the relationship between the local conditional means $x^{ik}(t)$ and the centralized conditional mean $x^k(t)$, assuming that $s(t) = k$. In the next two results, we develop similar relationships for the overall conditional distribution of the state $(x(t), s(t))$.

Theorem 2. Let $Y(t) = \{Y^1(t), \ldots, Y^N(t)\}$. Let $p(x(t), k \mid Y(t))$ denote the centralized conditional density of $(x(t), s(t))$ given $Y(t)$, and $p(x(t), k \mid Y^i(t))$ denote the local conditional density of $(x(t), s(t))$ of agent i. Then

$$p[x(t), k \mid Y(t)] = C\left(\frac{\prod_{i=1}^{N} p(x(t), k \mid Y^i(t))}{\prod_{i=1}^{N} p(x(t), k \mid Y^i(t-1))}\right) p(x(t), k \mid Y(t-1)), \quad (29)$$

where C is a normalizing constant, independent of x or k.

Proof. We will sketch the logic of the proof here. A rigorous proof appears in [12].

From Bayes' rule,

$$p(x(t), k \mid Y(t)) = \frac{p(y^1(t), \ldots, y^N(t) \mid x(t), k, Y(t-1))\,p(x(t), k \mid Y(t-1))}{p(y^1(t), \ldots, y^N(t) \mid Y(t-1))}$$

$$= \prod_{i=1}^{N} p(y^i(t) \mid x(t), k)\ \frac{p(x(t), k \mid Y(t-1))}{p(y^1(t), \ldots, y^N(t) \mid Y(t-1))} \quad (30)$$

because of the conditional independence of $y^i(t)$ and $y^j(t)$ given $x(t)$, k. Similarly,

$$p(x(t), k \mid Y^i(t)) = p(y^i(t) \mid x(t), k)\ \frac{p(x(t), k \mid Y^i(t-1))}{p(y^i(t) \mid Y^i(t-1))}. \quad (31)$$

Combining Eqs. (30) and (31) proves the theorem.

Corollary 1. Let $P^k(t)$ denote the centralized conditional probability that $s(t) = k$, given $Y(t)$. Then,

$$P^k(t) = \frac{Q^k(t)}{\sum_{j=1}^{K} Q^j(t)}, \quad (32)$$

where

$$Q^k(t) = \prod_{i=1}^{N}\left(\frac{P^{ik}(t)}{P^{ik}(t-1)}\left|\frac{\det M^{ik}(t)}{\det \Sigma^{ik}(t)}\right|^{1/2}\right)P^k(t)\left|\frac{\det \Sigma^k(t)}{\det M^k(t)}\right|^{1/2}$$

$$\times \exp\left\{-\frac{1}{2}\sum_{i=1}^{N}[x^{ik}(t)^T\Sigma^{ik}(t)^{-1}x^{ik}(t) - \bar{x}^{ik}(t)^T M^{ik}(t)^{-1}\bar{x}^{ik}(t)]\right\}$$
$$\times \exp\left\{-\frac{1}{2}[\bar{x}^k(t)M^k(t)^{-1}\bar{x}^k(t) - x^k(t)^T\Sigma^k(t)^{-1}x^k(t)]\right\}. \tag{33}$$

Proof. The corollary is an application of the results of Theorem 2, using the Gaussian densities of Eq. (14) and the relationships described in Theorem 1. For a complete proof, see [12].

Theorem 1 and Corollary 1 describe the coordinator's optimal algorithm. From the statistics $x^{ik}(t)$, the statistics $\bar{x}^{ik}(t+1)$, $x^k(t)$, and $\bar{x}^k(t+1)$ are computed using Eqs. (22), (16), and (17), respectively. Then, using $P^{ik}(t)$, $x^{ik}(t)$, $x^{ik}(t)$, $\bar{x}^{ik}(t)$, and $\bar{x}^k(t)$, the remaining centralized sufficient statistics, $P^k(t)$, are computed using Eqs. (32) and (33). Hence, this algorithm permits the coordinator to reconstruct the centralized sufficient statistics of the distribution $p(x(t), k \mid Y(t))$ from the communications $G^1(t), \ldots, G^N(t)$ at each time step.

One important feature of the hierarchical estimation problem presented above is that there is need for continuous communication between the coordinator and the local processors if we want the coordinator to achieve the centralized state estimate. This feature is in contrast with the results of hierarchical estimation for linear Gaussian systems in [11] and [13], where the reconstruction of the centralized conditional distribution of the state at any time t can be accomplished using only communications at that time. However, the results presented here suggest suboptimal solutions when the frequency of communications between the coordinator and the observation agents is limited as suggested in [12].

An important area of application for these results is the design of distributed multiobject tracking algorithms. As noted in Section II, multiobject tracking problems can be formulated as estimation problems for event-driven systems with dynamic events. Hence, the algorithm described in this subsection provides the basic theory for combining the estimates of distributed multiobject trackers. However, the design of practical multiobject tracking algorithms must incorporate several heuristic procedures to compensate for the exponential growth in the cardinality of the event space. Additional research is necessary to understand the effects of these procedures, and to design efficient procedures for combining distributed multiobject tracking estimates.

So far we developed the optimal estimation algorithm for a coordinator operating within a hierarchical estimation structure where observation agents transmit sufficient statistics of their information to the coordinator. In the next subsection we consider the coordinator's problem within a hierarchical estimation structure where there is limited communication between the coordinator and the observation agents.

C. HIERARCHICAL ESTIMATION WITH LIMITED COMMUNICATIONS

Consider again the system of Fig. 1 where the event-driven dynamical system is described by Eqs. (1) through (6) and the observations of the agents are described by Eqs. (7) through

(10). Without loss of generality in the theoretical if not practical development, we consider only the case of static event structure, as in the previous subsection.

We assume now that based on their measurements the observation agents report the event they judge most likely (i.e., the event with the maximum a posteriori probability) to the coordinator. The coordinator has to choose the event that minimizes the average probability of error associated with his decision. Contrary to the situations considered in Section III,B the reports of the observation agents to the coordinator are not sufficient statistics of their information; hence, the coordinator cannot reconstruct the centralized estimate of the state of the event-driven system. Moreover, the reports the coordinator receives from the observation agents may be conflicting with each other. Consequently, the coordinator is faced with the problem of combining the agents' estimates to produce his own estimate.

In this subsection we will briefly discuss the optimal algorithm for the consideration of this hierarchical estimation problem with limited communications; then we will propose a suboptimal estimation algorithm for the coordinator and illustrate its features with a simple example. For a complete treatment of the hierarchical estimation problem with limited communication, the reader should refer to [14].

We thus consider the hierarchical event estimation problem with limited communication under the following communication pattern:

(C.2) Based on his measurements each observation agent selects the event with the maximum *a posteriori probability* (MAP) and reports it to the coordinator.

Let $\{s^i(\tau), \tau \leq t, i = 1, 2, \ldots, N\}$ be the messages the coordinator has received from the local agents up until time t. The message $s^i(t)$ denotes the MAP estimate of agent i at time t. Let s be the value of the event for all times t. Using Bayes' rule, we obtain

$$\begin{aligned} p(s(t) &= k \mid s^i(t), t \leq t, i = 1, \ldots, N) \\ &= Cp(s(t) = k)p(s^1(1), \ldots, s^1(t), \\ &\qquad s^2(1), \ldots, s^N(t) \mid s(t) = k), \end{aligned} \tag{34}$$

where C is a constant independent of k. Hence, to compute its MAP estimate, the coordinator must compute the right-hand side of Eq. (34). The main difficulty arises from the term $p(s^1(1), \ldots, s^N(t) \mid s(t) = k)$. Computation of this term is extremely difficult because the communications $s^i(t)$ are conditionally correlated given s(t), since s(t) is only part of the dynamical state (x(t), s(t)).

Rather than pursuing the general case, we shall make some additional assumptions:

(A.1) Conditioned on knowledge of the event k, the trajectory x(t) is deterministic (i.e., x(0) is known and w(t) = 0 in Eq. (13)).

(A.2) The coordinator's processing is restricted to *memoryless* algorithms. That is, its estimate $\bar{s}(t)$ is a function of $s^1(t), \ldots, s^N(t)$ only.

Assumption (A.1) implies that the agents observations are mutually independent, conditioned on knowledge of the event. Hence, the estimates $s^i(t)$, $s^j(u)$ are also conditionally independent for $i \neq j$, and any t, u. Hence, in Eq. (34),

$$p(s^1(1), \ldots, s^N(t) \mid s(t) = k)$$

$$= \prod_{i=1}^{N} p(s^i(1), \ldots, s^i(t) \mid s(t) = k). \tag{35}$$

The computation of the right-hand side of Eq. (35) is still difficult. However, assumption (A.2) implies that the coordinator's problem is to construct the probability

$$p(s(t) = k \mid s^1(t), \ldots, s^N(t))$$

$$= Cp(s(t) = k)\prod_{i=1}^{N} p(s^i(t) \mid s(t) = k). \tag{36}$$

Eqaution (36) illustrates the key step in the coordinator's algorithm: Construction of the conditional probabilities $p(s^i(t) \mid s = k)$. This probability distribution depends on the statistics of the random variables in Eqs. (4) and (8), and in the processing used by the local agents in generating $s^i(t)$.

For the communication pattern (C.2), the local agent generates $s^i(t)$ as

$$s^i(t) = \max_{k=1,\ldots,K} p(s(t) = k \mid Y^i(t)). \tag{37}$$

Furthermore, by Bayes's rule,

$$p(s(t) = k \mid Y^i(t)) = \frac{p(Y^i(t) \mid s(t) = k)p(s(t) = k)}{p(Y^i(t))}. \tag{38}$$

Hence,

$$s^i(t) = \max_{k=1,\ldots,K} p(s(t) = k)p(Y^i(t) \mid s(t) = k). \tag{39}$$

Due to the assumption that the event structure is static, the first term $p(s(t) = k)$ is equal to $p(s(0) = k)$, which is known to the coordinator as part of the initial conditions. The second term can be computed as follows: Equations (3) and

(7) imply that $p(Y^i(t) \mid s(t) = k)$ is Gaussian; hence, we must compute the mean and covariance of the distribution of $Y^i(t)$. From Eqs. (3) and (7), the mean $m^{ik}(t)$ of $y^i(t)$ given $s(t) = s(0) = k$ is given by

$$\begin{aligned} m^{ik}(t) &= E\{y^i(t) \mid s(t) = k\} \\ &= C^i(k)\left\{(A(k))^t \overline{x}(0) + \sum_{s=1}^{t} (A(k))^{t-s} b(k)\right\} + d^i(k). \end{aligned} \tag{40}$$

Similarly, the conditional covariance $\Lambda^{ik}(t, s)$ of $y^i(t)$ and $y^i(s)$ given $s(t) = k$ is given (for $t \geq s$) by

$$\begin{aligned} \Lambda^{ik}(t, s) &= E\{(y^i(t) - m^{ik}(t))(y^i(s) - m^{ik}(s))^T \mid s(t) = k\} \\ &= C^i(k)(A(k))^t \Sigma(0)(A(k)^T)^s C^i(k)^T \\ &\quad + C^i(k)\sum_{r=1}^{s} (A(k))^{t-r} W(A(k)^T)^{s-r} C^i(k)^T \\ &\quad + V^i \delta(t - s). \end{aligned} \tag{41}$$

Let $\Lambda^{ik}(t)$ denote the covariance of $Y^i(t)$, and $M^{ik}(t)$ its mean. With this notation, we can rewrite Eq. (39) using the strictly monotone property of the ℓn function as

$$\begin{aligned} s^i(t) = \max_{k=1,\ldots,K} \Big\{ &\ell n\, p(s(t) = k) - \tfrac{1}{2}\, \ell n |\det \Lambda^{ik}(t)| \\ &- \tfrac{1}{2}(Y^i(t) - M^{ik}(t))^T (\Lambda^{ik}(t))^{-1} \\ &\times (Y^i(t) - M^{ik}(t)) \Big\}. \end{aligned} \tag{42}$$

Hence, the term $p(s^i(t) = \ell \mid s(t) = k)$ in the coordinator's algorithm in Eq. (36) can be evaluated as

$$\begin{aligned} p(s^i(t) &= \ell \mid s(t) = k) \\ &= p\Big(\Big\{Y^i(t): \ln p(s(t) = \ell) - \ln p(s(t) = m) \\ &\quad - \tfrac{1}{2} \ln\left|\det \Lambda^{il}(t)\right| + \tfrac{1}{2} \ln\left|\det \Lambda^{im}(t)\right| \\ &\quad - \tfrac{1}{2} (Y^i(t) - M^{il}(t))^T (\Lambda^{il}(t))^{-1} (Y^i(t) - M^{il}(t)) \\ &\quad + \tfrac{1}{2}(Y^i(t) - M^{im}(t))^T (\Lambda^{im}(t))^{-1} (Y^i(t) - M^{im}(t)) \geq 0, \\ &\qquad \text{for all } m = 1, 2, \ldots, K\Big\} \Big| \, s(t) = k\Big). \end{aligned} \tag{43}$$

The right-hand side of Eq. (43) is a Gaussian integral over the region specified by the inequalities on $Y^i(t)$, using the distribution $p(Y^i(t) \mid s(t) = k)$. This integral is difficult to evaluate in closed form; therefore, numerical techniques such as Gaussian quadrature and stochastic integration formulas [15, 22] must be used. An alternative approach pursued in [16] is to approximate the right-hand side of Eq. (43) by an upper bound; we will not pursue this approach here, but instead concentrate on illustrating how the coordinator uses the results of Eq. (43) to generate $p(s(t) = k \mid s^1(t), \ldots, s^N(t))$ from the communicated values $s^1(t), \ldots, s^N(t)$. Consider the following example.

Example. Assume that there are N agents and N events, with equal prior probability, and that agent i specializes in observing event i for all i = 1, ..., N. That is,

$$p(s^i(t) = i \mid s(t) = i) = E(t) \tag{44a}$$

$$p(s^i(t) = j \mid s(t) = i) = [1 - E(t)]/(N - 1) \quad \forall j \neq i \tag{44b}$$

$$p(s^i(t) = j \mid s(t) = j) = F(t) \quad \forall j \neq i \tag{44c}$$

$$p(s^i(t) = \ell \mid s(t) = j) = [1 - F(t)]/(N - 1) \quad \forall \ell \neq j, j \neq i \tag{44d}$$

where $E(t) > F(t)$ for all t, $E(t)$ and $F(t)$ are monotone increasing in t, $1 - E(t) \ll 1$, and $F(t) > 1/N$. Equation (44) says that agent i is much more reliable at detecting event i when event i is true than at detecting event j when event j is true. It also states that errors are uniformly distributed among other events. Assume that, at any time t, the coordinator has computed the parameters in Eq. (44) from the original event system parameters. At time t, the coordinator receives $s^1(t), \ldots, s^N(t)$.

Assume that

$$\begin{aligned} s^1(t) &= 1 \\ s^2(t) = s^3(t) = \cdots = s^{l+1}(t) &= 1 \\ s^{l+2}(t) = s^{l+3}(t) = \cdots = s^N(t) &= 2. \end{aligned} \tag{45}$$

Then, Eq. (36) becomes

$$\begin{aligned} p(s(t) = 1 \mid s^1(t), \ldots, s^N(t)) &= [E(t)F(t)^l(1 - F(t))^{N-l-1}(N - 1)^{l+1}] \\ &\quad \times [E(t)F(t)^l(1 - F(t))^{N-l-1}(N - 1)^{l+1} \\ &\quad + (1 - E(t))(1 - F(t))^l F(t)^{N-l-1}(N - 1)^{N-l-1} \\ &\quad + (N - 2)(1 - E(t))(1 - F(t))^{N-1}]^{-1}. \end{aligned} \tag{46}$$

Denote the denominator of Eq. (46) as D. Then,

$$\begin{aligned} p(s(t) = 2 \mid s^1(t), \ldots, s^N(t)) &= D^{-1}(1 - E(t))(1 - F(t))^l F(t)^{N-l-1}(N - 1)^{l+1}, \end{aligned} \tag{47}$$

and for $k > 2$,

$$\begin{aligned} p(s(t) = k \mid s^1(t), \ldots, s^N(t)) &= D^{-1}(1 - E(t))(1 - F(t))^{N-1}. \end{aligned} \tag{48}$$

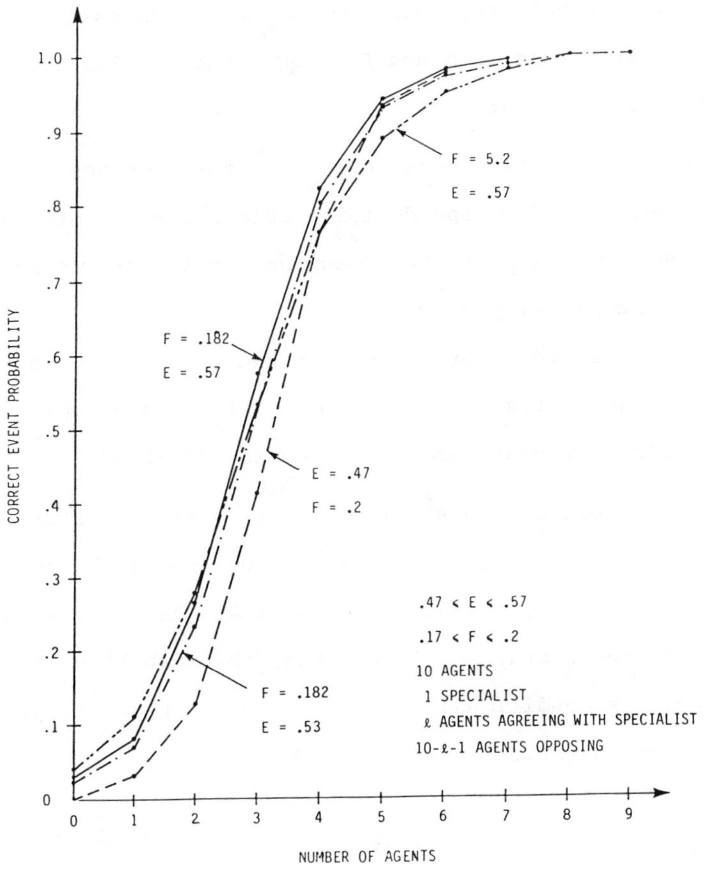

Fig. 5. Correct decision versus number of agents agreeing with specialist.

In Fig. 5 we show the numerical results obtained by Eqs. (46) and (47) for several values of E and F. We plot the probability that agent 1 (the specialist for event 1) is correct in his estimate as a function of l, the number of supporting agents. The results show that when five or more agents support the specialist then there will be an error of no more than 10% if the coordinator adopts the specialist's report as his own estimate. Furthermore, this conclusion is insensitive to significant variations in E and F. Thus, the results illustrate two important points:

(1) The proposed memoryless algorithm provides a meaningful and easily understood decision rule for the coordinator, e.g., "when the majority includes the specialist, it is safe to abide by the majority view."

(2) The coordinator's decision can be robust with respect to the probabilities $p(s^i(t) = k \mid s = l)$. Hence, the use of upper bounds for these probabilities is justified.

The probabilities $p(s^i(t) = k \mid s(t) = k)$ are referred to as *event observability indices* in [16]; they represent the accuracy of agent i in identifying event k. As the example illustrates, the coordinator uses these observability indices to construct the conditional probability of each event, given his limited communications.

D. SUMMARY

In this section we examined two hierarchical estimation structures. In the first structure, the coordinator receives sufficient statistics of the information of the local observation agents; for this structure, we derived an algorithm to allow the coordinator to reconstruct the centralized estimate of the state of the event-driven dynamical system. In the second structure, the communication between the coordinator and the local observation agents is limited, so that the coordinator receives only an estimate of the most likely event from each agent. We restricted the coordinator to use memoryless algorithms, and derived the optimal memoryless algorithm to construct the conditional probabilities of the events, given the communications by each agent. We demonstrated the algorithm using a simple example.

IV. DECENTRALIZED ESTIMATION STRUCTURES

A. *INTRODUCTION*

Our focus in this section is to develop distributed estimation algorithms for decentralized structures of estimation agents with no interagent communication and without a coordinating agent present. Such a structure is illustrated in Fig. 2. Since there is no coordination, each estimation agent processes its information to select a particular event as his estimate; the algorithms used in selecting these estimates must be designed to optimize an overall objective, reflecting system performance. The agents have different information available to select their estimates, and the overall group of estimates is evaluated in terms of a common objective; therefore, the problem of designing optimal algorithms for each agent becomes a *stochastic team problem*.

We will study two stochastic team problems involving the detection of events in event-driven systems: The decentralized Wald problem and the decentralized quickest detection problem. Both problems are extensions of classical statistical decision problems and incorporate multiple agents in a decentralized structure. Our results characterize the nature of the optimal decentralized algorithms, and provide insight into the design of effective decentralized estimation algorithms.

B. THE DECENTRALIZED WALD PROBLEM

Consider the event-driven system of Eqs. (3) to (7). Assume that the number of events is $K = 2$, that the event structure is static (i.e., $s(0) = s(t)$ for all t) and that Assumption (A.1) of Section III,C holds so that, conditioned on the event $s(t) = k$, the observations $y^i(t)$ are conditionally independent. For the sake of simple exposition, we will assume that the number of agents is $N = 2$.

The decentralized Wald problem is described as follows. At each time t, based on his observation set $Y^i(t)$, agent i must select one of three options:

a. declare $s^i(t) = 1$;

b. declare $s^i(t) = 2$;

c. declare nothing, and wait for another measurement.

Each agent may declare its event estimate only once.

Let $J(s^1, s^2; s)$ denote the cost of agent 1 estimating s^1 and agent 2 estimating s^2 when the true event is s. Let t^i denote the time at which agent i makes his estimate. Then, the decentralized Wald problem consists of selecting estimates $\gamma^i(Y^i(t))$, $i = 1, 2$ to minimize

$$J(\gamma^1, \gamma^2) = E\{ct^1 + ct^2 + J(s^1, s^2; s(0))\}. \tag{49}$$

Thus we see that the problem formulation models the important trade-off between making an estimate early, when it can be more useful, or waiting to make an estimate later, when it can be more accurate.

For the problem to be well posed, we must provide additional structure on J. In particular, we assume that

$$\begin{aligned} &J(1, s^2; 2) \geq J(2, s^2; 2), \quad J(1, s^2; 2) \geq J(1, s^2; 1) \\ &J(2, s^2; 1) \geq J(1, s^2; 1), \quad J(2, s^2; 1) \geq J(2, s^2; 2) \end{aligned} \tag{50}$$

with similar inequalities with s^1, s^2 reversed. The inequalities in Eq. (50) imply that it is always preferrable for each estimation agent to declare the correct event. Furthermore, we assume that agents must make a declaration before a terminal time T after which there are no more observations available.

Notice that, if

$$J(s^1, s^2; s) = J^1(s^1, s) + J^2(s^2, s), \tag{51}$$

then the decentralized Wald problem would decompose into two decoupled Wald problems, where agent i selects γ^i to minimize

$$J^i(\gamma^i) = E\{ct^i + J^i(s^i, s)\}. \tag{52}$$

In general, Eq. (51) does not hold, and the estimation problems of the two agents are coupled through the cost function (Eq. (49). Since each agent has different information, and the agents do not communicate, the decentralized Wald problem is a sequential team problem with static information structure [17,18]. Thus, the decomposition techniques of [18] can be used to determine the optimal strategies of each estimation agent, as follows.

Assume that the strategy of agent 2 is fixed as $\gamma^2(Y^2(t))$, and consider the problem faced by agent 1: He must select $\gamma^1(Y^1(t))$ such that (49) is minimized. Agent 1's problem is a stochastic centralized sequential decision problem with partial state observation, which will be solved using stochastic dynamic programming. Consider the decision problem faced by agent i at time t: Let $s^i(t)$ denote the declaration of agent i at time t, where $s^i(t) = 0$ means that the agent will wait for another measurement. Let $t \wedge t^i$ denote the minimum of t and t^i, where

$t^i = \min\{t: s^1(t) = 1 \text{ or } 2\}$. With this notation, the expression for $Y^i(t \wedge t^i)$ is

$$\begin{aligned} Y^i(t \wedge t^i) &= Y^i(t) \quad \text{if} \quad s^1(\tau) = 0, \quad \tau < t \\ &= Y^i(t^i) \quad \text{otherwise.} \end{aligned} \tag{53}$$

Using assumption A.1, we obtain

$$p(t^1, s^1, t^2, s^2 \mid Y^1(t)) = \sum_{s=1}^{2} p(t^1, s^1 \mid Y^1(t))p(t^2, s^2 \mid s(0) = s)p(s(0) = s \mid Y^1(t)). \tag{54}$$

To apply stochastic dynamic programming, we must identify the "state" of the stochastic system. Define the Markovian state $(\pi^1(t), t^1(t))$, where

$$\pi^1(t) = p(s(0) = 1 \mid Y^1(t \wedge t^1)). \tag{55}$$

The evolution of $\pi^1(t)$ is governed by Bayes's rule, and the decisions $s^1(t)$, as

$$\begin{aligned} \pi^1(t+1) &= \frac{\pi^1(t)p(y^1(t+1) \mid s=1)}{\pi^1(t)p(y^1(t+1) \mid s=1) + (1-\pi^1(t))p(y^1(t+1) \mid s=2)} \\ &\qquad \text{if } s^1(t) = 0,\ t^1(t) = t \\ &= \pi^1(t) \quad \text{otherwise.} \end{aligned} \tag{56}$$

The evolution of $t^1(t)$ is given by

$$\begin{aligned} t^1(t+1) &= t^1(t) + 1 \quad \text{if} \quad s^1(t) = 0,\ t^1(t) = t \\ &= t^1(t) \qquad \text{otherwise.} \end{aligned} \tag{57}$$

Consider the final time T; assume that $s^1(t) = 0$ for $t < T$. Then, the decision problem at time T consists of selecting

$s^1(T) = 1$ or 2 to minimize the cost-to-go

$$J^{1T} = cE\{t^2(T) \mid Y^1(T)\} + \min_{s^1(T)=1,2} E\{J(s^1(T),\ s^2(t^2(T));\ s) \mid Y^1(T)\}. \tag{58}$$

The last term of Eq. (58) can be rewritten using Eq. (54) as

$$\begin{aligned}
&\min_{s^1(T)=1,2} E\{J(s^1,\ s^2(t^2(T));\ s) \mid Y^1(T)\} \\
&= \min_{s^1(T)=1,2} \left\{ \sum_{s^2=1}^{2} \pi^1(T)p(s^2(t^2(T)) = s^2 \mid s = 1)J(s^1,\ s^2;\ 1) \right. \\
&\qquad + \sum_{s^2=1}^{2} (1 - \pi^1(T))p(s^2(t^2(T)) = s^2 \mid s = 2) \\
&\qquad\qquad \left. \times J(s^1,\ s^2;\ 2) \right\}.
\end{aligned} \tag{59}$$

Equations (58) and (59) lead to the first result:

Lemma 1. The optimal strategy for agent 1 at time T is

$$\gamma^{1*}(Y^1(T)) = \begin{cases} 1 & \text{if } \pi^1(t) \geq a(T)/b(T) \\ 2 & \text{otherwise,} \end{cases}$$

where

$$a(T) = \sum_{s^2=1}^{2} p(s^2(t^2(T)) = s^2 \mid s = 2) \times (J(1,\ s^2;\ 2) - J(2,\ s^2;\ 2)) \tag{60}$$

$$b(T) = \sum_{s^2=1}^{2} p(s^2(t^2(T)) = s^2 \mid s = 1) \times (J(2,\ s^2;\ 1) - J(1,\ s^2;\ 1)) + a(T). \tag{61}$$

Furthermore, the expected optimal cost $J(\pi^1(T),\ T)$ at time T is a concave function of $\pi^1(T)$.

The concavity of $J(\pi^1(T), T)$ follows from the linearity of Eq. (59) in $\pi^1(T)$. The optimal strategy compares $\pi^1(T)$ to a threshold value to select $s^1(t) = 1$ or 2.

Lemma 1 is the initial step in the dynamic programming algorithm. Assume that the optimal expected cost-to-go at time $t + 1$, given $Y^1(t + 1)$ and assuming $s^1(\ell) = 0$ for $\ell \leq t$, is given by $J^1(\pi^1(t + 1), t + 1)$, a concave function of $\pi^1(t + 1)$. The decision problem at time t is to select $s^1 = 0$, 1 or 2, given $Y^1(t)$, to minimize the expected cost-to-go

$$J^{1t} = E\{(ct^2(T) + J(s^1, s^2(t^2(T)); s)) \mid Y^1(t)\}I(s^1 \neq 0)$$

$$+ E\{(c + J^1(\pi^1(t + 1), t + 1)) \mid Y^1(t)\}I(s^1 = 0) \quad (62)$$

$$= cE\{t^2(T) \mid Y^1(t)\}$$

$$+ \sum_{s^2=1}^{2} \pi^1(t)p(s^2(t^2(T)) = s^2 \mid s = 1)J(s^1, s^2; 1)$$

$$+ \sum_{s^2=1}^{2} (1 - \pi^1(t))p(s^2(t^2(T)) = s^2 \mid s = 2)$$

$$\times J(s^1, s^2; 2) \quad \text{if} \quad s^1 \neq 0 \quad (63)$$

$$= c + E\{J^1(\pi^1(t + 1), t + 1) \mid Y^1(t)\}$$

$$\text{if} \quad s^1 = 0, \quad (64)$$

where $\pi^1(t + 1)$ is given in terms of $\pi^1(t)$ by Eq. (56).

Note that both (63) and (64) are concave functions of $\pi^1(t)$, [20], so that the minimum over $s^1(t) = 0, 1, 2$ is also a concave function of $\pi^1(t)$. Equations (62), (63), and (64) establish the dynamic programming recursion summarized in Theorem 3.

Theorem 3. The dynamic programming equation for agent 1 at time t, assuming $s^1(\tau) = 0$, $\tau < t$, is

$$
\begin{aligned}
J^1(\pi^1(t), t) &= \min\Bigg\{ \min_{s^1=1,2} \Bigg\{ E\{ct^2(T) \mid Y^1(t)\} \\
&\quad + \sum_{s^2=1}^{2} \pi^1(t) p(s^2(t^2(T)) = s^2 \mid s = 1) J(s^1, s^2; 1) \\
&\quad + \sum_{s^2=1}^{2} (1 - \pi^1(t)) p(s^2(t^2(T)) = s^2 \mid s = 1) \\
&\qquad \times J(s^1, s^2; 2) \Bigg\}, \\
&\quad c + E\{J^1(\pi^1(t + 1), t + 1) \mid Y^1(t)\} \Bigg\}. \qquad (65)
\end{aligned}
$$

Note that the inner minimization in Eq. (65) corresponds to $J^1[\pi^1(t), T]$. Hence, for all t, π^1

$$J^1(\pi^1, t) \leq J^1(\pi^1, T) \qquad (66)$$

and

$$J^1(\pi^1, t) \leq J^1(\pi^1, t + 1) + c. \qquad (67)$$

The inequality in Eq. (67) can be made tighter if we assume stationarity of the observation process, that is,

$$p(y(t) \mid s = i) = p(y(t + 1) \mid s = i) \quad \text{for all } t, i. \qquad (68)$$

Lemma 2. Assume Eq. (68) holds. Then,

$$J^1(\pi^1, t) \leq J^1(\pi^1, t + 1) \qquad (69)$$

Proof. By Eq. (66)

$$J^1(\pi^1, T - 1) \leq J^1(\pi^1, T).$$

Using induction and Eq. (65)

$$J^1(\pi^1, t) = \min\{J^1(\pi^1, T), c + E\{J^1(\pi^1(t + 1), t + 1) \mid Y^1(t)\}\}$$
$$\leq \min\{J^1(\pi^1, T), c + E\{J^1(\pi^1(t + 1), t + 2) \mid Y^1(t)\}\}$$
$$= J^1(\pi^1, t + 1),$$

completing the proof.

A complete characterization of agent 1's strategy is now available, which we summarize in Theorem 4.

Theorem 4. The optimal strategy for agent 1 at time t can be described in terms of thresholds $\alpha^1(t)$ and $\beta^1(t)$ as follows:

If $\pi^1(t) \leq \alpha^1(t)$, then $s^1(t) = 2$;

if $\pi^1(t) \geq \beta^1(t)$, then $s^1(t) = 1$;

otherwise, $s^1(t) = 0$.

The thresholds $\alpha^1(t)$, $\beta^1(t)$ are defined by the unique intersections of the concave curves $J^1(\pi^1, T)$ and $c + E\{J^1(\pi^1(t+1), t + 1) \mid Y^1(t)\}$.

Proof. The uniqueness of the thresholds follows from Eq. (65) the concavity of both functions, and the fact that

$$J^1(0, T) < c + E\{J^1(\pi^1(t + 1), t + 1) \mid Y^1(t)\}$$
$$< c + J^1(0, t + 1)$$
$$< c + J^1(0, T).$$

A similar inequality holds for $J^1(1, T)$. Hence, there are two distinct intersections $\alpha^1(t)$, $\beta^1(t)$, unless $J^1(\pi^1, t) = J^1(\pi^1, T)$ in which case $\alpha^1(t) = \beta^1(t) = a(T)/b(T)$, as in Lemma 1. The rest of the theorem follows from Theorem 3 and Lemma 2.

Now, Theorem 4 characterizes the optimal strategy for agent 1 for any arbitrary strategy γ^2 of agent 2. In particular, Theorem 4 holds for the optimal strategy of agent 2. Similarly,

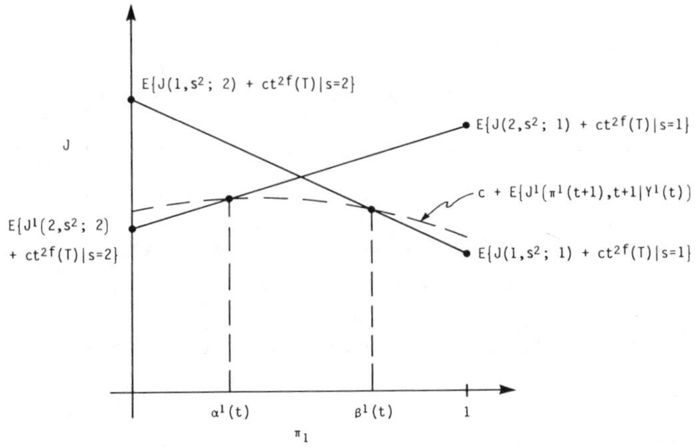

Fig. 6. Optimal strategy for agent 1.

a reciprocal argument establishes that the optimal strategy for agent 2 can be determined using thresholds $\alpha^2(t)$, $\beta^2(t)$ as in Theorem 4. According to the results of Lemma 1 and Theorem 4, these thresholds are coupled. Namely, the thresholds of agent 1 at any instant are coupled with the thresholds of agent 2 for all times.

The optimal decision rule and cost-to-go for agent 1 are illustrated in Fig. 6. Although Theorem 4 offers a complete characterization of the solution of the decentralized Wald problem, actual computation of this solution poses a difficult problem due to the coupling among the thresholds used by each agent. The design of practical, implementable algorithms to approximate the optimal strategy described in this section remains an area for future research.

C. THE DECENTRALIZED QUICKEST DETECTION PROBLEM

In the previous subsection, we studied a simple example of an event-driven dynamical system with two decentralized agents who jointly estimate the identity of a static event s. In this section, we will formulate and analyze a decentralized estimation problem where the event evolution will be dynamic. A more detailed presentation of the results in this section appears in [4].

Assume that the Markov chain s(t) has states 1 and 2, with initial state s(0) = 1 and transition probabilities

$$\begin{aligned} &q(1, 1) = 1 - q, \quad && q(2, 1) = 0 \\ &q(1, 2) = q, && q(2, 2) = 1. \end{aligned} \tag{70}$$

As in the previous subsection, we assume Assumption (A.1) holds; hence, each agent's observations are conditionally independent, given knowledge of the trajectory of the event s(t). We also assume that there are only two agents, and that no interagent communications occur.

The Markov chain of Eq. (70) has a single transition at a random time θ. Each agent has to estimate when this transition occurs. Let t^i denote the time at which agent i declares that the transition from s(t) = 1 to s(t) = 2 has occurred. Then, the decentralized quickest detection problem consists of selecting optimal agent estimation strategies γ^1, γ^2 to minimize the cost functional

$$J(\gamma^1, \gamma^1) = E\{J(t^1, t^2; \theta)\}, \tag{71}$$

where

$$\begin{aligned} J(t^1, t^2; \theta) = {} & c(t^1 - \theta)I(t^1 \geq \theta) + c(t^2 - \theta)I(t^2 \geq \theta) \\ & + I\{t^1 < \theta\}I\{t^2 < \theta\}. \end{aligned} \tag{72}$$

Notice that the objective in Eq. (72) represents a trade-off between each agent's possible delays in recognizing the event θ and the possibility that both agents declare the transition to have occurred before it actually does. The constant $c > 0$ is used to reflect the relative importance of these terms. As in the previous section, the decentralized quickest detection problem is a team problem, and can be analyzed in the same way.

The quickest detection problem with one agent has been solved in [9,19]. The optimal strategy consists of comparing a sufficient statistic for the observations, $p(s(t) = 1 \mid Y(t))$, to a time-invariant threshold. If the statistic is greater than the threshold, it is optimal to continue. The main result we shall prove in this subsection is that when two agents are present, the optimal strategy is again characterized by thresholds using local sufficient statistics. However, these thresholds are time varying and their computation requires the solution of two coupled sets of equations.

Consider a fixed strategy γ^2 for agent 2. Then, agent 1's problem consists of

$$\min_{\gamma^1} J^1(\gamma^1) = \min_{\gamma^1} E\{c(t^1 - \theta)I\{t^1 \geq \theta\} + I\{t^2 < \theta\}I\{t^1 < \theta\}\}. \tag{73}$$

Define $\pi^1(t)$ as

$$\pi^1(t) = p(s(t) = 1 \mid Y^1(t)) = p(\theta > t \mid Y^1(t)). \tag{74}$$

Note that

$$p(s(t + k) = 1 \mid Y^1(t)) = \pi^1(t)(1 - q)^k. \tag{75}$$

Now, the first term in Eq. (73) can be rewritten as

$$E\, c(t^1 - \theta)I\{t^1 \geq \theta\}\} = E\left\{c \sum_{t=1}^{t^1-1} I(s(t) = 2)\right\}$$

$$= E\left\{c \sum_{t=1}^{t^1-1} (1 - \pi^1(t))\right\}. \tag{76}$$

The second term can be simplified because of Assumption (A.1), to yield

$$E\{I\{t^2 < \theta\}I\{t^1 < \theta\}\}$$

$$= E\{E\{\{I\{\theta > t^1\}E\{I(t^2 < \theta \mid \theta\} \mid Y^1(t^1)\}\}. \tag{77}$$

Let $g^2(\theta) = E\{I(t^2 < \theta) \mid \theta\}$. Then,

$$E\{I(\theta > t^1)g^2(\theta) \mid Y^1(t^1)\}$$

$$= E\left\{\sum_{i=1}^{\infty} g^2(t^1 + i)p(\theta = t^1 + i \mid Y^1(t^2))\right\}$$

$$= E\left\{\sum_{i=1}^{\infty} g^2(t^1 + i)\pi^1(t^1)(1 - q)^{i-1}q\right\} \tag{78}$$

$$= \pi^1(t^1) \sum_{i=1}^{\infty} E(g(t^1 + i))(1 - q)^{i-1}q.$$

Hence, the problem for agent 1 can be expressed as the selection of a stopping time t, based on his observations $Y^1(t)$, to minimize

$$J^1(t^1) = E\left\{c \sum_{t=1}^{t^1-1} [1 - \pi^1(t)] + \pi^1(t^1)\right.$$

$$\left.\times \sum_{i=1}^{\infty} g^2(t^1 + i)q(1 - q)^{i-1}\right\}. \tag{79}$$

At time t, agent 1 must decide whether to declare $t^1 = t$ or continue, based on the value of $\pi^1(t)$, which summarizes the information $Y^1(t)$. By the principle of optimality

$$J^1[\pi^1(t), t] = \min\left\{\pi^1(t) \sum_{i=1}^{\infty} g^2(t+i)q(1-q)^{i-1},\ c(1-\pi^1(t)) + E\{J^1(\pi^1(t+1), t+1 \mid Y^1(t)\}\right\}, \tag{80}$$

where

$$\pi^1(t+1) = \frac{\pi^1(t)(1-q)p(y^1(t+1) \mid s(t+1)=1)}{\pi^1(t)(1-q)p(y^1(t+1) \mid s(t+1)=1) + [\pi^1(t)q + (1-\pi^1(t))]p(y^1(t+1) \mid s(t+1)=2)}. \tag{81}$$

Equation (80) is the dynamic programming recursion for the problem of agent 1. As in Section IV, B, we can establish the properties of $J^1(\pi, t)$.

Lemma 3. $J^1(\pi, t)$ is a concave function of π.

Proof. As in Section IV, B, $E\{J^1(\pi^1(t+1), t+1) \mid Y^1(t)\}$ is a concave function of $\pi^1(t)$. Hence, Eq. (80) establishes $J^1(\pi, t)$ as the minimum of two concave functions, proving the lemma.

Theorem 5. The optimal stopping time for agent 1 is

$$\tau^* = \min\{t\colon \pi^1(t) < \alpha^1(t)\}.$$

The threshold $\alpha^1(t)$ is determined by the solution of the equation

$$\pi^1(t) \sum_{i=1}^{\infty} g^2(t+i)q(1-q)^{i-1} = c(1-\pi^1(t)) + E\{J^1(\pi^1(t+1), t+1) \mid Y^1(t)\}. \tag{82}$$

Proof. For $\pi^1(t) = 0$, $c > 0$ implies that

$$\pi^1(t) \sum_{i=1}^{\infty} g^2(t + i)q(1 - q)^{i-1}$$

$$< c(1 - \pi^1(t)) + E\{J^1(\pi^1(t + 1), t + 1) \mid Y^1(t)\}. \quad (83)$$

Furthermore, for $\pi^1(t) = 1$, it is clear that

$$E\{J^1(\pi^1(t + 1), t + 1) \mid Y^1(t)\}$$

$$\leq \sum_{i=1}^{\infty} g^2(t + i)q(1 - q)^{i-1}.$$

Since the left-hand side of Eq. (82) is linear and the right-hand side concave, there is one intersection $\alpha^1(t)$. The rest of the lemma follows from standard dynamic programming arguments.

The optimal strategy at time t for agent 1 is illustrated in Fig. 7.

Since Lemma 3 and Theorem 5 hold for any fixed strategy γ^2 of agent 2, they hold for the optimal strategy. By summetry, the optimal strategies for both estimation agents consist of

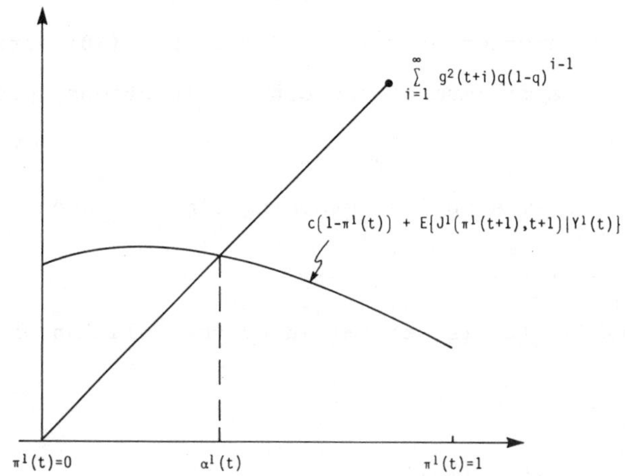

Fig. 7. Agent 1's optimal strategy.

thresholds where the threshold parameters $\alpha^1(t)$, $\alpha^2(t)$ are determined using the coupled dynamic programming equations of Theorem 5. In particular, note that, for any strategy γ^2 in Eq. (80), the first term in the minimization is time varying. Hence, even in the infinite horizon problem, the optimal thresholds will be time-varying, in contrast with the classical results for the quickest detection problem [19].

As in Section IV,B, the results of Theorem 5 are difficult to implement, because of the complexity of the equations defining the optimal thresholds. Further research is necessary to develop approximation techniques which are suitable for these computations.

D. SUMMARY

In this section, we studied two simple problems of designing optimal estimation algorithms for decentralized structures with no coordinating agent, where the performance of the agents is coupled through a common objective function. By formulating these problems as dynamic team problems, we developed characterizations of the optimal strategies. Even in these simple examples, the coupling through the cost function led to very complex equations characterizing the optimal strategies. Nevertheless, the qualitative insights into the structure of the optimal strategies might provide the basis for developing practical approximations to these strategies.

When the number of event states is greater than two, the complexity of the optimal algorithms increases tremendously. This is due to the fact that, in general, for K events, a (K - 2)-dimensional region is needed to partition the space of conditional probabilities into different decision regions. For K = 2, only a threshold point was necessary. For greater K, specification of these regions remains a formidable problem.

Another limitation of the results of this section is the absence of communication among the estimation agents. Coupled with Assumption (A.1), the absence of communication enabled us to establish that each agent's conditional probability distribution on the events was a sufficient statistic for constructing his team estimate. The use of dynamic programming arguments which we have developed depends critically on the absence of interagent communications. Extensions of these results to problems with communication will require signigicant additional research.

V. CONCLUSIONS

In this paper, we have presented a compendium of results concerning the design of optimal distributed estimation algorithm structures for event-driven dynamical systems. In particular, we focused on two classes of estimation structures: Hierarchical estimation structures and decentralized estimation structures. For the decentralized estimation structures, we considered two simple event-estimation problems and developed characterizations of the optimal algorithms. These characterizations highlighted the complexity of determining optimal algorithms, even for these simple examples. For such estimation structures, one should develop suboptimal algorithms based on the qualitative properties which we have derived in this paper.

For the hierarchical estimation structures, the limiting factor is the amount of communication allowed within the distributed estimation structure. In the extreme case where continuous communication is permitted, the coordinator can reconstruct the centralized state estimate of the event-driven dynamical system. Furthermore, approximations to the centralized estimate can be obtained using periodic communications. When the capacity of the communication channels is limited, we developed an optimal memoryless coordination algorithm for combining locally generated event estimates. The parameters of this algorithm are based on the statistics of the local processing algorithms, which can be computed numerically or approximated using probabilistic bounds.

In general, the design of optimal estimation algorithms given structural constraints on communications and information flow is a difficult problem. By focusing on event-driven systems, we have developed results for several estimation structures which highlight: (a) the complexity of the optimal algorithms; (b) the qualitative properties of these optimal algorithms; (c) the important role of assumptions such as conditional independence of observations; and (d) the trade-offs among estimator performance and communication requirements. The results of this paper provide a basis for the development of practical distributed estimation algorithms in the presence of structural constraints.

ACKNOWLEDGMENTS

Work sponsored by the Department of Energy, Division of Electric Energy Systems under Contract DE-AC02-80RA50418 and by the Air Force Office of Scientific Research under Contract F49620-81-C-0015.

REFERENCES

1. H. L. VAN TREES, "Detection, Estimation and Modulation Theory," Parts I, II, and III, Wiley, New York, 1968.

2. M. H. A. Davis, "Linear Estimation and Stochastic Control," Wiley, London, 1977.

3. R. R. TENNEY and N. R. SANDELL, JR., "Detection with Distributed Sensors," *IEEE Trans. Aerosp. and Electron. Syst. AES-17* (4), (1981).

4. D. TENEKETZIS and P. VARAIYA, "The Decentralized Quickest Detection Problem," in *IEEE Trans. Autom. Control AC-29* (7), 1984.

5. P. M. ANDERSON and A. A. FOUAD, "Power System Control and Stability," Iowa State Univ. Press, Ames, Iowa, 1977.

6. D. REID, "An Algorithm for Tracking Multiple Targets," *IEEE Trans. Autom. Control AC-24* (12), (1979).

7. K. R. PATTIPATI and N. R. SANDELL, JR., "A Unified View of State Estimation in Switching Environments," American Control Conference, San Francisco, California, pp. 458-465, June 1983.

8. A. A. B. PRITSKER and C. D. PEGDEN, "Introduction to Simulations and SLAM," Halsted, New York, 1979.

9. A. N. SHIRYAYEV, "Statistical Sequential Analysis," Translations of Mathematical Monographs, American Mathematical Society, 38, 1973.

10. D. T. MAGILL, "Optimal Adaptive Estimation of Sampled Processes," *IEEE Trans. Autom. Control AC-10* (1965).

11. J. L. SPEYER, "Computation and Transmission Requirements for a Decentralized Linear-Quadratic-Gaussian Control Problem," *IEEE Trans. Autom. Control AC-24*, 266-269 (1979).

12. D. A. CASTANON and D. TENEKETZIS, "Distributed Estimation Algorithms for Nonlinear Systems," to appear in *IEEE Trans. Autom. Control*.

13. A. S. WILLSKY, M. BELLO, D. A. CASTANON, B. C. LEVY, and G. VERGHESE, "Combining and Updating of Local Estimates and Regional Maps Along Sets of One-Dimensional Tracks," *IEEE Trans. Autom. Control AC-27* (4), (1982).

14. D. TENEKETZIS and Y. C. HO, "The Coordination Problem for Event Estimation of Event-Driven Dynamical Systems," ALPHATECH Technical Memorandum TM-131, September 1983.

15. J. P. IMHOF, "Computing the Distribution of Quadratic Forms in Normal Random Variables," *Biometrika*, 419 (1961).

16. D. TENEKETZIS, N. R. SANDELL, JR., L. C. KRAMER, and M. ATHANS, "Information Flow in Event-Driven Large-Scale Systems," ALPHATECH Technical Report TR-127, October 1981.

17. Y. C. HO, "Team Decision Theory and Information Structures," *Proc. IEEE 68* (6) (1980).

18. T. YOSHIKAWA, "Decomposition of Dynamic Team Decision Problems," *IEEE Trans. Autom. Control AC-23* (4) (1978).

19. A. N. SHIRYAYEV, "On Optimum Methods in Quickest Detection Problems," *Theory Probab. Appl. 16*, 712-717 (1971).

20. D. TENEKETZIS, "The Decentralized Wald Problem," Proceedings of the Large Scale Systems Symposium, Virginia Beach, October, 1982.

21. N. P. BUSLENKO, "Modelirovaniye Slozhnykh Sistem, Izdaniye Vtoroye," (Modeling of Complex Systems, Second Edition), Nauka, Moscow, 1978.

22. M. G. KENDALL, "Proof of Relations Connected with Tetrachoric Series and its Generalizations," *Biometrika 32*, 196 (1941).

Decentralized Control of Discrete Time Linear Systems with Incomplete Information

ALBERT B. CHAMMAS
Northrop Corporation
Electronics Systems Group
Century City, California

I. INTRODUCTION

The control of large-scale systems has been an active topic of research for many years (Sandell *et al.* [1]). Power, communication, and traffic networks are typical examples for such systems. The nature of large-scale systems imposes constraints on the information available to each controller. The lack of information can be about system parameters, and/or sensor measurements of its response. Most of the research performed on large-scale systems assumes that each controller has complete information about the system model, but has access to noisy measurements of a subset of its response. The exchange of sensor measurements via communication links between controllers allows for implementing standard optimum control laws. This

ISBN 0-12-012722-9

approach, however, requires complex communication links, large-scale estimator, and a feedback of each state or its estimate.

Decentralized feedback control tends to simplify the structure of the controller. For static linear quadratic Gaussian (LQG) team problems, Radner [2] showed that a unique team-optimal solution exists; that is, a linear function of the measurements available to each controller. Extensions of these results were obtained by Ho and Chu [3,4] to dynamic LQG team problems with nested information structures. Basar [5,6] extended Radner's results to obtain Nash equilibrium solutions for LQG problems with multiple-cost criteria. These results apply to LQG team problems with special information structure. In the general case, team-optimal solutions are nonlinear and are too difficult, if not impossible, to determine (Witsenhausen [7]). Constraining the class of admissible controls to be linear does not alleviate the complexity of the solution, since it requires infinite-dimensional estimators (Willman [8] and Rhodes [9]).

In this chapter, a different approach is presented for the decentralized control of discrete time linear systems with incomplete information. It is assumed that each controller has access to classical information structure, which consists of the system model, the statistics associated with uncertainties, and measurements of a subset of the state at discrete instants of time. The time interval of interest is divided into subintervals between output measurements. Each controller is constrained to use a linear function of its output measurements; the gains are allowed to vary at discrete instants of time between measurements. The gains are obtained from determining a Nash equilibrium point to a set of quadratic cost functions over each subinterval, sequentially. The decentralized controls thus obtained can be considered as a sequence of open-loop feedback strategies that are computed after each measurement. The approach presented here is similar to that of Chammas and Leondes [10], which was used for centralized LQG problems. This paper extends those results to obtain decentralized output feedback control laws for large-scale, discrete time linear systems, with multiple quadratic cost criteria and incomplete information. In particular, it is assumed that the jth controller has access only to a subset y_j of the system state X at discrete instants of time. The set of admissible decentralized controls Ω is defined by

$$\Omega = \{u_1[i, y_1(Nk)], \ldots, u_j[i, y_j(Nk)], \ldots, u_M[i, y_M(Nk)]\} \tag{1}$$

such that $u_j \in R^{r_j}$ for $j = 1, \ldots, M$ and

$$\begin{aligned} u_j[i, y_j(Nk)] &= C_j(i)y_j(Nk), \\ i &= Nk, Nk + 1, \ldots, [N(k + 1) - 1], \\ k &= k_0, k_0 + 1, \ldots, \end{aligned} \tag{2}$$

where $N \geq 1$ is a fixed integer that determines the frequency at which the output is sampled. It should be noted that the decentralized gains $C_j(i)$ are allowed to vary at discrete instants of time between output measurements.

Associated with each controller j is a quadratic cost function $J_j[[u_1, \ldots, u_j, \ldots, u_M, i, x[N(k + 1)]]$, which is defined over the interval $Nk \leq i < N(k + 1)$, for $k = k_0, k_0 + 1, \ldots, L - 1$.

Definition 1. A set of admissible controls $\Omega^* = \left\{\overset{*}{u}_1, \ldots, \overset{*}{u}_j, \ldots, \overset{*}{u}_M\right\}$ is said to be a sequential Nash equilibrium set if for j = 1, ..., M,

$$J_j\left[\overset{*}{u}_1, \ldots, \overset{*}{u}_j, \ldots \overset{*}{u}_M, i, x^*[N(k+1)]\right]$$
$$\leq J_j\left[\overset{*}{u}_1, \ldots, u_j, \ldots \overset{*}{u}_M, i, x[N(k+1)]\right], \tag{3}$$

where $k = k_0, k_0 + 1, \ldots, L - 1$.

It should be noted that Ω^* is determined by solving a standard Nash equilibrium problem over a sequence of time intervals $Nk \leq i < N(k + 1)$, starting at $k = k_0$, then $k = k_0 + 1, \ldots, k = L - 1$.

The objective of this chapter is to determine a sequential Nash equilibrium set Ω^* that is decentralized and admissible for discrete time linear systems with incomplete information. In Section II, the disturbance-free case is considered when the initial state of the system assumes a Gaussian distribution with known statistics. In Section III, the case when Gaussian white noise is present in the measurements and in the system dynamics is considered. The properties of the resultant decentralized closed-loop system are investigated in Section IV. It is shown that, in the absence of disturbances, the Nash equilibrium set of controls will drive the state of the system in finite time or asymptotically to the origin.

II. DISTURBANCE-FREE SYSTEMS

Consider the large-scale, discrete time linear system

$$X(i + 1) = \Phi(i + 1, i)X(i) + \sum_{j=1}^{M} B_j(i)u_j(i), \qquad i = 0, 1, \ldots, \tag{4}$$

where $X(i) \in R^n$, $u_j(i) \in R^{r_j}$. The jth controller has access only to the jth output of (4), which is given by

$$y_j(kN) = H_j(kN)X(kN), \qquad k = k_0, k_0 + 1, \ldots, \tag{5}$$

where $y_j(kN) \in R^{m_j}$ and $N \geq 1$ is an integer that determines the frequency at which the output is sampled relative to that of the control.

The initial state of the system is assumed to be a random variable with a Gaussian distribution. Its first- and second-order statistics are given by

$$E\{X(Nk_0)\} = \overline{X}_0; \qquad E\{X(Nk_0)X'(Nk_0)\} = \Sigma_0 > 0. \tag{6}$$

Associated with each controller j is a quadratic cost function

$$\begin{aligned} J_j\{u_1, \ldots, u_j, \ldots, u_M, i, X[N(k + 1)]\} \\ = \frac{1}{2}E\Bigg\{X'[N(k + 1)]F_j'[N(k + 1)]F_j[N(k +1)]X[N(k + 1)] \\ + \sum_{i=Nk}^{N(k+1)-1} u_j'(i)P_j(i)u_j(i)\Bigg\}, \end{aligned} \tag{7}$$

$$Nk \leq i < N(k + 1), \quad k = k_0, k_0 + 1, \ldots, L - 1.$$

The objective is to find a sequential Nash equilibrium set Ω^* that is admissible.

Theorem 1. The decentralized set of controls $\{\overset{*}{u}_1, \ldots, \overset{*}{u}_M\}$, where

$$\begin{aligned} \overset{*}{u}_j(i) = -P_j^{-1}(i)B_j'(i)\Phi'[N(k + 1), i + 1] \\ \times F_j'[N(k + 1)]\overset{*}{K}_j(Nk)\overset{*}{y}_j(Nk), \qquad Nk \leq i < N(k + 1), \\ j = 1, \ldots, M, \quad k = k_0, k_0 + 1, \ldots, L - 1, \end{aligned} \tag{8}$$

and $\overset{*}{K}_j(Nk)$ satisfy the set of matrix equations

$$F_j[N(k+1)]\left\{\sum_{l=1}^{M}\left[W_l[N(k+1), Nk]F_l'[N(k+1)]\overset{*}{K}_l(Nk)H_l(Nk)\right] \times \Sigma^*(Nk)H_j'(Nk) + \overset{*}{K}_j(Nk)H_j(Nk)\Sigma^*(Nk)H_j'(Nk)\right\}$$
$$= F_j[N(k+1)]\Phi[N(k+1), Nk]\Sigma^*(Nk)H_j'(Nk), \quad j = 1, \ldots, M, \tag{9}$$

with

$$\Sigma^*[N(k+1)] = \left\{\Phi[N(k+1), Nk] - \sum_{l=1}^{M} W_l[N(k+1), Nk]F_l'[N(k+1)]\overset{*}{K}_l(Nk)H_l(Nk)\right\} \times \Sigma^*(Nk)\left\{\Phi'[N(k+1), Nk] - \sum_{l=1}^{M} H_l'(Nk)\overset{*}{K}{}_l'(Nk)F_l[N(k+1)]W_l[N(k+1), Nk]\right\} \tag{10}$$

and

$$\Sigma^*(Nk_0) = \Sigma_0; \quad W_j[N(k+1), Nk] = \sum_{i=Nk}^{N(k+1)-1} \Phi[N(k+1), i+1]B_j(i)P_j^{-1}(i) \times B_j'(i)\Phi'[N(k+1), i+1] \tag{11}$$

is a sequential Nash equilibrium set for the cost functions (Eq. (7)) subject to the constraints of Eqs. (4)-(6) and (1) and (2). Furthermore, the state mean-square matrix of the decentralized closed-loop system is given by Eq. (10) and its mean by

$$\overline{X}^*[N(k+1)] = \left\{\Phi[N(k+1), Nk] - \sum_{l=1}^{M} W_l[N(k+1), Nk]F_l'[N(k+1)]\overset{*}{K}_l(Nk)H_l(Nk)\right\} \times \overline{X}^*(Nk) \tag{12}$$

$$\overline{X}^*(Nk_0) = \overline{X}_0. \tag{13}$$

The proof of the above theorem is given in the Appendix.

It should be noted that the decentralized gains $\left\{\overset{*}{K}_j(Nk), j = 1, \ldots M\right\}$ are determined by solving a set of M linear matrix equations, Eq. (9) forward in time, starting from $k = k_0$ and $\Sigma^*(Nk_0) = \Sigma_0$. These gains are then used to compute $\Sigma^*[N(k+1)]$ from Eq. (10).

Conditions for the solvability of Eq. (9) are difficult to obtain in general. For the special case when the problem of interest is that of a single controller u_1 and a single cost function J_1, the discrete output feedback gains $\overset{*}{K}_1(Nk)$ can be computed explicitly in terms of $\Sigma^*(Nk)$, provided $\left\{I + F_1' \times [N(k+1)]W_1[N(k+1), Nk]F_1[N(k+1)]\right\}$ is invertible. This special case is considered in the following corollary.

Corollary 1. The discrete time output feedback control law

$$\overset{*}{u}_1(i) = -P_1^{-1}(i)B_1'(i)\Phi'[N(k+1), i+1] \times F_1'[N(k+1)]\overset{*}{K}_1(Nk)y_1(Nk) \tag{14}$$

$$Nk \leq i < N(k+1), \qquad k = k_0,\ k_0 = L, \ldots, L-1,$$

minimizes sequentially the cost function

$$J_1(u_1, i, Nk) = \frac{1}{2} E\left\{X'[N(k+1)]F_1'[N(k+1)]F_1[N(k+1)]X[N(k+1)] + \sum_{i=Nk}^{N(k+1)-1} u_1'(i)P_1(i)u_1(i)\right\} \tag{15}$$

for $k = k_0, k_0 + 1, \ldots, L - 1$, subject to the constraints of Eqs. (4)-(6) and (1) and (2) with $J \equiv 1$, where

$$\overset{*}{K}_1(Nk) = \left\{I + F_1'[N(k+1)]W_1[N(k+1), Nk]F_1[N(k+1)]\right\}^{-1} \times F_1[N(k+1)]\Phi[N(k+1), Nk]\Sigma^*(Nk)H_1'(Nk) \times \left[H_1(Nk)\Sigma^*(Nk)H_1'(Nk)\right]^{\#} \tag{16}$$

and

$$\Sigma^*[N(k+1)] = \left\{\Phi[N(k+1), Nk] - W_1[N(k+1), Nk]F_1'[N(k+1)]\overset{*}{K}_1(Nk)H_1(Nk)\right\} \times \Sigma^*(Nk)\left\{\Phi'[N(k+1), Nk] - H_1'(Nk)\overset{*}{K}{}_1'(Nk)F_1[N(k+1)] \times W_1[N(k+1), Nk]\right\} \tag{17}$$

with

$$\Sigma^*(Nk_0) = \Sigma_0,$$

where in Eq. (16) $[M]^{\#}$ is used to denote the pseudo inverse of $[M]$.

Although the structure of the decentralized output feedback control laws (Eq. (8)) is simple, the finite time or asymptotic behavior of $\Sigma^*[Nk]$ and $\overline{X}^*(Nk)$ is too difficult to determine in general. For the case when each controller is penalizing only a weighted value of the state mean square, i.e., $P_j(i) \equiv 0$ for $j = i, \ldots, M$, the decentralized gains $\overset{*}{K}_j(Nk)$ can be determined explicitly, provided

$$\tilde{W}_j[N(k+1), Nk]$$

$$= \sum_{i=Nk}^{N(k+1)-1} \Phi[Nk, i+1]B_j(i)B_j'(i)\Phi'[Nk, i+1)] > 0 \qquad (18)$$

$$j = 1, \ldots, M, \quad k = k_0, k_0 + 1, \ldots, L - 1.$$

The above conditions[1] are satisfied if the system under consideration is discrete time controllable from each input. This case is summarized in the following theorem:

Theorem 2. The decentralized set of controls $\left\{\overset{*}{u}_1, \ldots, \overset{*}{u}_M\right\}$ where

$$\overset{*}{u}_j(i) = -B_j'(i)\Phi[Nk, i+1]\tilde{W}_j^{-1}[N(k+1), Nk]\overset{*}{K}_j(Nk)\overset{*}{y}_j(Nk),$$

$$Nk \le i < N(k+1), \qquad (19)$$

$$j = 1, \ldots, M, \quad k = k_0, k_0 + 1, \ldots, L - 1,$$

is a sequential Nash equilibrium set for the costs

$$\tilde{J}_j(u_1, \ldots, u_j, \ldots, u_M, i, Nk)$$

$$= \frac{1}{2} E\left\{X'[N(k+1)]F_j'[N(k+1)F_j[N(k+1)]X[N(k+1)]\right\}$$

$$k = k_0, k_0 + 1, \ldots L - 1, \quad j = 1, \ldots, M, \qquad (20)$$

subject to the constraints and assumptions of Eqs. (1) and (2), (4)-(6), and (18) where

$$K^*(Nk) \triangleq \left[\overset{*}{K}_1(Nk) \cdots \overset{*}{K}_j(Nk) \cdots \overset{*}{K}_M(Nk)\right]$$

$$= -\Sigma^*(Nk)H'(Nk)[H(Nk)\Sigma^*(Nk)H'(Nk)]^{\#} \qquad (21)$$

[1] *The arguments of Φ is different in the definition of $\tilde{W}_j[N(k+1), Nk)]$ and $W_j[N(k+1), Nk]$. This allows the gains $K^*(Nk)$ to have a structure similar to the Kalman filter gain.*

$$\Sigma^*[N(k + 1)] = \Phi[N(k + 1), Nk]$$
$$\times \{\Sigma^*(Nk) - \Sigma^*(Nk)H'(Nk)[H(Nk)\Sigma^*(Nk)H'(Nk)]^{\#}$$
$$\times H(Nk)\Sigma^*(Nk)\}\Phi'[N(k + 1), Nk] \quad (22)$$

with $\Sigma^*(Nk_0) = \Sigma_0$, $H(Nk)$ is the $m \times n$ matrix

$$H(Nk) = \begin{bmatrix} H_1(Nk) \\ \vdots \\ H_M(Nk) \end{bmatrix} \quad (23)$$

and $m \triangleq m_1 + \cdots + m_M$. The proof of the above theorem is similar to that of Theorem 1, and can be obtained by substituting $P_k(i) = 0$ in Eqs. (A.3) and (A.6) in the Appendix.

It is interesting to note that the decentralized gains $\overset{*}{K}_j(Nk)$ are specified in terms of the state mean-square matrix $\Sigma^*(Nk)$ and the combined observation matrix $H(Nk)$, and that the algorithms required to compute these gains can be easily implemented on line. Another interesting point is that for a single stage and a single-cost function, Eq. (19) reduces to the strategies obtained by Radner [2], Ho and Chu [3], and Basar [5]. In addition, the recursive relation (Eq. (22)) that determines the state mean-squared matrix of the decentralized closed-loop system is independent of $K^*(Nk)$ and has a structure similar to the discrete time Ricatti equation encountered in optimum filters and observers. This structure will be instrumental in establishing the properties of the decentralized closed-loop system. Furthermore, it should be noted that the decentralized control laws (Eq. (19)) are independent of the weighting matrices $F_j(Nk)$. Hence, $\left\{\overset{*}{u}_1, \ldots, \overset{*}{u}_M\right\}$ is an absolute minimum for $\tilde{J}_j(u_1, \ldots, u_M, i, Nk)$ and for all positive linear combinations of $\tilde{J}_j(u_1, \ldots, u_M, i, Nk)$. These results are summarized in the following proposition.

Proposition 1. Let $\left\{\overset{*}{u}_1, \ldots, \overset{*}{u}_M\right\}$ be the sequential Nash equilibrium set (Eqs. (19)-(23)) for the cost functions (Eq. 20)). Then for all $u_j \in \Omega$

$$\text{(i)} \quad \tilde{J}_j\left(\overset{*}{u}_1, \ldots, \overset{*}{u}_j, \ldots, \overset{*}{u}_M, i, Nk\right) \leq \tilde{J}_j(u_1, \ldots, u_j, \ldots u_M, i, Nk), \quad j = 1, \ldots, M \tag{24}$$

$$\text{(ii)} \quad \sum_{j=1}^{M} \alpha_j \tilde{J}_j\left(\overset{*}{u}_1, \ldots, \overset{*}{u}_M, i, Nk\right) \leq \sum_{j=1}^{M} \alpha_j \tilde{J}_j(u_1, \ldots, u_M, i, Nk), \qquad \alpha_j > 0. \tag{25}$$

The above proposition indicates that the Nash equilibrium set (Eqs. (19)-(23)) is also Parato optimal and globally optimal. Actually, the following proposition shows that the mean-square matrix of the optimum decentralized closed-loop system is less than that resulting from any admissible set of controls.

Proposition 2. Let $\left\{\overset{*}{u}_1, \ldots, \overset{*}{u}_M\right\}$ be the set of decentralized control laws defined by Eqs. (19)-(23) and let $\Sigma^*(Nk)$ be the resultant mean-square matrix of the state. Then for any admissible set of decentralized control laws $\{u_1, \ldots, u_M\}$

$$\Sigma^*(Nk) \leq \Sigma(Nk), \qquad k = k_0, k_0 + 1, \ldots, L - 1 \tag{26}$$

where $\Sigma(Nk)$ is the mean-square matrix of the state associated with $\{u_1, \ldots, u_M\}$.

Proof. By induction assume that for some k_i

$$\Sigma(Nk_i) \geq \Sigma^*(Nk_i) \tag{27}$$

for any $\{u_1, \ldots, u_M\} \in \Omega$. Then

$$\begin{aligned}\Sigma[N(k_i + 1)] &= \Phi[N(k_i + 1), Nk_i] \\ &\times \left\{I + \sum_{j=1}^{M} K_j(Nk_i)H_j(Nk_i)\right\}\Sigma(Nk_i) \\ &\times \left\{I + \sum_{j=1}^{M} H_j'(Nk_i)K_j'(Nk_i)\right\}\Phi'[N(k_i + 1), Nk_i]\end{aligned} \tag{28}$$

$$\begin{aligned}&\geq \Phi[N(k_i + 1), Nk_i] \\ &\times \left\{I + \sum_{j=1}^{M} K_j(Nk_i)H_j(Nk_i)\right\}\Sigma^*(Nk_i) \\ &\times \left\{I + \sum_{j=1}^{M} H_j'(Nk_i)K_j'(Nk_i)\right\}\Phi'[N(k_i + 1), Nk_i].\end{aligned} \tag{29}$$

Substituting for $\Sigma^*(Nk_1)$ from Eq. (22) into Eq. (29) we get

$$\begin{aligned}\Sigma[N(k_i + 1)] \geq \Sigma^*[N(k_i + 1)] &+ \Phi[N(k_i + 1), Nk_i] \\ &\times \Big\{\Sigma^*(Nk_i)H'(Nk_i)\left[H(Nk_i)\Sigma^*(Nk_i)H'(Nk_i)\right]^{\#} \\ &\times H(Nk_i)\Sigma^*(Nk_i) \\ &+ \sum_{j=1}^{M} K_j(Nk_i)H_j(Nk_i)\Sigma^*(Nk_i) \\ &\times \sum_{j=1}^{M} H'(Nk_i)K_j'(Nk_i)\Big\}\Phi'[N(k_i + 1), Nk_i]\end{aligned}$$

hence

$$\Sigma[N(k_i + 1)] \geq \Sigma^*[N(k_i + 1)]. \tag{30}$$

Since $\Sigma(Nk_0) \geq \Sigma^*(Nk_0)$, Eq. (26) follows by induction. Q.E.D.

In the remainder of this section, the behavior of the optimum decentralized closed-loop system over a finite time interval will be considered. In particular, it will be shown that under suitable observability assumption the initial state of the closed-loop system will tend to zero for almost all sample paths[2] in a finite time interval. However, before proceeding, the following definitions and lemma are needed.

Definition 2. System Eq. (4) is said to be completely observable at Nk_0 from its combined inputs with index ν if there exist a finite ν such that the matrix

$$M_{\nu,k_0}(N) = \left[H'(Nk_0) \;\vdots\; \Phi'[N(k_0+1), Nk_0]H'[N(k_0+1)] \;\vdots\; \cdots \;\vdots\; \Phi'[N(\nu-1), Nk_0]H'[N(\nu-1)]\right] \tag{31}$$

has full rank.

In the sequel, let R{M} and N{M} denote the range and null space of a matrix M, and assume that $\Phi[i+1, i]$ is invertible.

Lemma 1. Let $\Sigma^*[N(k+1)]$ be given by Eq. (22); then

$$N\left\{\Phi[Nk_0, N(k+1)]\Sigma^*[N(k+1)]\Phi'[Nk_0, N(k+1)]\right\} \supset R\{M_{k,k_0}(N)\}. \tag{32}$$

The proof of the above lemma can be found in [10].

Theorem 3. Assume that the system in Eq. (4) is completely observable at Nk_0 from its combined inputs with index ν, and let the decentralized controls be given by Eqs. (19)-(23). Then

$$\Sigma^*[N(k_0+\nu)] = 0 \tag{33}$$

[2]*Except for a set of initial conditions of measure zero, the state will tend to zero in a finite time interval.*

and

$$\overline{X}^*[N(k_0 + \nu)] = 0 \tag{34}$$

where $\Sigma^*[N(k_0 + \nu)]$ and $\overline{X}^*[N(k_0 + \nu)]$ are the state mean-square matrix and the mean of the optimum decentralized closed-loop system.

Proof. Since Eq. (4) is completely observable at Nk_0 with index ν, it follows that $M_{\nu,k_0}(N)$ has a full rank n. Hence from Lemma 1,

$$\Sigma^*[N(k_0 + \nu)] = 0. \tag{35}$$

But noting that $\Sigma^*[N(k_0 + \nu)]$ can be rewritten as

$$\begin{aligned}\Sigma^*[N(k_0 + \nu)] = \Bigg\{ \prod_{i=k_0}^{k_0+\nu-1} & \Phi[N(i + 1), Ni] \\ & \times [I - \Sigma^*(Ni)H'(Ni)[H(Ni)\Sigma^*(Ni)H'(Ni)]^{\#}H(Ni)]\Bigg\} \\ & \times \Sigma^*(Nk_0)\Bigg\{ \prod_{i=k_0}^{k_0+\nu-1} [I - H'(Ni) \\ & \qquad \times [H(Ni)\Sigma^*(Ni)H'(Ni)]^{\#}H(Ni)\Sigma^*(Ni)] \\ & \qquad \times \Phi'[N(i + 1), Ni]\Bigg\}.\end{aligned} \tag{36}$$

Since $\Sigma^*(Nk_0) = \Sigma_0 > 0$, it follows that

$$\begin{aligned}\prod_{i=k_0}^{k_0+\nu-1} & \Phi[N(i + 1), Ni][I - \Sigma^*(Ni)H'(Ni)[H(Ni)\Sigma^*(Ni)H'(Ni)]^{\#}] \\ & \times H(Ni) = 0.\end{aligned} \tag{37}$$

Substituting for $\{u_1, \ldots, u_M\}$ from Eqs. (19)-(23) into Eq. (4)

and taking the expected value, it can be seen that

$$\overline{X}^*[N(k_0 + \nu)] = \left\{ \prod_{i=k_0}^{k_0+\nu-1} \Phi[N(i + 1), Ni] \times [I - \Sigma^*(Ni)H'(Ni)[H(Ni)\Sigma^*(Ni)H'(Ni)]^{\#}] \times H(Ni) \right\} \overline{X}_0. \tag{38}$$

Hence, it follows from Eqs. (37) and (38) that

$$\overline{X}^*[N(k_0 + \nu)] = 0. \qquad \text{Q.E.D.}$$

Since the initial state of the system under consideration is assumed to have a Gaussian distribution, the above theorem implies that, except for a set of initial conditions of measure zero, the state of the decentralized closed-loop system will tend to zero in a finite time interval. Actually, it will be shown in Section IV that the decentralized set of controls (Eqs. (19)-(23)) is a dead-beat set of controls. The information structure required to implement the Nash equilibrium strategies (Eqs. (19)-(23)) is classical in the sense that each controller requires knowledge of the system model $\{\Phi(i + 1), B_j(i), H_j(i), j = 1, \ldots, M \; \forall_i\}$; the statistics of the uncertainties $\{\Sigma_0, \overline{X}_0\}$, the structure of the cost functions, and his output measurements, $y_j(N_k)$. The Nash strategies (Eqs. (8)-(11)) require in addition the weighting matrices $\{P_j(i), F_j(N_k), \forall_i, \forall_k, j = 1, \ldots, M\}$ of the cost functions. The on-line information exchange requirements are minimal since most of the above parameters can be predetermined off-line.

III. STOCHASTIC LINEAR SYSTEMS

In this section we consider the decentralized optimum control of large-scale, discrete time linear systems, with uncertainty in the measurements and in the system dynamics. The system under consideration is given by

$$X(i + 1) = \Phi(i + 1, i)X(i) + \sum_{j=1}^{M} B_j(i)u_j(i)$$
$$+ D(i)W(i), \quad i = 0, 1, \ldots, \tag{39}$$

where $X(i) \in R^n$, $u_j(i) \in R^{r_j}$. The uncertainty $W(i)$ in the system model is assumed to be a Gaussian stochastic process with

$$E\{W(i)\} = 0,$$
$$E\{W(i)W'(k)\} = \tilde{Q}(i)\delta(i - k), \tag{40}$$

where $\tilde{Q}(i)$ is a positive semidefinite $p \times p$ matrix, bounded for all i, and $\delta(\ )$ is the Dirac delta function.

The jth controller has access only to measurements of a subset of the state at discrete instants of time. These measurements are corrupted by noise and are given by

$$y_j(Nk) = H_j(Nk)X(Nk) + v_j(Nk), \quad k = 0, 1, \ldots, \tag{41}$$

where $y_j(Nk) \in R^{m_j}$; $N \geq 1$ is an integer that determines the frequency at which the output is sampled relative to that of the control. The measurement noise $v_j(Nk)$ is assumed to be a Gaussian stochastic process with

$$E\{v_j(Nk)\} = 0,$$
$$E\{v_i(Nk)v_j'(Nl)\} = R_{ij}(Nk)\delta[N(k - l)], \tag{42}$$

where $R_{ij}(Nk)$ is an $m_i \times m_j$ matrix.

The initial state of the system is assumed to have a Gaussian distribution with

$$E\{X(Nk_0)\} = \overline{X}(Nk_0),$$
$$E\{X(Nk_0)X'(Nk_0)\} = \Sigma(Nk_0) = \Sigma_0 > 0. \tag{43}$$

Furthermore, it will be assumed that

$$E\{W(i)v'(Nk)\} = 0,$$
$$E\{W(i)X'(Nk_0)\} = 0, \qquad E\{v(Nk)X'(Nk_0)\} = 0. \tag{44}$$

Throughout the following let the m × m matrix R be given by

$$R = \begin{bmatrix} R_{11} & R_{12} & \cdots & R_{1m} \\ \vdots & \vdots & & \vdots \\ R_{1m} & R_{2m} & & R_{mm} \end{bmatrix} > 0. \tag{45}$$

Theorem 4. The set of decentralized control laws $\left\{\overset{*}{u}_1, \ldots, \overset{*}{u}_j, \ldots, \overset{*}{u}_M\right\}$, where

$$\overset{*}{u}_j(i) = -P_j^{-1}(i)B_j'(i)\Phi'[N(k+1), i+1]$$
$$\times F_j'[N(k+1)]\overset{*}{K}_j(Nk)y^*(Nk), \qquad Nk \le i < N(k+1),$$
$$k = k_0, k_0 + 1, \ldots, L-1, \quad j = 1, \ldots, M, \tag{46}$$

is a sequential Nash equilibrium set for the cost functions

$$J_j(u_1, \ldots, u_j, \ldots, u_m, i, Nk)$$
$$= \frac{1}{2} E\left\{X'[N(k+1)]F_j'[N(k+1)]F_j[N(k+1)]X[N(k+1)]\right.$$
$$\left. + \sum_{i=Nk}^{N(k+1)-1} u_j'(i)P_j(i)u_j(i)\right\}, \qquad j = 1, \ldots, M,$$
$$k = k_0, k_0 + 1, \ldots, L-1 \tag{47}$$

subject to the constraints and assumptions of Eqs. (1) and (2) and Eqs. (39)-(45), where the $\overset{*}{K}_j(Nk)$ satisfy the set of M linear matrix equations.

$$F_j[N(k+1)]\left\{\sum_{l=1}^{M}\left[W_l[N(k+1), Nk]F_l'[N(k+1)]\overset{*}{K}_l(Nk)H_l(Nk)\right]\right.$$
$$\left.\times\ \Sigma^*(Nk)H_j'(Nk)\right\}$$
$$+\sum_{l=1}^{M} W_l[N(k+1), Nk]F_l'[N(k+1)]\overset{*}{K}_l(Nk)R_{lj}(Nk)$$
$$+\overset{*}{K}_j(Nk)\left[H_j(Nk)\Sigma^*(Nk)H_j'(Nk) + R_{jj}(Nk)\right]$$
$$= F_j[N(k+1)]\Phi[N(k+1), Nk]\Sigma^*(Nk)H_j'(Nk),$$
$$j = 1, \ldots, M, \tag{48}$$

and

$$\Sigma^*[N(k+1)] = \left\{\Phi[N(k+1), Nk]\right.$$
$$\left.-\sum_{j=1}^{M} W_j[N(k+1), Nk]F_j'[N(k+1)]\overset{*}{K}_j(Nk)\right\}$$
$$\times\ \Sigma^*(Nk)\left\{\Phi'[N(k+1), Nk]\right.$$
$$-\sum_{j=1}^{M} H_j'(Nk)\overset{*}{K}{}_j'(Nk)F_j[N(k+1)]$$
$$\left.\times\ W_j[N(k+1), Nk]\right\}$$
$$\times\sum_{l=1}^{M}\sum_{j=1}^{M} W_j[N(k+1), Nk]F_j'[N(k+1)]$$
$$\times\ \overset{*}{K}_j(Nk)R_{jl}\overset{*}{K}{}_l'(Nk)F_l'[N(k+1)]$$
$$\times\ W_l[N(k+1), Nk] + Q[N(k+1), Nk] \tag{49}$$

with $\Sigma^*(Nk_0) = \Sigma_0$; $W_j[N(k+1), Nk]$ is given by Eq. (11) and

$$Q[N(k+1), Nk] = \sum_{i=Nk}^{N(k+1)} \Phi[N(k+1), i+1]D(i)\tilde{Q}(i)D'(i)$$
$$\times\ \Phi'[N(k+1), i]. \tag{50}$$

The proof of this theorem is given in the Appendix.

The computation required to determine the decentralized set of gains is relatively simple. First, the set of M linear matrix equations (Eq. (48)) is solved for $K^*(Nk)$, starting from the initial condition $\Sigma^*(Nk_0)$. These gains are then used to determine $\Sigma^*[N(k + 1)]$ from Eq. (49). This sequence is repeated for $k = k_0, \ldots, L - 1$ to determine an admissible Nash equilibrium set over the interval of interest. Conditions for the solvability of Eq. (48) are too difficult to determine in general. In the special case of a single controller and a single cost function, the optimum gain can be computed explicitly if $\{I + F_1'[N(k + 1)]W_1[N(k + 1), Nk]F_1[N(k + 1)]\}$ is invertible. In this case, the gain is given by

$$\begin{aligned} K_1^*(Nk) &= \{I + F_1'[N(k + 1)]W_1[N(k + 1), Nk]F_1[N(k + 1)]\}^{-1} \\ &\quad \times F_1[N(k + 1)]\Phi[N(k + 1), Nk] \\ &\quad \times \Sigma^*(Nk)H_1'(Nk)\left[H_1(Nk)\Sigma^*(Nk)H_1'(Nk) + R_{11}\right]^{-1}, \end{aligned} \tag{51}$$

where $\Sigma^*(Nk)$ is determined recursively from Eq. (49) with $j = l = 1$.

Another case of interest is when each controller penalizes only a weighted mean-square value of the state at the sampling times, i.e., $P_j(i) \equiv 0$ for $j = 1, \ldots, M$. In this case, the decentralized gains $K_j^*(Nk)$ can be computed explicitly if the system under consideration is completely controllable from each input. These results are summarized in the following theorem.

Theorem 5. The set of decentralized control laws $\left\{\overset{*}{u}_1, \ldots, \overset{*}{u}_M\right\}$ given by

$$\overset{*}{u}_j(i) = -B_j'(i)\Phi'[Nk, i+1]\tilde{W}_j^{-1}[N(k+1), Nk]\overset{*}{K}_j(Nk)\overset{*}{y}_j(Nk),$$
$$Nk \leq i < N(k+1), \quad j = 1, \ldots, M,$$
$$k = k_0, k_0 + 1, \ldots, k_0 + L - 1 \tag{52}$$

is a sequential Nash equilibrium set for the costs

$$\tilde{J}_j[u_1, \ldots, u_j, \ldots, u_M, i, Nk]$$
$$= \frac{1}{2} E\left\{X'[N(k+1)]F_j'[N(k+1)]F_j[N(k+1)]X[(k+1)]\right\},$$
$$j = 1, \ldots, M; \quad k = k_0, k_0 + 1, \ldots, k_0 + L - 1. \tag{53}$$

Subject to the constraints and assumptions (Eqs. (39)-(45) and (18)), where

$$K^*(Nk) \triangleq \left[\overset{*}{K}_1(Nk) \cdots \overset{*}{K}_j(Nk) \cdots \overset{*}{K}_M(Nk)\right]$$
$$= \Sigma^*(Nk)H'(Nk)[H(Nk)\Sigma^*(Nk)H'(Nk) + R(Nk)]^{-1} \tag{54}$$

$H(Nk)$ is the $m \times n$ combined observability matrix of Eq. (23), $R(Nk)$ is given by Eq. (45) and

$$\Sigma^*[N(k+1)] = \Phi[N(k+1), Nk][\Sigma^*(Nk) - \Sigma^*(Nk)H'(Nk)$$
$$\times [H(Nk)\Sigma^*(Nk)H'(Nk) + R(Nk)]^{-1}$$
$$\times H(Nk)\Sigma^*(Nk)]\Phi'[N(k+1), Nk] + Q(Nk) \tag{55}$$

with $\Sigma^*(Nk_0) = \Sigma_0$. Furthermore, the state mean-square matrix of the closed-loop system is given by Eq. (55) and its mean $\overline{X}^*(Nk)$ by

$$\overline{X}^*[N(k+1)] = \Phi[N(k+1), Nk]\{I - K^*(Nk)H(Nk)\}\overline{X}^*(Nk)$$
$$\overline{X}^*(Nk_0) = \overline{X}_0. \tag{56}$$

The proof of the above theorem is similar to that of Theorem 4, and can be obtained by substituting $P_j(i) = 0$ in Eq. (A.12) of the Appendix, then proceeding in a similar fashion.

It is interesting to note that the decentralized gains $\overset{*}{K}_j(Nk)$ are obtained by partitioning a combined gain $K^*(Nk)$ that has the same structure as the Kalman gain. Similarly, the state mean-square matrix $\Sigma^*(Nk)$ of the decentralized closed-loop system is obtained from a recursive matrix equation of the Riccati type, whose properties are well known [11,12]. These properties will be used in the sequel to establish the asymptotic properties of the decentralized control laws (Eqs. (54) and (55)).

Results similar to those obtained in Section II can be developed. In particular, it can be shown that for any set of admissible controls

$$\Sigma^*[N(k + 1)] \leq \Sigma[N(k + 1)],$$
$$k = k_0, k_0 + 1, \ldots, L - 1, \qquad (57)$$

where $\Sigma^*[N(k + 1)]$ is the state mean-square matrix associated with the decentralized set of controls (Eqs. (52)-(55)). By noting that these control laws are independent of the weighting matrices $F_j[N(k + 1)]$, it can be deduced that $\left\{\overset{*}{u}_1, \ldots, \overset{*}{u}_M\right\}$, besides being a sequential Nash equilibrium set, is a sequential Parato-optimal set and a sequential optimal control set for the cost function (Eq. (53)).

The information exchange requirements for implementing the Nash equilibrium strategies (Eqs. (46)-(49) and (52)-(55)) are the same as those outlined in the previous section, with the added information requirements about $\{D(i), \tilde{Q}(i), R_j(Nk), \forall i, k\}$.

IV. FINITE TIME CONTROL AND STABILITY

The deterministic properties of the decentralized closed-loop system are now considered. Of particular interest are the finite time and asymptotic behavior of the state in the absence of disturbances. Specifically, consider the large-scale, discrete time system described by Eqs. (4) and (5), and assume that N, the integer that determines the frequency at which the output is sampled relative to that of the control, is chosen such that

$$\tilde{W}_j[N(k+1), Nk] \text{ is invertible for } j = 1, \ldots, M. \tag{58}$$

It should be noted that condition Eq. (58) is satisfied if system Eq. (4) is completely controllable from each input. Throughout this section, it will be assumed that the initial state $X(Nk_0)$ is unknown and that the jth controller ($j = 1, \ldots, M$) has access only to the jth output.

Definition 3. System Eq. (4) is said to be finite time controllable at Nk_0 by decentralized output feedback if, given any $X_L \in R^n$, there exists a set of controls

$$\{u_1(i, y_1(kN), \ldots, u_j(i, y_j(kN), X_L),$$
$$\ldots, u_M(i, y_j(kN), X_L)\}$$

such that $X[N(k_0 + L)] = X_L$ for some finite integer L.

Theorem 6. Assume that Eq. (58) is satisfied, then system (4) is finite time controllable by decentalized output feedback if and only if it is completely observable at Nk_0 from its combined inputs.

Proof. (i) Necessity is well known.

(ii) Sufficiency: Let $X_L \in R^n$ be an arbitrary state and consider the decentralized set of controls

$$u_j(i) = -B'(i)\Phi'[Nk, i + 1]\tilde{W}_j^{-1}[N(k + 1), Nk]$$
$$\times \left\{\overset{*}{K}_j(Nk)[y_j(Nk) - H_j(Nk)X_L] - \Phi[Nk, N(k + 1)]X_L + X_L\right\},$$
$$Nk \leq i < N(k + 1), \quad j = 1, \ldots, M,$$
$$k = k_0, k_0 + 1, \ldots, k_0 + L - 1, \tag{59}$$

where $\tilde{W}_j[N(k + 1), Nk]$ is given by Eq. (18) and $\overset{*}{K}_j(Nk)$ is given by Eqs. (21)-(23). Substituting Eq. (58) into Eq. (4) we get

$$X[N(k + 1)] = \Phi[N(k + 1), Nk]$$
$$\times \left\{I - \sum_{j=1}^{M} \overset{*}{K}_j(Nk)H_j(Nk)\right\}[X(Nk) - X_L] + X_L. \tag{60}$$

Equation (60) can be rewritten as

$$X[N(k + 1)] - X_L = \Phi[N(k + 1), Nk]$$
$$\times \{I - K^*(Nk)H(Nk)\}[X(Nk) - X_L], \tag{61}$$

where $K^*(Nk)$ is given by Eq. (21) and $H(Nk)$ is defined by Eq. (23). Since Eq. (4) is completely observable at Nk_0 from its combined inputs, it follows that $M_{\nu,k_0}(N)$ has full rank for some finite ν. Hence, from Lemma 1, we have

$$N\left\{\Phi[Nk_0, N(k_0 + \nu)]\Sigma^*[N(k_0 + \nu)]\Phi'[Nk_0, N(k_0 + \nu)]\right\}$$
$$= R^n \tag{62}$$

and since $\Phi[Nk_0, N(k_0 + \nu)]$ is nonsingular

$$N\left\{\Sigma^*[N(k_0 + \nu)]\right\} = R^n. \tag{63}$$

But from Eq. (22) $\Sigma^*[N(k_0 + \nu)]$ can be rewritten as

$$\Sigma^*[N(k_0 + \nu)]$$
$$= \prod_{i=k_0}^{k_0+\nu-1} \Phi[N(i + 1), Ni]\{I - \Sigma^*(Ni)H'(Ni) \times [H(Ni)\Sigma^*(Ni)H'(Ni)]^{\#}H(Ni)\}$$
$$\times \Sigma^*(Nk_0) \prod_{i=k_0}^{k_0+\nu-1} \{I - H'(Ni)[H(Ni)\Sigma^*(Ni)H'(Ni)]^{\#}H(Ni) \times \Sigma^*(Ni)\Phi'[N(i + 1), Ni]\}. \tag{64}$$

Since $\Sigma^*(Nk_0) = \Sigma_0 > 0$, it follows from Eqs. (64) and (63) that

$$N\left\{\prod_{i=k_0}^{k_0+\nu-1} \Phi[N(i + 1), Ni]\right\}\{I - \Sigma^*(ni)H'(Ni) \times [H(Ni)\Sigma^*(Ni)H'(Ni)]^{\#}H(Ni)\} = R^n. \tag{65}$$

Substituting for $K^*(Nk)$ from Eq. (23), Eq. (61) can be rewritten as

$$X[N(k_0 + \nu)] - X_L = \prod_{i=k_0}^{k_0+\nu-1} \Phi[N(i + 1), Ni] \times \{I - \Sigma^*(Ni)H'(Ni) \times [H(Ni)\Sigma^*(Ni)H'(Ni)]^{\#}H(Ni)\} \times [X(Nk_0) - X_L]. \tag{66}$$

From Eqs. (66) and (65) it can be deduced that

$$X[N(k_0 + \nu)] = X_L. \qquad \text{Q.E.D.}$$

It should be noted that the decentralized output feedback control set (Eq. (58)) is basically the Nash equilibrium set (Eqs. (19)-(23)) modified to account for a desired nonzero terminal state. Actually, it can be shown that the Nash equilibrium set is a dead-beat set of decentralized control laws that will drive the state to the origin in at most $[\mu n]$ steps. A tighter bound on the number of steps required to drive the state to the origin will be established in the following corollary.

Corollary 1. Let μ_j denote the minimum ℓ for which $\tilde{W}_j[\ell(k+1), \ell k]$ is invertible and define

$$\mu = \max\{\mu_j\} \qquad j = 1, \ldots, M. \tag{67}$$

Assume that system Eq. (4) is completely observable from its combined inputs with index ν. Then the decentralized set of controls $\{u_1(i, y_1(\mu k)), \ldots, u_M(i, y_M(\mu k))\}$, where

$$u_j(i, y_j(\mu k) = -B_j'(i)\Phi'(\mu k, i+1)\tilde{W}^{-1} \times [\mu(k+1), \mu k]\overset{*}{K}_j(\mu k)y_j(\mu k), \tag{68}$$

$$\mu k \leq i < \mu(k+1), \quad j = 1, \ldots, M, \quad k = k_0, \ldots, k_0 + \nu - 1,$$

and $K^*(\mu k)$ is given by Eqs. (21)-(23), will drive the system to the origin in at most $[\mu\nu]$ steps.

It is interesting to compare the above results with dead-beat controller-observers. It is well known [13] that a dead-beat observer requires, at most, ν steps to determine the initial state of the system, while a dead-beat controller requires, at most, μ steps to drive a known initial state to the origin. Hence, a dead-beat controller-observer will drive an unknown initial state to the origin in, at most, $\mu + \nu$ steps, which is less than the number of steps required by the output feedback control law (Eq. (68)).

In many applications of decentralized control, the design objective is to obtain an asymptotically stable closed-loop system. Under suitable assumptions, the Nash equilibrium set

(Eqs. (52)-(55)) will result in an asymptotically stable decentralized closed-loop system. These assumptions are

$$0 < \alpha_{1j}I \leq \tilde{W}_j[N(k+1), Nk)] \leq \alpha_{2j}I < \infty, \qquad j = 1, \ldots, M, \ \forall k \tag{69}$$

$$0 < \beta_1 I \leq \sum_{k=l-q}^{l-1} \Phi[Nl, N(k+1)]Q[N(k+1), Nk] \times \Phi'[Nl, N(k+1)] \leq \beta_2 I < \infty, \qquad \forall l \geq q \tag{70}$$

$$||\Phi[Nl, Nq]|| < \alpha_3 |N(l - q)|, \qquad \forall l, q \tag{71}$$

$$0 < \gamma_1 I \leq \sum_{k=l-q}^{l} \Phi'[Nk, Nl]H'(Nk)R^{-1}(Nk)H(Nk)\Phi[Nk, Nl] < \gamma_2 I < \infty, \qquad \forall l \geq q \tag{72}$$

where α_{1j}, α_{2j}, α_3, β_1, β_2, γ_1, and γ_2 are real constants.

Theorem 7. If Eqs. (69)-(72) are satisfied, then the Nash equilibrium set $\left\{\overset{*}{u}_1(i, y_1(kN)), \ldots, \overset{*}{u}_M(i, y_M(kN))\right\}$ will result in a closed-loop system that is uniformly asymptotically stable in the large, where

$$\overset{*}{u}_j(i) = -B_j'(i)\Phi'[Nk, i+1]\tilde{W}_j^{-1}[N(k+1), Nk] \times \overset{*}{K}_j(Nk)y_j(Nk) \qquad Nk \leq i < N(k+1), \quad k = k_0, k_0 + 1, \ldots, j = 1, \ldots, M \tag{73}$$

and $\overset{*}{K}_j$ is given by Eqs. (54) and (55). The proof of the above theorem is given in the Appendix.

In the time invariant case, assumptions (69)-(72) are relaxed to

$$[\Phi, B_j] \text{ is a controllable pair for } j = 1, \ldots, M; \tag{74}$$

$$[\Phi^N, H] \text{ is an observable pair;} \tag{75}$$

$[\Phi^N, G]$ is a controllable pair where $GG' = Q$; (76)

and the Nash equilibrium set is discrete time periodic with period N. These results are summarized in the following theorem.

Theorem 8. Assume that Eqs. (74)-(76) are satisfied, then the set of periodic Nash equilibrium set of control laws $\{\overset{*}{u}_1, \ldots, \overset{*}{u}_m\}$, with

$$\overset{*}{u}_j[i, y_j(Nk)] = -B_j'\Phi'^{Nk-i-1}W_j^{-1}(N)\tilde{K}_j y_j(Nk),$$

$$Nk \leq i < N(k+1), \quad k = 0, 1, \ldots, \quad j = 1, \ldots, M, \tag{77}$$

result in an asymptotically stable closed-loop system. $\tilde{K}_j$ is obtained from partitioning the combined gain $\tilde{K}$, which is given by

$$\tilde{K} \triangleq \left[\tilde{K}_1 \cdots \tilde{K}_j \cdots \tilde{K}_M\right] = \tilde{\Sigma}H'[H\tilde{\Sigma}H' + R]^{-1}, \tag{78}$$

where $\tilde{\Sigma}$ is the positive definite solution of the matrix equation

$$\tilde{\Sigma} = \Phi^N\{\tilde{\Sigma} - \tilde{\Sigma}H'[H\tilde{\Sigma}H' + R]^{-1}H\tilde{\Sigma}\}\Phi'^N + Q \tag{79}$$

and

$$W_j(N) = \sum_{i=0}^{N-1} \Phi^{-(i+1)}B_jB_j'\Phi'^{-(i+1)}. \tag{80}$$

The results presented in Theorems 7 and 8 represent a generalization of those obtained by Chammas and Leondes [14] about the stabilization of linear systems by discrete output feedback.

V. CONCLUSIONS

The approach presented in this chapter for the decentralized control of large-scale, discrete time-linear systems is different than the standard LQG approach in at least two aspects.

(1) The decentalized feedback gains are allowed to vary at discrete instants of time between output measurements, i.e.,

the control sampling rate is higher than that of the measurements.

(2) The time interval of interest is divided into a sequence of subintervals; the decentralized controls are then determined by finding a Nash equilibrium point for a set of quadratic cost functions over each subinterval, sequentially.

The main advantage of the proposed approach is that the gains can be computed on-line, using relatively simple algorithms. Furthermore, the resultant close-loop system is asymptotically stable in the large, provided that some standard assumptions are satisfied.

APPENDIX

Proof of Theorem 1. Let the set of admissible controls Ω be given by Eqs. (1) and (2); then for any $u_j[i, y(Nk)] \in \Omega$, the state of system Eq. (4) at the sampling times Nk is given by

$$X[N(k+1)] = \Phi[N(k+1), Nk]X[Nk] + \sum_{l=1}^{M}\left(\sum_{i=Nk}^{N(K+1)-1} \Phi[N(k+1), i+1]B_l(i)C_l(i)y_l(Nk)\right). \tag{A.1}$$

Defining $\Sigma[N(k+1)] = E\{X[N(k+1)]X'[N(k+1)]\}$, then from (A.1)

$$\begin{aligned}\Sigma[N(k+1)] = {} & \left\{\Phi[N(k+1), Nk] + \sum_{l=1}^{M}\sum_{i=Nk}^{N(k+1)-1} \Phi[N(k+1), i+1]\right.\\ & \left.\times B_l(i)C_l(i)H_l(Nk)\right\}\Sigma(Nk)\\ & \times\left\{\Phi'[N(k+1), Nk] + \sum_{l=1}^{M} H_l'(Nk)\sum_{i=Nk}^{N(K+1)-1}\right.\\ & \left.\times C_l'(i)B_l'(i)\Phi'[N(k+1), i+1]\right\}.\end{aligned} \tag{A.2}$$

Using the trace operator tr, Eq. (7) can be rewritten as

$$J_j(C_1, \ldots, C_j, \ldots C_M, i, Nk)$$

$$= \frac{1}{2} \operatorname{tr}\left\{F_j[N(k+1)]\Sigma[N(k+1)]F_j'[N(k+1)]\right\}$$

$$+ \sum_{i=Nk}^{N(k+1)-1} P(i)C_j(i)H_j(Nk)\Sigma(Nk)H_j'(Nk)C_j'(i),$$

$$Nk \leq i < N(k+1); \quad k + k_0, k_0 + 1, \ldots, L - 1. \tag{A.3}$$

The problem under consideration is now equivalent to finding a sequential Nash equilibrium set of output feedback gains $\left\{\overset{*}{C}_1(i), \ldots, \overset{*}{C}_j(i), \ldots, \overset{*}{C}_M(i)\right\}$ such that for $J = 1, \ldots, M$ and $k - k_0, k_0 + 1, \ldots, L - 1$ the inequality

$$J_j\left(\overset{*}{C}_1, \ldots, \overset{*}{C}_j, \ldots, \overset{*}{C}_M, i, Nk\right)$$

$$\leq \left(\overset{*}{C}_1, \ldots, C_j, \ldots, \overset{*}{C}_M, i, Nk\right) \tag{A.4}$$

is satisfied subject to the constraints of Eqs. (A.2) and (6).

The sequential Nash equilibrium set is determined by using standard calculus of variation techniques, over each sequence of N samples, starting at Nk_0. Let $\left\{\overset{*}{C}_1(i), \ldots, \overset{*}{C}_j, \ldots, \overset{*}{C}_M(i)\right\}$ be a Nash equilibrium set of output gains for $Nk \leq i < N(k+1)$, and let $\delta C_j(i)$ be a first-order variation in the jth gain over the interval $Nk \leq i < N(k+1)$. Simple computation shows that the first-order variation in the jth cost function is given by

$$\delta J_j\left(\overset{*}{C}_1, \ldots, \overset{*}{C}_j + \delta C_j, \ldots, \overset{*}{C}_M, i, Nk\right)$$

$$= \operatorname{tr}\Bigg[F_j[N(k+1)]\Bigg\{\Phi[N(k+1), Nk]$$

$$+ \sum_{l=1}^{M} \sum_{i=Nk}^{N(k+1)-1} \Phi[N(k+1), i+1]B_l(i)\overset{*}{C}_l(i)H_l(Nk)\Bigg\}$$

$$\times\ \Sigma^{*}(Nk)H'(Nk)\sum_{i=Nk}^{N(K+1)-1}\delta C_j'(i)B_j'(i)$$

$$\left.\times\ \Phi'[N(k+1),\ i+1]F_j'[N(k+1)]\right]$$

$$+\ \mathrm{tr}\left\{\sum_{i=Nk}^{N(k+1)-1}P_j(i)\overset{*}{C}_j(i)H_j(Nk)\Sigma^{*}(Nk)H_j'(Nk)\delta C_j'(i)\right\}. \qquad (A.5)$$

Let

$$\overset{*}{C}_j(i) = -P_j^{-1}(i)B_j'(i)\Phi'[N(k+1),\ i+1]$$

$$\times\ F_j'[N(k+1)]\overset{*}{K}_j(Nk). \qquad (A.6)$$

Then substituting from Eq. (A.6) into Eq. (A.5) we get

$$\delta J_j\left(\overset{*}{C}_1,\ \ldots,\ \overset{*}{C}_j+\delta C_j,\ \ldots,\ \overset{*}{C}_M,\ i,\ Nk\right)$$

$$= \mathrm{tr}\Bigg[F_j[N(k+1)]\Bigg[\Phi[N(k+1),\ Nk]$$

$$-\ \sum_{l=1}^{M}\left(W_l[N(k+1),\ Nk]F_l'(Nk)\overset{*}{K}_l(Nk)H_l(Nk)\right)$$

$$-\ \overset{*}{K}_j(Nk)H_j(Nk)\Bigg]\Sigma^{*}(Nk)H_j'(Nk)\sum_{i=Nk}^{N(k+1)-1}\delta C_j'(i)B_j'(i)$$

$$\times\ \Phi'[N(k+1),\ i+1]F_j'[N(k+1)]\Bigg], \qquad (A.7)$$

where $W_j[N(k+1),\ Nk]$ is given by Eq. (11).

From Eq. (A.7) it can be seen that if the set of gains $\overset{*}{K}_j(Nk)$ satisfies the equation

$$F_j[N(k+1)]\Bigg\{\sum_{l=1}^{M}\left[W_l[N(k+1),\ Nk]F_l'[N(k+1)]\overset{*}{K}_l(Nk)H_l(Nk)\right]$$

$$\times\ \Sigma^{*}(Nk)H_j'(Nk)\ +\ \overset{*}{K}_j(Nk)H_j(Nk)\Sigma^{*}(Nk)H_j'(Nk)\Bigg\}$$

$$= F_j[N(k+1)]\Phi[N(k+1),\ Nk]\Sigma^{*}(Nk)H_j'(Nk) \qquad (A.8)$$

for $j = 1, \ldots, M$ and $k = k_0, k_0 + 1, \ldots, L - 1$, then

$$\delta J_j\left(\overset{*}{C}_1, \ldots, \overset{*}{C}_j + \delta\overset{*}{C}_j, \ldots, \overset{*}{C}_M, i, Nk\right) \equiv 0 \tag{A.9}$$

for $j \equiv 1, \ldots, M$, $k = k_0, k_0 + 1, \ldots, L - 1$. Similarly simple computation shows that if $\overset{*}{C}_j(i)$ is given by Eq. (A.6), where $\overset{*}{K}_j(Nk)$ satisfies Eq. (A.8), then $\delta^2 J_j\left(\overset{*}{C}_1, \ldots, \overset{*}{C}_j + \delta C_j, \ldots, \overset{*}{C}_M, i, Nk\right)$, the second-order variation in the jth cost is given by

$$\begin{aligned}
&\delta^2 J_j\left(\overset{*}{C}_1, \ldots, \overset{*}{C}_j + \delta C_j, \ldots, \overset{*}{C}_M, i, Nk\right) \\
&\quad = \frac{1}{2} \operatorname{tr}\Bigg\{F_j[N(k + 1)] \\
&\qquad \times \Bigg\{\left[\sum_{i=Nk}^{N(k+1)-1} \Phi[N(k + 1), i + 1]B_j(i)\delta C_j(i)\right] \\
&\qquad\qquad \times H_j(Nk)\Sigma^*(Nk)H_j'(Nk) \\
&\qquad \times \left[\sum_{i=1}^{N(k+1)-1} \delta C_j'(i)B_j'(i)\Phi'[N(k + 1), i + 1]\right]\Bigg\} \\
&\qquad\qquad \times F_j'[N(k + 1)] \\
&\qquad + \sum_{i=1}^{N(K+1)-1} P_j(i)\delta C_j(i)H_j(Nk)\Sigma^*(Nk)H_j'(Nk)\delta C_k'(i)\Bigg\}
\end{aligned} \tag{A.10}$$

for $j = 1, \ldots, M$ and $k = k_0, k + 1, \ldots, L - 1$. But Eq. (A.10) is positive semidefinite. Hence

$$\begin{aligned}
&J_j\left(\overset{*}{C}_1, \ldots, \overset{*}{C}_j, \ldots, \overset{*}{C}_M, i, Nk\right) \\
&\quad \geq J_j\left(\overset{*}{C}_1, \ldots, C_j, \ldots, \overset{*}{C}_M, i, Nk\right).
\end{aligned} \tag{A.11}$$

Q.E.D.

Proof of Theorem 4. Let $\left\{\overset{*}{u}_1, \ldots, \overset{*}{u}_M\right\}$ be an admissible, sequential Nash equilibrium set. Then the first-order variation $\delta J_j\left[\overset{*}{u}_1, \ldots, \overset{*}{u}_j + \delta u_j, \ldots, \overset{*}{u}_M, i, Nk\right]$ in the jth controller cost is given by

$$\delta J_j\Big[\overset{*}{u}_1, \ldots, \overset{*}{u}_j + \delta u_j, \ldots, \overset{*}{u}_M, i, Nk\Big]$$

$$= \operatorname{tr}\Bigg[F_j[N(k+1)]\Bigg\{\Phi[N(k+1), Nk] + \sum_{l=1}^{M}\sum_{i=Nk}^{N(k+1)-1} \Phi[N(k+1), i+1]B_l(i) \times \overset{*}{C}_l(i)[H_l(Nk)\Sigma^*(Nk)\Big[H_j'(Nk) + R_{lj}(Nk)\Big]\Bigg\}$$

$$\times \sum_{i=Nk}^{N(k+1)-1} \delta C_j'(i)B_l'(i)\Phi'[N(k+1), i+1]F_j'[N(k+1)]\Bigg]$$

$$+ \operatorname{tr}\Bigg\{\sum_{i=Nk}^{N(k+1)-1} P_j(i)\overset{*}{C}_j(i)\Big[H_j(Nk)\Sigma^*(Nk)H_j'(Nk) + R_{jj}(Nk)\Big]\delta C_j'(i)\Bigg\}. \qquad \text{(A.12)}$$

Let $\overset{*}{C}_j(i)$ be given by

$$\overset{*}{C}_j(i) = -P_j^{-1}(i)B_j'(i)\Phi'[N(k+1), i+1] \times F_j'[N(k+1)]\overset{*}{K}_j(Nk) \qquad \text{(A.13)}$$

for $j = 1, \ldots, M$. Then Eq. (A.12) can be rewritten as

$$\delta J_j\Big[\overset{*}{C}_1, \ldots, \overset{*}{C}_j + \delta C_j, \ldots, \overset{*}{C}_M, i, Nk\Big]$$

$$= \operatorname{tr}\Bigg[F_j[N(k+1)]\Bigg\{\Phi[N(k+1), Nk]\Sigma^*(Nk)H_j'(Nk) - \sum_{l=1}^{M} W_l[N(k+1), Nk]F_j'[N(k+1)] \times \overset{*}{K}_l(Nk)H_l(Nk)\Sigma^*(Nk)H_j'(Nk) + R_{lj}(Nk)\Bigg\}$$

$$- \overset{*}{K}_j(Nk)\Big[H_j(Nk)\Sigma^*(nk)H_j'(Nk) + R_{jj}(Nk)\Big]\Bigg]$$

$$\times \sum_{i=Nk}^{N(k+1)-1} \delta C_j'(i)B_l'(i)\Phi'[N(k+1), i+1]F_j'[N(k+1)]. \qquad \text{(A.14)}$$

From Eq. (A.14) it can be seen that if $\overset{*}{K}_j(Nk)$ satisfies Eq. (48) for j = 1, ..., M then

$$\delta J_j\left[\overset{*}{C}_1, \ldots, \overset{*}{C}_j + \delta C_j, \ldots, \overset{*}{C}_M, i, Nk\right] \equiv 0$$

for j = 1, ..., M. Similarly, it can be shown that for $\left\{\overset{*}{u}_1, \ldots, \overset{*}{u}_j, \ldots, \overset{*}{u}_M\right\}$,

$$\delta^2 J_j\left[\overset{*}{C}_1, \ldots, \overset{*}{C}_j + \delta C_j, \ldots, \overset{*}{C}_M, i, Nk\right] \geq 0 \tag{A.15}$$

for j = 1, ..., M. Q.E.D.

Proof of Theorem 7. Substituting the decentralized set of controls Eq. (A.16) into Eq. (71) we get

$$\begin{aligned} X[N(k+1)] &= \Phi[N(k+1), Nk] \\ &\quad \times \{I - \Sigma^*(Nk)H'(Nk)[H(Nk)\Sigma^*(Nk)H'(Nk) \\ &\quad + R(Nk)]^{-1}H(Nk)\}X(Nk). \end{aligned} \tag{A.16}$$

Let $P^*(Nk)$ be given by

$$\begin{aligned} P^*(Nk) &= \{\Sigma^*(Nk) - \Sigma^*(Nk)H'(Nk)[H(Nk)\Sigma^*(Nk)H'(Nk) + R(Nk)]^{-1} \\ &\quad \times H(Nk)\Sigma^*(Nk)\}. \end{aligned} \tag{A.17}$$

Then it was shown in Deyst [15,16] that if Eqs. (70) and (72) are satisfied, then $P^*(Nk)$ is bounded from above and below for every k, specifically

$$\frac{\beta_1}{1 + \beta_1\gamma_2} I \leq P^*(Nk) \leq \left\{\frac{1}{\gamma_1} + \frac{q\gamma_2^2\beta_2}{\gamma_1^2}\right\} I \tag{A.18}$$

where q is an integer.

Consider the function

$$\begin{aligned} &V\{X[N(k+1)], N(k+1)\} \\ &\quad = X'[N(k+1)]\Phi'[Nk, N(k+1)] \\ &\qquad \times P^{*-1}(Nk)\Phi[Nk, N(k+1)]X[N(k+1)]. \end{aligned} \tag{A.19}$$

From Eq. (71) it can be seen that

$$I\,\alpha_3^{-2}(N) \leq \Phi'[Nk, N(k+1)]\Phi[Nk, N(k+1)]$$
$$\leq \alpha_3^2(N)\,I\,. \qquad (A.20)$$

Combining Eqs. (A.20) and (A.18), we get

$$\frac{\gamma_1^2\alpha_3^{-2}}{\gamma_1 + N\gamma_2^2\beta_2}\,I \leq \Phi'[Nk, N(k+1)]P^{*-1}(Nk)\Phi[Nk, N(k+1)]$$
$$\leq \frac{1+\beta_1\gamma_2}{\beta_1}\,\alpha_3^2\,I. \qquad (A.21)$$

Hence $V[X[N(k+1)], N(k+1)]$ is uniformly bounded from above and below for each k, i.e., there exist continuous, nondecreasing scalar functions

$$\delta_1[\|X[N(k+1)]\|] \quad \text{and} \quad \delta_2[\|X[N(k+1)]\|]$$

such that, $\delta_1(0) = \delta_2(0) = 0$ and

$$0 < \delta_1[\|X[N(k+1)]\|] \leq V\{X[N(k+1)], N(k+1)\}$$
$$\leq \delta_2[\|X[N(k+1)]\|] < \infty$$
$$\forall k. \qquad (A.22)$$

Hence, Eq. (A.19) is a Lyapunov function. To show that Eq. (A.16) is uniformly asymptotically stable in the large, we need to show that for some finite q there exists a negative definite function $\delta_3[\|X[N(k+1)]\|]$ such that $\forall k > q$

$$V\{X[N(k+1)], N(k+1)\} - V\{X[N(k-q+1)], N(k-q+1)\}$$
$$\leq \delta_3[\|X[N(k+1)]\|]. \qquad (A.23)$$

Substituting for $X[N(k+1)]$ from Eq. (A.16) into Eq. (A.19) we get

$$V\{X[N(k+1)], N(k+1)\} = X'[Nk]\Sigma^{*-1}(Nk) - X'(Nk)H'(Nk)$$
$$\times [H(Nk)\Sigma^*(nk)H'(Nk) + R(Nk)]^{-1}$$
$$\times H(Nk)X(Nk). \qquad (A.24)$$

Since

$$\Sigma^*(Nk) = \Phi[Nk, N(k-1)]P^*[N(k-1)]\Phi'[Nk, N(k-1)] + Q[Nk, N(k-1)] \quad (A.25)$$

it follows that

$$\Sigma^*(Nk) \geq \Phi[Nk, N(k-1)]P^*[N(k-1)]\Phi'[N(k-1)] \quad (A.26)$$

from which it can be deduced that

$$\Phi'[N(k-1), Nk]P^{*-1}[N(k-1)]\Phi[N(k-1), Nk] \geq \Sigma^{*-1}(Nk). \quad (A.27)$$

Combining (A.27), (A.19), and (A.24) we get

$$V\{X[N(k+1)], N(k+1)\} \leq V\{X[Nk], Nk\} - X'(Nk)H'(Nk) \times [H(Nk)\Sigma^*(Nk)H'(Nk) + R(Nk)]^{-1} \times H(Nk)X(Nk). \quad (A.28)$$

Repeating the above for k - 1, ..., k - q we get

$$V\{X[N(k+1), N(k+1)]\} - V\{X[N(k-q)], N(k-q)\} \leq - \sum_{i=(k-q)}^{k} X'(Ni)H'(Ni) \times [H(Ni)\Sigma^*(Ni)H'(Ni) + R(Ni)]^{-1} H(Ni)X(Ni). \quad (A.29)$$

But from Eq. (A.25)

$$[R(Ni) + H(Ni)\Sigma^*(Ni)H'(Ni) = R(Ni) + H(Ni)\{\Phi[Ni, N(i-1)]P^*[N(i-1)]\Phi'[Ni, Ni-1)] + Q[Ni, N(i-1)]\}H'(Ni). \quad (A.30)$$

and since $\Phi[Ni, N(i-1)]P^*[N(i-1)]\Phi'[Ni, N(i-1)]$ is bounded from above and below, it follows that there exists an $\eta > 0$ such that

$$R[Ni] + H(Ni)\Sigma^*(Ni)H'(Ni) \leq R(Ni) + \eta H(Ni)H'(Ni) < \infty. \quad (A.31)$$

From Eqs. (A.31) and (A.29) we have

$$V\{X[N(k+1)], N(k+1)\} - V\{X[N(k-q)], N(k-q)\}$$
$$\leq - \sum_{i=k-q}^{k} X'(Ni)H'(Ni)[R(Ni) + \eta H(Ni)H'(Ni)]^{-1}$$
$$\times H(Ni)X(Ni). \tag{A.32}$$

But Eq. (71) implies that Eq. (4) is completely observable and since observability is invariant under output feedback, it follows from Eq. (A.32) that

$$V\{X[N(k+1)], N(k+1)\} - V\{X[N(k-q)], N(k-q)\}$$
$$\leq \delta_3 \|X[N(k+1)]\| < 0 \tag{A.33}$$

from which it can be concluded that Eq. (A.16) is uniformly asymptotically stable in the large. Q.E.D.

REFERENCES

1. N. R. SANDELL *et al.*, *IEEE Trans. Automat. Control AC-23*, 108 (1978).
2. R. RADNER, *Ann. Mach. Statist. 33*, 857 (1962).
3. Y. C. HO and K. C. CHU, *IEEE Trans. Automat. Control AC-17*, 15 (1972).
4. K. C. CHU, *IEEE Trans. Automat. Control AC-17*, 22 (1972).
5. T. BASAR, *IEEE Trans. Automat. Control AC-20*, 320 (1975).
6. T. BASAR, *IEEE Trans. Automat. Control AC-23*, 233 (1978).
7. H. S. WITSENHAUSEN, *SIAM J. Control Optim. 6*, 131 (1968).
8. W. WILLMAN, *IEEE Trans. Automat. Control AC-14*, 504 (1969).
9. I. B. RHODES and D. G. LUENBERGER, *IEEE Trans. Automat. Control AC-14*, 476 (1969).
10. A. B. CHAMMAS and C. T. LEONDES, *IEEE Trans. Automat. Control AC-23*, 921 (1978).
11. W. W. HAGER and L. L. HOROWITZ, *SIAM J. Control Optim. 14*, 295 (1976).
12. E. T. TSE, "Electronics Systems Laboratory," Report No. 412, Massachusetts Institute of Technology (1970).

13. E. TSE and M. ATHANS, *IEEE Trans. Automat. Control AC-15*, 416 (1970).

14. A. B. CHAMMAS and C. T. LEONDES, "Proc. Joint Automatic Control Conf.," 1656 (1977).

15. J. J. DEYST and C. F. PRICE, *IEEE Trans. Automat. Control AC-13*, 702 (1968).

16. J. J. DEYST, *IEEE Trans. Automat. Control AC-18*, 562 (1973).

Decentralized Control Using Time-Varying Feedback

BRIAN D. O. ANDERSON

JOHN B. MOORE

Department of Systems Engineering
Institute of Advanced Studies
Australian National University
Canberra, Australia

I. FIXED MODES AND DECENTRALIZED CONTROL

A. *WHAT ARE FIXED MODES?*

Consider a finite-dimensional time-invariant linear system, possibly with multiple inputs and outputs, and suppose that the system is either not completely controllable or not completely observable. Then, as is well known, no matter what feedback controller one connects to the system, so long as the controller has available to it the system inputs and outputs and nothing more, the modes which are uncontrollable or unobservable will remain as modes of the closed-loop system. If the controller

ISBN 0-12-012722-9

is linear, finite-dimensional and time-invariant, this means that the closed-loop characteristic polynomial will have a zero or zeros which are independent of the particular control design, and which identify the system *fixed modes*. Such fixed modes also have the interpretation of being the eigenvalues associated with the uncontrollable or unobservable part of the system matrix. If the modes are unstable, there is then no way that the system can be controlled so as to achieve any of the common design objectives – be they based on optimal control, pole positioning, or whatever. On the other hand, if there are no fixed modes, or if there are such modes which are stable, it is possible to select one of an array of design procedures to advance a particular objective.

In this chapter we study the possibility of observing and controlling the modes of a system when the controllers are constrained to being *decentralized*. (The term is explained below.) Of particular concern to us will be the exploration of the fixed mode idea, introduced above in our recollection of results applying with conventional, or *centralized*, controllers. To do this, we must first clarify our meaning of the word decentralized, and this is best done with the aid of Fig. 1, which illustrates the *two-channel* case. The system's inputs and outputs are each supposed to be divided into two sets (any one scalar input or output can, if desired, be in more than one set). The control structure is then such that the channel 1 inputs can be derived by feedback of channel 1 outputs, but can in no way depend on channel 2 inputs or outputs. The analogous statement is true for the channel 2 inputs. Of course, one can also consider three-channel, four-channel, etc., generalizations. The key ideas however remain much the same.

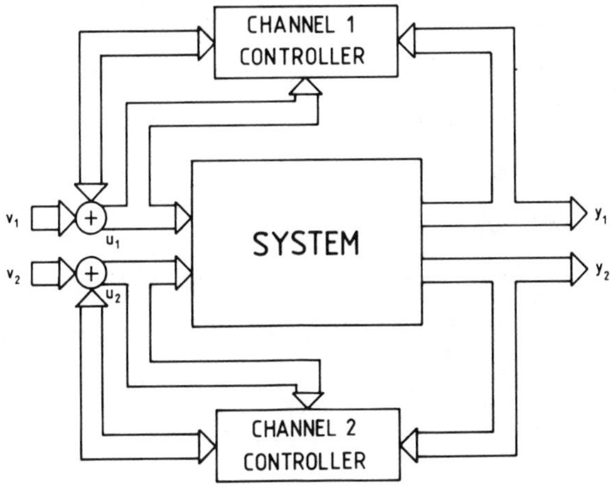

Fig. 1. Prototype system with decentralized controller.

Decentralized control structures are typically appropriate for large-scale systems. For example, most power systems normally contain more than one generator, and at each generator measurements are taken on that generator and local controls applied to it. Though in any power system, there is naturally some measure of centralized control, total centralization would be out of the question on grounds such as complexity, reliability, difficulty of update in times of expansion, and so on. Many social systems also exhibit elements of decentralized control — a company with several operating divisions for example, in which each operating division has autonomy.

Now suppose that the system being controlled is linear, finite-dimensional, and time-invariant. Suppose further that it is represented by state-variable equations which are controllable and observable. (This minimality is equivalent to there being no *centralized* fixed modes, or fixed modes of the type described in the first paragraph, if centralized controllers are used.) Next, suppose that decentralized controllers are used. Then there are some key consequences.

(1) If the controllers are restricted to being linear, and nondynamic, i.e., $u_i = K_i y_i + v_i$ for some constants K_i, it is possible for the closed-loop characteristic to have a zero s_0 which is independent of the K_i; see [1]. An example appears in the next section.

(2) If the controllers are permitted then to be linear, time-invariant, and finite-dimensional, the new characteristic polynomial still has the same zero, s_0, which is for obvious reasons termed a *decentralized fixed mode.*

By analogy with the centralized case, one might imagine that in these circumstances, one is encountering an unobservable or uncontrollable mode. Pursuing the analogy, one might therefore conclude that the use of nonlinear/time-varying/distributed controllers will not allow elimination of the decentralized fixed mode with characteristic frequency s_0. As it turns out, however, the analogy is *not* safe to pursue: under circumstances set out later in the chapter, one can eliminate the mode — *by using linear, time-varying controllers.* This means that for linear, time-invariant systems which are to be controlled via a decentralized controller, the controller may have to be time-varying, if the closed loop is to be stable, or to have a prescribed degree of stability.

The first clue that such a result might be possible was provided by [2], which showed that, using a mixed closed-loop/open-loop decentralized strategy the state of a wide class of systems could be forced to zero. This result allowed an arbitrary initial state, and encompassed some systems with decentralized fixed modes (though not all). If it were true that the decentralized fixed mode had the same characteristics and properties as the centralized fixed mode, the result would not have been achievable.

We have referred above to the possibility of eliminating a decentralized fixed mode by using a time-varying controller. It perhaps should be emphasized that removing an unstable fixed mode is one thing; specifying a decentralized controller design to achieve, for example, a prescribed degree of stability is another. Once we have described how the fixed mode can be eliminated, we shall describe how controller design can be approached. However, we caution the reader that we are far from being able to answer such questions as: How much performance do we lose, or more generally how do we characterize the various trade-offs, in replacing a centralized controller by a decentralized controller?

B. DECENTRALIZED FIXED MODES — AN EXAMPLE

Consider the transfer fraction matrix

$$W(s) = \begin{bmatrix} \dfrac{1}{s(s+1)} & \dfrac{1}{s-1} \\[2ex] \dfrac{s-1}{s(s+1)} & \dfrac{1}{s+1} \end{bmatrix}. \tag{1}$$

It is not hard to check that a minimal state variable realization is defined by

$$\dot{x} = \begin{bmatrix} 1 & 0 & 0 & 0 \\ 0 & 0 & 0 & 0 \\ 0 & 0 & -1 & 0 \\ 0 & 0 & 0 & -1 \end{bmatrix} x + \begin{bmatrix} 0 & 1 \\ 1 & 0 \\ 1 & 0 \\ 0 & 1 \end{bmatrix} \begin{bmatrix} u_1 \\ u_2 \end{bmatrix} \tag{2a}$$

$$y = \begin{bmatrix} 1 & 1 & -1 & 0 \\ 0 & -1 & 2 & 1 \end{bmatrix} x. \tag{2b}$$

Now suppose decentralized constant feedback is applied, i.e.,

$$u_1 = k_1 y_1 + v_1 \tag{3a}$$

$$u_2 = k_2 y_2 + v_2. \tag{3b}$$

Here, k_1 and k_2 are constant gains, and v_1 and v_2 are external inputs. The feedback is decentralized since u_1 is allowed to depend only on y_1 (rather than y_1 and y_2), and u_2 is allowed to depend only on y_2. The closed-loop system matrix is

$$\begin{bmatrix} 1 & 0 & 0 & 0 \\ 0 & 0 & 0 & 0 \\ 0 & 0 & -1 & 0 \\ 0 & 0 & 0 & -1 \end{bmatrix} + \begin{bmatrix} 0 & 1 \\ 1 & 0 \\ 1 & 0 \\ 0 & 1 \end{bmatrix} \begin{bmatrix} k_1 & 0 \\ 0 & k_2 \end{bmatrix} \begin{bmatrix} 1 & 1 & -1 & 0 \\ 0 & -1 & 2 & 1 \end{bmatrix}$$

$$= \begin{bmatrix} 1 & -k_2 & 2k_2 & k_2 \\ k_1 & k_1 & -k_1 & 0 \\ k_1 & k_1 & -1 - k_1 & 0 \\ 0 & -k_2 & 2k_2 & -1 + k_2 \end{bmatrix}.$$

The closed-loop characteristic polynomial is now the characteristic polynomial of this matrix, which can be evaluated as

$$(s - 1)\Big[s^3 + s^2(2 - k_2) + s(1 - k_1 - k_2 - k_1k_2) + k_1 - 2k_1k_2\Big].$$

The key point is that $s = 1$ *is a zero of the closed-loop characteristic polynomial, irrespective of the values assumed by* k_1, k_2. As such, $s = 1$ is an example of *a decentralized fixed mode.*

C. *CHARACTERIZATION OF DECENTRALIZED FIXED MODES*

The first formal treatment of decentralized fixed modes appeared in [1]. However, this reference did not indicate how one could characterize fixed modes without first evaluating the characteristic polynomial of the closed-loop system and then observing somehow that it had a zero that was invariant with respect to k_1, k_2 selections. We indicate here several characterizations.

State Variable Characterization [3]

Suppose the system is

$$\dot{x} = Ax + B_1u_1 + B_2u_2, \quad y_1 = C_1'x, \quad y_2 = C_2'x \tag{4}$$

and is minimal. (The superscript prime denotes matrix transposition.) Suppose also the feedback is of the form $u_i = K_iy_i + v_i$, $i = 1, 2$. Then there is a decentralized fixed mode if and only if for some eigenvalue λ of A, one of the following conditions holds:

$$\text{rank}\begin{bmatrix} \lambda I - A & B_1 \\ C_2' & 0 \end{bmatrix} < \dim A, \qquad \text{rank}\begin{bmatrix} \lambda I - A & B_2 \\ C_1' & 0 \end{bmatrix} < \dim A. \tag{5}$$

Remarks.

(1) For the example above, take $\lambda = 1$ and check that the first condition holds:

$$\text{rank}\begin{bmatrix} \lambda I - A & B_1 \\ C_2' & 0 \end{bmatrix}$$

$$= \text{rank}\begin{bmatrix} 0 & 0 & 0 & 0 & 0 \\ 0 & 1 & 0 & 0 & 1 \\ 0 & 0 & 2 & 0 & 1 \\ 0 & 0 & 0 & 2 & 0 \\ 0 & -1 & 2 & 1 & 0 \end{bmatrix} = 3 < 4 = \dim A. \tag{6}$$

(2) More than two channels can be considered; see [3] for details of the form taken by the extensions to (5).

(3) The conditions (5) are a subset of those necessary to ensure that a decentralized system is observable and controllable from one channel alone, after constant gain feedback has been applied around the second channel [4-6]. This idea is important for the sequel, so we develop it further here. But observe first that for the example of Section II, if $u_2 = k_2y_2$,

then (as shown by simple algebra) there is lack of controllability from u_1, irrespective of k_2. Now to understand the result of [4-6] further, suppose the second condition in (5) holds for $x = s_0$, an eigenvalue of A. Since

$$\begin{bmatrix} s_0 I - A & B_2 \\ C_1' & 0 \end{bmatrix} \begin{bmatrix} I & 0 \\ -K_2 C_2' & I \end{bmatrix} = \begin{bmatrix} s_0 I - A - B_2 K_2 C_2' & B_2 \\ C_1' & 0 \end{bmatrix}$$

the rank of the right-hand side is less than dim A for all K_2. A fortiori

$$\operatorname{rank}\begin{bmatrix} s_0 I - A - B_2 K_2 C_2' \\ C_1' \end{bmatrix} < \dim A. \tag{7}$$

This is a condition for unobservability of the pair $[A + B_2 K_2 C_2', C_1]$. Since it is perhaps not well known, we indicate how it relates to a more familiar condition. From (7) we conclude there exists $w \neq 0$ with

$$\begin{bmatrix} s_0 I - A - B_2 K_2 C_2' \\ C_1' \end{bmatrix} w = 0$$

whence

$$C_1' w = 0, \qquad \left(A + B_2 K_2 C_2'\right)^i w = s_0^i w$$

and so

$$C_1'\left(A + B_2 K_2 C_2'\right)^i w = 0.$$

In summary, the second condition of (5) implies that if feedback $u_2 = K_2 y_2$ is applied around channel 2, the resulting one-channel system is unobservable for all K_2. The unobservable mode is s_0, while the unobservable state may depend on K_2.

It is also easy to see that if the second condition of (5) holds and feedback $u_1 = K_1 y_1$ is used to create a one-channel system with input u_2 and output y_2, then this system will be uncontrollable for all K_1. Similar results also hold if the first condition in (5) holds.

The main result of [4-6] proves this type of result both ways. We shall note the precise formulation subsequently.

Matrix Fraction Characterization [3][1]

Suppose that $W(s) = A^{-1}(s)B(s)$ is a left matrix fraction description of $W(s)$, with $A(s)$, $B(s)$ coprime polynomial matrices. Define $A_i(s)$, $B_i(s)$ for $i = 1, 2$ by rewriting $A(s)y(s) = B(s)u(s)$ as

$$A_1(s)y_1 + A_2(s)y_2 = B_1(s)u_1 + B_2(s)u_2. \tag{8}$$

Then there is a decentralized fixed mode at s_0, which is necessarily a zero of $\det A(s)$, if and only if one of the following conditions holds:

$$\begin{aligned} &\operatorname{rank}[A_1(s_0) \quad B_1(s_0)] < \dim A_1(s_0) \\ &\operatorname{rank}[A_2(s_0) \quad B_2(s_0)] < \dim A_2(s_0). \end{aligned} \tag{9}$$

Transfer Fraction Matrix Characterization [7]

Suppose that

$$\begin{bmatrix} y_1(s) \\ y_2(s) \end{bmatrix} = \begin{bmatrix} W_{11}(s) & W_{12}(s) \\ W_{21}(s) & W_{22}(s) \end{bmatrix} \begin{bmatrix} u_1(s) \\ u_2(s) \end{bmatrix}. \tag{10}$$

Then if s_0 is a simple zero of the open-loop characteristic polynomial, it is also a decentralized fixed mode if and only

[1] *This section can be omitted by the reader unfamiliar with matrix fraction descriptions of linear finite-dimensional systems.*

if the following is true:

$$W(s) = \left[\begin{array}{c|c} \text{No entry has a pole at } s_0 & s_0 \text{ is a simple zero of characteristic polynomial of this block} \\ \hline \text{Every entry has a zero at } s_0 & \text{No entry has a pole at } s_0 \end{array}\right]. \quad (11)$$

Should s_0 be a multiple zero of the open-loop characteristic polynomial, the transfer function matrix characterization, in contrast to the state variable and matrix fraction characterizations, becomes more complicated. See [7] for details.

The example of Section I,B is immediately seen as conforming to the pattern for W(s) in Eq. (11), with $s_0 = 1$.

There is an important intuitive idea behind the above pattern for W(s). Let us suppose that W(s) is a 2×2 matrix, and that we apply feedback in two stages. In the first stage feedback $u_2 = k_2 y_2$ is applied around channel 2 as illustrated in Fig. 2. In the second stage (not illustrated), feedback $u_1 = k_1 y_1$ will be applied around the resulting one-channel system.

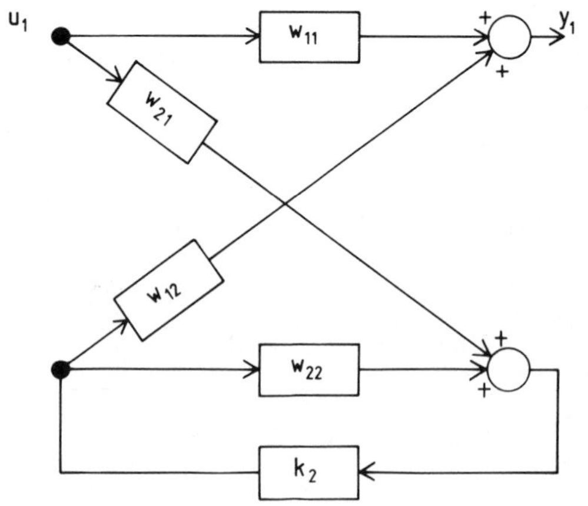

Fig. 2. System with control round channel 2.

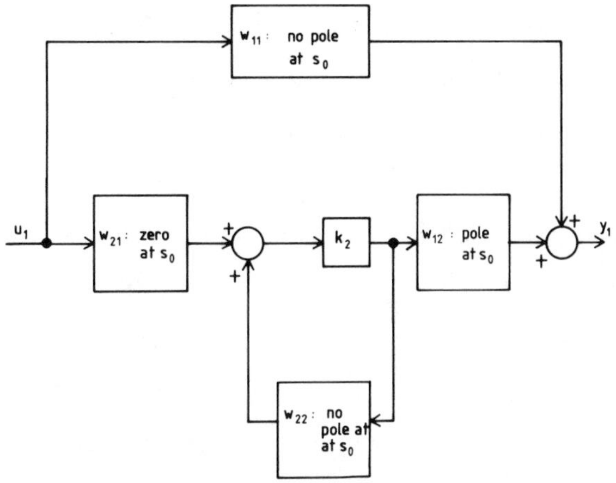

Fig. 3. Redrawing of scheme of Fig. 2.

Consider the redrawing of the Fig. 2 scheme as in Fig. 3 with W(s) possessing the structure of Eq. (11). It is immediately clear that there is a pole-zero cancellation between w_{21} and w_{12}, and that this cancellation exists for all k_2. Therefore, the one-channel system will be uncontrollable. (Of course, if w_{21} has the pole and w_{12} the zero, s_0 will be an unobservable mode for the one-channel system.) Consequently, whatever value of k_1 is selected for the feedback around the one-channel system, s_0 will remain as a zero of the closed-loop characteristic polynomial. Since s_0 is then invariant with respect to the choice of k_1 and k_2, it is a decentralized fixed mode.

Figure 3 also illustrates, at least intuitively, several other important ideas.

(1) If $w_{21}(s) \equiv 0$, then plainly there is no decentralized control strategy which could vary any of the poles of w_{12} which are not poles of w_{11} or w_{22}. Thus a prerequisite for eliminating a fixed mode associated with a pole of w_{12} only is that

$w_{21} \not\equiv 0$; similarly, a prerequisite for eliminating a fixed mode associated with a pole of w_{21} is that $w_{12} \not\equiv 0$. Such conditions are termed *connectivity conditions*.

(2) If k_2 is not a constant feedback law, but is replaced by $k_2(s)$, the transfer function of a time-invariant dynamic system, the pole-zero cancellation will still take place, and so the fixed mode will remain. For rational $k_2(s)$, this is established in [1] and for possibly irrational $k_2(s)$, in [3].

(3) If k_2 is a time-varying operator of some description, for example, a periodically switched, piecewise constant gain, then the pole-zero cancellation will *in general no longer occur*.

This is because, as is well known, a linear time-invariant integro-differential operator and a linear time-varying operator do not commute [example: With $D \equiv d/dt$,

$$Dk(t)[x(t)] = k(t)D[x(t)] + \dot{k}(t)x(t),$$

i.e., $Dk(t) \neq k(t)D$ unless $\dot{k}(t) \equiv 0$]. Such commutativity would be needed in Fig. 3 in order to juxtapose w_{21} and w_{12}. Of course, without the pole-zero cancellation, there is no fixed mode. So this argument suggests that we could eliminate the fixed mode by making k_2 time varying.

(4) Let us consider a different form of intuitive argument for the same conclusion as the remark above. With w_{12} possessing an unstable pole at s_0, we know that to stabilize it, there would need to be a possibility for signals at the frequency s_0 to enter w_{12}. On the other hand signals with frequency s_0 cannot pass through w_{21}. Now suppose that k_2 varies sinusoidally at frequency $j\omega_0$, where $s_0 + j\omega_0$, $s_0 - j\omega_0$ are not zeros of w_{21}. Then if a signal at frequency $s_0 \pm j\omega_0$ enters w_{21}, it will leave it, and then be modulated by k_2 with the result that the

output of k_2 can contain a frequency s_0. This is the prerequisite for eliminating the unstable pole. This intuitive argument also gives some insight into what sort of period would be appropriate: one should select $T = 2\pi/\omega_0$ so that $s_0 \pm j\omega_0$ is not close to s_0, or, for that matter, to any other zero s_1 of w_{21}. If the time variation in k_2 is not sinusoidal, but nevertheless periodic, the conclusion is less clear, since the "modulating action" is more complex.

Note that these arguments do not show definitively that one is able to eliminate a fixed mode, let alone that one can, for example, stabilize using a decentralized controller a system with an unstable fixed mode. They simply open the door to showing that it might be possible, as was done in [8] and as explained in the remainder of this chapter.

II. ELIMINATING DECENTRALIZED FIXED MODES WITH TIME-VARYING CONTROLLERS

A. *THE TECHNICAL LEMMAS*

We consider a system in state variable form:

$$\dot{x} = Ax + B_1u_1 + B_2u_2, \quad y_1 = C_1'x, \quad y_2 = C_2'x \tag{12}$$

and begin by asking the question, *When, with feedback of the form* $u_2 = K_2(t)y_2$, *will the system be observable from* y_1? We first derive two necessary conditions.

It is clear on intuitive grounds that we need centralized observability as

$$\left\{A,\ [C_1'\ C_2']'\right\} \text{ is completely observable.} \tag{13}$$

Formally, if this condition were not satisfied, $\left\{A + B_2K_2(t)C_2',\ [C_1'\ C_2']'\right\}$ would not be observable (observability is preserved with output feedback), and a fortiori $\left\{A + B_2K_2(t)C_2', C_2\right\}$ would be unobservable.

The second necessary condition is

$$\text{Either } [A, C_1] \text{ is observable, or } C_1'(sI - A)^{-1}B_2 \not\equiv 0. \qquad (14)$$

If the first alternative holds, then it is trivial that $K_2(t) \equiv 0$ ensures observability from output 1. [Actually, it then follows that almost any constant control law $u_2 = K_2y_2$ ensures observability. For the observability condition can be formally viewed as one requiring that the rank of a certain matrix take a certain value, where the entries of this matrix are entries of $C_1'\left(A + B_2K_2C_2'\right)^i$ for $i = 0, \ldots, \dim A - 1$. Regarding the entries of K_2 as variables, observability then follows if and only if at least one of a number of determinants, which evaluate as multivariable polynomials in the entries of K_2, is nonzero. If a multivariable polynomial is nonzero for one choice of variables, it will be nonzero for almost all such choices. The selection $K_2 \equiv 0$ guarantees one of the polynomials is nonzero.]

Suppose then the first alternative in Eq. (14) fails. We first give an intuitive argument for the necessity of the second alternative. With the first alternative failing, it is evidently necessary to somehow pass information contained in the observations at the second output to the first output. This is done by passing the y_2 information to the second input, via $u_2 = K_2y_2$, and then allowing the internal system connection from u_2 to y_1 — defined by the transfer function matrix $C_1'(sI - A)^{-1} \times B_2$ — to carry the information right through to y_1. If, however, $C_1'(sI - A)^{-1}B_2 \equiv 0$, no information can get through via this mechanism.

Now we turn to a formal argument for the necessity of Eq. (14). With $u_2 = K_2(t)y_2$, the closed-loop transition matrix $\phi_{K_2}(t, \sigma)$ satisfies.

$$\dot{\phi}_{K_2}(t, \sigma) = A\phi_{K_2}(t, \sigma) + B_2K_2(t)C_2'\phi_{K_2}(t, \sigma)$$

whence

$$\phi_{K_2}(t, \sigma) = e^{A(t-\sigma)} + \int_\sigma^t e^{A(t-\tau)}B_2K_2(\tau)C_2'\phi_{K_2}(\tau, \sigma)\, d\tau.$$

Now if $C_1'(sI - A)^{-1}B_2 \equiv 0$, then $C_1'e^{A(t-\sigma)}B_2 \equiv 0$ for all t, σ, and we have

$$C_1'\phi_{K_2}(t, \sigma) = C_1'e^{A(t-\sigma)}.$$

The observability Grammian associated with $[A + B_2K_2(t)C_2', C_1]$ is now

$$W(s, s + L) \triangleq \int_s^{s+L} \phi_{K_2}'(t, s)C_1C_1'\phi_{K_2}(t, s)\, dt$$

$$= \int_s^{s+L} [e^{A(t-s)}]'C_1C_1'e^{A(t-s)}\, dt \tag{15}$$

and is accordingly nonsingular for all $L > 0$ if and only if $[A, C_1]$ is observable.

Having now seen the two necessary conditions Eq. (13) and Eq. (14) which are prerequisites to securing observability from channel 1 via feedback around channel 2, it is appropriate to recall the precise form of the result of [4-6], which indicates when constant feedback around channel 2 will suffice.

Theorem 1. Consider the system Eq. (12). Then Eq. (13), Eq. (14), and

$$\text{rank}\begin{bmatrix} \lambda I - A & B_2 \\ C_1' & 0 \end{bmatrix} \geq \dim A \tag{16}$$

for all λ constitute necessary and sufficient conditions for the existence of a K_2 such that $[A + B_2K_2C_2', C_1]$ is observable.

We stress that Eqs. (13) and (14) have been shown to be necessary conditions for the existence of a control law with K_2 constant *or* time-varying, which achieve observability of $[A + B_2K_2C_2', C_1]$. However, we have not asserted that Eq. (16) is necessary for the existence of a time-varying gain, and indeed the thrust of this chapter is to show that Eqs. (13) and (14) alone are the necessary and sufficient conditions for the existence of a time-varying gain guaranteeing observability of $[A + B_2K_2(t)C_2', C_1]$. Even should Eq. (16) fail, i.e., even if there are decentralized fixed modes, there is, as we shall show, no difficulty in achieving observability.

Our first result is for plants with u_2, y_2 scalar:

Lemma 1. Assume the observability condition Eq. (13) holds and $C_1'(sI - A)^{-1}B_2 \not\equiv 0$. Let $K_2(t) \equiv 0$ on $[s, s_1]$ and $K_2(t) \equiv K_2 \neq 0$ on $[s_1, s + L]$ for arbitrary s_1, L with $s < s_1 < s + L$. Suppose further that u_2, y_2 are scalar. Then $W(s, s + L)$, see Eq. (15), is nonsingular.

Proof. Suppose temporarily that $C_1'(sI - A)^{-1}B_2$ is scalar and that $W(s, s + L)\gamma = 0$ for some $\gamma \neq 0$, to obtain a contradiction. Using the definition of $W(\cdot, \cdot)$ in Eq. (15) (first equality only!), we see that

$$C_1'e^{A(t-s)}\gamma = 0, \quad t \in [s, s_1]$$

$$C_1'e^{\left(A+B_2K_2C_2'\right)(t-s_1)}e^{As_1}\gamma = 0, \quad t \in [s_1, s + L).$$

Set $\delta = e^{As_1}\gamma$ and recognize that $\alpha'e^{At}\beta \equiv 0$ on an interval if and only if $\alpha' A^i \beta = 0\ \forall i$. Then for all i

$$C_1' A^i \delta = 0, \quad C_1'\left(A + B_2 K_2 C_2'\right)^i \delta = 0.$$

Let q be the least nonnegative integer for which $C_1' A^q B_2 \neq 0$. Note that q exists since $C_1'(sI - A)^{-1} B_2 \neq 0$. Then the second equation implies (using the first) that

$$\begin{bmatrix} C_1'A^qB_2K_2 & 0 & & \cdot & \cdot \\ * & C_1'A^qB_2K_2 & & \cdot & \cdot \\ * & * & C_1'A^qB_2K_2 & \cdot & \cdot \\ * & * & * & \cdot & \cdot \\ & & & \cdot & \cdot \end{bmatrix} \begin{bmatrix} C_2' \\ C_2'A \\ C_2'A^2 \\ \cdot \\ \cdot \end{bmatrix} \delta = 0$$

whence for all i

$$C_2' A^i \delta = 0. \tag{17}$$

But now $C_1' A^i \delta = 0$ and $C_2' A^i \delta = 0$, with $\delta \neq 0$. This contradicts the observability assumption (13).

Now suppose $C_1'(sI - A)^{-1} B_2$ is a vector, and let C_{1j}' denote the jth row of C_1, and

$$W_j(s, s + L) \triangleq \int_s^{s+L} \phi_{K_2}'(t, s) C_{1j} C_{1j}' \phi_{K_2}(t, s)\, dt. \tag{18}$$

Then

$$W(s, s + L) = \sum_j W_j(s, s + L) \tag{19}$$

and $W(s, s + L)\gamma = 0$ if and only if $W_j(s, s + L)\gamma = 0$, since each $W_j(s, s + L)$ is individually nonnegative definite. Arguing as above, we conclude that for all j, i

$$C_{1j}' A^i \delta = 0, \quad C_2' A^i \delta = 0 \tag{20}$$

and again, Eq. (13) is violated. ∇∇∇

In Lemma 1, u_2 and y_2 are restricted to being scalars. We now remove this restriction. The idea is as follows. Suppose that $C_1'(sI - A)^{-1}B_{2j} \neq 0$. Then we use $K_2(t)$ to switch in turn each component of y_2 to the jth component of u_2. More specifically:

Lemma 2. With notation as above, suppose that Eq. (13) holds and that the jth column of $C_1'(sI - A)^{-1}B_2$ is not identically zero. Let e_i denote a unit vector with 1 in the ith position, and let p_2 denote the dimension of y_2. Take

$$\begin{aligned}
K_2(t) &\equiv 0, && t \in [s, s_1] \\
K_2(t) &\equiv k_{12}e_je_1', && t \in [s_1, s_2] \\
K_2(t) &\equiv k_{22}e_je_2', && t \in [s_2, s_3] \\
&\vdots \\
K_2(t) &\equiv k_{p_2 2}e_je_{p_2}', && t \in [s_{p_2}, s + L]
\end{aligned} \tag{21}$$

with $s < s_1 < s_2 < \cdots s + L$, and $k_{i2} \neq 0$ for all i. Then $W(s, s + L)$ is nonsingular.

Proof. Suppose for convenience that C_1' has only one row. In the contrary case, the argument can be extended, just as for Lemma 1. Then $W(s, s + L)\gamma = 0$ implies

$$\begin{aligned}
&C_1' \exp[A(t - s)]\gamma = 0, \quad t \in [s, s_1] \\
&C_1' \exp\left[\left(A + B_{2j}k_{12}e_1'C_2'\right)(t - s_1)\right] \exp(As_1)\gamma = 0, \quad t \in [s_1 s_2] \\
&C_1' \exp\left[\left(A + B_{2j}k_{22}e_2'C_2'\right)(t - s_2)\right] \exp\left[\left(A + B_{2j}k_{12}e_1'C_2'\right)(s_2 - s_1)\right] \\
&\quad \times \exp(As_1)\gamma = 0, \quad t \in [s_2, s_3] \\
&\vdots
\end{aligned} \tag{22}$$

Arguing as in the proof of Lemma 1, the first two equations imply, for $\delta_1 = e^{As_1}\gamma$, and all i

$$C_1'A^i\delta_1 = 0, \quad e_1'C_2'A^i\delta_1 = 0.$$

Let $\delta_2 = \exp[(A + B_2k_{12}e_1'C_2')(s_2 - s_1)]\delta_1$. Then it is easy to see that

$$C_1'A^i\delta_2 = 0, \quad e_1'C_2'A^i\delta_2 = 0. \tag{23}$$

Now take the first of these identities with Eq. (22). One obtains by the same arguments

$$e_2'C_2'A^i\delta_2 = 0.$$

Proceeding in this fashion, we construct a vector δ_{p_2}, nonzero if and only if γ is nonzero, such that, for $j = 1, 2, \ldots, p_2$, and all i

$$C_1'A^i\delta_{p_2} = 0, \quad e_j'C_2'A^i\delta_{p_2} = 0. \tag{24}$$

Equivalently,

$$C_1'A^i\delta_{p_2} = 0, \quad C_2'A^i\delta_{p_2} = 0. \tag{25}$$

This provides a contradiction to an assertion that $W(s, s + L)$ is nonsingular. ∇∇∇

Let us summarize. To have $W(s + L)$ nonsingular, it is enough

(1) to have $[A, C_1]$ observable (then one can take $K_2(t) \equiv 0$);

(2) if $[A, C_1]$ is not observable, to have $C_1'(sI - S)^{-1}B_2 \not\equiv 0$ and to have

$$\operatorname{rank}\begin{bmatrix} \lambda I - A & B_2 \\ C_1' & 0 \end{bmatrix} \geq \dim A$$

for all λ (then almost all constant K_2 will suffice);

(3) if $[A, C_1]$ is not observable, and if

$$\text{rank}\begin{bmatrix} s_0 I - A & B_2 \\ C_1' & 0 \end{bmatrix} < \dim A$$

for some s_0 (which is then a decentralized fixed mode), to have $C_1'(sI - A)^{-1}B_2 \neq 0$ (then a switched K_2 of the form described in Lemmas 1 and 2 will suffice).

Let us add one final piece of intuition to points (2) and (3) above. If $[A, C_1]$ is not observable, we need to get the information seen by channel 2 through somehow to the output of channel 1. If $K_2 = 0$, then on channel 1, we are observing only what C_1 allows us to observe. But if $K_2 \neq 0$, the output information on channel 2 is fed back to influence the input of channel 2 and then, because $C_1'(sI - A)^{-1}B_2 \neq 0$, some of this shows up at the channel 1 output. That part of the state which C_1 could not observe (and which C_2 can then observe) shows up, in an admittedly mangled fashion at output 1; as it turns out, the processing can sometimes be unraveled and the state then observed.

However, it may be the case that the separate contributions to y_1 [the direct contribution associated with $C_1'(sI - A)^{-1}B_1$ and that due to feedback of y_2 and u_2 and transmission through $C_1'(sI - A)^{-1}B_2$] are not separately resolvable when K_2 is constant. Why then will time-varying K_2 allow resolution? If $K_2 = 0$, the first contribution alone is present, and can be evaluated; then when $K_2 \neq 0$, the first contribution can be, in crude terms, subtracted off, allowing evaluation of the second contribution.

This is not inconsistent with there being a fixed mode with frequency s_0; for one value of K_2, one particular state is unobservable, and for a different value of K_2, a different state is unobservable. No one state is unobserved for all values of K_2, so that time variation of K_2 permit observation of all states.

B. FORMAL RESULTS

Let us suppose that there is given the decentralized two-channel system $\{A, [B_1\ B_2], [C_1\ C_2]\}$ where $\left\{A, \left[C_1'\ C_2'\right]'\right\}$ is completely observable, $C_1'(sI - A)^{-1}B_2 \neq 0$, and there is a decentralized fixed mode s_0 such that

$$\text{rank}\begin{bmatrix} s_0 I - A & B_2 \\ C_1' & 0 \end{bmatrix} < \dim A.$$

Let $K_2(\cdot)$ be periodic with period L and vary as described in Lemma 2. Let τ be an arbitrary time and consider any interval $[\tau, \tau + 2L]$. Then this contains a subinterval $[s + mL, s + (m + 1)L]$ for some integer m, and so

$$W(\tau, \tau + 2L) \geq W(s + mL, \quad s + (m + 1)L) = W(s, s + L).$$

Thus $W(\tau, \tau + 2L)$ is bounded below away from zero uniformly for $\tau \in (-\infty, \infty)$. It is also bounded above for all τ, as is easily seen. Hence the pair $\left[A + B_2K_2(t)C_2', C_1\right]$ is uniformly completely observable [9-11]. (The significance of this is explained further below.)

Of course, if $[A, C_1]$ is observable, or if it is not observable but there is no fixed mode of the type described, the above conclusion is still valid. However, the use of a time-varying feedback law is not essential to achieve observability.

It is not hard now to see that if $K_2(t)$ takes *any* ρ differing piecewise constant values where $\rho > p_2 + 1$, and is periodic, the uniform complete observability condition still holds. The observability is characterized by the failure of certain multivariable equalities in the entries of K_2 at each of its constant values. Now, there exist periodic gain selections for which the equalities do not all hold, so that for almost all such selections they will fail to hold. (To extend from $p_2 + 1$ to $p_2 + 2$ and then $p_2 + 3$, ... distinct values of K_2, regard any set of $p_2 + 1$ values as a set of $p_2 + 2$ specialized so that two values are the same.)

Now consider the controllability question. By duality, it is clear that we need to require $\{A, [B_1\ B_2]\}$ controllable. If $[A, B_1]$ is controllable, then almost any $K_2(t)$, constant or time-varying and including $K_2(t) \equiv 0$, will ensure controllability from channel 1. If $[A, B_1]$ is not controllable, it is necessary that $C_2'(sI - A)^{-1}B_1 \not\equiv 0$. Then if there are no fixed modes, almost any fixed K_2 will ensure that $[A + B_2K_2C_2', B_1]$ is completely controllable. If there are fixed modes, then K_2 should take at least dim $u_2 + 1$ distinct piecewise constant values in a periodic fashion. For almost all selections of such values, $[A_2 + B_2K_2(t)C_2', B_1]$ will be uniformly completely controllable.

Notice that with K_2 nonzero and with $C_2'(sI - A)^{-1}B_1 \not\equiv 0$, any generic input applied on channel 1 will give rise to a signal at the input of channel 2. In this way, even though $[A, B_1]$ may not be controllable, one will have some opportunity to influence all the states.

By combining the controllability and observability results we see that if $\{A, [B_1\ B_2], [C_1\ C_2]\}$ is controllable and observable, and if $C_2'(sI - A)^{-1}B_1 \not\equiv 0$, $C_1'(sI - A)^{-1}B_2 \not\equiv 0$ then the following applies:

(1) *If there are no fixed modes, almost any constant* K_2 *will ensure* $[A + B_2K_2C_2', B_1, C_1]$ *is controllable and observable.*

(2) *If there are fixed modes almost any selection of a piecewise constant, periodic* $K_2(t)$ *taking at least* $\max(\dim u_2 + 1, \dim y_2 + 1)$ *distinct values will ensure that* $[A_2 + B_2K_2(t)C_2', B_1, C_1]$ *is uniformly completely controllable and observable.*

If $C_2'(sI - A)^{-1}B_1 \equiv 0$, we need $[A, B_1]$ completely controllable and if $C_1'(sI - A)^{-1}B_2 \equiv 0$, we need $[A, C_1]$ completely observable for these conclusions to remain true.

What now is the significance of these conditions? If (1) holds, then conventional linear system design methods can be applied to channel 1 to position poles, minimize a linear-quadratic index, etc. If (2) holds, then linear-quadratic design methods may be applied [11] to secure an exponentially stable state estimator and an exponentially stabilizing state feedback law. The estimator and feedback law will then have periodic gains [12].

In case we work in discrete time, the same results hold, save that $[A + B_2K_2(t)C_2', B_1, C_1]$ may have uncontrollable/unobservable modes at the origin. (These modes of course are unlikely to create any difficulties in a control problem.) Since any periodic discrete-time system can be treated as a time-invariant system (by redefining the sampling interval as one period), other techniques of linear system theory, e.g., those appropriate to pole positioning, can be applied to the single-channel design problem.

Another important observation is that even for a system with no decentralized fixed modes, it may be easier to control if time-varying feedback is used on channel 2 than if constant feedback is used. Indeed, this will certainly be the case if the given system is close to having a fixed mode, in the sense, for example, that the structure of Eq. (11) for W(s) could be achieved if poles or zeros were perturbed slightly.

Last, we comment that we have discovered examples where with $m_2 = p_2 > 1$, only two different piecewise constant values are required for $K_2(t)$, in order to make a system with a fixed mode observable and controllable from channel 1. This means that it may be possible to improve on the main result.

C. MULTICHANNEL SYSTEMS

Up to now, we have studied two-channel systems. Now we discuss p-channel systems for $p > 2$. With each channel of a p-channel system, associate a node of a p-node graph, and draw a directed arc connecting node i to node j just in the case $C_j'(sI - A)^{-1}B_i \not\equiv 0$. A path $\{j_1\ j_2 \cdots j_r\}$ from node j_1 to j_r is a set of arcs connecting j_1 to j_2 to $j_3 \cdots$ to j_r. In the p-channel system, if there is nonzero (decentralized) feedback from output to input in each of channels $j_1, j_2, \ldots, j_r$, and if $\{j_1\ j_2 \cdots j_r\}$ is a path, it will be possible for signals inserted at the input j_1 to affect the output of all channels j_i along the path — irrespective of whether there is an arc connecting j_1 to j_i.

A system is termed strongly connected if there is a path between any two nodes. It is not hard to see that a system is strongly connected if and only if for every partition of the channels into disjoint sets A and B we have $C_A'(sI - A)^{-1}B_B \not\equiv 0$. An alternative condition is that there is no ordering of the channels for which the system transfer function matrix is block triangular.

In [5], it is explained that every time-invariant system can be regarded as a collection of strongly coupled subsystems which have only one-way, or no, connections between them.

Moreover, many questions of decentralized control can be analyzed by considering them in relation to the individual strongly connected subsystems.

Let us now note the variation to the idea required if periodic gains are present. In the definition of connectivity for a constant gain system above, where a transfer function matrix must not be identically zero, we require that the corresponding collection of transfer function matrices be all not identically zero, where each transfer function is now associated with an interval in which the gains are constant. Thus if in the time-invariant case, there is a connectivity condition $C'(sI - A)^{-1}B \not\equiv 0$ and if A is replaced by a periodically varying A(t), switching between A_1 and A_2, we require that $C'(sI - A_1)^{-1}B \not\equiv 0$ and $C'(sI - A_2)^{-1}B \not\equiv 0$.

We now assert:

Lemma 3. Consider a p-channel strongly connected system and suppose a (p - 1)-channel system is formed by putting feedback of the form $u_p = -K_p y_p$ around the pth channel, with K_p periodic and piecewise constant. Then for generic K_p, the resulting (p - 1)-channel system is strongly connected.

Proof. Consider any two nodes j_1, j_r of the graph associated with the (p - 1)-channel system derived after introducing feedback to the original p-channel system. Before the introduction of this feedback, these two nodes, regarded as nodes of the graph of the p-channel system, define the end points of a path because the p-channel system is strongly connected. We distinguish

Case 1: The path does not include node p;

Case 2: The path includes node p.

Let W_{ji} denote $C_j(sI - A)^{-1}B_i$ (or the collection of such quantities), and $\overline{W}_{ji}$ denote the corresponding quantity resulting after feedback. Under case 1, we have $W_{j_2 j_1} \not\equiv 0, \ldots, W_{j_r j_{r-1}} \not\equiv 0$. Since for one specialized feedback, viz., $u_p \equiv 0$, we have $\overline{W}_{j_2 j_1} = W_{j_2 j_1} \not\equiv 0, \ldots, \overline{W}_{j_r j_{r-1}} = W_{j_r j_{r-1}} \not\equiv 0$ it follows that for almost all feedback, i.e., generically, we must have $\overline{W}_{j_2 j_1} \not\equiv 0, \ldots, \overline{W}_{j_r j_{r-1}} \not\equiv 0$; i.e., a path connects j_1 to j_r for the (p - 1)-channel system — the same path in effect as in the p-channel system.

For case 2, suppose the path is $j_1, j_2, \ldots, j_k, p, j_{k+2}, \ldots, j_r$. Arguing as for case 1, we know that generically $\overline{W}_{j_2 j_1} \not\equiv 0, \ldots, \overline{W}_{j_k j_{k-1}} \not\equiv 0, \overline{W}_{j_{k+3} j_{k+2}} \not\equiv 0, \ldots, \overline{W}_{j_r j_{r-1}} \not\equiv 0$. We must show that generically, $\overline{W}_{j_{k+2} j_k} \not\equiv 0$. If $W_{j_{k+2} j_k} \not\equiv 0$, we can apply the case 1 argument. So assume that $W_{j_{k+2} j_k} \equiv 0$. Then

$$\overline{W}_{j_{k+2} j_k} = -W_{j_{k+2} p} K_p (I + W_{pp} K_p)^{-1} W_{p j_k}$$

as an easy calculation shows. Since $W_{j_{k+2} p} \not\equiv 0$, and K_p is arbitrary, we have for generic K_p that $\overline{W}_{j_{k+2} j_k} \not\equiv 0$. Consequently in the graph of the (p - 1)-channel system, there is a path $j_1, \ldots, j_k, j_{k+2}, \ldots, j_r$ connecting nodes j_1 to j_r. This establishes the strong connectivity result.

We remark that the above result is actually true for more complicated (e.g., dynamic) feedback. However, we need only the present form.

It is not hard to verify that if a system with periodic time-varying gains is not strongly connected, it can be decomposed into a collection of strongly connected subsystems which can only have one-way connections between them and that, as for the time-invariant case, decentralized control questions must be analyzed by considering the individual subsystems. Accordingly, to explain the main ideas of the section, we confine attention to a three-channel, strongly connected system.

Suppose we aim to use feedback on channels 2 and 3 to provide (uniform) controllability and observability at input and output 1. Temporarily consider channels 1 and 2 together as a single channel *A*. It is immediately clear that unless using channel *A* one can observe and control the system with a feedback gain around channel 3, there is no possibility of doing the same with channel 1, given feedback around channels 2 and 3.

Using the earlier ideas, we see observability and controlliability from channel A can be achieved by feedback around channel 3; in case there are no fixed modes, this feedback around channel 3 can be constant, and almost any constant feedback gain suffices. If, however, there is a decentralized fixed mode associated with the channel *A*, channel 3 pair a constant gain will not suffice, but a piecewise constant periodic gain taking at least ρ_3 different values [$\rho_3 = 1 + \max(\dim u_3, \dim y_3)$] will suffice.

With this feedback, there now results a system with two channels, 1 and 2, which is possibly periodically time varying, and which is uniformly controllable and observable. By virtue of Lemma 3 it is, at least for generic periodic or constant gains around channel 3, strongly connected. The question arises as to whether we can now apply feedback around channel 2 to make the system uniformly controllable and observable from channel 1. The answer is yes; we shall argue simply the observability.

If this two-channel system is time invariant, the result is immediate by the earlier results. So suppose that it is described by $\{A(t), [B_1\ B_2]\}$ where $A(t)$ is periodic and piecewise constant. Let us assume that $A(t)$ in fact takes the value $\bar{A}$ in $[s, s + T_1)$, $\tilde{A}$ in $[s + T_1, s + T)$. Observability means that if there exists γ for which

$$\begin{bmatrix} C_1' \\ C_2' \end{bmatrix} e^{\bar{A}t}\gamma = 0, \qquad \begin{bmatrix} C_1' \\ C_2' \end{bmatrix} e^{\tilde{A}t} e^{\bar{A}T_1}\gamma = 0$$

then $\gamma = 0$. [This can be checked by examining the observability Grammian over $(s, s + T)$.] Equivalently (take $\delta = e^{\bar{A}T_1}\gamma$), the equations

$$\begin{bmatrix} C_1' \\ C_2' \end{bmatrix} e^{\bar{A}t}\delta = 0, \qquad \begin{bmatrix} C_1' \\ C_2' \end{bmatrix} e^{\tilde{A}t}\delta = 0$$

imply $\delta = 0$. If the "frozen" systems $\{\bar{A}, [B_1\ B_2], [C_1\ C_2]\}$ and $\{\tilde{A}, [B_1\ B_2], [C_1\ C_2]\}$ were to have no fixed modes (other than any associated with lack of centralized controllability and observability), then constant feedback around channel 2 would generically produce uniform controllability and observability at channel 1. However, it is obvious from the definition of fixed modes that if the original three-channel system has fixed modes, so must each of the frozen two-channel systems. We now explain what is done in this case.

For convenience, suppose that y_2 is a scalar. We then take $u_2 = K_2(t)y_2$ where $K_2(t) = 0$, $t \in [s, s_1)$, $K_2(t) = \bar{K}_2$, $t \in [s_1, s + T_1)$, $K_2(t) = 0$, $t \in [s + T_1, s_2)$, $K_2(t) = \tilde{K}_2$, $t \in [s_2, s + T)$ with $K_2(t)$ periodic. If γ_1 is a null vector of the observability Grammian over $[s, s + T]$ of $\left\{A(t) + B_2K_2(t)C_2', C_1\right\}$, then

$C_1' \exp(\bar{A}t)\gamma_1 = 0$

$$C_1' \exp\left[\left(\bar{A} + B_2\bar{K}_2C_2'\right)t\right]\exp(\bar{A}s_1)\gamma_1 = 0$$

$$C_1' \exp(\tilde{A}t)\ \exp\left[\left(A + B_2\bar{K}_2C_2'\right)(T_1 + s - s_1)\right]\ \exp(\bar{A}s_1)\gamma = 0$$

$$C_1' \exp\left[\left(\tilde{A} + B_2\tilde{K}_2C_2'\right)t\right]\exp\left(\tilde{A}(s_2 - s - T_1)\right)$$

$$\times \exp\left[\left(A + B_2\bar{K}_2C_2'\right)(T_1 + s - s_1)\right]\ \exp(As_1)\gamma_1 = 0. \tag{26}$$

Arguing as earlier, and using the fact that $C_1'(sI - \bar{A})^{-1}B_2 \not\equiv 0$ in the light of strong connectivity, we conclude from the first two equations that

$$C_1'e^{\bar{A}t}\gamma_1 = 0, \quad C_2'e^{\bar{A}t}\gamma_1 = 0$$

for all t, and in fact if $\delta = \exp\left[\left(\bar{A} + B_2\bar{K}_2C_2'\right)(T_1 + s - s_1)\right] \times \exp(\bar{A}s_1)\gamma_1$, then

$$C_1'e^{\bar{A}t}\delta = 0, \quad C_2'e^{\bar{A}t}\delta = 0. \tag{27}$$

In a similar manner the last two equations in Eqs. (26) yield

$$C_1'e^{\tilde{A}t}\delta = 0, \quad C_2'e^{\tilde{A}t}\delta = 0. \tag{28}$$

However, as argued above, the observability of the two-channel system implies that in Eqs. (27) and (28) we have $\delta = 0$, and thus $\gamma = 0$; i.e., the single-channel system is observable.

The above analysis applies for scalar y_2. The earlier techniques can be used to derive the result for vector y_2.

The procedure for coping with a p-channel system when $p > 3$ is a straightforward extension of the procedure for a three-channel system. Assuming the p-channel system is strongly connected and meets a centralized controllability and observability condition, one successively applies feedback around channels p, p - 1, ..., 2. The feedback can be constant only if there are no fixed modes associated with any of the frozen systems encountered at any stage in the procedure. Otherwise, it must be periodic and piecewise constant, taking a certain minimum number of values that is readily computable at each stage. The end result is that for generic values for all the feedback gains, the one-channel system is uniformly controllable and observable.

D. AREAS FOR FURTHER STUDY

The results presented here open up further areas for research on linear decentralized control. Let us indicate several of these.

(1) Suppose a system is to have a decentralized controller structure and the aim is to observe and control it from one channel having put feedback (periodic if need be) around the other channel. How should one systematically select the value of the feedback around the second channel and the period in the nonconstant case, for example, to achieve a good compromise between system performance for a nominal plant and robustness to plant uncertainty or variations?

(2) Presumably, if piecewise constant periodic feedback around channel 2 ensures uniform observability and controllability from channel 1, many, if not almost all, periodic feedbacks which are not piecewise constant will have the same effect. How can such feedbacks be characterized?

(3) The controller structures studied in this chapter have no dynamics in all but one channel. The controller on the remaining channel has dynamics with state variable dimension approximately equal to that of the system being controlled. How could one distribute the controller complexity more evenly across the different channels?

(4) Recent unpublished work of which the authors are aware shows that piecewise constant, periodic feedback controllers around a periodic single-input, single-output system operating in discrete time can very frequently be used to generate a deadbeat response. This raises questions as to whether such ideas could be wedded to the ideas of this chapter to show that decentralized, piecewise constant, periodic controllers could provide a deadbeat response for a very wide class of systems.

REFERENCES

1. S. H. WANG and E. J. DAVISON, *IEEE Trans. Automat. Control AC-18*, 24 (1973).

2. H. KOBAYASHI, H. HANAFUSA, and T. YOSHIKAWA, *IEEE Trans. Automat. Control AC-23*, 182 (1978).

3. B. D. O. ANDERSON and D. J. CLEMENTS, *Automatica 17*, 703 (1981).

4. J. P. CORFMAT and A. S. MORSE, *SIAM J. Control Optim. 14*, 163 (1976).

5. J. P. CORFMAT and A. S. MORSE, *Automatica 12*, 479 (1976).

6. J. M. POTTER, B. D. O. ANDERSON, and A. S. MORSE, *IEEE Trans. Automat. Control AC-24*, 491 (1979).

7. B. D. O. ANDERSON, *IEEE Trans. Automat. Control AC-27*, (1982).

8. B. D. O. ANDERSON and J. B. MOORE, *IEEE Trans. Automat. Control AC-26*, 1133 (1981).

9. L. M. SILVERMAN and B. D. O. ANDERSON, *SIAM J. Control 6*, 121 (1968).

10. B. D. O. ANDERSON and J. B. MOORE, "Linear Optimal Control," Prentice-Hall, Englewood Cliffs, New Jersey, 1971.

11. R. E. KALMAN, *Bol. Soc. Matem. Mexicana*, 102, (1960).

12. J. R. BROUSSAND, p. 125, "Proc. 20th IEEE Conf. on Decision and Control," San Diego, 1981.

Structural Dynamic Hierarchical Stabilization and Control of Large-Scale Systems

P. P. GROUMPOS

Energy Research Center
Department of Electrical Engineering
Cleveland State University
Cleveland, Ohio

I. INTRODUCTION

One of the main thrusts in systems research over the last few years has been the development of theories for large-scale systems (LSS), and multilevel hierarchical systems (MHS) [1-10].

ISBN 0-12-012722-9

LSS, in general, are complex and involve a large number of variables. In addition, time lags, nonlinearities, uncontrollability, nonobservability, and lack of overall stability are often the rule rather than the exception; and, in many cases, the complex systems are sparse. Despite the high efficiency of modern large computers, the formidable complexity of LSS makes the problem under consideration here, *the control and stability of the system*, impossible to treat as an overall "one-piece" solution. Indeed, such a consideration is not only difficult but unrealistic.

Solutions may be numerically intractable (poor convergence or even nonconvergence). There is also a possibility that in some applications, a "one-piece" approach may either be simply impossible (insufficient computer memory), too costly (undesired computation time), or too complex and cumbersome to be implemented. Present systems and methods can be classified as

(1) centralized systems (general classical or modern centralized techniques);

(2) large-scale systems and distributed systems (decentralized or general LSS techniques); and

(3) multilevel hierarchical systems (general hierarchical theories).

Today, it is widely accepted that most systems cannot be considered small but rather complex and that they interact with a number of other subsystems around them. Therefore, general centralized techniques and their extensions cannot be used to analyze today's complex systems except on some small isolated subsystems. In this chapter, the challenging problem of controlling and stabilizing LSS as well as MHS is addressed.

Theories which have been developed for LSS and/or MHS have been used for controlling large complex systems. The recent book by Jamshidi [10] treats a considerable number of these approaches and includes illustrative algorithms for many of them.

The challenging problem of "controlling" a LSS is discussed in Section II. A new dynamic hierarchical control is defined in Section III, while an algorithm for a structural pole placement and stabilization of LSS is provided in Section IV. The need for a unified approach to the general controlling problem of LSS is addressed in Section V. A summary and closing remarks follow in Section VI.

II. CONTROLLING LARGE-SCALE SYSTEMS

The control of any system is a problem that demands careful consideration. This is even more the case when a control law is to be designed for large-scale systems since some situations defy resolution because of the following reasons:

(1) Knowledge of the system is usually inexact. Mathematical modeling of LSS is still, at best, an art. Presently, we can say only that aggregated and highly imprecise models of large complex systems exist.

(2) There is a wide variety of problems (i.e., stability, controllability, observability, speed of response, insensitivity to disturbance and parameter variation, choice of identification of critical parameters) which often need to be addressed simultaneously.

(3) The constraints associated with each subsystem and the overall system are different, often numerous, and not known to all subsystems. There is a structure of semiautonomous

controllers functioning to meet "local" objectives as well as contributing to "overall" objectives.

(4) Since there is more than one controller, a control law needs to take this into consideration in conjunction with the fact that different and often unrelated information is available at each controller at different times or at different frequencies.

(5) The exchange or transference of the whole state vector throughout a large complex system is often impractical, uneconomical, and even impossible.

(6) There exists a qualitative goal of efficient, secure, and reliable operation expressed in terms of a number of more specific, quantitative performance measures ("local" plus "global") which are possibly incommensurable, conflicting, and presently not well formulated.

(7) The system frequently extends over a significant spatial region and exhibits a wide range of dynamic frequencies.

Some of the above reasons (3,5-7) have been described as characteristic of LSS by Athans [13]. Due to this untidy situation, a significant portion of research on LSS has dealt with the general "control problem of LSS" [1-13]. These research efforts have been motivated by the inadequacy of centralized (classical or modern) control theories to address satisfactorily the above-mentioned reasons for a control law for large complex systems.

For example, with techniques such as linear-quadratic (LQ) optimal control or pole placement [36], it is possible to achieve improved system performance by using the key concept of state feedback. However, it is often impossible to instrument a feedback system to the extent required for full state feedback because of reason 5 above. The "control problem of LSS" is ultimately concerned with feedback of either state or output. Hence, linear problems are those most often studied since nonlinear feedback control theory is not yet well developed; this study will also concentrate on the former.

Consider a LSS which is assumed to be composed of a number of dynamic interconnected subsystems being described by a continuous or discrete state model. In this model, N controllers are considered, each having a set of actuators and sensors. The key assumption here is that each controller has available at each instant of time, only a *subset of the LSS information*. Hence, the general "control problem of LSS" is characterized by a *multicontroller structure* in which each controller generates only a subset of the overall control effort for the LSS based on a limited set of information. Despite this multicontroller structure assumption, the overall control law may still be designed in a completely centralized way.

There are several different approaches to the control and stabilization of LSS. In the interest of presenting the most complete picture possible of this complex problem, we briefly discuss three of these approaches. Due to space constraints, we minimize mathematical and theoretical development in the following three approaches. However, their significant points will be outlined.

A. *DECENTRALIZED TECHNIQUES*

As early as 1970, the question has been raised about the conditions under which there exists a set of appropriate local feedback control laws that will stabilize and control a *complete system*. Several different versions of this problem have been formulated and examined by Aoki [14]. Using concepts of dynamic compensation, Davison and his co-workers addressed the same problem more extensively, [15,16,19,20].

Consider a linear time-invariant multivariable system with N local control stations described by

$$\dot{x}(t) = Ax(t) + \sum_{i=1}^{N} B_i u_i(t) \qquad (1)$$

$$y_i(t) = C_i x(t), \quad i = 1, 2, \ldots, N,$$

where $x(t) \in R^n$ is the state of the system, $u_i(t) \in R^{m_i}$; $\Sigma_{i=1}^{N} m_i = m$, and $y_i(t) \in R^{p_i}$; $\Sigma_{i=1}^{N} p_i = p$ are the input and output, respectively, of the ith local control station. The *decentralized stabilization* problem is to find *N local* output feedback control laws with *dynamic compensation* for (1) of the form

$$u_i(t) = Q_i z_i(t) + K_i y_i(t) + v_i(t) \qquad (2)$$

$$\dot{z}_i(t) = S_i z_i(t) + R_i y_i(t) \qquad (3)$$

such that the overall system

$$\begin{bmatrix} \dot{x}(t) \\ \dot{z}(t) \end{bmatrix} = \begin{bmatrix} A + BK & BQ \\ RC & S \end{bmatrix} \begin{bmatrix} x(t) \\ z(t) \end{bmatrix} + \begin{bmatrix} B \\ 0 \end{bmatrix} v(t) \qquad (4)$$

is asymptotically stable. In Eq. (4), $K = \text{diag}\{K_i\}$, $Q = \text{diag}\{Q_i\}$, $R = \text{diag}\{R_i\}$, $S = \text{diag}\{S_i\}$, $B = \{B_1, B_2, \ldots, B_N\}$, $C = \{C_1, C_2, \ldots, C_N\}^T$, and $v(t) = \{v_1(t), v_2(t), \ldots, v_N(t)\}^T$. If we let $\mathscr{K} = \{K \mid K = \text{block diag}(K_1, K_2, \ldots, K_N);\ K_i \in R^{m_i \times p_i}, i = 1, 2, \ldots, N\}$, the fixed modes of system (1) relative to $\mathscr{K}$ are the eigenvalues of $A + BK$, $K \in \mathscr{K}$, which are invariant under feedback. A necessary and sufficient condition for the decentralized stabilization of (1) using only local dynamic compensation is that all the fixed modes of the system (C, A, B) with respect to $\mathcal{K}$ lie on the open left-half complex plane. Around the same time as Davison and Wang's work, Corfmat and Morse reexamined the same problem. In their papers [17,18], they introduced the concept of complete systems which are those that can be made both controllable and observable *through a single channel*. Using ideas from graph theory, they obtained certain results (e.g., single-channel controllability and observability imply strong connectedness). Moreover, they gave explicit and more complete characteristics of conditions for determining when a closed-loop spectrum of a k-channel linear system can be freely assigned or stabilized in terms of "artificial" subsystem properties. Some interesting observations have been made [4] for these approaches. From a practical point of view, dynamic compensation around a single or even around a few selected components may require impractically large gains. In addition, it is often undesirable for geographically dispersed systems, such as transportation, energy, or communication systems. Although this general decentralized synthesis technique is constructive, it may not always prove to be the best way to construct decentralized control systems, particularly for systems known to possess "weak couplings" between channels. Furthermore, the stability and "control" of an entire LSS is determined only after *all local* controllers have been applied. Several extensions have been obtained by others and some are mentioned in [12].

When actual synthesis of decentralized controllers is considered further, constraints and limitations emerge. In practical terms, it is generally impossible to connect all decentralized controllers to a system simultaneously. The notion of sequential stability was then developed by Davison and Gesing

[19] in which it was desired to implement a realistic robust decentralized controller in a sequential way so that only *one* local controller at a control station was connected to the system at any time. *Only one local controller was permitted to be adjusted.* Surprisingly, it was shown that any ordering of the controllers could be applied to the plant and the resultant system would still remain stable. However, some ordering may produce a "more satisfactory" speed of response than other orderings. When the ith controller possesses a limited knowledge of the model of an LSS to be stabilized, then a different problem is present. This problem was addressed by Davison and Ozguner [20], but again in the framework of the general decentralized servomechanism problem [16]. This approach again requires local output feedback controls and "centralized" synthesis techniques with the only difference being that each controller possesses only a *detailed local model* of the controlled plant. Moreover, the number of dynamic control agents have been increased.

B. MULTILEVEL TECHNIQUES

In general, these techniques address the important question of how a dynamic LSS is to be decomposed and structurally controlled. Using either physical characteristics of a complex system or certain properties of its dynamic model, in general, a set of *local* controllers followed by another set of *global* controllers are considered. Various approaches with respect to this general multilevel concept have been proposed during the last decade or so [1-8,10,21-24].

Only that work which is related to the stabilization problem of LSS will be considered here. The work of Siljak and his colleagues seems to be that most related to this discussion.

In reviewing this approach, it is more convenient to write the state equation of (1) in the input decentralized form.

$$S_i: \quad \dot{x}_i(t) = A_i x_i(t) + \sum_{j=1}^{N} A_{ij} x_j(t) + B_i u_i(t) \tag{5}$$

where $x_i(t) \in R^{n_i}$ is the state and $u_i(t) \in R^{m_i}$ is the input of the ith subsystem, respectively, and $x_j(t) \in R^{n_j}$ for $j = 1, 2, \ldots, N$ and $j \neq i$ are the states of the other subsystems connected to the ith subsystem. The matrices A_{ii} and A_{ij} are appropriately defined and model the local plant dynamics and the interactions between the ith and jth subsystems, respectively. To stabilize the overall system S, composed of $S_1, S_2, \ldots, S_N$, the following decentralized multilevel control is applied [7,21]:

$$u_i(t) = u_i^l(t) + u_i^g(t) \tag{6}$$

where $u_i^l(t)$ is the local control law chosen as

$$u_i^l(t) = -K_i^T x_i(t) \tag{7}$$

with constant feedback gains $K_i \in R^{n_i}$; $u_i^g(t)$ is the global control law chosen as

$$u_i^g(t) = -\sum_{j=1}^{N} K_{ij}^T x_j(t) \tag{8}$$

with constant feedback gains $K_{ij} \in R^{n_j}$. The controllability assumption of all the pairs (A_i, B_i) guarantees the existence of of the local feedback law (7) such that the spectrum of $A_i - B_i K_i^T$ denoted by $\sigma\left(A_i - B_i K_i^T\right) < C^-$. Each uncoupled subsystem is stabilized with a degree of exponential stability depending on the desired location of the eigenvalues only of the local closed-loop subsystem. However, local and global controllability are not sufficient for decentralized stabilization via local feedback as shown by Wang in [25]. To conclude stability of the overall system $\underline{S}$ it is necessary to implement a global control as given by (8). The use of a vector Lyaponov function has been suggested [7]; its components are quadratic Lyaponov functions for the individual subsystems. In this context, the global control law (8) is to be applied with the matrices K_{ij} chosen to guarantee the stability of the aggregate system through the use of the Sevastyanov-Kotelyanskii necessary and sufficient conditions for the stability of a Metzler matrix. In essence, the global feedback gains are chosen to minimize the effect of the interactions between subsystems which are regarded under this approach as degrading perturbation terms. Hence, the computations required for the global feedback gains and the evaluation of its robust characteristics depend explicitly on the parameters of the interconnection matrices A_{ij}. Furthermore, the whole multilevel stabilization process *might have to be designed more than once*. This depends on appropriate choice of the eigenvalues for the decoupled subsystems. Once the subsystem eigenvalues are prescribed, then the local and global feedback control laws can be computed uniquely. If the necessary and sufficient conditions are not met, a reassignment of the subsystem's eigenvalues is required. Several extensions are mentioned in [12].

C. SINGULAR PERTURBATION TECHNIQUES

In general, perturbation methods are useful for dealing with an LSS system that can be approximated by a system of simpler structure. Mathematically, the difference in response between the actual and approximate systems is modeled as a perturbation term driving the latter. Perturbation methods are usually divided into two main subclasses: Weak coupling and strong coupling approaches [2].

The second approach, which is based on the notion of a singular perturbation, i.e., a perturbation term in the left-hand side of a differential equation, is the only one considered here since it is related to the discussed work. The singular perturbation approach lowers the model order by first neglecting the fast phenomena. It then improves the approximation by re-introducing their effects as "boundary layer" corrections calculated in separate time scales. Further improvements can be made by asymptotic expansion methods.

Using this basic philosophy, Chow and Kokotovic [26] investigated the eigenvalue problem in a two-time scale system. A matrix norm condition was given under which the small eigenvalues of the system will be sufficiently separated from the large eigenvalues. A feedback control design was developed in which two gain matrices were used for placing the small and large eigenvalues separately. In another paper by Chow and Kokotovic [27], conditions for complete separation of slow and fast regulator designs were formulated. In that approach, the system is considered to be composed of slow and fast subsystems.

Subsequently, the notion of multiparameter perturbation suitable for LSS was introduced by Khalil and Kokotovic. First, the notion of multimodeling for LSS with several decision makers is introduced [28]. The multimodeling is approached as a multiparameter singular perturbation in the sense that each decision maker designs feedback strategy using results of Chow and Kokotovic [27] and based on a simplified view of the overall system. Assuming that the interactions between fast subsystems are weak, conditions for a feedback design to be satisfactory were given. To avoid the weak coupling limitation, a more general multiparameter perturbation for linear time varying systems was considered in [29] where strong, fast interactions were allowed. The so-called "block D-stability" property of the interacting fast subsystems was considered and several tests for block D stability were proposed. In another development [30], the problem of decentralized stabilization by *many* decision makers using *different* models of the LSS was considered. Using the multimodeling approach [28] and multiparameter perturbation techniques [29], a two-step stabilization procedure was developed. An LSS is composed of interconnected subsystems which have distinguishable fast and slow parts and so are represented by singularly perturbed models. The objective here is to find *local* state feedback control laws with x_i the slow and z_i the fast states of subsystem S_i of the form

$$u_i = K_{is}x_i + K_{if}z_i, \quad i = 1, 2, \ldots, N, \tag{9}$$

which will make the closed-loop system asymptotically stable for all sufficiently small singular perturbation parameters ϵ which lie in a set H defined by some bounds, incorporating physical characteristics of the system. To stabilize an LSS composed of interconnected subsystems with slow and fast parts, the stability of the boundary layer system is first ensured and then the stability of the reduced system. The following two steps are proposed:

Step 1. Substitute $u_i = \tilde{u}_i + K_{if}z_i$ in the original LSS and choose K_{if} such that the fast interconnected system satisfied a boundary layer stability condition; and

Step 2. Set $\epsilon_i = 0$ and eliminate z_i, the fast states, so that a reduced interconnected slow system is obtained which depends on the choices of F_{if} from step 1.

The stabilization procedure is then completed by choosing $u_i = K_{ir}x_i$ such that the closed loop reduced system is asymptotically stable.

Many interesting questions were raised by Khalil and Kokotovic [30] and partially answered. For example, how does the choice of the K_{if} affect the structure of the reduced system? When does a subsystem designer choose the feedback gains K_{if} associated with the fast states without any information about the dynamics of the other subsystems? How is this approach related to other decentralized control techniques such as the ones discussed in Subsections A and B? Similar questions will be raised in Section V.

III. TWO-LEVEL STRUCTURAL DYNAMIC HIERARCHICAL CONTROL (SDHC)

In the previous section, it was pointed out that stabilizing or controlling an LSS is not an easy or straightforward task. The many different approaches [1-10], some of which were briefly discussed in the previous section, show the importance of the problem. Taking into consideration reasons 1-7 of Section II and carefully considering the many approaches, it was thought that a structural control law [11,12] for LSS would be very constructive and most beneficial. It is believed [1,6] and seems natural that most LSS composed of N interconnected subsystems would operate in a more efficient and robust way if some kind of overall coordinated control effort is designed. Since the simplest type of hierarchical structure is the two-level one [1], it seems logical for us to turn our attention to a two-level structural dynamic hierarchical control (SDHC) concept, and to define it.

Definition. Given a LSS composed of N dynamic interconnected subsystems, a two-level structural dynamic hierarchical control law is defined when a *dynamic coordinator* is considered and interacting with the N subsystems and the design of the overall control consists of N control laws $u_i(t)$ associated with N subsystems and of a control law $u_0(t)$ associated with the dynamic coordinator resulting in the following structural feedback gain:

$$\begin{bmatrix} K_1 & & & & & & K_{10} \\ & K_2 & \ddots & & \bigcirc & & K_{20} \\ & & & & & & \vdots \\ & & & \bullet & & & \\ & & \bigcirc & & \ddots & K_N & K_{N0} \\ K_{01} & K_{02} & \cdots & & \cdots & K_{0N} & K_0 \end{bmatrix}. \tag{10}$$

The structural form (10) is referred to as blocked arrow canonical form (BACAF) due to its resemblance to an arrow; (10) is often referred to as bordered block diagonal form (BBDF) in network and power analysis and matrix theory. Since BACAF is used for modeling two-level dynamic hierarchical systems (DYHIS) [12], this terminology will be used here.

The ith subsystem S_i and the dynamic coordinator G are described by

$$S_i: \quad \dot{x}_i(t) = A_i x_i(t) + \sum_{\substack{j=1 \\ i \neq j}}^{N} A_{ij} x_j(t) + B_i u_i(t) + A_{i0} x_0(t) \tag{11}$$

$$G: \quad \dot{x}_0(t) = A_0 x_0(t) + \sum_{i=1}^{N} A_{0i} x_i(t) + B_0 u_0(t), \tag{12}$$

where $x_i(\cdot)$, $u_i(\cdot)$ and $x_0(\cdot)$, $u_0(\cdot)$ are n_i-, m_i-, n_0-, and m_0-dimensional state and control vectors, A_i, A_{ij}, A_{i0}, A_{0i}, A_0, B_i, and B_0 are constant matrices of appropriate dimensions.

When state feedback is considered, the following control law would result in a closed-loop two-level SDHC:

N control laws associated with the N subsystems

$$u_i(t) = K_i x_i(t) + K_{i0} x_0(t), \qquad i = 1, 2, \ldots, N; \tag{13}$$

a control law associated with the dynamic coordinator G

$$u_0(t) = K_0 x_0(t) + \sum_{i=1}^{N} K_{0i} x_i(t). \tag{14}$$

K_i, K_0, K_{i0}, and K_{0i} are appropriate dimensional feedback gains to be determined depending on the problem under consideration (stabilization, optimization, or pole placement).

Equations (11) and (12) can be combined as follows:

$$\begin{bmatrix} \dot{x}(t) \\ \dot{x}_0(t) \end{bmatrix} = \begin{bmatrix} A & C \\ E & A_0 \end{bmatrix} \begin{bmatrix} x(t) \\ x_0(t) \end{bmatrix} + \begin{bmatrix} B & 0 \\ 0 & B_0 \end{bmatrix} \begin{bmatrix} u(t) \\ u_0(t) \end{bmatrix} \tag{15}$$

where C and E represent the overall interconnection structure between the N subsystems and the coordinator. Suppose now that each subsystem S_i has a limited knowledge of the overall LSS model [12,20,28] and say that A_{ij} from Eq. (11) is not known by the ith subsystems and so can be momentarily ignored. Then, when the two-level SDHC (13) and (14) are applied to (15) where A is a block diagonal matrix, the following closed-loop system is obtained

$$\begin{bmatrix} \dot{x}_1(t) \\ \dot{x}_2(t) \\ \vdots \\ \dot{x}_N(t) \\ \dot{x}_0(t) \end{bmatrix} = \begin{bmatrix} A_1 + B_1K_1 & & & \bigcirc & A_{10} + B_1K_{10} \\ & A_2 + B_2K_2 & & & A_{20} + B_2K_{20} \\ \vdots & \bigcirc & \ddots & & \vdots \\ & & & A_N + B_NK_N & A_{N0} + B_NK_{N0} \\ A_{01} + B_0K_{01} & A_{02} + B_0K_{02} & \cdots & A_{0N} + B_0K_{0N} & A_0 + B_0K_0 \end{bmatrix} \times \begin{bmatrix} x_1(t) \\ x_2(t) \\ \vdots \\ x_N(t) \\ x_0(t) \end{bmatrix}. \tag{16}$$

The closed-loop overall system (16) takes a BACAF structure. The important thing about the BACAF structure is that it clearly shows which relationships exist or could be obtained between the N subsystems and the coordinator G. For example, the stability and pole placement problem of the overall system (15) can be studied by evaluating the strength of interaction between each individual subsystem and the coordinator [12,31].

It is important to reflect on some generalities about the BACAF structure of (16). It was obtained by neglecting the interactions between the N subsystems and assuming a two-level SDHC. In essence, this is in line with the assumption that subsystems would prefer to be autonomous, and so only local information should be processed first. Hence, only K_i, i = 1, 2, ..., N, need to be determined. If there were no interconnections between the subsystems, then this should suffice. But since this is not true, global information is processed and there is then a need to consider algorithms for achieving this as well as to study their impact on the overall system. The proposed two-level SDHC approach here explores the basic characteristics of two-level dynamical hierarchical systems [12], and, as can be seen from the next section, presents a totally new approach to the control and stabilization problem of LSS.

IV. STRUCTURAL STABILIZATION OF LARGE-SCALE SYSTEMS

A. *THEORETICAL DEVELOPMENT*

The approach here is to use the conceptual two-level SDHC defined in the previous section in stabilizing LSS. The interesting question here is that if a two-level SDHC approach is to be used, under what conditions can the overall LSS be stabilized, including the dynamic coordinator.

Let us investigate a related problem, namely, under what conditions all poles of (15) can be placed arbitrarily. Clearly, Eq. (15) assumes the presence of a dynamic coordinator and hence a two-level SDHC approach can be utilized. Before we outline any algorithm for stabilizing a LSS, let us first answer a *basic question* which seems to be the key to this approach. Let us rewrite the closed-loop overall LSS, Eq. (16), into the following form:

$$\begin{bmatrix} \dot{x}(t) \\ \dot{x}_0(t) \end{bmatrix} = \begin{bmatrix} \Lambda & C \\ E & G \end{bmatrix} \begin{bmatrix} x(t) \\ x_0(t) \end{bmatrix} \tag{17}$$

where $\Lambda = \text{diag}\{\Lambda_1, \Lambda_2, \ldots, \Lambda_n\}$, $\Lambda_i = A_i + B_iK_i$, $C = \{C_1, C_2, \ldots, C_N\}^T$, $C_i = A_{i0} + B_iK_{i0}$, $E = \{E_1, E_2, \ldots, E_N\}$, $E_i = A_{0i} + B_0K_{0i}$, and $G = A_0 + B_0K_0$. The following theorem addresses the pole assignment problem of (17).

Theorem 1. Let the Λ matrix of (17) be composed of one-dimensional subsystems with elements λ_i such that $\lambda_i \neq \lambda_j$ for all $i \neq j$. Then there exist *unique* products $k_i = e_i c_i$ and a *unique scalar coordinator* g such that all poles of the two-level system, Eq. (17), can be placed arbitrarily. The proof is provided in Appendix A.

Remark. The dynamic coordinator is of the first order and the g and products $k_i = e_i c_i$ are *uniquely determined.*

If the Λ matrix has repeated eigenvalues but is diagonalizable, then the coordinator G and the interconnection matrices C and E can easily be determined by simply extending Theorem 1 and applying the proper simple elementary similarity transformation (EST) [12]. If the Λ matrix of (17) is composed of subsystems S_i, each assuming a Jordan block, then the following theorem resolves the question of the complexity of E, C, and G for the poles of the system (17) to be placed arbitrarily.

Theorem 2. Let the matrix Λ of Eq. (17) be composed of Jordan blocks $J_i^{n_i \times n_i}$ with a corresponding eigenvalue λ_i. If $\lambda_i \neq \lambda_j$ for all $i \neq j$, then there is a *unique first-order* coordinator, g. The interconnection matrices E and C become simple row and column vectors, respectively. Moreover, only the n_ith entry of the $\underline{C}$ column vector need be nonzero, which can be taken as one. Then the row vector $e = \{e_1, e_2, \ldots, e_N\}$ can uniquely be determined and all poles of the overall LSS, Eq. (17), can be placed arbitrarily.

The proof of this theorem can be found in [11]. In addition, in [11] all other cases with respect to the structure of the coordinator and of the interconnection matrices E and C have been investigated.

From the above, we can say that a two-level structural stabilization approach to LSS would strongly depend on the N subsystems structure and dynamics. Let us outline one possible way of developing such an approach.

B. *A TWO-LEVEL STRUCTURAL STABILIZATION PROCEDURE*

Step 1. Assume a dynamic coordinator without specifying its structure or dynamics so that it interacts with all subsystems. A two-level DYHIS has been formed.

Step 2. Apply N local control laws by using only local states and of the form

$$u_i(t) = K_i x_i(t) \tag{18}$$

and place all those poles that can be placed arbitrarily, based on the controllability characteristics of the pairs (A_i, B_i).

Step 3. Use the following similarity transformation:

$$\begin{bmatrix} x(t) \\ x_0(t) \end{bmatrix} = \begin{bmatrix} P & 0 \\ 0 & I \end{bmatrix} \begin{bmatrix} \bar{x}(t) \\ \bar{x}_0(t) \end{bmatrix} \tag{19}$$

such that the resulting system

$$\begin{bmatrix} \dot{\bar{x}}(t) \\ \dot{\bar{x}}_0(t) \end{bmatrix} = \begin{bmatrix} P^{-1}(A + BK^l)P & P^{-1}C \\ E & A_0 \end{bmatrix} \begin{bmatrix} \bar{x}(t) \\ \bar{x}_0(t) \end{bmatrix} + \begin{bmatrix} P^{-1}B \\ 0 \end{bmatrix} u_i^0(t) + \begin{bmatrix} 0 \\ B_0 \end{bmatrix} u_0(t) \tag{20}$$

where K^l = block diag$\{K_1, K_2, \ldots, K_N\}$ is chosen according to local feedback law (18) and where $P^{-1}(A + BK^l)P \to J$ in Jordan canonical form. The $P^{-1}C$ operation need not be performed before step 4.

Step 4. Depending on the dynamics (the Jordan forms) of the N subsystems, determine the structure of the coordinator G and of the interconnection matrices E and C.

Step 5. For each subsystem, use the additional control

$$u_i^0(t) = \{K_{10}, K_{20}, \ldots, K_{N0}\}^T x_0(t). \tag{21}$$

Step 6. For the coordinator, use the control law (14)

$$u_0(t) = \sum_{i=1}^{N} K_{0i}x_i(t) + K_0x_0(t). \tag{22}$$

Step 7. Stabilize the overall two-level DYHIS for the *closed-loop BACAF structure* resulting from steps 2 through 6 by selecting the appropriate values of K_i, K_{i0}, K_{0i}, and K_0.

Before we consider any examples, it would be worthwhile to present and briefly discuss some interesting observations.

C. *SOME INTERESTING OBSERVATIONS*

Neither subsystem nor overall controllability is needed for the two-level structural stabilization procedure.

The structure and complexity of the dynamic coordinator and its interconnections with the N subsystems strongly depend on the dynamics of the subsystems. The similarity transformation (19) does not directly affect the dynamic coordinator as can be seen by (20). However, it can reveal important information about the resulting two-level DYHIS.

The BACAF two-level closed-loop DYHIS is guaranteed to be stable [11].

No recursive or any sequential control connection is required.

The "decentralized" control law K_i can be designed using either Siljak's method [7] or Wang and Davison's method [15].

The nice two-level SDHC and the subsequent stabilization procedure proposed here can open up real possibilities for a robust overall control law. This claim can be substantiated as follows: If *any* or *all* local control laws of step 2 fail, the dynamic coordinator can provide a control law such that the closed-loop two-level DYHIS will be stable. In the case where *all* N local controls fail, then a zero-diagonal BACAF feedback gain, resulting from combining steps 5 and 6, can be determined for overall stability of the system. On the other hand, if a complete decentralized control law can be designed and is reliable, then any global control law would be obsolete and a dynamic coordinator would not need to be considered. Hence, the control and stabilization of a LSS can be accomplished by a structural mixture of local control laws and/or a hierarchical control law.

The proposed two-level structural stabilization procedure can provide a way to treat systems with fixed modes. It has been shown [12,31] that for the stabilization of a LSS with r unstable fixed modes at most, an rth-order dynamic coordinator is required. Some interest in analyzing LSS with fixed modes has been developed lately [32,33] and so the proposed two-level SDHC is to be further explored.

Another very important remark to be made is how easy it is to compute the characteristic equation of a BACAF with a single row and column E and C, respectively, and a scalar coordinator g for Eq. (16). This is shown in Appendix A in the proof of Theorem 1, and more extensively in [11] and [12]. This is very important because it enables us to calculate part of the required feedback gains in a very easy and straightforward way.

D. EXAMPLES

Various examples could be used to illustrate the usefulness of this new two-level SDHC to the control and stabilization problem of LSS. However, due to space limitations the following two will make the points clear.

Example 1

Let us assume two subsystems S_i, $i = 1, 2$, having the following dynamics:

$$A_i = \begin{bmatrix} \gamma_i & 0 \\ 0 & a_i \end{bmatrix} b_i = \begin{bmatrix} 0 \\ b_i \end{bmatrix}$$

$\gamma_i > 0$, $a_i < 0$, and $\gamma_i \neq \gamma_j$, $a_i \neq a_j$ for $i \neq j$. Furthermore, let the interconnection between the subsystems S_1 and S_2 be

$$A_{12} = A_{21} = \begin{bmatrix} 0 & 1 \\ 0 & 0 \end{bmatrix}.$$

The pairs (A_i, b_i), $i = 1, 2$, are not controllable and so local feedback cannot be used to stabilize the subsystems since $\gamma_i > 0$. Furthermore, the overall system (A, B) where

$$A = \begin{bmatrix} A_1 & A_{12} \\ A_{21} & A_2 \end{bmatrix} \quad \text{and} \quad B = \begin{bmatrix} b_1 & 0 \\ 0 & b_2 \end{bmatrix}$$

is not controllable and hence the decentralized approach where a global feedback control is to be designed, cannot be used to stabilize the system since there are uncontrollable modes.

The two-level structural hierarchical stabilization approach introduced here can stabilize the overall system. Since $\gamma_i \neq \gamma_j$ and $a_i \neq a_j$ for $i \neq j$, we could look into a scalar dynamic coordinator. We can apply local feedback control laws to relocate the a_i, $i = 1, 2$, to any other desired stable region as long as it is not to the points γ_i, $i = 1, 2$, let us say to α_i, $i = 1, 2$, and such that $\alpha_i \neq \alpha_j$, $i \neq j$. Then a similarity transformation can be used to obtain the Jordan form of the $\bar{A} = A + BK$ resulting system. The eigenvalues of $\bar{A}$ are now $\lambda_i = \gamma_i$, $i = 1, 2$, and $\lambda_j = \alpha_j$, $j = 1, 2$. The Jordan blocks are of dimension one and indeed a scalar dynamic coordinator sufficed for the overall stability of the system. The closed-loop two-level DYHIS, skipping the details of the other steps of the algorithm and keeping in mind the proof of Theorem 1 of Appendix A where $e_i = -1$ takes the form

$$\begin{bmatrix} \dot{\bar{x}}_1 \\ \dot{\bar{x}}_2 \\ \dot{\bar{x}}_3 \\ \dot{\bar{x}}_4 \\ \dot{\bar{x}}_0 \end{bmatrix} = \begin{bmatrix} \gamma_1 & & & & c_1 \\ & \alpha_1 & & \bigcirc & c_2 \\ & & \gamma_2 & & c_3 \\ & \bigcirc & & \alpha_2 & c_4 \\ -1 & -1 & -1 & -1 & g \end{bmatrix} \begin{bmatrix} \bar{x}_1 \\ \bar{x}_2 \\ \bar{x}_3 \\ \bar{x}_4 \\ \bar{x}_0 \end{bmatrix}. \tag{23}$$

The characteristic equation $f(\lambda)$ of the closed-loop BACAF structure is easily computed (Appendix A and [12]) and is

$$f(\lambda) = \sum_{i=1}^{4} c_i \prod_{\substack{j=1 \\ i\neq j}}^{4} (\lambda - \lambda_i) + (\lambda - g) \prod_{i=1}^{4} (\lambda - \lambda_i) \tag{24}$$

where the λ_i are the diagonal elements of the BACAF matrix, Eq. (23). If the desired closed-loop eigenvalues are λ_i^d, i = 1, 2, 3, 4, 5 (one for the dynamic coordinator), then the characteristic equation can be computed from $f_d(\lambda) = \prod_{i=1}^{5} \left(\lambda - \lambda_i^d\right)$. By equating like coefficients in $f(\lambda)$ and $f_d(\lambda)$, a set of five simultaneous linear equations results which can uniquely be solved and so specify the c_i and g (Theorem 1).

We can point out here that local decentralized control laws did not have to be used such that the $a_i < 0$, i = 1, 2, being related to α_i, i = 1, 2. Still, the proposed approach would guarantee the stability of the overall system with a scalar dynamic coordinator. However, the loss (or nonrequirement) of a dynamic coordinator and hence the proposed two-level structural approach would result in an unstable system overall. A similar example was used in a slightly different way when comparing two different methodologies [34].

Example 2

In this example, we will demonstrate only the nice way of calculating the c and g of a BACAF structure. Suppose that three subsystems S_1, S_2, and S_3 have first-order dynamics with modes of operation at 1, -2, and 3, respectively. There are not any local controllers to control-stabilize them. A dynamic coordinator is required to control-stabilize these three subsystems. The desired closed-loop poles are required to be at -4, -3, -2, and -1.

The resultant closed-loop two-level DYHIS is

$$\begin{bmatrix} \dot{x}_1 \\ \dot{x}_2 \\ \dot{x}_3 \\ \dot{x}_0 \end{bmatrix} = \begin{bmatrix} 1 & & \bigcirc & c_1 \\ & -2 & & c_2 \\ \bigcirc & & 3 & c_3 \\ -1 & -1 & -1 & g \end{bmatrix} \begin{bmatrix} x_1 \\ x_2 \\ x_3 \\ x_0 \end{bmatrix}. \tag{25}$$

The characteristic equation using (24) is

$$f(\lambda) = c_1(\lambda + 2)(\lambda - 3) + c_2(\lambda - 1)(\lambda - 3) + c_3(\lambda - 1)(\lambda + 2) + (\lambda - 1)(\lambda + 2)(\lambda - 3)(\lambda - g). \tag{26}$$

The desired characteristic equation is

$$f_d(\lambda) = \lambda^4 + 9\lambda^3 + 28\lambda^2 + 38\lambda + 24 \tag{27}$$

when expanding and grouping like power terms of (26) and then matching like power coefficients of (26) and (27), and using the results of Appendix A, we find that g = -11 while c_1, c_2, and c_3 are the unique solution of Ac = y where

$$A = \begin{bmatrix} 1 & 1 & 1 \\ 1 & 4 & -1 \\ -6 & 3 & -2 \end{bmatrix}$$

and $y = [1, -11, -90]^T$. The determinant of A is nonzero, A = 30; $c_1 = 13.33$, $c_2 = -7.73$, and $c_3 = 6.6$.

Although these two examples are simple, they do illustrate the major distinctions of the two-level SDHC approach. First, it can be used when other decentralized techniques fail and second, the BACAF structure needs to be formed *once* which guarantees overall stability of the system. Furthermore, the feedback BACAF gain can be determined in a very simple way.

V. TOWARD A UNIFIED APPROACH FOR THE CONTROL OF LARGE-SCALE SYSTEMS

A. *THE NEED FOR A UNIFIED APPROACH*

In the previous sections we considered and discussed different approaches to the control problems of LSS. It is of interest to note that there are even more than we can mention here, i.e., those of Stackelberg [5], structural perturbation [24], and other multilevel methods [6-10].

A number of basic questions are appropriate here: How are all these different approaches related to each other? Are there basic generic properties that can and need to be addressed for the controlling problem of LSS? Why should we consider *only* dynamic compensation or *only* general "multilevel structures" in controlling LSS? How does the Stackelberg approach relate to multilevel and the proposed two-level SDHC? How much dynamic compensation can we afford in controlling LSS? How are multimodeling approaches [28,30] related to the proposed two-level SDHC approach? How can all these different approaches actually be implemented using "parallel processing structures?"

A final basic question: Are we headed toward a unified approach for the control problem of LSS? This author feels that we are and in the stabilization problem of LSS is encouraged by the recent reports of Davison and Ozguner [20], Khalil and Kokotovic [30], and Kuo and Loparo [33]. Indeed the challenging situation arising from 1 to 7 in Section II can be addressed only with a unified approach.

There can be numerous examples where "generic" properties of the different approaches can be identified but yet not fully explored and carefully evaluated. Here it will be shown that the multimodeling approach and the proposed two-level SDHC approach have some common characteristics. To be more precise, let us consider N interconnected subsystems of a LSS using the multimodeling approach [28-30].

$$\begin{bmatrix} \epsilon_1 \dot{z}_1 \\ \epsilon_2 \dot{z}_2 \\ \vdots \\ \epsilon_N \dot{z}_N \\ \dot{x}_0 \end{bmatrix} = \begin{bmatrix} A_{11} & \epsilon_{12}A_{12} & & \epsilon_{1N}A_{1N} & A_{10} \\ \epsilon_{21}A_{21} & A_{22} & & \epsilon_{2N}A_{2N} & A_{20} \\ \vdots & \vdots & \ddots & \vdots & \vdots \\ \epsilon_{N1}A_{N1} & \epsilon_{N2}A_{N2} & & A_{NN} & A_{N0} \\ A_{01} & A_{02} & \cdots & A_{0N} & A_0 \end{bmatrix} \begin{bmatrix} z_1 \\ z_2 \\ \vdots \\ z_N \\ x_0 \end{bmatrix}$$

$$+ \begin{bmatrix} B_{11} & & \bigcirc \\ & B_{22} & & \\ \bigcirc & & \ddots & \\ & & & B_{NN} \\ B_{01} & B_{02} & \cdots & B_{0N} \end{bmatrix} \begin{bmatrix} u_1 \\ u_2 \\ \vdots \\ u_N \end{bmatrix} \qquad (28)$$

where the z_i are the fast states with dimensionalities n_i, x_0 is the slow state with dimensionality n_0, and the u_i are local controls with dimensionalities m_i, and all matrices are appropriately dimensioned.

Now under the usual assumption, the fast subsystems are uncoupled, i.e., $\epsilon_{ij} = 0$; and in addition assume the slow subsystem with state x_0 is a controller. u_0 with dimensionality m_0 is to interact with the fast subsystems through $\{B_{10}, B_{02}, \ldots, B_{0N}\}^T$ and B_0 with the slow state. Then the overall system would become

$$\begin{bmatrix} \epsilon_1 \dot{z}_1 \\ \epsilon_2 \dot{z}_2 \\ \vdots \\ \epsilon_N \dot{z}_N \\ \dot{x}_0 \end{bmatrix} = \begin{bmatrix} A_{11} & & \bigcirc & & A_{10} \\ & A_{22} & & & A_{20} \\ \bigcirc & & \ddots & & \vdots \\ & & & A_{NN} & A_{N0} \\ A_{01} & A_{02} & \cdots & A_{0N} & A_0 \end{bmatrix} \begin{bmatrix} z_1 \\ z_2 \\ \vdots \\ z_N \\ x_0 \end{bmatrix} + \begin{bmatrix} B_{11} & & \bigcirc & & B_{10} \\ & B_{22} & & & B_{20} \\ \bigcirc & & \ddots & & \vdots \\ & & & B_{NN} & B_{N0} \\ B_{01} & B_{02} & \cdots & B_{0N} & B_0 \end{bmatrix} \begin{bmatrix} u_1 \\ u_2 \\ \vdots \\ u_N \\ u_0 \end{bmatrix}. \quad (29)$$

If we compare the above result with the two-level DYHIS representation of LSS when a structural SDHC approach is to be developed, Eq. (16), the resemblance is very noticeable. Both the A and B matrices of the "modified multimodeling" approach take BACAF structures and the control and stability problem of the combined slow and fast subsystem can be studied with the approach outlined briefly above when appropriately modified.

B. A GENERAL INTEGRATED INFORMATION-CONTROL SYSTEM FUNCTIONALIZATION

We are told today that the hardware technology has provided us with a whole new world of digital devices and that now the problem is how to use them. After you know what you want to do, how do you arrange all these powerful microcomputing systems to do the job for you? This increasing computer power, at decreasing cost in smaller packages, continues to strengthen the concept of, and open new horizons on, distributed systems in complex process control. Today, besides the theoretical considerations, the advantages of more reliability, increased flexibility, assurance of survivability, better expandability, and lower cost are the key motivating forces behind the use of *decentralized* and *hierarchical control* in all complex man-made systems. However, to effectively use this concept, there is a need to reconsider the *general concept of control for LSS and MHS*.

It is essential to understand *what* the control and related information "control-functions" should be and how they should be distributed before considering how to actually design an effective "overall control law" for LSS and MHS. There is a need to consider the controls and information in a kind of *integrated information control concept* [35] as a first step toward a more *general system functionalization*. This concept is illustrated in Fig. 1.

The first basic and major division should be between global and local "functions." Furthermore, this can be generally divided into the two following major functional categories:

1. *System actual control functions* which are related to changing a given process of a more complex system in such a way that certain objectives are met. (For example, in the interconnected power case, changing the valve position of a machine or the speed governor setting for a machine or a bus voltage.)

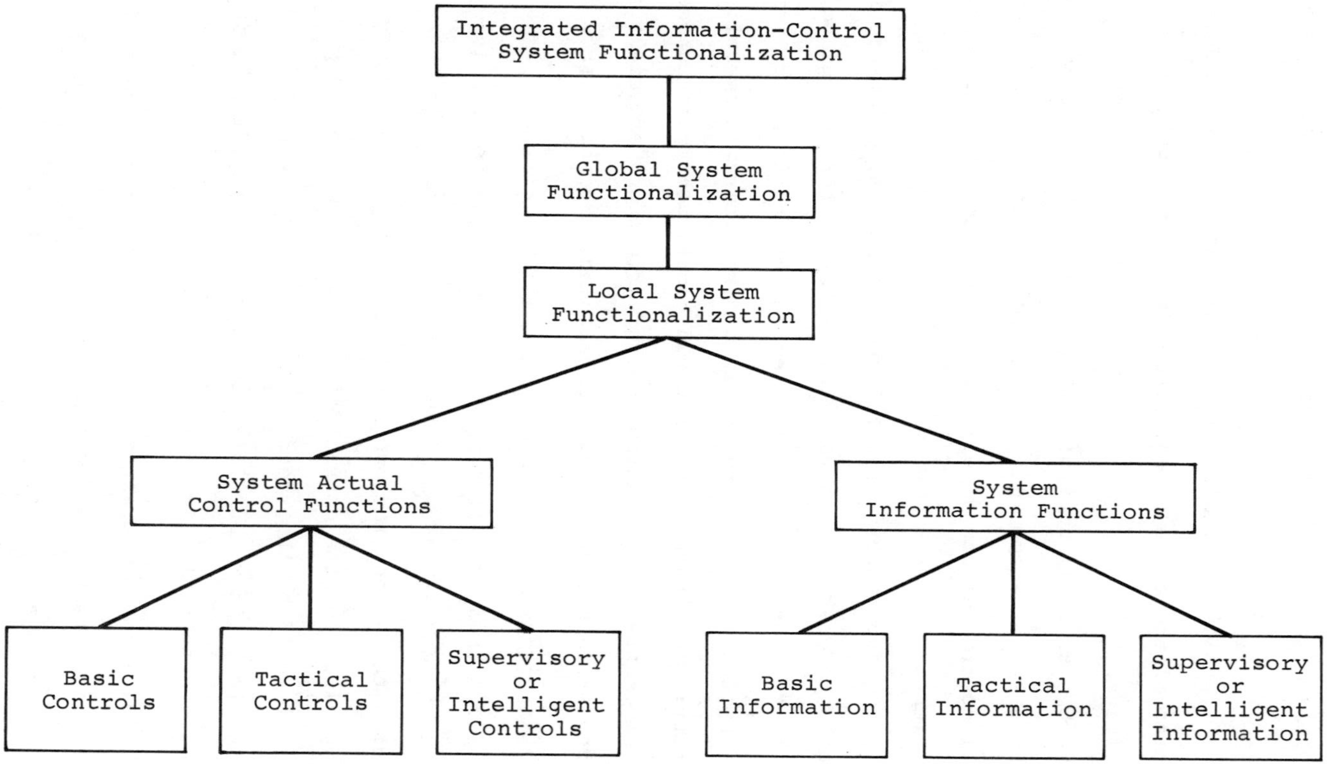

Fig. 1. The integrated information-control system functionalization concept.

In addition, we need to have further basic divisions (examples given are for the above-mentioned interconnected power case):

a. basic control, which changes specific variables of units of the system, e.g., speed-governor setting, bus voltage;

b. tactical controls, which are related to changing the state of a complex system resulting in a better overall control strategy, e.g., economic dispatch, unit commitment;

c. supervisory or intelligent controls, which are related to changing a given process for better understanding the state of the complex system and trying to change certain functions so as to obtain a more desirable overall state; e.g., such controls would constitute load and energy management, load shedding, using various and efficient energy storage systems, system planning, and maintenance scheduling.

2. *System information functions* which are to keep informing the various subsystem of the complex system as to what is happening throughout the overall system and perhaps even giving some guidance for the correction of a problem. In the power case, it would be the speed governor, the net power flow from one area to another, bus voltages, and operating frequencies. As in 1, further divisions are needed:

a. basic information – data of short-term value, such as the estimation and display of a single-state variable, e.g., change of power angle with respect to reference for ith machine, change of speed of the ith machine, change of bus voltage, and relaying;

b. tactical information — data of medium-term value which would give a better picture of the complex process, e.g., change of load demand, availability of power from other power generating units, cost effective scheduling of power changes;

c. intelligent or strategic information — of long-term value and possibly able to change the overall structure and operation of the system, e.g., availability of energy sources, possible future expansion of generating units and transmission capacity, adoption of new and more efficient devices or components, increasing the reliability of control centers, weather forecasting, and similar uses.

From the above description of system functionalization, we could have local system actual control functions and local system information functions or local tactical controls and local tactical information, or global tactical controls and global intelligent or strategic information, etc. If we take all the above into consideration, we have the following definition of an intelligent integrated control (I^2C).

Definition. An intelligent integrated control approach is defined as a collection of local and global control designs that incorporate appropriately the above control system functionalization concept in such a way that a *set* of local and global objectives are satisfied.

How to analyze, arrange, and synthesize such a complex I^2C for LSS is still a wide open question. It is not an easy problem, but a unified theory for dealing with it should emerge within the next few years since it seems near at hand now.

The proposed two-level structural dynamical hierarchical control approach is, however, a step in the right direction.

Research areas here are many, challenging, wide open, and very promising; some of these are

structural pole placement of LSS in the presence of fixed modes;

new optimality criteria;

new BACAF-stability concept to be developed and investigated and compared to D stability;

comparison of today's techniques, including generic properties and relationship to the I^2C concept;

more precise and mathematical definition for integrated-information control system functionalization (perhaps done in a systematic way) that would allow existing large complex systems to be used for development of I^2C strategies;

exploration of the characteristics of the BACAF structure and use of the proposed two-level SDHC approach for the estimation and optimization problems of LSS;

parallel processing implementation of today's LSS approaches.

VI. SUMMARY AND CLOSING REMARKS

The general stabilization and control problem of LSS has been addressed in this chapter. The special reasons which make this problem very difficult have been outlined. Three different approaches for the stabilization of LSS were briefly reviewed.

A new two-level SDHC approach was introduced. An algorithm for stabilizing LSS using the two-level SDHC approach was outlined, and two examples show its contribution to a solution of the stabilization problem of LSS. The interesting observations in Section IV,C justify further investigation of the two-level SDHC approach. As indicated earlier, this new approach would stabilize LSS when other techniques fail. Furthermore, the feedback gain matrix assumes a nice structure with computational advantages.

A fundamental question of the need to develop a unified approach for the control problem of LSS was addressed in detail. The proposed general system functionalization and the definition of an I^2C approach seem very promising for future research studies. Subsystem integration within the scope and objectives of an overall LSS is currently a very real problem. How to approach and further accomplish this integration with new techniques of LSS (and MHS) is a challenge. The two-level SDHC approach addresses this integration problem in a promising way. Nevertheless, further work on the general control problem of large complex systems is needed; using these results should lead to a unified control theory. Such a theory would help very much in the design of future complex systems.

APPENDIX A: PROOF OF THEOREM 1

Assume we have

$$\dot{\underline{x}} = \begin{bmatrix} \lambda_1 & & \bigcirc & \underline{C}_1 \\ & \lambda_2 & & \underline{C}_2 \\ & & \ddots & \vdots \\ \bigcirc & & \lambda_n & \underline{C}_n \\ -E_1 & -E_2 & \cdots \;\; -E_n & G \end{bmatrix} \underline{x}. \tag{A.1}$$

The complexity of the coordinator is determined via the required structural complexity of $\underline{C}$, which guarantees that (λ, C) is controllable. $\underline{C}$ must have as many columns as the largest dimensionality of Jordan blocks associated with the BACAF [12]. Here then $\underline{C}$ should be a single-column vector $c = [c_1, c_2, c_3, \ldots, c_n]^T$. Hence, the coordinator G should be a scalar dynamic g, and so $\underline{E}$ would be a row vector $e = [e_1, e_2, e_3, \ldots, e_n]$. For simplicity, we set $e_i = -1$, $i = 1, 2, \ldots, n$. Then the question of determining g and $\underline{C}$ needs to be resolved.

The recursive form of the *characteristic equation* ($|\lambda I - A|$) of Eq. (A.1) (which is an arrow-type matrix) when incorporating the change of notation (with $\underline{C}$ and $\underline{E}$ as defined above) can be shown to be [11]

$$p_p(\lambda) = (\lambda - \lambda_k)p_{k+1}(\lambda) + c_k q_{k+1}(\lambda) \tag{A.2}$$

$$q_k(\lambda) = q_{k+1}(\lambda)(\lambda - \lambda_k) \tag{A.3}$$

with final conditions

$$p_{n+1}(\lambda) = \lambda - g, \qquad q_{n+1}(\lambda) = 1$$

with g being a scalar; note that

$$q_k(\lambda) = \prod_{i=k}^{n} (\lambda - \lambda_i). \tag{A.4}$$

If (A.4) is incorporated in (A.2) and also let k - j be the index, then

$$p_{k-j}(\lambda) = (\lambda - \lambda_{k-j})p_{k-j+1}(\lambda) + c_{k-j} \prod_{i=k-j+1}^{n} (\lambda - \lambda_i). \tag{A.5}$$

Let $k = j + 1$; (A.5) becomes

$$p_1(\lambda) = (\lambda - \lambda_1)p_2(\lambda) + c_1 \prod_{i=2}^{n} (\lambda - \lambda_i) \tag{A.6}$$

which is the characteristic equation of the *overall two-level closed-loop DYHIS*. Now $p_1(\lambda)$ is an $(n + 1)$th order polynomial where $p_2(\lambda)$ is an nth order polynomial. Let $p_2(\lambda) = \Sigma_{i=0}^{n} a_i\lambda^i$ and $\prod_{i=2}^{n}(\lambda - \lambda_i) = \Sigma_{i=0}^{n-1} b_i\lambda^i$ where the a_i and b_i are constants with $a_n = b_{n-1} = 1$. If we expand $p_1(\lambda)$ (Eq. (A.6)) taking into consideration the above notation, we have the following $(n + 1)$th order polynomial

$$\begin{aligned} &\lambda^{n+1} + \lambda^n(a_{n-1} - \lambda_1) + \lambda^{n-1}(a_{n-2} - \lambda_1 a_{n-1} + c_1) \\ &\quad + \lambda^{n-2}(a_{n-3} - \lambda_1 a_{n-2} + c_1 b_{n-2}) \\ &\quad + \cdots + \lambda(a_0 + \lambda_1 a_1 + c_1 b_1) + c_1 b_0 - \lambda_1 a_0. \end{aligned} \tag{A.7}$$

To fit the n + 1 poles to arbitrary desired values, it is necessary and sufficient to set the coefficients of the above polynomial (A.7) to match the desired characteristic polynomial $\lambda^{n+1} + d_n\lambda^n + \cdots + d_1\lambda + d_0$. Since the b_i are fixed by the given λ_i, then the design parameters are c_1 and the a_i, so we require that (A.8) has a unique solution:

$$\begin{bmatrix} b_0 & -\lambda_1 & & & \bigcirc & & \\ b_1 & 1 & -\lambda_1 & & & & \\ b_2 & 0 & 1 & -\lambda_1 & & & \\ \vdots & \vdots & & \ddots & \ddots & & \\ 1 & 0 & \vdots & \vdots & 0 & 1 & -\lambda_1 \\ 0 & 0 & & & & 0 & 1 \end{bmatrix} \begin{bmatrix} c_1 \\ a_0 \\ a_1 \\ \vdots \\ a_n \\ a_{n-1} \end{bmatrix} = \begin{bmatrix} d_0 \\ d_1 \\ d_2 \\ \vdots \\ d_{n-1} \\ d_n \end{bmatrix}. \tag{A.8}$$

The determinant of (A.8) can easily be computed by recursive expansion along the appropriate rows and columns and is found to be

$$\Delta = \lambda_1^{n-1} + \lambda_1^{n-2} b_{n-2} + \lambda_1^{n-3} b_{n-3} + \cdots + \lambda_1 b_1 + b_0. \tag{A.9}$$

Then the question is, Under what conditions is $\Delta = 0$? By the previous definition of the b_i, which we repeat as $\Sigma_{i=0}^{n-1} b_i\lambda^i = \prod_{i=2}^{n}(\lambda - \lambda_1)$, it is clear that the roots of (A.9) are $\lambda_1 = \lambda_2$,

$\lambda_1 = \lambda_3, \ldots, \lambda_1 = \lambda_n$. Thus,

$$\Delta = (\lambda_1 - \lambda_2)(\lambda_1 - \lambda_3) \cdots (\lambda_1 - \lambda_n). \tag{A.10}$$

However, $\Delta \neq 0$ since $\lambda_1 \neq \lambda_j$ for all i, j - 1, 2, ..., n is assumed by the theorem. Hence, $\Delta \neq 0$ and so c_1 and $a_0, a_1, \ldots, a_{n-1}$ can be uniquely determined by the solution of (A.8) which exists and is unique. Since $a_0, a_1, \ldots, a_{n-1}$ are independent of c_1, the same procedure can be used to sequentially find c_2, then c_3, and finally c_n.

The determination of the scalar coordinator g still remains to be explained. Let us write a *nonrecursive* form of the characteristic equation for the arrow form (A.1) (when C_i and E_i are assumed as defined above.)

$$f(\lambda) = \sum_{j=1}^{n} c_i \prod_{\substack{i=1 \\ i\neq j}}^{n} (\lambda - \lambda_i) + (\lambda - g)\prod_{i=1}^{n} (\lambda - \lambda_i). \tag{A.11}$$

It is clear from (A.11) that g will be determined from the second term of $f(\lambda)$ (in other words, of the coefficient of the λ^n power). The parameters c_i, which can be determined as outlined earlier, *will not be part of the coefficients of the* λ^{n+1} *and* λ^n *power*. Expanding the second term of (A.11), we have

$$(\lambda - g)\left(\lambda^n + f_{n-1}\lambda^{n-1} + f_{n-2}\lambda^{n-2} + \cdots + f_1\lambda + f_0\right) \tag{A.12}$$

where the f_i are functions of the λ_1. Furthermore, (A.12) can be written, after multiplication and grouping like power terms, as

$$\lambda^{n+1} + (f_{n-1} - g)\lambda^n + (f_{n-2} - gf_{n-1})\lambda^{n-1} + \cdots + gf_0. \tag{A.13}$$

Again, let the desired characteristic polynomial be

$$\lambda^{n+1} + d_n\lambda^n + \cdots + d_1\lambda + d_0. \tag{A.14}$$

To determine g we need to match the coefficients of the λ^n powers. So we have

$$f_{n-1} - g = d_n$$

and hence

$$g = f_{n-1} - d_n. \tag{A.15}$$

Therefore, g can always be determined and be unique.

This completes the proof of Theorem 1.

APPENDIX B: TWO-LEVEL DYNAMICAL HIERARCHICAL SYSTEMS (DYHIS)

In Section III of this chapter, we introduced a two-level SDHC. This was sought as a natural approach but also because it stems from a belief that there is a need to address a new class of systems, dynamically involved throughout any structure (decentralized, distributed, or multilevel) [12]. It is believed by this author that the class of dynamical hierarchical systems is a new class of systems structure, although it has many features and characteristics common to LSS and MHS [12].

Briefly, a DYHIS is assumed to be composed of a finite number of dynamic interconnected subsystems but which must consider some kind of hierarchical infrastructure. It is important to stress here that *all subsystems* are considered dynamic, regardless of the level they might occupy with respect to a hierarchical structure. Hence, any problem (optimization, stabilization, or estimation and control) needs to be addressed within the framework of the dynamic infrastructure of a hierarchical pyramid. A solution to any of these problems will have constraints imposed by this assumption. Let us take, for example, the optimization problem of a special class of two-level DYHIS [12].

In this class of two-level DYHIS, the task of controlling and coordinating N dynamic subsystems $S_1, S_2, \ldots, S_n$ is carried out by a dynamic coordinator G. The N subsystems are assumed to be in the first level while the coordinator is at the second level of a hierarchy. For the sake of simplicity, the N subsystems exchange state information *only* between themselves and the dynamic coordinator and not with each other. Figure 2 shows such a two-level DYHIS, with Eq. B.1 in Fig. 3 describing it. The justification for this simple structure is given in [12].

A two-level DYHIS of this form is considered since

(1) it is the simplest type of hierarchical structure;

(2) the problem of controlling and coordinating N subsystems fits into this structure;

(3) it exhibits the most essential and crucial characteristics of most DYHIS; and [12]

(4) more complex DYHIS and LSS can be built using two-level DYHIS in a modular fashion.

Hence, to investigate the interlevel relationship of a two-level DYHIS is extremely important and of great interest to

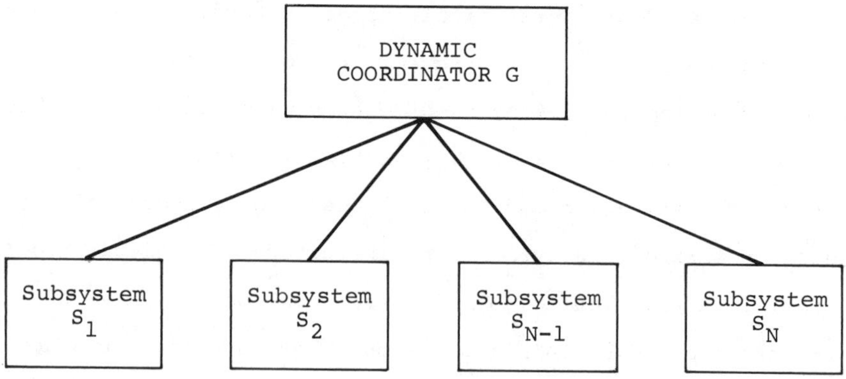

Fig. 2. A structural two-level DYHIS.

$$\begin{bmatrix} \dot{x}_1 \\ \dot{x}_2 \\ \vdots \\ \dot{x}_N \\ \dot{x}_0 \end{bmatrix} = \begin{bmatrix} A_{11} & & \bigcirc & & A_{10} \\ & A_{22} & & & A_{20} \\ & \bigcirc & \ddots & & \vdots \\ & & & A_{NN} & A_{N0} \\ A_{01} & A_{02} & \cdots & A_{0N} & A_0 \end{bmatrix} \begin{bmatrix} x_1 \\ x_2 \\ \vdots \\ x_N \\ x_0 \end{bmatrix}$$

$$+ \begin{bmatrix} B_{11} & & \bigcirc & & B_{10} \\ & B_{22} & & & B_{20} \\ & \bigcirc & \ddots & & \vdots \\ & & & B_{NN} & B_{N0} \\ B_{01} & B_{02} & \cdots & B_{0N} & B_0 \end{bmatrix} \begin{bmatrix} u_1 \\ u_2 \\ \vdots \\ \\ u_0 \end{bmatrix} \qquad (B.1)$$

Fig. 3. A BACAF state model representation for the structural two-level DYHIS of Fig. 2.

engineers and to scientists. What is important here is to understand the relationship between the N subsystems and the coordinator and the different roles they play.

If we now consider one subsystem S_i and the coordinator G, then we have the following optimization problem:

$$\min_{u_i(t)} J_i + \min_{u_0(t)} J_0 \qquad (B.2)$$

where

$$J_i = x_i^T(T)H_i x_i(T) + \frac{1}{2}\int_0^T \Big[x_i^T(t)Q_i x_i(t) + u_i^T(t)R_i u_i(t) + x_i^T(t)Q_{i0}x_0(t) + x_0^T(t)Q_{i0}^T x_i(t)\Big]\, dt \qquad (B.3)$$

with $H_i \geq 0$, $Q_i \geq 0$, $R_i > 0$, and $Q_{i0} = Q_{i0}^T \geq 0$ and

$$J_0 = x_0^T(T)H_0 x_0(T) + \frac{1}{2}\int_0^T \Big[x_0^T(t)Q_0 x_0(t) + u_0^T(t)R_0 u_0(t) + \sum_{i=1}^{N} \Big(x_0^T(t)Q_{0i}x_i(t) + x_i(t)Q_{0i}^T x_0(t)\Big)\Big]\, dt \qquad (B.4)$$

with $H_0 \geq 0$, $Q_0 \geq 0$, $R_0 > 0$, and $Q_{0i} = Q_{0i}^T \geq 0$ subject to

$$S_i: \quad \dot{x}_i(t) = A_i x_i(t) + B_i u_i(t) + A_{i0} x_0(t) \tag{B.5}$$

$$G: \quad \dot{x}_0(t) = A_0 x_0(t) + B_0 u_0(t) + \sum_{i=1}^{N} A_{0i} x_i(t). \tag{B.6}$$

Notice that the coordinator G has some knowledge about the states of all other subsystems through the last term of Eq. (B.6). Furthermore, note that the penalizing matrice Q is not strictly diagonal as has been assumed in other approaches, but it takes a BACAF structure (if the problem posed here is carefully studied).

Let us now form the following Hamiltonian

$$H = H_i + H_0 \tag{B.7}$$

where

$$\begin{aligned} H_i = \frac{1}{2}\Big[& x_i^T(t) Q_i x_i(t) + u_i^T(t) R_i u_i(t) \\ & + x_i^T(t) Q_{i0} x_0(t) + x_0^T(t) Q_{i0}^T x_i(t) \Big] \\ & + p_i^T(t)\,[A_i x_i(t) + B_i u_i(t) + A_{i0} x_0(t)] \end{aligned} \tag{B.8}$$

and

$$\begin{aligned} H_0 = \frac{1}{2}\Big[& x_0^T(t) Q_0 x_0(t) + u_0^T(t) R_0 u_0(t) \\ & + \sum_{i=1}^{N} \left(x_0^T(t) Q_{0i} x_i(t) + x_i(t) Q_{0i}^T x_0(t) \right) \Big] \\ & + p_0^T(t) \left[A_0 x_0(t) + B_0 u_0(t) + \sum_{i=1}^{N} A_{0i} x_i(t) \right] \end{aligned} \tag{B.9}$$

where $p_i(t)$ and $p_0(t)$ are the usual arbitrary Lagrange multipliers [36].

Following the well-known variational approach to optimal control problems, we have the following necessary conditions for optimality [36].

For the H_i subsystem

$$\dot{x}_i^*(t) = \partial H_i/\partial p_i$$

$$= A_i x_i^*(t) + B_i u_i^*(t) + A_{i0} x_0^*(t) \quad (B.10)$$

$$\dot{p}_i^*(t) = -\partial H_i/\partial x_i$$

$$= -Q_i x_i^*(t) - A_i^T p_i^*(t) - Q_{i0} x_0^*(t) \quad (B.11)$$

$$0 = \partial H_i/\partial u_i$$

$$= R_i u_i^*(t) + B_i^T p_i(t). \quad (B.12)$$

For the dynamic coordinator

$$\dot{x}_0^*(t) = \partial H_0/\partial p_0$$

$$= A_0 x_0^*(t) + B_0 u_0^*(t) + \sum_{i=1}^{N} A_{0i} x_i^*(t) \quad (B.13)$$

$$\dot{p}_0^*(t) = -\partial H_0/\partial x_0$$

$$= -Q_0 x_0^*(t) - A_0^T p_0^*(t) - \sum_{i=1}^{N} Q_{0i} x_i^*(t) \quad (B.14)$$

and

$$0 = \partial H_0/\partial u_0$$

$$= R_0 u_0^*(t) + B_0^T p_0^*(t). \quad (B.15)$$

If the solution takes the form of

$$p_i^*(t) = K_i(t) x_i^*(t)$$

and

$$\overset{*}{p}_0(t) = K_0(t)\overset{*}{x}_0(t)$$

then the solutions of (B.10) to (B.12) and (B.13) to (B.15) bring us the following conditions:

$$\Big(\dot{K}_i(t) + A_i^T K_i(t) + K_i(t)A_i - K_i(t)B_i R_i^{-1} B_i^T K_i(t) + Q_i\Big)x_i(t) + (K_i(t)A_{i0} + Q_{i0})x_0(t) = 0 \tag{B.16}$$

and

$$\Big(\dot{K}_0(t) + A_0^T K_0(t) + K_0(t)A_0 - K_0(t)B_0 R_0^{-1} B_0^T K_0(t) + Q_0\Big)x_0(t) + \sum_{i=1}^{N} (K_0(t)A_{0i} + Q_{0i})x_i(t) = 0. \tag{B.17}$$

Since these must hold true for *all time*, *all subsystems* and *the coordinator*, we have the following equations:

$$\dot{K}_i(t) = -K_i(t)A_i - A_i^T K_i(t) + K_i(t)B_i R_i^{-1} B_i^T K_i(t) - Q_i; \quad K_i(T) = H_i \tag{B.18}$$

$$K_i(t)A_{i0} + Q_{i0} = 0 \quad \text{for} \quad i = 1, 2, \ldots, N \tag{B.19}$$

and

$$\dot{K}_0(t) = -K_0(t)A_0 - A_0^T K_0(t) + K_0(t)B_0 R_0^{-1} B_0^T K_0(t) - Q_0; \quad K_0(T) = H_0 \tag{B.20}$$

$$K_0(t)A_{0i} + Q_{0i} = 0 \quad \text{for} \quad i = 1, 2, \ldots, N. \tag{B.21}$$

Note that Eqs. (B.18) and (B.20) are the usual nonlinear Riccati differential equations which can easily be solved backward in time assuming that the dimensionality of each of the N subsystems and of the dynamic coordinator are relatively small. They will be much smaller than any centralized approach that was to be used to solve the overall LSS (B.1).

The control laws $u_i(t)$ and $u_0(t)$ given now by

$$\overset{*}{u}_i(t) = -R_i^{-1}B_i^TK_i(t)\overset{*}{x}_i(t) \tag{B.22}$$

$$\overset{*}{u}_0(t) = -R_0^{-1}B_0^TK_0(t)\overset{*}{x}_0(t) \tag{B.23}$$

will be "optimal" if conditions (B.19) and (B.21) hold. These two conditions tell us how the N subsystems and the dynamic coordinator should be interconnected between themselves. Since these are to hold for all times, we can have interconnections which should be time varying, namely,

$$A_{i0}(t) = -K_i^{-1}(t)Q_{i0} \tag{B.24}$$

$$A_{0i}(t) = -K_0^{-1}(t)Q_{0i}. \tag{B.25}$$

These can be interpreted as the conditions where neutral interconnections can exist between the N subsystems and the coordinator, for all time. In other words, the overall optimum which could be attained by a centralized controller is obtained through a two-level DYHIS structure and a set of local control laws of the form (B.22) and a coordinator's control of the form (B.23). Conditions (B.24) and (B.25) become time invariant at steady-state. These results can be compared to those of the perturbational approach [37], where the basic idea is to classify the interconnections beneficial, detrimental, or neutral.

Equations (B.19) and (B.21) can be used to generate a two-level strategy with compensatory signal which would account for the interconnection effects between the N subsystems and the dynamic coordinator only. Here the role of the global controller of the perturbational approach [37] is assumed by the dynamic coordinator [12].

What is interesting here is that the two-level dynamic hierarchical system and the associated structural control strategy can address problems of LSS from a modular point. Subsystems can be easily added or deleted in a two-level DYHIS in a simple way and the subsequent analysis becomes very simple. The BACAF structure of two-level DYHIS is simple, straightforward, and its characteristics, such as stability, pole placement, and the generation of a two-level control strategy, can be easily determined. The modularity characteristic of the two-level DYHIS and the associated structural control strategy can be used in a very challenging way to address an interesting problem of cooperative and noncooperative systems. A LSS would be considered an active cooperative DYHIS if a two-level SDHC could be designed resulting in a performance cost which is better or equal to a cost attained if a centralized control approach was used. An interesting research area would be to develop a concept of active cooperative LSS.

REFERENCES

1. M. D. MESAROVIC, D. MACKO, and Y. TAKAHARA, "Theory of Hierarchical Multilevel Systems," Academic Press, New York, 1970.

2. P. V. KOKOTOVIC, R. E. O'MALLEY, and P. SANNUTI, "Singular Perturbations and Order Reduction in Control Theory — An Overview," *Automatica 12*, 123-132 (1976).

3. M. S. MAHMOUD, "Multilevel Systems Control and Applications: A Survey," *IEEE Trans. Systems Man Cybernet. SMC-7*, 125-143 (1977).

4. SANDELL, *et al.*, "Survey of Decentralized Control Methods for Large Scale Systems," *IEEE Trans. Automat. Control AC-23*, 108-128 (1978).

5. J. B. CRUZ, JR., "Leader-Follower Strategies for Multilevel Systems," *IEEE Trans. Automat. Control AC-23*, 244-255 (1978).

6. M. G. SINGH, "Dynamic Hierarchical Control," North-Holland, Amsterdam, 1977.

7. D. D. SILJAK, "Large-Scale Dynamic Systems: Stability and Structure," North-Holland, Amsterdam, 1978.

8. W. FINDEISEN, *et al.*, "Control and Coordination in Hierarchical Systems," Wiley, New York, 1980.

9. R. F. DRENICK, "Large Scale System Theory in the 1980's," *J. Large Scale Systems 2*, 29-43 (1981).

10. M. JAMSHIDI, "Large-Scale Systems: Modeling and Control," North-Holland, Amsterdam, 1983.

11. P. P. GROUMPOS, "A State Space Approach to Hierarchical Systems," Ph.D. Dissertation, State University of New York at Buffalo, 1979.

12. P. P. GROUMPOS, "Dynamical Hierarchical Systems (DYHIS)," TR-ELE 80-1, Cleveland State University, Cleveland, Ohio, 1980.

13. M. ATHANS, "Advances and Open Problems on the Control of Large Scale Systems," pp. 2371-2382, in "Proc. IFAC Congress," Helsinki, 1978.

14. M. AOKI, "On Feedback Stabilizability of Decentralized Dynamic Systems," *Automatica 8*, 163-173 (1972).

15. S. H. WANG and E. J. DAVISON, "On the Stabilization of Decentralized Control Systems," *IEEE Trans. Automat. Control AC-18*, 473-478 (1973).

16. E. J. DAVISON, "The Robust Decentralized Control of a General Servomechanism Problem," *IEEE Trans. Automat. Control AC-21*, 14-24 (1976).

17. J. P. CORFMAT and A. S. MORSE, "Stabilization with Decentralized Feedback Control," *IEEE Trans. Automat. Control AC-18*, 673-682 (1973).

18. J. P. CORFMAT and A. S. MORSE, "Decentralized Control of Linear Multivariable Systems," *Automatica 12*, 479-495 (1976).

19. E. J. DAVISON and W. GESING, "Sequential Stability and Optimization of Large Scale Decentralized Systems," *Automatica 15*, 307-324 (1979).

20. E. J. DAVISON and U. OZGUNER, "Decentralized Synthesis of the Decentralized Robust Servomechanism Problem," Paper WAI-A, in "Proc. 1980 Joint Automatic Control Conf.," August 13-15, 1980, San Francisco, California.

21. D. D. SILJAK and M. B. VUKCEVIC, "Large Scale Systems: Stability, Complexity, Reliability," *J. Franklin Inst. 301*, 49-69 (1976).

22. D. D. SILJAK and M. B. Vukcevic, "Decentralization, Stabilization and Estimation of Large-Scale Systems," *IEEE Trans. Automat. Control AC-21*, 363-366 (1976).

23. D. D. SILJAK and M. B. Vukcevic, "A Multilevel Optimization of Large Scale Dynamic Systems," *IEEE Trans. Automat. Control AC-21*, 79-84 (1976).

24. M. K. SUNDARESHAN, "Decentralized and Multilevel Controllability of Large-Scale Systems," *Internat. J. Control 30*, 71-80 (1979).

25. S. H. WANG, "An Example in Decentralized Control Systems," *IEEE Trans. Automat. Control AC-23*, 938 (1978).

26. J. H. CHOW and P. V. KOKOTOVIC, "Eigenvalue Placement in Two-Time-Scale Systems," pp. 321-326, in "Large Scale Systems: Theory and Applications (G. Guardabassi and A. Locatelli, eds.), IFAC Symp. Udide, Italy, June 1976.

27. J. H. CHOW and P. V. KOKOTOVIC, "A Decomposition of Near-Optimum Regulators for Systems with Slow and Fast Modes," *IEEE Trans. Automat. Control AC-21*, 701-705 (1976).

28. H. K. KHALIL and P. V. KOKOTOVIC, "Control Strategies for Decision Makers Using Different Models of the Same Systems," *IEEE Trans. Automat. Control AC-23*, 289-298 (1978).

29. H. K. KHALIL and P. V. KOKOTOVIC, "D-Stability and Multiparameter Singular Perturbation," *SIAM J. Control Optim. 17*, 56-65 (1979).

30. H. K. KHALIL and P. V. KOKOTOVIC, "Decentralized Stabilization of Systems with Slow and Fast Modes," pp. 108-112, in "Proc. 1979 Joint Automatic Control Conf.," Denver, Colorado, June 1979.

31. P. P. GROUMPOS and K. A. LOPARO, "Structural Control of Large Scale Systems," pp. 422-426, in "Proc. of the 1980 IEEE CDC," Albuquerque, New Mexico, December 10-12, 1980.

32. B. D. O. ANDERSON and J. B. MOORE, "Time-Varying Feedback Laws for Decentralized Control," pp. 519-524, in "Proc. of the 19th IEEE CDC," Albuquerque, New Mexico, December 10-12, 1980.

33. G. S. KUO and K. A. LOPARO, "Decentralized Fixed Modes and Stabilization in Large-Scale Systems," pp. 874-877, in "Proc. of 1982 ACC," Arlington, Virginia, June 14-16, 1982.

34. K. A. LOPARO and P. P. GROUMPOS, "Stabilization in Large Scale Systems," pp. 357-360, in "Proc. of 3rd Inter. Symposium on Large Engineering Systems," St. John's Newfoundland, Canada, July 1980.

35. P. P. GROUMPOS, "Control System Functionalization of Command-Control-Communications (C^3) Systems via Two-Level DYHIS," pp. 309-330, in "Proc. of 4th MIT/ONR Workshop on C^3 Problems," June 15-28, San Diego, California, 1981.

36. B. D. O. ANDERSON and J. B. MOORE, "Linear Optimal Control," Prentice-Hall, Englewood Cliffs, New Jersey, 1971.

37. M. K. SUNDARESHAN, "Generation of Multilevel Control and Estimation Schemes for Large Scale Systems: A Perturbational Approach," *IEEE Trans. Systems Man Cybernet. SMC-7*, 144-152 (1977).

Decentralized Design of Decentralized Controllers

BENJAMIN FRIEDLANDER

Systems Control Technology, Inc.
Palo Alto, California

I. INTRODUCTION

The increasing complexity of engineering, economic, and other large-scale systems has stimulated extensive research in recent years. Decentralized controllers are a practical necessity in such systems since factors such as computational complexity, communications costs, and reliability make centralized control strategies infeasible. The analysis and design of decentralized controllers received considerable attention as evidenced by the large number of publications in this area (see,

ISBN 0-12-012722-9

for example, the references in [1,2] and the categories "decentralized control" and "large-scale systems" in [3]).

Many of the proposed design procedures for decentralized controllers involve solutions of problems whose dimension equals that of the full system. As an example, consider the design of optimal controllers (in the linear quadratic Gaussian sense) subject to structural constraints [4,5]. Various gradient algorithms were proposed for solving the nonlinear equations involved in the computation of the controller parameters [6,7]. The evaluation of the gradient, at each iteration step, was shown to involve the solution of a Lyapunov equation of dimension equal to that of the full system. For large-scale systems, this may involve an excessive amount of computation, preventing the practical application of this design method. This computational issue is particularly important if the design procedure needs to be repeated often due to changes in system parameters (e.g., set-point changes), or the addition/deletion of subsystems (for maintenance or system growth).

In this chapter we propose a procedure for computing decentralized controller parameters by solving a set of problems, each of a relatively low dimension. This procedure has the attractive property that each local controller can be computed based on locally available information only. Thus, the communication requirements between subsystems are minimized. Furthermore, the proposed technique lends itself to on-line implementation which provides the system with the capability of adapting to parameter variations or structural changes.

The basic idea of our approach can be described as follows. Consider a large-scale system consisting of N interconnected subsystems $\{S_i, i = 1, \ldots, N\}$. Denote by S_i^c the systems

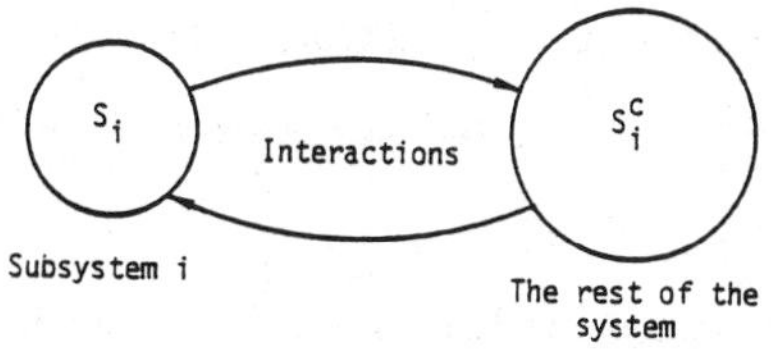

Fig. 1. The system, as viewed from subsystem i.

consisting of all subsystems except subsystem i, as depicted in Fig. 1. Assume for a moment that all the subsystems in S_i^c have determined their local controller parameters (not necessarily optimally). Using the procedures described in [6,7], it is possible to compute for S_i the controller parameters which minimize the quadratic cost function. Next we fix these controller parameters and repeat the same procedure for the next subsystem. Cycling through all the subsystems in this manner will eventually yield the optimum decentralized control solution. This procedure is essentially a sequential implementation of the gradient method.

So far, the method described above offers no advantages over the centralized gradient techniques presented in [6,7] since at each step a high-dimensional problem needs to be solved. Consider, however, the possibility of replacing S_i^c by a *reduced-order model* $\bar{S}_i^c$, in the process of computing the parameters of subsystem i. In other words, we design the local controller based on the assumption that the total system is $\{S_i, \bar{S}_i^c\}$ rather than $\{S_i, S_i^c\}$. If the reduced-order model $\bar{S}_i^c$ is close to S_i^c in some sense, we may expect that the resulting controller will yield performance that is close to the optimum. This notion can be made more precise as will be indicated in Section V. Using a low-order model $\bar{S}_i^c$ $\left(\text{assuming dimension } \{\bar{S}_i^c\} \ll \text{dimension } \{S_i^c\}\right)$ greatly simplifies the computations required at each step of the iterative gradient algorithm. The dimension of the problem that needs to be solved by subsystem i will be the sum of the dimensions of S_i and $\overline{S}_i^c$.

The key to the application of this idea is to find the reduced-order model for S_i^c. This can be done, for example, by using system identification techniques to estimate the model parameters. The interaction variables $\left(\text{between } S_i \text{ and } S_i^c\right)$ will be the inputs and outputs of the system to be identified. If system identification is performed on-line, we can obtain an adaptive controller design procedure. Note that each local controller is designed based on a different model since $\left\{S_i, \overline{S}_i^c\right\} \neq \left\{S_j, \overline{S}_j^c\right\}$ for $i \neq j$. By choosing different orders for $\overline{S}_i^c$ we can cover the whole range from optimal decentralized control $\left(\text{letting } \overline{S}_i^c = S_i^c\right)$ to a completely "selfish" control (letting $\overline{S}_i^c = 0$, in which case each subsystem uses a control law that optimizes its own cost function while completely ignoring the rest of the system). By choosing the order of $\overline{S}_i^c$ we can trade off computational complexity vs performance.

In the following sections we develop in more detail the concepts described above. In Section II we present a centralized gradient procedure for computing the parameters of the optimal discrete-time decentralized controller. In Section III we discuss a number of ways for performing the design in a decentralized manner using reduced-order modeling and some other ideas. In Section IV we present an example of designing a decentralized controller by the reduced-order modeling approach. In Section V we analyze some of the properties of the decentralized control system obtained by this design procedure.

II. DISCRETE-TIME OPTIMAL DECENTRALIZED CONTROL

In this section we develop a method for computing a decentralized optimal stochastic control law for discrete-time multi-input multi-output systems. Our derivation follows closely the ideas of Geromel and Bernussou in [6] and is, in fact, an extension of their work to the discrete-time case.

Consider a large-scale system, consisting of N subsystems of dimensions $\{n_i,\ i = 1, \ldots, N\}$. The system is linear and time-invariant, and can be described by the state equation

$$x(k + 1) = Ax(k) + Bu(k) + Dw(k) \tag{1}$$

where

$x(k)$ is the state vector of dimension $n = \Sigma_{i=1}^{N} n_i$;

$u(k) = \left[u_1^T(k), \ldots, u_N^T(k)\right]^T$ is the input vector, where $u_i(k)$ are the individual inputs to the N subsystems, $\dim u_i(k) = m_i$ and $\dim u(k) = m = \Sigma_{i=1}^{N} m_i$;

$w(k) = \left[w_1^T(k), \ldots, w_N^T(k)\right]^T$ is a zero-mean white-noise disturbance vector, where $w_i(k)$ are the individual disturbances to the N subsystems, $\dim w_i(k) = p_i$, and $\dim w(k) = p = \Sigma_{i=1}^{N} p_i$;

A is the system matrix, naturally partitioned as $A = (A_{ij})_{1 \leq i,j \leq n}$, where $\dim A_{i,j} = n_i \times n_j$;

B is the input matrix, $B = \text{block diag}\{B_i,\ 1 \leq i \leq N\}$, where $\dim B_i = n_i \times m_i$;

D is the disturbance matrix, $D = \text{block diag}\ \{D_i,\ 1 \leq i \leq N\}$, $D_i = n_i \times p_i$;

The disturbance vector covariance matrix is assumed to be of the form $W \triangleq Ew(k)w^T(k) = \text{block diag}\{W_i,\ 1 \leq i \leq N\}$ where $\dim W_i = p_i \times p_i$. In other words, disturbances in different subsystems are assumed to be uncorrelated.

We assume a linear, completely decentralized, state-feedback control law, i.e.,

$$u(k) = -Kx(k) \tag{2}$$

where $K = \text{block diag}\{K_i, i = 1, \ldots, N\}$, $\dim K_i = m_i \times n_i$. The cost to be minimized is given by

$$J = E\{x^T(k)Qx(k) + u^T(k)Ru(k)\} \tag{3}$$

where x(k) and u(k) are assumed to be wide-sense stationary (i.e., the system is at a stochastic steady state), making J independent of k. The matrix Q is assumed to be positive semi-definite and the matrix R to be positive definite. Furthermore,

$$Q = \text{block diag}\{Q_i, 1 \leq i \leq N\}, \quad \text{where} \quad \dim Q_i = n_i,$$

$$R = \text{block diag}\{R_i, 1 \leq i \leq N\}, \quad \text{where} \quad \dim R_i = m_i.$$

Using the control law (2) we can express J as

$$J = E\{x^T(k)Qx(k) + x^T(k)K^TRKx(k)\}$$

$$= E\{x^T(k)[Q + K^TRK]x(k)\} = \text{tr}\{[Q + K^TRK]\Pi\}, \tag{4}$$

where

$$\Pi \triangleq E\{x(k)x^T(k)\}.$$

As is well known [8], Π satisfies the discrete Lyapunov equation

$$\Pi - F\Pi F^T = DWD^T \tag{5}$$

where $F \triangleq A - BK$ is the closed-loop system matrix.

To get an algorithm for computing the optimal decentralized control law, we need an expression for the gradient matrix $\partial J/\partial K$. To this end let us perturb K to $K + \delta K$, where $\delta K \to 0$, and compute the correspondingly perturbed cost function $J + \delta J$. Assume that $\Pi(K + \delta K) = \Pi + \delta\Pi$, and proceed as follows[1]:

$$\begin{aligned} J + \delta J &= \mathrm{tr}\{[Q + (K^T + \delta K^T)R(K + \delta K)][\Pi + \delta\Pi]\} \\ &\approx \mathrm{tr}\{[Q + K^TRK + \delta K^TRK + K^TR\delta K][\Pi + \delta\Pi]\} \\ &\approx \mathrm{tr}\{[Q + K^TRK]\Pi\} + 2\mathrm{tr}\{\delta K^TRK\Pi\} \\ &\quad + \mathrm{tr}\{[Q + K^TRK]\delta\Pi\}. \end{aligned} \tag{6}$$

Hence

$$\delta J \approx 2\mathrm{tr}\{\delta K^TRK\Pi\} + \mathrm{tr}\{[Q + K^TRK]\delta\Pi\}. \tag{7}$$

To continue, we need to express $\delta\Pi$ in terms of δK and the other matrices. By definition, $\Pi + \delta\Pi$ satisfies

$$(\Pi + \delta\Pi) - (F - B\delta K)(\Pi + \delta\Pi)(F^T - \delta K^TB^T) = DWD^T. \tag{8}$$

Expanding, we get

$$\begin{aligned} &\Pi + \delta\Pi - (F - B\delta K)(\Pi + \delta\Pi)(F^T - \delta K^TB^T) \\ &\quad \approx \Pi + \delta\Pi - F\Pi F^T - F\delta\Pi F^T + B\delta K\Pi F^T + F\Pi\delta K^TB^T. \end{aligned} \tag{9}$$

Thus

$$\delta\Pi - F\delta\Pi F^T \approx -BK\Pi F^T - F\Pi K^TB^T. \tag{10}$$

We now introduce a matrix P as the solution of the discrete Lyapunov equation:

$$P - F^TPF = Q + K^TRK. \tag{11}$$

Then

$$\begin{aligned} \mathrm{tr}\{[Q + K^TRK]\delta\Pi\} &= \mathrm{tr}\{[P - F^TPF]\delta\Pi\} \\ &= \mathrm{tr}\{[P\delta\Pi - F^TPF\delta\Pi]\} \\ &= \mathrm{tr}\{P[\delta\Pi - F\delta\Pi F^T]\} \\ &\approx -\mathrm{tr}\{P[B\delta K\Pi F^T - F\Pi\delta K^TB^T]\} \\ &= -2\mathrm{tr}\{\delta K^TB^TPF\Pi\}. \end{aligned} \tag{12}$$

[1]*We use the known rules tr AB = tr BA, tr A = tr* A^T *many times in the sequel. Also, the symbol ≈ means equality up to first-order terms.*

Substituting into (7) will give

$$\delta J = 2\mathrm{tr}\{\delta K^T RK\Pi\} - 2\mathrm{tr}\{\delta K^T B^T PF\Pi\}$$

$$= 2\mathrm{tr}\{\delta K^T [RK - B^T PF]\Pi\}. \tag{13}$$

Thus, finally

$$\partial J/\partial K = 2[RK - B^T P(A - BK)]\Pi, \tag{14a}$$

where

$$\Pi - (A - BK)\Pi(A - BK)^T = DWD^T, \tag{14b}$$

$$P - (A - BK)^T P(A - BK) = Q + K^T RK. \tag{14c}$$

A simple check of this result is given by the well-known unconstrained solution to the optimal stochastic control problem. Setting the right-hand side of (14a) to zero and solving for K, we get

$$K = (R + B^T PB)^{-1} B^T PA. \tag{15}$$

This, together with (14c), are classical results. An efficent algorithm for solving the Lyapunov equations (14b) and (14c) is presented in the Appendix. Once we have an expression for $\partial J/\partial K$, a local constrained optimal gain K can be found using a *feasible directions method*, as in [9]. At the ith step $\partial J/\partial K_i$ is computed using (14) and then "masked" so as to retain only the block-diagonal entries, compatible with the blocks of K. Then K is updated by

$$K_{i+1} = K_i - \alpha_{i+1}(\partial J/\partial K_i), \tag{16}$$

where the step size α_{i+1} has to satisfy

$$J(K_{i+1}) \leq J(K_i). \tag{17}$$

The step size α_{i+1} can be varied in an adaptive manner, as described in [6]. Finally, note that the method described here is not restricted to block-diagonal constraints. By an appropriate masking of $\partial J/\partial K$, arbitrary constraints can be imposed on K. See [7] for a relevant discussion.

III. DECENTRALIZED COMPUTATION OF THE CONTROLLER PARAMETERS

As we have seen above, the main computational burden in evaluating the gradient matrix $\partial J/\partial K$ is the solution of two Lyapunov equations (14b) and (14c). This is usually not a serious problem, even for large-scale systems, if the computation can be done off-line, as a part of the system design. However, in an adaptive environment, when the system parameters are identified in real time, the equations have to be solved on-line. In such cases it is desirable to solve the equations in a decentralized manner, where each of the subsystems is responsible for part of the computations. In this section we discuss two decentralized methods of solving the Lyapunov equations.

A. REDUCED-ORDER MODELING

The basic idea of using reduced-order models to achieve a decentralized design procedure was described in the introduction. Here we present some of the issues involved in more detail. First, rewrite Eq. (1) as

$$\begin{bmatrix} x_i(k+1) \\ x_i^c(k+1) \end{bmatrix} = \begin{bmatrix} A_i & A_{i1}^c \\ A_{i2}^c & A_i^c \end{bmatrix} \begin{bmatrix} x_i(k) \\ x_i^c(k) \end{bmatrix} + \begin{bmatrix} B_i & 0 \\ 0 & B_i^c \end{bmatrix} \begin{bmatrix} u_i(k) \\ u_i^c(k) \end{bmatrix} + \begin{bmatrix} D_i & 0 \\ 0 & D_i^c \end{bmatrix} \begin{bmatrix} w_i(k) \\ w_i^c(k) \end{bmatrix}, \tag{18}$$

where x_i, x_i^c are the states of sybsystem S_i and of S_i^c. The covariance of $\left[w_i^T \; w_i^{cT}\right]^T$ is $\mathrm{diag}\left\{W_i, W_i^c\right\}$. The state matrices as well as the other system parameters are partitioned accordingly. The cost function is similarly written as

$$\begin{aligned} J &= E\left\{x_i^T(k)Q_i x_i(k) + u_i^T(k)R_i u_i(k)\right\} \\ &\quad + E\left\{x_i^{cT}(k)Q_i^c x_i^c(k) + u_i^{cT}(k)R_i^c u_i^c(k)\right\} \\ &= J_i + J_i^c. \end{aligned} \tag{19}$$

Assume that the system S_i^c is already operating in closed loop with $u_i^c(k) = -K_i^c x_i^c(k)$. Thus, Eq. (18) can be rewritten as

$$\begin{bmatrix} x_i(k+1) \\ x_i^c(k+1) \end{bmatrix} = \begin{bmatrix} A_i & A_{i1}^c \\ A_{i2}^c & F_i^c \end{bmatrix} \begin{bmatrix} x_i(k) \\ x_i^c(k) \end{bmatrix} + \begin{bmatrix} B_i u_i(k) \\ 0 \end{bmatrix} + \begin{bmatrix} D_i w_i(k) \\ D_i^c w_i^c(k) \end{bmatrix}, \tag{20a}$$

where

$$F_i^c = A_i^c - B_i^c K_i^c = \text{closed-loop state matrix.} \tag{20b}$$

The cost function J_i^c can be rewritten as

$$J_i^c = E\left\{x_i^{cT}\underbrace{\left[Q_i^c + K_i^{cT}R_i^c K_i^c\right]}_{G_i^c}x_i^c\right\}. \tag{21}$$

Using an identification algorithm or model reduction technique, we find a reduced-order model

$$\begin{bmatrix} x_i(k+1) \\ \bar{x}_i^c(k+1) \end{bmatrix} = \begin{bmatrix} A_i & \bar{A}_{i1}^c \\ \bar{A}_{i2}^c & \bar{F}_i^c \end{bmatrix} \begin{bmatrix} x_i(k) \\ \bar{x}_i^c(k) \end{bmatrix} + \begin{bmatrix} B_i u_i(k) \\ 0 \end{bmatrix} + \begin{bmatrix} D_i w_i(k) \\ \bar{D}_i^c \bar{w}_i^c(k) \end{bmatrix}, \tag{22}$$

with noise covariance diag$\left\{W_i, \overline{W}_i^c\right\}$. A somewhat more difficult problem is to relate the cost function J_i^c to the states of the reduced-order model. In other words, it is necessary to estimate $\overline{G}_i^c$ so that

$$J_i^c \cong E\left\{\overline{x}_i^{cT}\overline{G}_i\overline{x}_i^c\right\}. \tag{23}$$

Under some simplifying assumptions (e.g., that $\overline{G}_i^c$ is a diagonal matrix) it is possible to estimate the elements of $\overline{G}_i^c$ by performing a least-squares fit, using an observer for the states $\overline{x}_i^c$. In the special case where minimum variance control is considered, it is possible to estimate $\overline{G}_i^c$ directly, provided that the outputs of all the subsystems are available to subsystem i. In this case $R_i = 0$ and $Q_i = H_i^T H_i$ where

$$y_i(k) = H_i x_i(k) = \text{the output of subsystem } i. \tag{24}$$

The output matrix H_i can be estimated during the identification procedure, providing direct estimate of $\overline{G}_i^c = \overline{H}_i^{cT}\overline{H}_i^c$. In fact, by using a convenient canonical form (e.g., $H_i = [1, 0, \ldots, 0]$) no estimation is necessary.

The algorithm derived in Section II will now be applied to the reduced-order system (22) and (24) to compute the gain K_i of subsystem i. Then we proceed to the next subsystem, and the whole process is repeated.

The procedure described above can be implemented in many different ways depending on what information is available to the local subsystem (interconnections only, outputs of all subsystems, or inputs of all subsystems), and depending on the particular system identification or model reduction technique used. In Section IV we present an example illustrating the type of results that can be obtained using this procedure.

By running this algorithm continuously, we can obtain a truly adaptive control technique. If the system is time-invariant, the algorithm will eventually converge; i.e., the gradients $\partial J/\partial K_i$ will become very small. By monitoring the magnitude of these gradients, we can detect changes in the system. If the gradients become sufficiently large, the design procedure will be repeated to readjust the controllers.

B. DESIGN BY SIMULATION

Here we present a different approach to the design of optimal decentralized controllers. This approach is computationally simpler than the one described before, but it requires more communication between the subsystems to perform the design. The proposed procedure is based on the computation of each of the matrices P and Π in (14b and (14c) by running a certain simulation.

Let F be a stable matrix, i.e., $|\lambda_i| < 1$ for all eigenvalues $\{\lambda_i\}$ of F. Let V be a symmetric positive semidefinite matrix. Then, as is well known, the solution to the Lyapunov equation

$$X - FXF^T = V, \tag{25}$$

is given by

$$X = \sum_{i=0}^{\infty} F^i V (F^T)^i. \tag{26}$$

The dimensions of X, F, V are $n \times n$ and let $\text{rank}(V) = r$, $r \leq n$. Then V can be expressed as

$$V = LL^T, \tag{27}$$

where L is full-rank $n \times r$ matrix. Define

$$x(i) \triangleq F^i L. \tag{28}$$

Then

$$X = \sum_{i=0}^{\infty} x(i)x^T(i). \tag{29}$$

Next note that x(i) is the response at time i of the autonomous system

$$x(k + 1) = Fx(k) \tag{30}$$

to the "multi-experiment" initial condition $x(0) \equiv 1$.

Going back to the Lyapunov equations, consider first (14b). The matrix A - BK is just the closed-loop system matrix of the system under consideration, hence it should be stable (and well damped) in most practical cases. A decentralized simulation of the system can be constructed, matching exactly the structure of the true system.

The ℓth subsystem simulates its own dynamics $A_{\ell,\ell} - B_\ell K_\ell$ and its various interconnections $\{A_{\ell,j}, j \neq \ell\}$. These interconnections of course parallel the actual interconnections. Thus, the information flow for the simulation matches the true information flow in the system. Once such a simulation is constructed, Eq. (14b) can be solved as described above by using the appropriate initial conditions, running the simulation, and summing according to (29) until convergence is obtained. As was said before, the closed-loop system is usually well damped, leading to fast convergence.

As for Eq. (14c), its solution calls for simulating the *adjoint* system:

$$x(k + 1) = (A - BK)^T x(k). \tag{31}$$

This is achieved by letting the ℓth subsystem simulate its own adjoint $A^T_{\ell,\ell} - K^T_\ell B^T_\ell$ and its interconnections $\left\{A^T_{j,}\ , j \neq \ell\right\}$. Note that the interconnections in the adjoint system are the same as in the original system, except that the direction of information flow is reversed. Otherwise the solution is the same as in the previous case. Note that

(i) $(A - BK)^T$ has the same eigenvalues as $A - BK$, thus both simulations will converge at the same rate.

(ii) The right-hand side (14c) is usually of low rank. The rank of K^TRK is bounded by m while the rank of Q is usually low if an output-weighting criterion is used.

The local gradient $\partial J/\partial K_i$ is finally computed using Eq. (14a).

IV. AN EXAMPLE

To see the kind of performance achievable by the reduced-order modeling technique, consider the following example, consisting of two interconnected subsystems S_1 (fourth order) and S_2 (first order).

$$A = \left[\begin{array}{cccc|c} 0 & 1 & 0 & 0 & 0 \\ 0 & 0 & 1 & 0 & 0 \\ 0 & 0 & 0 & 1 & 0 \\ 0.1 & -0.31 & -0.234 & 1.12 & -5.0 \\ \hline 0.025 & 0 & 0 & 0 & 0.5 \end{array}\right];$$

$$B = \left[\begin{array}{c|c} 0 & 0 \\ 0 & 0 \\ 0 & 0 \\ 1 & 0 \\ \hline 0 & 1 \end{array}\right]$$

$$Q = \text{diag}\{1,\ 0,\ 0,\ 0,\ 1\}; \qquad R = \text{diag}\{1,\ 1\};$$

$$DWD^T = \text{diag}\{0,\ 0,\ 0,\ 1,\ 0\}.$$

Before any control has been applied we have $J = 1101.6$ and the open-loop poles are $\lambda_i = -0.572,\ 0.219 \pm j0.519,\ 0.877 \pm j0.439$.

We want to improve system performance (i.e., reduce the cost function J) by applying feedback control. First we note that applying *optimal centralized control* gives J = 16.47 and the closed-loop poles are $\lambda_i = -0.422, 0.033 \pm j0.368, 0.247 \pm j0.121$. The optimal feedback gain matrix is

$$K = \left[\begin{array}{cccc|c} 0.0498 & 0.156 & -0.135 & 0.577 & -2.65 \\ \hline 0.0145 & 0.0138 & 0.0693 & -0.0553 & 0.905 \end{array}\right].$$

Applying the *optimal decentralized control* to these two subsystems results in a higher cost of J = 37.46, with closed-loop poles $\lambda_i = -0.738, -0.0473 \pm j0.496, 0.528 \pm j0.354$, and gain matrix

$$K = \left[\begin{array}{cccc|c} 0.00263 & -0.248 & -0.001 & 0.374 & 0 \\ \hline 0 & 0 & 0 & 0 & 1.02 \end{array}\right].$$

If instead we apply decentralized controller gain computed by *"selfish" optimization* we get J = 59.74, $\lambda_i = -0.619, -0.005 \pm j0.588, 0.672 \pm j0.413$, and

$$K = \left[\begin{array}{cccc|c} 0.0634 & -0.174 & -0.217 & -0.639 & 0 \\ \hline 0 & 0 & 0 & 0 & 0.266 \end{array}\right].$$

Note the difference between the cost function of the selfish control (59.74) and the optimal decentralized control (37.46). The results obtained by reduced-order modeling are expected to lie somewhere in between.

We tested the effect of reduced-order modeling by setting the gain K_1 of the larger subsystem S_1 to its optimal decentralized value. Then we computed the gain K_2, using a reduced-order model for S_1. The model reduction was achieved in this case by taking the characteristic polymonial of the first subsystem.

$$a^4(z) = 1 - 0.746z^{-1} + 0.233z^{-2} + 0.062z^{-3} - 0.0974z^{-4}$$

and using the "inverse Levinson" algorithm [13] to compute a set of orthogonal polynomials. This procedure gives

$$a^1(z) = 1 - 0.595z^{-1}$$

$$a^2(z) = 1 - 0.744z^{-1} + 0.25z^{-2},$$

$$a^3(z) = 1 - 0.747z^{-1} + 0.258z^{-2} - 0.0011z^{-3}.$$

The resulting performance and the controller parameters are summarized in the following tabulation:

Order of $\bar{S}_1$	K_2	J	*Closed-loop poles* λ_i
1	0.958	37.758	$-0.710,\ -0.042 \pm j0.518,\ 0.540 \pm j0.357$
2	1.01	37.467	$-0.732,\ -0.046 \pm j0.500,\ 0.530 \pm j0.354$
3	1.05	37.521	$-0.751\ \ -0.049 \pm j0.486,\ 0.523 \pm j0.353$
4	1.00	37.493	$-0.728,\ -0.046 \pm j0.504,\ 0.532 \pm j0.355$

Note that using a reduced-order model of order 1 already gives very close to the optimum cost. If on the other hand subsystem 2 employs selfish control (i.e., reduced-order model of order zero), we get J = 71.622,

$$\lambda_i = -0.553,\ 0.073 \pm j0.651,\ 0.693 \pm j0.377,$$

$$K = \left[\begin{array}{cccc|c} 0.00263 & -0.248 & -0.001 & 0.374 & 0 \\ \hline 0 & 0 & 0 & 0 & 0.266 \end{array}\right].$$

Thus, it is important to take into account the presence of S_1 in the design of the controller for S_2. This example is not a conclusive proof of the feasibility of the proposed technique. It illustrates, however, that using even very low-order models in the design procedure can significantly improve performance over that of the selfish controller, at a small increase in computational complexity.

V. ANALYSIS OF THE REDUCED-ORDER MODELING APPROACH

The properties of the system designed by the above-mentioned procedure are analyzed in this section. We consider a single subsystem and assume that the rest of the system is fixed. This represents a single step in the iterative design procedure described in earlier sections. Global analysis of the iterative design procedure is not available at this time.

To derive the properties of the control system we find it convenient to use an input/output description of the various subsystems, rather than use the state-space formulation of Sections II-IV. This requires the introduction of some new notation.

Consider the system depicted in Fig. 2 and described by

$$y_1 = L_{11}e_1 + L_{12}e_2 \tag{32a}$$

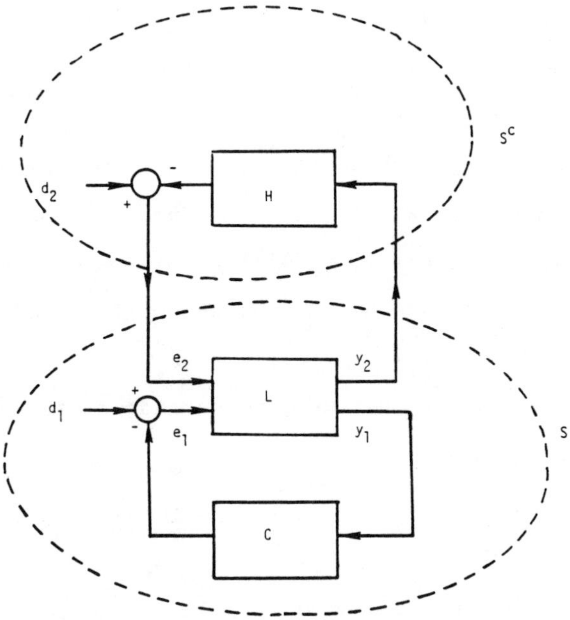

Fig. 2. A decentralized control system.

$$y_2 = L_{21}e_1 + L_{22}e_2 \tag{32b}$$

$$e_1 = d_1 - Cy_1 \tag{32c}$$

$$e_2 = d_2 - Hy_2 \tag{32d}$$

where e_1, y_1, and d_1 are the local subsystem error, output and disturbance signals, respectively. The local subsystem is defined by the dynamic operators $\{L_{ij}, i, j = 1, 2\}$. The signals y_2, e_2 represent the interaction between the local subsystem S and the rest of the system S^c. The disturbance signal d_2 represents the effects of noise and input signals in S^c, on the local subsystem S. The operator H represents the interaction dynamics as viewed from the input and output of the subsystem. The dynamic operator C is the local controller.

The controller is to be designed, as before, assuming complete knowledge of the local subsystem $\{L_{ij}, i, j = 1, 2\}$. The rest of the system is represented by a reduced order model $\bar{H}$ which is related to the full-order model by

$$H = (I + \Delta)\bar{H}. \tag{33}$$

The operator Δ represents the modeling error. This error is not known and its presence introduces an uncertainty into the design problem. We assume, however, knowledge of some bound on the effects of this error, as will be discussed later. The disturbances d_1, d_2 are not known, except for the fact that they belong to some set D, i.e., $(d_1', d_2) \in D$.

The key questions that need to be addressed are:

(i) Under what conditions on the modeling error (Δ) and the disturbance signals (D) is it possible to stabilize the complete system?

(ii) Under what conditions is it possible to design the local controller so that the closed-loop subsystem behavior will satisfy specifications on command response, sensitivity, etc.?

(iii) Should the controller structure be fixed or adaptive? An adaptive controller may improve system performance in view of the unavoidable plant uncertainty.

To answer these questions, we first reorganize the system depicted in Fig. 3 so as to separate out the modeling error Δ. Let z and v be defined by

$$v = \bar{H}y_2 = \bar{H}L_{21}e_1 + \bar{H}L_{22}e_2 \quad \text{(cf. (32b))} \tag{34a}$$

$$z = \Delta v. \tag{34b}$$

From Eq. (32) it follows that

$$e_1 = d_1 - CL_{11}e_1 - CL_{12}e_2 \tag{35a}$$

$$e_2 = d_2 - \bar{H}L_{21}e_1 - \bar{H}L_{22}e_2 - z. \tag{35b}$$

The system defined by Eqs. (34) and (35) can be rewritten as

$$e = T_{ed}d - T_{ed}\begin{bmatrix} 0 \\ I \end{bmatrix} z \tag{36a}$$

where

$$T_{ed} = \left\{ I + \begin{bmatrix} C & 0 \\ 0 & \bar{H} \end{bmatrix} \begin{bmatrix} L_{11} & L_{12} \\ L_{21} & L_{22} \end{bmatrix} \right\}^{-1} \tag{36b}$$

$$e = \left[e_1^T, e_2^T\right]^T \tag{36c}$$

$$d = \left[d_1^T, d_2^T\right]^T. \tag{36d}$$

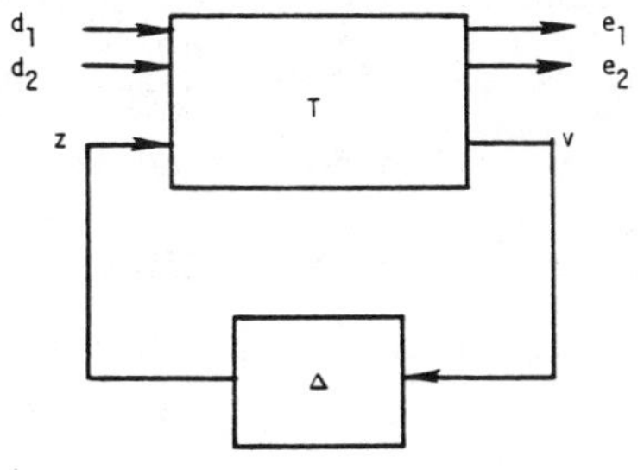

Fig. 3. The interconnection system (isolating the modeling error).

Next we combine Eqs. (34b) and (36a) to give

$$\begin{bmatrix} e \\ v \end{bmatrix} = \begin{bmatrix} T_{ed} & T_{ez} \\ T_{vd} & T_{vz} \end{bmatrix} \begin{bmatrix} d \\ z \end{bmatrix} \tag{37a}$$

where

$$T_{ez} = -T_{ed} \begin{bmatrix} 0 \\ I \end{bmatrix} \tag{37b}$$

$$T_{vd} = \overline{H}[L_{21} \;\; L_{22}]T_{ed} \tag{37c}$$

$$T_{vz} = -\overline{H}[L_{21} \;\; L_{22}]T_{ed} \begin{bmatrix} 0 \\ I \end{bmatrix} \tag{37d}$$

(cf. (34a), (36a)).

Figure 3 depicts the system corresponding to these equations. The relationship between the disturbances d and the error e can be written more explicitly by combining (37a) and (34b):

$$e = T_{ed}d + T_{ez}\Delta v \tag{38}$$

$$v = T_{vd}d + T_{vz}\Delta v \tag{39a}$$

or

$$v = (I - T_{vz}\Delta)^{-1}T_{vd}d. \tag{39b}$$

Thus,

$$e = T(\Delta)d \tag{40a}$$

where

$$T(\Delta) = T_{ed} + T_{ez}(I - \Delta T_{vz})^{-1}\Delta T_{vd}. \tag{40b}$$

This expression is identical to the one presented in [16] for describing uncertain linear time invariant systems. Theorem 2 in [16] leads directly to the following result.

Theorem. Consider the system defined by Eqs. (37) and (32). The linear time invariant operators T and Δ are assumed to be stable. Define

$$\delta(\omega) = \overline{\sigma}[\Delta(e^{j\omega})], \quad \forall \omega \in R \tag{41}$$

where

$$\overline{\sigma}[A] = \left[\max_i \lambda_i(A^*A)\right]^{1/2} = \text{maximum singular value of } A \tag{42}$$

$\lambda_i(M)$ = ith eigenvalue of M.

Then:

(i) The system $T(\Delta)$ is stable if

$$\delta(\omega)\overline{\sigma}\left[T_{vz}(e^{j\omega})\right] < 1, \quad \forall\omega \in R. \tag{43}$$

(ii) The error e is bounded in L_2-norm by[2]

$$||e||_2 \le \overline{\rho}||d||_2, \quad \overline{\rho} = \sup_{\omega\in R} \rho(\omega) \tag{44a}$$

where

$$\rho(\omega) = \overline{\sigma}\left[T_{ed}(e^{j\omega})\right] + \frac{\delta(\omega)\overline{\sigma}\left[T_{ez}(e^{j\omega})\right]\overline{\sigma}\left[T_{vd}(e^{j\omega})\right]}{1 - \delta(\omega)\overline{\sigma}\left[T_{vz}(e^{j\omega})\right]}. \tag{44b}$$

Proof. A consequence of the small-gain theorem [15, p. 40] or Theorem 2 in [16].

Since T_{ed}, T_{ez}, T_{vd}, T_{zv}, and Δ are stable by assumption, $T(\Delta)$ will be stable if $(I - \Delta T_{vz})^{-1}$ is stable. By the contraction principle [15, p. 28] this will happen if

$$\overline{\sigma}\left[\Delta(e^{j\omega})T_{vz}(e^{j\omega})\right] \le \delta(\omega)\overline{\sigma}\left[T_{vz}(e^{j\omega})\right] < 1 \quad \forall\omega \in R. \tag{45}$$

[2] *The* L_p*-norm of the function* $x(t)$ *is defined by*

$$||x||_p = \lim_{T\to\infty} ||x||_{Tp},$$

where

$$||x||_{Tp} = \left[\int_0^T |x(t)|^p\, dt\right]^{1/p}, \quad \textit{and} \quad |x(t)| = [x^T(t)x(t)]^{1/2}.$$

This is the multivariable version of the requirement that the loop gain be smaller than unity to ensure stability of a feedback system. Next note that

$$\|e\|_2 = \|T(\Delta)d\|_2 \leq \sup_{\omega \in R} \overline{\sigma}[T(\Delta(e^{j\omega}))]\,\|d\|_2. \tag{46}$$

By direct application of norm inequalities [15] we get

$$\overline{\sigma}[T(\Delta(e^{j\omega}))] \leq \overline{\sigma}\left[T_{ed}(e^{j\omega})\right] + \frac{\overline{\sigma}\left[T_{ez}(e^{j\omega})\right]\delta(\omega)\overline{\sigma}\left[T_{vd}(e^{j\omega})\right]}{1 - \delta(\omega)\overline{\sigma}\left[T_{vz}(e^{j\omega})\right]} = \rho(\omega). \tag{47}$$

Equation (44) follows from (46) and (47).

This theorem answers two of the questions posed earlier. Equation (43) provides a bound for the modeling error: given the model for the local subsystem $\{L_{1j},\ 1,\ j = 1,\ 2\}$, a reduced-order model $\overline{H}$ for the rest of the system and a specific controller design, we can compute $\overline{\sigma}\left[T_{vz}(e^{j\omega})\right]$. The stability of the system will be assured provided that $\delta(\omega) < 1/\overline{\sigma}\left[T_{vz}(e^{j\omega})\right]$. The same equation can be used to evaluate various controller designs, given knowledge of the bound $\delta(\omega)$ on the modeling error. The condition $\overline{\sigma}\left[T_{vz}(e^{j\omega})\right] < 1/\delta(\omega)$ can be translated into design requirements for the controller C. (However, it is difficult to obtain an explicit set of requirements except in relatively simple cases.)

The bound $\delta(\omega) = \overline{\sigma}[\Delta(e^{j\omega})]$ will generally not be known a priori, but can be determined experimentally. From Eq. (35b) it follows that

$$z = \Delta\overline{H}y_2 = d_2 - e_2 - \overline{H}y_2. \tag{48}$$

Using the fact that

$$\overline{\sigma}[A] = \sup_{x \neq 0} \frac{\|Ax\|_2}{\|x\|_2}, \tag{49}$$

we get

$$\delta(\omega) = \sup_{d_2, y_2, e_2} \frac{\|d_2 - e_2 - \bar{H}y_2\|}{\|\bar{H}y_2\|}$$

$$\leq \sup_{d_2, y_2} \frac{\|d_2\|}{\|\bar{H}y_x\|} + \sup_{y_2, e_2} \frac{\|e_2 + \bar{H}y_2\|}{\|\bar{H}y_2\|}. \quad (50)$$

This quantity can be evaluated by applying a set of test signals y_2 (of frequency ω) to the system S^c and measuring the error e_2 (at the same frequency). Since the disturbance d_2 is unknown, we must assume a bound on its norm, e.g., $\|d_2\| \leq J_d(\omega)$.

The second part of the theorem (44) can be used to evaluate the acceptable disturbance level, given a specified bound on the error norm, e.g., $\|e\|_2 \leq J_e$. The error norm will meet design specifications provided that $\|d\|_2 \leq J_e/\bar{\rho}$. Note that to guarantee stability we only need $d \in L_2$ (in fact a weaker condition will suffice). However, to achieve a specified performance level we need the stronger condition above.

Equation (44) can also be used to specify design requirements for the controller. Consider the case where we are given bounds on the error norm $\|e\|_2 \leq J_e$ and the disturbance norm $\|d\|_2 \leq J_d$. To satisfy both bounds we must have

$$\rho(\omega) \leq J_e/J_d \quad \forall\omega \in R. \quad (51)$$

The equation above can be used to evaluate a given controller C. It also specifies a complicated nonlinear relation in C, which needs to be evaluated in conjuction with the stability condition (45).

The theorem and the subsequent discussion were given in the context of linear time invariant systems. Similar results can be obtained for a more general class of time-varying, possibly nonlinear systems. To do this assume that the various operators in the systems depicted in Figs. 2 and 3 are causal and map L_{pe} into itself.[3] For any such operator M it is possible to define a gain $\gamma_p(\cdot)$ as

$$\gamma_p(M) = \sup_{\substack{x \in L_{pe} \\ x \neq 0}} \frac{\|Mx\|_p}{\|x\|_p}. \tag{52}$$

The theorem will be modified simply by replacing $\overline{\sigma}[\cdot]$ with $\gamma_p(\cdot)$. Thus, the main results will be:

(i) The system $T(\Delta)$ is L_p stable if

$$\gamma_p(\Delta)\gamma_p(T_{vz}) < 1. \tag{53}$$

(ii) The error e is bounded in L_p-norm by

$$\|e\|_p \leq \overline{\rho}\|d\|_p \tag{54a}$$

where

$$\overline{\rho} = \gamma_p)T_{ed}) + \frac{\gamma_p(\Delta)\gamma_p(T_{ez})\gamma_p(T_{vd})}{1 - \gamma_p(\Delta)\gamma_p(T_{vz})}. \tag{54b}$$

The proof follows the same steps as before.

Note that these results are more conservative than the corresponding results for the linear time invariant case. The various bounds and inequalities above involve global properties, whereas earlier they applied pointwise (i.e., for every frequency ω). This is, apparently, the price that has to be paid for the greater generality of the results in (53) and (54).

[3] *The normed function space of dimension n is defined by*

$$L_p^n = \left\{x\colon [0, \infty) \to R^n, \ \|x\|_p < \infty\right\}$$

and its extension by

$$L_{pe}^n = \left\{x\colon [0, T] \to R^n, \ \|x\|_{Tp} < \infty, \ \forall T < \infty\right\}.$$

In the discussion so far we assumed a fixed controller structure. An interesting alternative is the use of an adaptive controller which will "tune" itself to give the best achievable performance. An adaptive controller will be considered if it is not possible to satisfy the design equations developed earlier by a fixed controller, or if an a priori reduced-order model H is not available. The performance of the adaptive controller can be analyzed using a recently developed framework for treating such controllers in the presence of unmodeled dynamics [17].

VI. CONCLUDING REMARKS

As is evident from the discussion above, the idea of using multiple rediced-order models for designing decentralized controllers is still at a preliminary stage of development. Some of the key issues requiring further investigation are global convergence analysis of the iterative design procedure, development of efficient techniques for reduced order modeling, and analysis of the effects of structural perturbations (i.e., connection or removal of subsystems).

The basic approach presented in this chapter can be extended in several directions. Our ultimate goal is to develop an adaptive control technique which performs the complete design procedure on-line. The analysis and design of multiple interacting adaptive controllers represents a challenging problem. The proposed approach can be combined with the concept of hierarchical control. Instead of each subsystem performing the design independently, it can coordinate its efforts with a central supervisor. The supervisor may control overall system behavior by specifying the cost functions to be used by each subsystem, or more directly by providing each subsystem with a reduced-order model of the outside world. These and other extensions are currently under investigation.

Finally, we note that the approach discussed in this chapter is only one of many techniques for designing decentralized controllers. We refer the reader to the vast literature on the methods of dynamic decomposition, aggregation, perturbation, etc. [1,2]. It is hoped that our particular approach will complement existing techniques and provide new insights into the inherent complexities of large-scale systems.

APPENDIX. EFFICIENT SOLUTION OF DISCRETE LYAPUNOV EQUATIONS

Consider the Lyapunov equation:

$$X - AXA^T = B \tag{A.1}$$

where A, X, B are all $n \times n$ matrices and where B is a symmetric matrix. This equation is linear in the unknown parameters X. Since there are n^2 unknown parameters, Eq. (A.1) is equivalent to a set of n^2 simultaneous linear equations. The solution of such equations will generally require proportional to n^6 operations (multiplications and additions), and require $\sim n^4$ words of storage. In this appendix we present a solution technique that requires on the order of $\sim n^3 m$ operations, where $m = \text{rank } B$, and $\sim n^2$ words of storage. The proposed technique is similar to that described in [10]. See also [14] for a somewhat different approach. A brief derivation follows.

The matrix B can always be written as

$$B = \sum_{i=1}^{m} \sigma_i b_i b_i^T, \tag{A.2}$$

where $\sigma_i = \pm 1$ and $m = \text{rank } B$. Let X_i be the solution to

$$X_i - AX^iA^T = b_ib_i^T; \quad 1 \leq i \leq m. \tag{A.3}$$

Then clearly

$$X = \sum_{i=1}^{m} \sigma_i X_i \tag{A.4}$$

is the solution of (A.1). To solve (A.3), let $a(z)$ be the characteristic polynomial of A, i.e.,

$$a(z) = \det(zI - A) = z^n + a_1 z^{n-1} + \cdots + a_n. \tag{A.5}$$

Also let

$$C_i = \left[b_i,\ Ab_i,\ \ldots,\ A^{n-1}b_i\right]$$

$$= \text{controllability matrix of } \{A,\ b_i\} \tag{A.6}$$

$$A_c = \begin{bmatrix} -a_1 & -a_2 & \cdots & & -a_n \\ 1 & 0 & \cdots & & 0 \\ 0 & 1 & \cdots & & 0 \\ \vdots & \vdots & & & \vdots \\ 0 & 0 & \cdots & 1 & 0 \end{bmatrix}$$

$$= \text{controller canonical form of the matrix } A, \tag{A.7}$$

$$A_{co} = \begin{bmatrix} 0 & 0 & \cdots & 0 & -a_n \\ 1 & 0 & & \vdots & \vdots \\ 0 & 1 & & & \\ \vdots & \vdots & & 0 & \\ 0 & 0 & \cdots & 1 & -a_1 \end{bmatrix}$$

$$= \text{controllability canonical form of the matrix } A, \tag{A.8}$$

$$U = \begin{bmatrix} 1 & a_1 & \cdots & a_{n-1} \\ 0 & 1 & \cdots & a_{n-2} \\ \vdots & \vdots & & \vdots \\ 0 & 0 & \cdots & 1 \end{bmatrix}$$

$$= \text{upper triangular Toeplitz matrix.} \tag{A.9}$$

The following two identities are easy to verify ((A.10) uses Cayley-Hamilton theorem):

$$AC_i = C_i A_{co} \tag{A.10}$$

$$A_{co} U = U A_c . \tag{A.11}$$

See [11] for a more detailed discussion of these identities. We can now state and prove the main result:

Theorem. Let

$$\tilde{X} - A_c \tilde{X} A_c^T = e_1 e_1^T, \tag{A.12}$$

where $e_1^T = [1, 0, \ldots, 0]$. Then

$$X_i = C_i U \tilde{X} U^T C_i^T, \tag{A.13}$$

is a solution of (A.3).

Proof. Using (A.10) and (A.11) we can write

$$\begin{aligned} X_i - AX_i A^T &= C_i U \tilde{X} U^T C_i^T - AC_i U \tilde{X} U^T C_i^T A^T \\ &= C_i U \tilde{X} U^T C_i^T - C_i A_{co} U \tilde{X} U^T A_{co}^T C_i^T \\ &= C_i U \tilde{X} U^T C_i^T - C_i U A_c \tilde{X} A_c^T U^T C_i^T \\ &= C_i U \left[\tilde{X} - A_c \tilde{X} A_c^T\right] U^T C_i^T \\ &= C_i U e_1 e_1^T U^T C_i^T = C_i e_1 e_1^T C_i^T = b_i b_i^T . \end{aligned} \tag{A.14}$$

Remarks.

(i) Note that controllability of $\{A, b_i\}$ is not required, i.e., C_i is allowed to be singular.

(ii) $\tilde{X}$ is known to be Toeplitz, i.e.,

$$\tilde{X} = \begin{bmatrix} x_0 & x_1 & \cdots & x_{n-1} \\ x_1 & & \ddots & \vdots \\ \vdots & \ddots & & x_1 \\ x_{n-1} & \cdots & x_1 & x_0 \end{bmatrix}. \tag{A.15}$$

Moreover, $\tilde{X}$ can be efficiently computed by solving

$$\left\{\begin{bmatrix} 1 & a_1 & \cdots & a_n \\ & 1 & \ddots & \vdots \\ & & & a_1 \\ 0 & & & 1 \end{bmatrix} + \begin{bmatrix} 0 & & & a_n \\ & & \cdot^{\cdot^{\cdot}} & a_{n-1} \\ & & & \vdots \\ a_n & a_{n-1} & \cdots & 1 \end{bmatrix}\right\}\begin{bmatrix} x_n \\ x_{n-1} \\ \vdots \\ 1/2x_0 \end{bmatrix} = \begin{bmatrix} 0 \\ 0 \\ \vdots \\ I \end{bmatrix}. \tag{A.16}$$

Using, for example, the technique presented in [12].

(iii) Finally, the solution to (A.1) is obtained by

$$X = \sum_{i=1}^{m} \sigma_i C_i U\tilde{X}U^T C_i^T. \tag{A.17}$$

ACKNOWLEDGMENTS

The work presented in this chapter is the result of a joint research effort. The algorithms in Section II and in the Appendix were derived by Dr. B. Porat, who was also responsible for the numerical results in Section IV. The analysis in Section V is based directly on material provided by Dr. R. L. Kosut.

This work was supported by the Air Force Office of Scientific Research under Contract F4920-81-C-0051.

REFERENCES

1. *IEEE Trans. Automat. Control AC-23 (2)*, Special Issue on large-scale systems and decentralized control (1978).

2. D. D. ŠILJAK, "Large-Scale Dynamic Systems — Stability and Structure," Elsevier North-Holland, Amsterdam (1978).

3. *IEEE Trans. Automat. Control AC26 (4)*, Control system society 25th Anniversary index (1981).

4. R. L. KOSUT, "Suboptimal Control of Linear Time-Invariant Systems Subject to Control Structure Constraints," *IEEE Trans. Automat. Control AC-15 (5)*, 557-563 (1970).

5. W. S. LEVINE and M. ATHANS, "On the Determination of the Optimal Constant Output Feedback Gains for Linear Multivariable Systems," *IEEE Trans. Automat. Control AC-15*, 44-48 (1970).

6. J. C. GEROMEL and J. BERNUSSOU, "An Algorithm for Optimal Decentralized Regulation of Linear Quadratic Interconnected Systems," *Automatica 15*, 489-491 (1979).

7. C. J. WENK and C. H. KNAPP, "Parameter Optimization in Linear Systems with Arbitrary Constrained Controller Structure," *IEEE Trans. Automat. Control AC-25 (3)*, 496-500 (1980).

8. K. J. ASTRÖM, "Introduction to Stochastic Control Theory," Academic Press, New York, 1970.

9. L. S. LASDON, "Optimization Theory for Large Systems," Macmillan, New York (1970).

10. N. J. YOUNG, "Formulae for the solution of Lyapunov matrix equations," *Internat. J. Control 31*, 159-179 (1980).

11. T. KAILATH, "Linear Systems," Prentice-Hall, Englewood Cliffs, New Jersey (1980).

12. G. A. MERCHANT and T. W. PARKS, "Efficient Solution of a Toeplitz-Plus-Hankel Coefficient Matrix System of Equations," *IEEE Trans. Acoust. Speech Signal Process. ASSP-30 (1)*, 40-44 (1982).

13. N. LEVINSON, "The Wiener RMS (root mean square) error criterion in filter design and prediction," *J. Math. Phys. 25*, 261-278 (1947).

14. R. R. BITMEAD, "Explicit Solutions of the Discrete-Time Lyapunov Matrix Equation and Kalman-Yakubovich Equations," *IEEE Trans. Automat. Control AC-26 (6)*, 1291-1294 (1981).

15. C. A. DESOER and M. VIDYASAGAR, "Feedback Systems: Input/Output Properties," Academic Press, New York, 1975.

16. R. L. KOSUT, "Analysis of Performance Robustness for Uncertain Multivariable Systems," in Proc. IEEE Conf. on Decision and Control," Orlando, Florida, December 1982.

17. R. L. KOSUT and B. FRIEDLANDER, "Performance Robustness Properties of Adaptive Control Systems," in Proc. IEEE Conf. on Decision and Control," Orlando, Florida, December 1982.

Decentralized Control Using Local Models for Large-Scale Systems

E. J. DAVISON

Department of Electrical Engineering
University of Toronto
Toronto, Canada

Ü. ÖZGÜNER

Department of Electrical Engineering
The Ohio State University
Columbus, Ohio

I. INTRODUCTION

This chapter is concerned with the problem of synthesizing decentralized controllers for a plant subject to the following constraints: (a) no central authority will be used in the

ISBN 0-12-012722-9

controller synthesis; and (b) each control agent of the plant possesses only a local mathematical model of the plant, which, in general, may vary from agent to agent. This type of problem, called "decentralized control using local models," occurs often in practice, in particular, in large-scale systems where it may be virtually impossible to obtain a mathematical model of the complete overall system; what often can be obtained in practice, however, is a local model of the overall system based on the inputs and outputs of a given control agent of the plant (obtained, for example, by carrying out identification techniques on the agent's local inputs and local outputs). For example, in chemical process control and in power systems consisting of multi-interconnected areas, it is often the case that a control agent in a given part of the plant may have available a fairly representative model of the plant as seen by its inputs and outputs.

The general problem to be considered then is: given that a complete overall model of the large-scale system is not necessarily available to any control agent, but only local models of the system as seen from agent to agent, to what extent can the local agents synthesize a controller for the overall system to achieve some common desired objective, e.g., stability, robust tracking, or regulation?

In solving this problem, the constraint of *sequential stability* is introduced; this deals with the practical requirement that in any realistic synthesis of a large-scale system, the control agents cannot simultaneously apply their controllers, and so it is essential that when a particular control agent applies his own controller, the resultant closed-loop system should remain stable.

The chapter is divided into six sections. Section II deals with the decentralized robust servomechanism problem and obtains existence conditions and a controller characterization which solves the problem. Section III deals with the robust decentralized servomechanism problem subject to sequential stability. Section IV defines the local model problem and deals with the robust stabilization problem and robust decentralized servomechanism problem with sequential stability using local models. Section V considers the case of the expanding system problem. Here it is desired to determine under what conditions one can connect a new subsystem to an existing decentralized controlled system and find a controller for this subsystem, using a local model, without the requirement of having to retune the previous controllers found in the system. Section VI deals with the retunability problem. This deals with the case of determining under what type of conditions the controllers of an interconnected system can be retuned, using only local models, when the system is subject to structural perturbations.

II. THE DECENTRALIZED SERVOMECHANISM PROBLEM

The following decentralized servomechanism problem is initially considered. A system has ν local control stations, each of which has outputs to be regulated, and in addition has s local control stations in which there are no outputs to be regulated but in which there do exist outputs which can be measured and used for control purposes. In this problem framework, the s control stations can be used to assist in the control of the outputs of the ν control stations which are to be regulated.

The plant consisting of $\nu + s$ local control stations is assumed to be described by the following linear time-invariant system:[1]

$$\dot{x} = Ax + \sum_{i=1}^{\nu+s} B_i u_i + E\omega$$

$$\begin{aligned} y_i^m &= C_i^m x + D_i^m u_i + F_i^m \omega, && i = 1, 2, \ldots, \nu + s \\ y_i &= C_i x + D_i u_i + F_i \omega, && i = 1, 2, \ldots, \nu \\ e_i &= y_i - y_i^{ref}, && i = 1, 2, \ldots, \nu \end{aligned} \tag{1}$$

where $x \in R^n$ is the state, $u_i \in R^{m_i}$, and $y_i^m \in R^{r_i^m}$ are the input and measurable outputs of the ith control station ($i = 1, 2, \ldots, \nu + s$), $\omega \in R^\Omega$ is a disturbance vector, and $e_i \in R^{r_i}$ ($i = 1, 2, \ldots, \nu$) is the error in the system which is the difference between the output $y_i \in R^{r_i}$ to be regulated and the specified reference input y_i^{ref} ($i = 1, 2, \ldots, \nu$). Let

$$B \triangleq (B_1, B_2, \ldots, B_\nu),$$

$$C \triangleq \begin{bmatrix} C_1 \\ C_2 \\ \vdots \\ C_\nu \end{bmatrix}, \quad F \triangleq \begin{bmatrix} F_1 \\ F_2 \\ \vdots \\ F_\nu \end{bmatrix}, \quad C_m \triangleq \begin{bmatrix} C_1^m \\ C_2^m \\ \vdots \\ C_\nu^m \end{bmatrix},$$

$$\hat{B} \triangleq [B_{\nu+1}, B_{\nu+2}, \ldots, B_{\nu+s}],$$

[1] *Throughout the paper, the following type of notation may be used: λ_i, $i = 1, 2, \ldots, \ell$, $\ell \geq 0$ where ℓ is a nonnegative integer. If $\ell = 0$, this notation means that the term λ_i does not exist and is to be deleted.*

$$y_{ref} \triangleq \begin{bmatrix} y_1^{ref} \\ y_2^{ref} \\ \vdots \\ y_\nu^{ref} \end{bmatrix}, \quad e \triangleq \begin{bmatrix} e_1 \\ e_2 \\ \vdots \\ e_\nu \end{bmatrix},$$

$$D \triangleq \text{block diag}(D_1, D_2, \ldots, D_\nu),$$

$$\hat{C}_m \triangleq \begin{bmatrix} C_{\nu+1}^m \\ C_{\nu+2}^m \\ \vdots \\ C_{\nu+s}^m \end{bmatrix}.$$

The disturbance vector ω is assumed to satisfy

$$\dot{z}_1 = \mathscr{A}_1 z_1, \qquad \omega = \hat{\mathscr{C}}_1 z_1, \tag{2}$$

where $z_1 \in R^{\hat{n}_1}$ and where $(\hat{\mathscr{C}}_1, \mathscr{A}_1)$ is observable and $z_1(0)$ is not known. The specified reference input vector y_{ref} is assumed to satisfy

$$y_{ref} = G\rho, \qquad \dot{z}_2 = \mathscr{A}_2 z_2, \qquad \rho = \hat{\mathscr{C}}_2 z_2, \tag{3}$$

where $z_2 \in R^{\hat{n}_2}$, $(\hat{\mathscr{C}}_2, \mathscr{A}_2)$ is observable, and y_{ref} is measurable.

It is assumed without loss of generality that

$$\text{rank}\begin{pmatrix} E \\ F \end{pmatrix} = \text{rank}\,\hat{\mathscr{C}}_1 = \Omega$$

and

$$\text{rank } G = \text{rank}\,\hat{\mathscr{C}}_2 = \dim(\rho).$$

In addition, it is assumed for nontriviality that $\max(\Omega, \dim(\rho)) \geq 1$, $\sigma(\mathscr{A}_1) \subset \mathbb{C}^+$, $\sigma(\mathscr{A}_2) \subset \mathbb{C}^+$ where $\sigma(\cdot)$ denotes the set of eigenvalues of $(\cdot)$ and $\mathbb{C}^+$ denotes the closed right-half complex plane. It is assumed that the outputs y_i^m are the only outputs which are available for measurement at the ith control station ($i = 1, 2, \ldots, \nu + s$).

In this problem it is desired to solve the *robust decentralized servomechanism problem* [1,2] for (1), so that the outputs y_i, $i = 1, 2, \ldots, \nu$ asymptotically track y_i^{ref}, $i = 1, 2, \ldots, \nu$, respectively. It is assumed for nontriviality that $\max(\nu, s) \geq 1$, which implies that the cases $s = 0$ or $\nu = 0$ may be allowed in the problem formulation. If $s = 0$, then this implies that (1) has outputs to be asymptotically regulated at all control stations. If $\nu = 0$ (a pathological case), then this implies that (1) has no output at any control station to be asymptotically regulated; in this case the controllers to be found are to be used solely for improving the response of the closed-loop system.

The following definitions are required in the development to follow:

Let the minimal polynomial of $\mathscr{A}_1$, $\mathscr{A}_2$ be denoted by $\Lambda_1(s)$, $\Lambda_2(s)$, respectively, and let the zeros of the least common multiple of $\Lambda_1(s)$, $\Lambda_2(s)$ (multiplicities included) be given by

$$\lambda_1, \lambda_2, \ldots, \lambda_q. \tag{4}$$

Let the coefficients δ_i, $i = 1, 2, \ldots, q$, be given by the coefficients of the polynomial $\prod_{i=1}^{q}(\lambda - \lambda_i)$ where the λ_i are given by (4), i.e.,

$$\lambda^q + \delta_q\lambda^{q-1} + \delta_{q-1}\lambda^{q-2} + \cdots + \delta_2\lambda + \delta_1 = \prod_{i=1}^{q}(\lambda - \lambda_i) \tag{5}$$

Let $\mathscr{C}$ be a $q \times q$ companion matrix given by

$$\mathscr{C} \triangleq \begin{bmatrix} 0 & 1 & 0 & \cdots & 0 \\ 0 & 0 & 1 & & 0 \\ \vdots & \vdots & \vdots & & \vdots \\ -\delta_1 & -\delta_2 & -\delta_3 & \cdots & -\delta_q \end{bmatrix}. \tag{6}$$

Let

$$\overset{*}{C}_m \in R^{(r_m+r)\times(n+r)} \qquad \text{and} \qquad \hat{C}_m^* \in R^{\hat{r}_m \times (n+r)}$$

where

$$r \triangleq \sum_{i=1}^{\nu} r_i, \quad r_m \triangleq \sum_{i=1}^{\nu} r_i^m, \quad \hat{r}_m \triangleq \sum_{i=\nu+1}^{\nu+s} r_i^m$$

be given as follows:

$$\overset{*}{C}_m \triangleq \begin{bmatrix} \overset{*}{C}_1 \\ \overset{*}{C}_2 \\ \vdots \\ \overset{*}{C}_\nu \end{bmatrix}, \quad \hat{C}_m^* \triangleq \begin{bmatrix} \overset{*}{C}_{\nu+1} \\ \overset{*}{C}_{\nu+2} \\ \vdots \\ \overset{*}{C}_{\nu+s} \end{bmatrix} \tag{7}$$

where

$$\overset{*}{C}_1 \triangleq \begin{bmatrix} C_1^m & 0 & 0 & \cdots & 0 \\ 0 & I_{r_1} & 0 & \cdots & 0 \end{bmatrix}$$

$$\overset{*}{C}_2 \triangleq \begin{bmatrix} C_2^m & 0 & 0 & \cdots & 0 \\ 0 & 0 & I_{r_2} & \cdots & 0 \end{bmatrix}$$

$$\vdots$$

$$\overset{*}{C}_\nu \triangleq \begin{bmatrix} C_\nu^m & 0 & 0 & \cdots & 0 \\ 0 & 0 & 0 & \cdots & I_{r_\nu} \end{bmatrix}$$

$$\overset{*}{C}_{\nu+1} \triangleq \begin{pmatrix} C_{\nu+1}^m & 0 & 0 & \cdots & 0 \end{pmatrix}$$

$$\overset{*}{C}_{\nu+2} \triangleq \begin{pmatrix} C_{\nu+2}^m & 0 & 0 & \cdots & 0 \end{pmatrix}$$

$$\vdots$$

$$\overset{*}{C}_{\nu+s} \triangleq \begin{pmatrix} C_{\nu+s}^m & 0 & 0 & \cdots & 0 \end{pmatrix}.$$

The following result is now obtained for a solution to the robust decentralized servomechanism problem.

Theorem 1 [1,2]. A necessary and sufficient condition that there exists a solution to the robust decentralized servomechanism problem for (1) such that $e(t) \to 0$ as $t \to \infty$ for all disturbances described by (2) and for all specified reference inputs described by (3) and such that the closed-loop system is stable is that the following conditions all hold:

(1) $$\left\{\begin{pmatrix} C_m \\ \hat{C}_m \end{pmatrix}, A, (B, \hat{B})\right\}$$

has no unstable decentralized fixed modes with respect to K [3].

(2) The decentralized fixed modes with respect to K of the q systems

$$\left\{\begin{pmatrix} \overset{*}{C}_m \\ \hat{C}_m^* \end{pmatrix}, \begin{pmatrix} A & 0 \\ C & \lambda_j I \end{pmatrix}, \begin{pmatrix} B & \hat{B} \\ D & 0 \end{pmatrix}\right\}, \qquad j = 1, 2, \ldots, q$$

do not contain λ_j, $j = 1, 2, \ldots, q$, respectively.

(3) y_i^m, $i = 1, 2, \ldots, \nu$ must contain [1] the output y_i, $i = 1, 2, \ldots, \nu$, respectively.

A. CONTROLLER STRUCTURE

Assume that Theorem 1 holds; then any controller which regulates (1) has the following structure [1,2]:

$$u_i = K^i \xi_i + \hat{x}_i, \qquad i = 1, 2, \ldots, \nu$$

$$u_i = \hat{x}_i, \qquad i = \nu + 1, \nu + 2, \ldots, \nu + s, \tag{8}$$

where $\xi_i \in R^{r_i q}$ is the output of the *decentralized servocompensator* given by [1]

$$\dot{\xi}_i = \overset{*}{\mathscr{C}}_i \xi_i + \overset{*}{\mathscr{B}}_i e_i, \qquad e_i = y_i - y_i^{ref},$$

$$i = 1, 2, \ldots, \nu, \tag{9}$$

where

$$\overset{*}{\mathscr{C}}_i \triangleq T_i \text{ block diag}\underbrace{(\mathscr{C}, \mathscr{C}, \ldots, \mathscr{C})}_{r_i \text{ matrices}} T_i^{-1}, \quad \overset{*}{\mathscr{B}}_i = T_i \mathscr{B}_i$$

where T_i is a nonsingular real matrix, $\mathscr{C}$ is defined in (6), and $\mathscr{B}_i$ is given as follows:

$$\mathscr{B}_i \triangleq \text{block diag}\underbrace{(\gamma, \gamma, \ldots, \gamma)}_{r_i \text{ matrices}}$$

where $\gamma \in R^q$ is given by $\gamma = (0, 0, \ldots, 0, 1)'$.

$\hat{x}_i$, $i = 1, 2, \ldots, \nu + s$, is the output of a *decentralized stabilizing compensator* given by

$$\begin{aligned} \dot{\eta}_i &= \Lambda_i^0 \eta_i + \Lambda_i^1 \xi_i + \Lambda_i^2 \hat{y}_i^m \\ \hat{x}_i &= \bar{K}^i \eta_i + K_0^i \hat{y}_i^m, \quad i = 1, 2, \ldots, \nu, \end{aligned} \tag{10a}$$

$$\begin{aligned} \dot{\eta}_i &= \Lambda_i^0 \eta_i + \Lambda_i^2 \hat{y}_i^m \\ \hat{x}_i &= \bar{K}^i \eta_i + K_0^i \hat{y}_i^m, \quad i = \nu + 1, \nu + 2, \ldots, \nu + s, \end{aligned} \tag{10b}$$

where $\hat{y}_i^m \triangleq y_i^m - D_i^m u_i$, $i = 1, 2, \ldots, \nu + s$, and where K_0^i, K^i, $\bar{K}^i$, Λ_i^0, Λ_i^1, Λ_i^2 are found (using the algorithm of [3]) to stabilize (assign specified symmetric eigenvalues to) the following augmented system:

$$\begin{bmatrix} \dot{x} \\ \dot{\xi}_1 \\ \vdots \\ \dot{\xi}_\nu \end{bmatrix} = \left[\begin{array}{c|ccc} A & 0 & \cdots & 0 \\ \hline \overset{*}{\mathscr{B}}_1 C_1 & \overset{*}{\mathscr{C}}_1 & \cdots & 0 \\ \vdots & \vdots & & \vdots \\ \overset{*}{\mathscr{B}}_\nu C_\nu & 0 & \cdots & \overset{*}{\mathscr{C}}_\nu \end{array}\right] \begin{bmatrix} x \\ \xi_1 \\ \vdots \\ \xi_\nu \end{bmatrix} + \left[\begin{array}{c|c} B & \hat{B} \\ \hline \text{block diag} & \\ \left(\overset{*}{\mathscr{B}}_1 D_1, \ldots, \overset{*}{\mathscr{B}}_\nu D_\nu\right) & 0 \end{array}\right] \left[\begin{array}{c} u_1 \\ \vdots \\ u_\nu \\ \hline u_{\nu+1} \\ \vdots \\ u_{\nu+s} \end{array}\right],$$

$$\begin{bmatrix} \hat{y}_i^m \\ \xi_i \end{bmatrix} = \begin{bmatrix} C_i^m x \\ \xi_i \end{bmatrix}, \qquad i = 1, 2, \ldots, \nu$$

$$\hat{y}_i^m = C_i^m x, \qquad i = \nu + 1, \nu + 2, \ldots, \nu + s, \tag{11}$$

where system (11) has decentralized modes equal to the decentralized fixed modes (if any) of

$$\left\{ \begin{pmatrix} C_m \\ \hat{C}_m \end{pmatrix}, A, (B, \hat{B}) \right\}.$$

Remark 1. The resulting closed-loop system obtained after applying the decentralized servocompensator and decentralized stabilizing compensator may have as its eigenvalues any preassigned stable symmetric set of eigenvalues, together with the decentralized modes (if any) of

$$\left\{ \begin{pmatrix} C_m \\ \hat{C}_m \end{pmatrix}, A, (B, \hat{B}) \right\}.$$

III. THE ROBUST DECENTRALIZED SERVOMECHANISM PROBLEM WITH SEQUENTIAL STABILITY

The previous results (Theorem 1) obtained do not consider the practical details of how one may apply the decentralized controllers obtained to the plant. The purpose of this section is to introduce the notion of a *sequential stability constraint* which enables one to realistically connect the decentralized controllers to the plant.

The notion of *sequential stability* in the synthesis of decentralized controls is concerned with the property of a synthesis technique which allows the decentralized controllers for a system to be connected to the system *one at a time* (in a sequential way) *such that the controlled system remains stable at all times*. The motivation for introducing this constraint is that it generally *is impossible to connect all decentralized controllers to a system simultaneously* (i.e., due to the difficulties of communication etc., there will always be some time lag associated with applying the controllers). It will be shown that provided the plant is open-loop asymptotically stable, it is possible to introduce a synthesis technique which solves the robust decentralized servomechanism problem subject to this sequential stability constraint.

Definition. Assume that the plant (1) is open-loop asymptotically stable. Consider now applying decentralized controllers S_i, $i = 1, 2, \ldots, \bar{\nu}$, $\bar{\nu} \triangleq \nu + s$, where S_i is a dynamic compensator with inputs y_i, $\hat{y}_i^m$, y_i^{ref} and output u_i, to (1). Then, if the resultant closed-loop system obtained by applying the decentralized controllers S_i, $i = 1, 2, \ldots, k$, to (1) is stable for $k = 1, 2, \ldots, \bar{\nu}$, the controllers S_i, $i = 1, 2, \ldots, \bar{\nu}$, are called *sequentially stable controllers with respect to control agent order* $(1, 2, \ldots, \bar{\nu})$ [4].

Assume now with no loss of generality that the controller synthesis for (1) is to be carried out in the control agent order $1, 2, \ldots, \bar{\nu}$. The following definition is made.

Given the system (1), then the *robust decentralized servomechanism problem with sequential stability* consists of solving the following problem: find a decentralized controller for (1) so that:

(1) there is a solution to the robust decentralized servomechanism problem; and

(2) the controller synthesis is carried out by applying a series of sequentially stable controllers with respect to control agent order $(1, 2, \ldots, \bar{\nu})$ [4].

The following result is then obtained [4]:

Theorem 2. Consider the system (1) in which A is assumed to be asymptotically stable; then there exists a solution to the robust decentralized servomechanism problem with sequential stability for (1) if and only if there exists a solution to the robust decentralized servomechanism problem for (1) (given by Theorem 1).

Remark 2. It may be observed that *the requirement of sequential stability* in the robust decentralized servomechanism problem *has not added any extra conditions to be satisfied* (other than the plant to be open-loop stable) over the standard robust decentralized servomechanism problem. It is also to be observed that *any* ordering of the controllers can be applied to the plant. Some ordering however may produce a "more satisfactory" speed of response than other orderings; *all* ordering however will always result in the system being stabilized.

The following result is now obtained for the special case when the disturbances and reference signals are of the polynomial-sinusoidal type.

Theorem 3. Consider the system (1) in which A is assumed to be asymptotically stable, and assume that $\mathrm{Re}(\lambda_i) = 0$, $i = 1, 2, \ldots, q$ where λ_i is given by (4), and that there exists a solution to the robust decentralized servomechanism problem (given by Theorem 1); then there exists a solution to the decentralized robust servomechanism problem with sequential stability such that the decentralized stabilizing compensator [see (10)] has order zero.

When the conditions of Theorem 3 hold, this implies that the decentralized robust controller which solves the servomechanism problem has *minimum order* (equal to rq).

The results obtained in Theorem 2 and 3 are an extension of the results obtained in [4], which only considered the case when $s = 0$. The proof of the results follow directly on using arguments identical to those used in [4].

IV. THE ROBUST DECENTRALIZED SERVOMECHANISM PROBLEM USING LOCAL MODELS

The following definition will now be made to describe what is meant by an agent's local model of a plant. Assume, with no loss of generality, that the controller synthesis is to be carried out in the control agent order $(1, 2, \ldots, \nu, \nu + 1, \nu + 2, \ldots, \nu + s)$.

Consider the plant (1) with $\omega \equiv 0$, $y_{ref} \equiv 0$ given by

$$\dot{x} = Ax + (B_1, B_2, \ldots, B_{\nu+s})\begin{bmatrix} u_1 \\ u_2 \\ \vdots \\ u_{\nu+s} \end{bmatrix}$$

$$\begin{aligned} y_1^m &= C_1^m x + D_1^m u_1 \\ y_2^m &= C_2^m x + D_2^m u_2 \\ &\vdots \\ y_{\nu+s}^m &= C_{\nu+s}^m x + D_{\nu+s}^m u_{\nu+s}. \end{aligned} \tag{12}$$

Assume that the control

$$u_i = K_i \hat{y}_i^m + v_i, \quad i = 1, 2, \ldots, \nu + s, \tag{13}$$

where

$$\hat{y}_i^m \triangleq y_i^m - D_i^m u_i, \quad i = 1, 2, \ldots, \nu + s,$$

has been applied to (12). In addition, assume that the following controllers have been applied to control agents 1, 2, ..., i - 1 where $i \geq 2$:

$$v_j = K^j \xi_j + \hat{x}_j, \quad j = 1, 2, \ldots, i - 1,$$

$$i \in [2, 3, \ldots, \nu], \tag{13a}$$

where ξ_j is the output of a decentralized servocompensator given by (9) and $\hat{x}_j$ is the output of a decentralized stabilizing compensator given by (10a), and

$$v_j = K^j \xi_j + \hat{x}_j, \quad j = 1, 2, \ldots, \nu,$$

$$v_j = \hat{x}_j, \quad j = \nu + 1, \nu + 2, \ldots, i - 1,$$

$$i \in [\nu + 1, \nu + 2, \ldots, \nu + s], \tag{13b}$$

where $\hat{x}_j$ is the output of a decentralized stabilizing compensator given by (10b).

Definition. Let the minimal state realization of the closed-loop system obtained by applying the controller (13), (13a), and (13b) to the plant (12) for control agent i (with input v_i and output y_i^m) be called the *ith agent's local model of the plant (12) with respect to feedback gains* (K_i, $i = 1, 2, \ldots, \nu + s$) *and controllers* (13a), (13b) or more briefly *the ith agent's local model* of the controlled plant [5].

A synthesis procedure which solves the decentralized robust servomechanism problem with sequential stability, in which each control agent is assumed to possess only a local model of the controlled plant and in which there exists no central decision making authority, is called a *decentralized synthesis procedure for solving the decentralized robust servomechanism problem with sequential stability.*

The following assumptions are made in this decentralized synthesis problem.

A. ASSUMPTIONS

(1) It is assumed that each control agent possesses only a local model of the controlled plant, and that there exists no central decision making authority.

(2) It is assumed that each control agent knows the class of disturbances and reference signals associated with the plant, i.e., each control agent knows the values of $\lambda_1, \lambda_2, \ldots, \lambda_q$ of (4).

(3) It is assumed that each control agent has the same performance criterion, i.e., that the closed-loop system be stable and that the eigenvalues of the resultant closed loop system all lie in a certain stable preassigned symmetric region of the complex plane denoted by $\mathbb{C}_g^-$ (except for any decentralized fixed modes of

$$\left\{\begin{pmatrix} C_m \\ \hat{C}_m \end{pmatrix}, A, (B, \hat{B})\right\}$$

which may lie outside of $\mathbb{C}_g^-$).

In this problem formulation, it is assumed that the ith agent's local model of the controlled plant can be obtained in either of two ways as follows:

(a) by taking a fundamental approach and applying the laws of physics, etc., to that part of the plant which is relevant to the control agent's local inputs and outputs;

(b) by using identification techniques. During this modeling/identification procedure, it is obviously assumed that no changes have occurred in the rest of the plant until the local model has been obtained.

The following result is obtained:

Theorem 4 [5]. Consider system (1) in which A is assumed to be asymptotically stable. Then there exists a solution to the decentralized synthesis for the robust decentralized servomechanism problem with sequential stability if and only if there exists a solution to the robust decentralized servomechanism problem (given by Theorem 1).

Assume now with no loss of generality that the order of the controllers to be applied to the plant is in the order 1, 2, 3, ..., ν, $\nu + 1$, $\nu + 2$, ..., $\nu + s$ and that Theorem 4 holds. Then the following algorithm can be used to find a decentralized synthesis for the problem [5].

B. *ALGORITHM I (DECENTRALIZED SYNTHESIS SOLUTION)*

Step 1: Apply the output feedback control

$$u_i = K_i \hat{y}_i^m + v_i, \quad i = 1, 2, \ldots, \nu + s, \tag{14}$$

sequentially to the plant, where $K_i \in R^{m_i \times r_i^m}$ are arbitrary nonzero matrices (chosen from a pseudorandom number generator say) chosen "small enough" so as to maintain stability of the closed-loop plant.

Step 2: Using centralized synthesis [6-8] and knowledge of agent 1's local model of the controlled plant, apply the servocompensator (9) with i = 1 to the terminals of control agent 1 and apply a stabilizing compensator $v_1 = K^1 \xi_1 + \hat{x}_1$, where ξ_1 is is given by (9) and $\hat{x}_1$ is given by (10a) so that the resultant closed-loop system is stable and has a desired dynamic response, i.e., so that all noncentralized fixed modes [9] of agent 1's local model of the controlled plant are shifted into $\mathbb{C}_g^-$. The resultant system then has the property that y_1 is regulated.

Step 3: Repeat the centralized synthesis procedure of step 2 for each control agent 2, 3, ..., ν sequentially, using as control inputs v_i, $i = 2, 3, \ldots, \nu$, respectively, and knowledge of the agent's local model of the controlled plant. The resultant system then has the property that $y_1, y_2, \ldots, y_\nu$ are all regulated.

Step 4: Using centralized synthesis techniques and knowledge of agent $(\nu + 1)$'s local model of the controlled plant, apply a stabilizing compensator $v_{\nu+1} = \hat{x}_{\nu+1}$ where $\hat{x}_{\nu+1}$ is given by (10b) so that the resultant closed-loop system has a desired dynamic response, i.e., so that all noncentralized fixed modes of the local model of the controlled plant with respect to agent $\nu + 1$ are shifted into $\mathbb{C}_g^-$.

Step 5: Repeat the centralized synthesis procedure of step 4 for each control agent $\nu + 2, \nu + 3, \ldots, \nu + s$, sequentially using as control inputs v_i, $i = \nu + 2, \nu + 3, \ldots, \nu + s$, respectively, and knowledge of the agent's local model of the controlled plant.

Step 6: Stop. The resultant system then has the property that $y_1, y_2, \ldots, y_\nu$ are all asymptotically regulated and that the closed-loop system is stable with a desired dynamic response, i.e., the eigenvalues of the resultant closed-loop system are all contained in $\mathbb{C}_g^-$ except for those decentralized fixed modes (if any) of

$$\left\{\begin{pmatrix} C_m \\ \hat{C}_m \end{pmatrix}, A, (B, \hat{B})\right\}$$

which may lie outside of $\mathbb{C}_g^-$.

Properties of Algorithm I.

(1) There always exists an $\epsilon > 0$ so that in step 1 of Algorithm I

$$\forall K_i \in \left(R^{m_i \times r_i^m} \,\middle|\, \|K_i\| < \epsilon\right), \qquad i = 1, 2, \ldots, \nu + s,$$

$$A + \sum_{i=1}^{k} B_i K_i C_i^m \text{ is asymptotically stable.}$$
$$\forall k \in [1, 2, \ldots, \nu + s].$$

(2) For almost all [10] K_i, $i = 1, 2, \ldots, \nu + s$ for almost all K^j, $j = 1, 2, \ldots, \nu$, and for almost all Λ_j^0, K_0^j, $j = 1, 2, \ldots, \nu + s$ [see (10a), (10b)], obtained by using Algorithm I, steps 2-5 of Algorithm I can be carried out so that the resultant closed-loop system has its eigenvalues contained in $\mathbb{C}_g^-$, except for those decentralized fixed modes (if any) of

$$\left\{\begin{pmatrix} C_m \\ \hat{C}_m \end{pmatrix}, A, (B, \hat{B})\right\}$$

which may lie outside of $\mathbb{C}_g^-$, if and only if Theorem 1 holds.

Remark 3. The only reason for imposing the requirement that the plant be open-loop stable in Theorem 4 is to satisfy the sequential stability constraint requirement. If this requirement is relaxed, then Theorem 4 still applies for the case of unstable plants.

Discussion. In the decentralized synthesis problem, the plant model (1) is not known to any control agent, and since no central decision making authority is available, the conditions for a solution to the problem cannot be explicitly determined by any control agent. However, it is known by Theorem 4 that Algorithm I will produce a desired controller synthesis for "almost all controller gains" if and only if a solution to the problem exists. Thus, the method for solving the decentralized servomechanism problem is to proceed with Algorithm I, and if at steps 2 and 3 a controller agent cannot solve his local synthesis problem, this implies that for "almost all controller gains" used, there exist no solution to the decentralized servomechanism problem, i.e.,

(a) if Theorem 1 holds, then a solution will exist to the decentralized synthesis for the robust decentralized servomechanism problem using Algorithm I for almost all controller gains;

(b) if Theorem 1 does not hold, then a solution will not exist to the decentralized synthesis for the robust decentralized servomechanism problem using Algorithm I for any choice of controller gains (or controllers).

In the problem discussed with $\nu = 0$, then a complete solution to the pole-assignment problem for the decentralized control problem using decentralized synthesis (i.e., using only local models) is obtained. In this case, it follows from [5] that steps 1-3 of Algorithm I can be deleted and only steps 4-6 of Algorithm I are now required to solve the problem.

C. POLE-ASSIGNMENT PROBLEM USING DECENTRALIZED SYNTHESIS

Given the plant

$$\dot{x} = Ax + (B_1, B_2, \ldots, B_s)\begin{bmatrix} u_1 \\ u_2 \\ \vdots \\ u_s \end{bmatrix}$$

$$\hat{y}_i^m = C_i^m x, \quad i = 1, 2, \ldots, s, \tag{15}$$

where all quantities are defined as before and $\nu = 0$, find a decentralized synthesis so as to assign all poles of the resultant controlled system into $\mathbb{C}_g^-$ (except for those decentralized fixed modes, if any, of $(\hat{C}_m, A, \hat{B})$ which lie outside of $\mathbb{C}_g^-$).

D. *ALGORITHM II (POLE-ASSIGNMENT DECENTRALIZED SYNTHESIS)*

Assume with no loss of generality that the control synthesis is to proceed in the control agent order 1, 2, ..., s.

Step 1: Using centralized synthesis and a knowledge of agent 1's local model of the plant [i.e., the minimal realization of (C_1^m, A, B_1)], apply a stabilizing compensator

$$u_1 = K_0^1 \hat{y}_1^m + \bar{K}^1 \eta_1, \quad \dot{\eta}_1 = \Lambda_1^0 \eta_1 + \Lambda_1^2 \hat{y}_1^m \tag{16}$$

to control agent 1 so that

$$\begin{bmatrix} A + B_1 K_0^1 C_1^m & B_1 \bar{K}^1 \\ \Lambda_1^2 C_1^m & \Lambda_1^0 \end{bmatrix} \tag{17}$$

has all its eigenvalues, except for those eigenvalues which correspond to the centralized fixed modes [9] of (C_1^m, A, B_1) contained in $\mathbb{C}_g^-$.

Step 2: Using centralized techniques and knowledge of control agent 2's local model of the resultant controlled plant (i.e., the minimal realization of (15), (16) with respect to input u_2 and output $\hat{y}_2^m$) apply a stabilizing compensator

$$u_2 = K_0^2 \hat{y}_2^m + \bar{K}^2 \eta_2, \quad \dot{\eta}_2 = \Lambda_2^0 \eta_2 + \Lambda_2^2 \hat{y}_2^m \tag{18}$$

to control agent 2's terminals, so that

$$\begin{bmatrix} A + B_1 K_0^1 C_1^m + B_2 K_0^2 C_2^m & B_1 \bar{K}^1 & B_2 \bar{K}^2 \\ \Lambda_1^2 C_1^m & \Lambda_1^0 & 0 \\ \Lambda_2^2 C_2^m & 0 & \Lambda_2^0 \end{bmatrix} \tag{19}$$

has all its eigenvalues, except for those eigenvalues which correspond to the decentralized fixed modes of

$$\left\{ \begin{pmatrix} C_1^m \\ C_2^m \end{pmatrix}, A, (B_1, B_2) \right\},$$

contained in $\mathbb{C}_g^-$. This is always possible to do for almost all K_0^1, Λ_1^0.

Step s: Using centralized techniques and knowledge of control agent s's local model of the plant, apply a stabilizing compensator

$$u_s = K_0^s \hat{y}_s^m + \overline{K}^s \eta_s, \qquad \dot{\eta}_s = \Lambda_s^0 \eta_s + \Lambda_s^2 \hat{y}_s^m$$

to control agent s so that

$$\begin{bmatrix} A + \sum_{i=1}^{s} B_i K_0^i C_i^m & B_1 \overline{K}^1 & \cdots & B_s \overline{K}^s \\ \Lambda_1^2 C_1^m & \Lambda_1^0 & \cdots & 0 \\ \vdots & \vdots & & \vdots \\ \Lambda_s^2 C_s^m & 0 & & \Lambda_s^0 \end{bmatrix}$$

has its eigenvalues contained in $\mathbb{C}_g^-$, except for those decentralized fixed modes, if any, of $\left(\hat{C}_m, A, \hat{B}\right)$ which lie outside of $\mathbb{C}_g^-$. This is always possible to do for almost all K_0^i, Λ_i^0, $i = 1, 2, \ldots, s - 1$. Stop.

Remark 4. In this procedure, it may turn out that the minimal realization of the plant at steps $k_1, k_2, \ldots$ is identically zero; if this is the case, then it is essential that the stabilizing compensator $u_i = K_0^i \hat{y}_i^m$, $i = k_1, k_2, \ldots$ still be applied (where the K_0^i are arbitrary "small" nonzero gain matrices) in order for the algorithm to proceed, i.e., it it necessary that $K_0^i \neq 0$, $i = 1, 2, \ldots, s$, in general for the algorithm to proceed.

Remark 5. If the sequential stability constraint is relaxed, then Algorithms I and II are still applicable for the case of unstable open-loop plants (1), provided that (1) has no unstable decentralized fixed modes.

Remark 6. Note that the controllers obtained in Algorithms I and II are, in general, not unique with respect to the control agent order sequence chosen.

Discussion. In Algorithms I and II, the decentralized synthesis uses at each control station a local model which, in general, incorporates the compensator dynamics of the preceding control stations. This implies that the local models of the plant obtained under open-loop conditions cannot, in general, be used to construct local controllers for the system. The question may be asked, To what extent is the requirement of using a local model of the plant which incorporates preceding controller dynamics actually necessary?

Simple examples may be constructed to show that this requirement, in general, is necessary.

E. APPLICATION OF DECENTRALIZED SYNTHESIS RESULTS

Consider the robust servomechanism problem for the following centralized multivariable system [6]:

$$\begin{aligned} \dot{x} &= Ax + Bu + E\omega \\ y &= Cx + F\omega \\ y_m &= C_m x + F_m \omega, \end{aligned} \tag{20}$$

where $u \in R^m$ are the inputs, $x \in R^n$ is the state, $y \in R^r$ are the outputs to be regulated, y_m are the measurable outputs and $\omega \in R^\Omega$ are the disturbances. Let the reference inputs y_{ref} be described by (3) and the disturbances ω be described by (2).

There has been much interest recently in trying to apply single-input-single-output design methods to solve this multivariable servomechanism problem, e.g., see [11]. The following application of the previous results shows how this multivariable problem can be solved using only single-input-single-output methods.

The following result is obtained which enables this to be done [5].

Theorem 5. Assume there exists a solution to the robust centralized servomechanism problem [6] for (20) and let the controller

$$u = Ky_m + Gv \tag{21}$$

be applied to (20). Then for almost all $K \in R^{m \times r_m}$ and for almost all $G \in R^{m \times r}$.

(1) There exists a solution to the robust decentralized servomechanism problem for the following system:

$$\begin{aligned} \dot{x} &= (A + BKC_m)x + BGv + E\omega \\ y &= Cx + F\omega \\ y_m &= C_m x + F_m \omega \end{aligned} \tag{22}$$

with ν control agents, where $\nu \in [1, 2, \ldots, r]$, with any ordering of inputs and measurable outputs at each control station, provided only that at each control station the number of local control inputs is chosen to be equal to the number of local outputs to be regulated.

(2) The decentralized fixed modes of (22) are equal to the centralized fixed modes of (20).

Remark 7. If A in (20) is asymptotically stable, then the choice of K = 0 in Theorem 5 can always be made.

It is seen therefore that if there exists a solution to the centralized robust servomechanism problem for (20) and if A is asymptotically stable, then Theorem 5 implies that the decentralized synthesis procedure (Algorithm I) can be applied to solve (20); in particular if $y_m = y$, then for almost all G, there exists a solution to the following decentralized servomechanism problem

$$\dot{x} = Ax + \sum_{i=1}^{r} \overset{*}{B}_i v_i + E\omega$$
$$y_i = C_i x + F_i \omega, \quad i = 1, 2, \ldots, r, \tag{23}$$

where $BG \triangleq \left(\overset{*}{B}_1, \overset{*}{B}_2, \ldots, \overset{*}{B}_r\right)$, $F' \triangleq \left(F_1', F_2', \ldots, F_r'\right)$, $C' \triangleq \left(C_1', C_2', \ldots, C_r'\right)$ which has the property that the decentralized fixed modes of (23) are equal to the centralized fixed modes of (20). This decentralized problem can be solved by applying a sequence of single-input-single-output design methods in each control loop using Algorithm I. In this case, the closed-loop system will always remain stable and all controllable-observable modes of the system can be assigned.

V. THE EXPANDING SYSTEM PROBLEM

The following type of problem is now considered. Assume that a decentralized controller has been applied to the plant (1), so that the overall closed loop system is asymptotically stable, and such that robust tracking and regulation occurs in each of the system's local control agents. Suppose now that a new subsystem S_{new}, which has outputs to be regulated, is to be connected to S. It is desired to determine when it is possible to find a local controller for S_{new} (using only a local model of the resultant system obtained from the control agent associated with S_{new}) so that its outputs and all previous outputs are regulated, without the requirement of having to retune the previous controllers associated with the original plant (1).

This is called the *expanding system problem* for (1), and occurs often in large-scale systems, e.g., in industrial process control systems.

In particular, assume that a solution exists for the robust decentralized servomechanism for (1), i.e., that Theorem 1 is satisfied, and that a controller (8) has been applied to (1) to solve the robust decentralized servomechanism problem. Let the resultant closed-loop system be described by:

$$S: \quad \begin{aligned} \dot{x} &= \mathscr{A}x + (\mathscr{E}_1, \mathscr{E}_2)\begin{pmatrix}\omega \\ y_{ref}\end{pmatrix} \\ e &= Hx + (F, -I)\begin{pmatrix}\omega \\ y_{ref}\end{pmatrix} \end{aligned}$$

where $\mathscr{A}$ is asymptotically stable, and e is the error in the system.

Let the subsystem S_{new}, which is to be connected to S, be described by:

$$S_{new}: \quad \begin{aligned} \dot{\bar{x}} &= \bar{A}\bar{x} + \bar{B}\bar{u} + \bar{E}\bar{\omega}, \quad \bar{x} \in R^{\bar{n}}, \quad \bar{y} \in R^{\bar{r}}, \quad \bar{u} \in R^{\bar{m}} \\ \bar{y} &= \bar{C}\bar{x} + \bar{D}\bar{u} + \bar{F}\bar{\omega} \\ \bar{y}_m &= \bar{C}_m\bar{x} + \bar{D}_m\bar{u} + \bar{F}_m\bar{\omega} \\ \bar{e} &= \bar{y} - \bar{y}_{ref} \end{aligned} \tag{24}$$

where $\bar{u}$ is the input, $\bar{y}$ is the output to be regulated, $\bar{y}_m$ is the measurable output, $\bar{e}$ is the error in the system and where $\bar{\omega}$, $\bar{y}_{ref}$ are disturbances, reference input signals which satisfy (2), (3), respectively. Assume that S_{new} is controllable and observable, and that there exists a solution to the centralized robust servomechanism problem [6] for S_{new} (taken in isolation), i.e., assume for (24) that the following conditions all hold:

(a) $(\bar{C}_m, \bar{A}, \bar{B})$ is controllable and observable

(b) $\operatorname{rank}\begin{bmatrix} \bar{A} & -\lambda_i I & \bar{B} \\ \bar{C} & & \bar{D} \end{bmatrix} = \bar{n} + \bar{r}, \quad i = 1, 2, \ldots, q,$

(c) y is contained in y_m (i.e., y can be measured).

Assume now that there exist interconnections between S and S_{new}, so that S_{new} may be connected to S in the following general composite way:

$$\begin{bmatrix} \dot{x} \\ \dot{\bar{x}} \end{bmatrix} = \begin{bmatrix} \mathscr{A} & \mathscr{B}_1\mathscr{K}_1\mathscr{C}_1 \\ \mathscr{B}_2\mathscr{K}_2\mathscr{C}_2 & \bar{A} \end{bmatrix}\begin{bmatrix} x \\ \bar{x} \end{bmatrix} + \begin{bmatrix} 0 \\ \bar{B} \end{bmatrix}\bar{u} + \begin{bmatrix} \mathscr{E}_1 & \mathscr{B}_1\mathscr{K}_1\mathscr{G}_1 \\ \mathscr{B}_2\mathscr{K}_2\mathscr{G}_2 & \bar{E} \end{bmatrix}\begin{bmatrix} \omega \\ \bar{\omega} \end{bmatrix} + \begin{bmatrix} \mathscr{E}_2 \\ 0 \end{bmatrix} y_{ref}$$

$$\bar{y}_m = \begin{bmatrix} 0 & \bar{C}_m \end{bmatrix}\begin{bmatrix} x \\ \bar{x} \end{bmatrix} + \bar{D}_m\bar{u} + \begin{pmatrix} 0 & \bar{F}_m \end{pmatrix}\begin{bmatrix} \omega \\ \bar{\omega} \end{bmatrix}$$

$$\bar{y} = [0 \quad \bar{C}]\begin{bmatrix} x \\ \bar{x} \end{bmatrix} + \bar{D}\bar{u} + (0 \quad \bar{F})\begin{bmatrix} \omega \\ \bar{\omega} \end{bmatrix} \tag{25}$$

$$\bar{e} = \bar{y} - \bar{y}_{ref}$$

$$e = (H, 0)\begin{bmatrix} x \\ \bar{x} \end{bmatrix} + (F, 0)\begin{bmatrix} \omega \\ \bar{\omega} \end{bmatrix} - y_{ref}$$

where $\mathscr{B}_1$, $\mathscr{B}_2$, $\mathscr{C}_1$, $\mathscr{C}_2$, $\mathscr{G}_1$, $\mathscr{G}_2$, $\mathscr{K}_1$, and $\mathscr{K}_2$ are arbitrary.

The following result is now obtained as a solution to this expanding system problem [12]:

Theorem 6. Consider the interconnected composite system (25) subject to assumptions (a)-(c); then:

(1) There exists a solution to the robust centralized servomechanism problem for (25) so that the resultant closed loop syste

is asymptotically stable, and such that $\bar{e} \to 0$ as $t \to \infty$, $e \to 0$ as $t \to \infty$ for all disturbances $\begin{pmatrix} \omega \\ \bar{\omega} \end{pmatrix}$ and for all reference signals $\begin{pmatrix} y_{ref} \\ \bar{y}_{ref} \end{pmatrix}$ described by (2), (3) respectively for almost all interconnection gains $\mathcal{K}_1$, $\mathcal{K}_2$.

(2) The centralized fixed modes of

$$\left\{ \begin{pmatrix} 0 & \bar{C}_m \end{pmatrix}, \begin{pmatrix} \mathcal{A} & \mathcal{B}_1\mathcal{K}_1\mathcal{C}_1 \\ \mathcal{B}_2\mathcal{K}_2\mathcal{C}_2 & \bar{A} \end{pmatrix}, \begin{pmatrix} 0 \\ \bar{B} \end{pmatrix} \right\}$$

are contained in sp($\mathcal{A}$) for almost all interconnection gains $\mathcal{K}_1$, $\mathcal{K}_2$.

Remark 8. Theorem 6 says that for *all* interconnection matrices $\mathcal{B}_1$, $\mathcal{B}_2$, $\mathcal{C}_1$, $\mathcal{C}_2$ and for almost all interconnection gain matrices $\mathcal{K}_1$, $\mathcal{K}_2$, one can solve the expanding system problem using only a local model of the composite system obtained from the S_{new} control agent, without the need of retuning the previous controllers used in S.

It should be noted that the assumption of $\left(\bar{C}_m, \bar{A}, \bar{B}\right)$ being controllable and observable is an *essential* assumption to make in order that Theorem 6 be true for arbitrary interconnections existing between S and S_{new}. In particular, simple counterexamples can be found to show that if $\left(\bar{C}_m, \bar{A}, \bar{B}\right)$ is only stabilizable and detectable, then there may exist interconnection matrices so that (25) has unstable centralized fixed modes for all interconnection gains $\mathcal{K}_1$, $\mathcal{K}_2$. This result may give some insight into the observation in practice that there may or may not be "immense difficulties" associated with the control of a system when a new subsystem is added to the existing controlled system.

VI. THE RETUNABILITY PROBLEM

The following type of question is now asked: given a large-scale decentralized system which is made up of a number of interconnected subsystems, What happens if certain subsystems or groups of subsystems are connected and/or disconnected? This type of question arises in large power/energy systems, communication networks, and C^3I systems in general. In this section, it is desired to determine, in particular, under what conditions the control agents of an interconnected system can readjust their controllers, using only local models, to solve the robust decentralized servomechanism problem when the overall system is subject to structural perturbations.

Assume that the plant (1) consists of ν interconnected subsystems, and is given as follows:

$$\dot{x} = \begin{bmatrix} A_{11} & A_{12} & \cdots & A_{1\nu} \\ A_{21} & A_{22} & \cdots & A_{2\nu} \\ \vdots & \vdots & & \vdots \\ A_{\nu 1} & A_{\nu 2} & \cdots & A_{\nu\nu} \end{bmatrix} x + \begin{bmatrix} B_1 & 0 & \cdots & 0 \\ 0 & B_2 & \cdots & 0 \\ \vdots & \vdots & & \vdots \\ 0 & 0 & \cdots & B_\nu \end{bmatrix} \begin{bmatrix} u_1 \\ u_2 \\ \vdots \\ u_\nu \end{bmatrix} + \begin{bmatrix} E_1 \\ E_2 \\ \vdots \\ E_\nu \end{bmatrix} \omega$$

$$\begin{bmatrix} y_1 \\ y_2 \\ \vdots \\ y_\nu \end{bmatrix} = \begin{bmatrix} C_1 & 0 & \cdots & 0 \\ 0 & C_2 & \cdots & 0 \\ \vdots & \vdots & & \\ 0 & 0 & \cdots & C_\nu \end{bmatrix} x + \begin{bmatrix} F_1 \\ F_2 \\ \vdots \\ F_\nu \end{bmatrix} \omega \tag{26}$$

$$\begin{bmatrix} y_1^m \\ y_2^m \\ \vdots \\ y_\nu^m \end{bmatrix} = \begin{bmatrix} C_1^m & 0 & \cdots & 0 \\ 0 & C_2^m & \cdots & 0 \\ \vdots & \vdots & & \vdots \\ 0 & 0 & \cdots & C_\nu^m \end{bmatrix} x$$

where

$$A_{ii} \in R^{n_i \times n_i}, \; B_i \in R^{n_i \times m_i}, \; C_i \in R^{r_i \times n_i}, \; C_i^m \in R^{r_i^m \times n_i},$$

$$i = 1, 2, \ldots, \nu.$$

Here

$$u_i \in R^{m_i}, \; y_i \in R^{r_i}, \; y_i^m \in R^{r_i^m}$$

are the input, output to be regulated, and measurable output, respectively, of the ith control agent corresponding to the ith subsystem, $i = 1, 2, \ldots, \nu$. The error in the system is given by $e_i \triangleq y_i - y_i^{ref}$, $i = 1, 2, \ldots, \nu$, where y_i^{ref} is the reference input signal for the ith control agent. The disturbance signal ω and reference input signal $y_{ref} \triangleq \left(y_1^{ref'}, y_2^{ref'}, \ldots, y_\nu^{ref'}\right)'$ is assumed to satisfy (2), (3), respectively.

The following definitions are required in the development to follow:

Definitions. Let the directed graph $G:(N, L)$ define the interconnection structure of the interconnected system (26). Here each subsystem S_j, $j \in [1, 2, \ldots, \nu]$, is denoted by a node $j \in [1, 2, \ldots, \nu]$ and each nonzero interconnection from S_i to S_j by an oriented link $\ell_{ij} \in L$ connecting node i to node j in the graph. Obviously the existence of a link ℓ_{ij} implies $A_{ij} \neq 0$ and vice versa. A subgraph $G_T:(N_T, L_T)$ is a collection of nodes $N_T \subset N$ and a related set L_T of all links connecting the nodes N_T in the original graph. Denote the set of nodes remaining outside the subgraph G_T by N_T^- and the outgoing links from N_T to N_T^- (if any) by L_T^-.

Given (26) and given $N_T \subset N$ with k elements (say), define now the matrix A_{N_T} as follows:

$$A_{N_T} \triangleq \begin{bmatrix} A_{t_1t_1} & A_{t_1t_2} & \cdots & A_{t_1t_k} \\ A_{t_2t_1} & A_{t_2t_2} & \cdots & A_{t_2t_k} \\ \vdots & \vdots & & \vdots \\ A_{t_kt_1} & A_{t_kt_2} & \cdots & A_{t_kt_k} \end{bmatrix} \tag{27}$$

where $t_i \neq t_j$ for $i \neq j$, and where $t_j \in N_T$, $j = 1, 2, \ldots, k$, and define

$$\begin{aligned} B_{N_T} &\triangleq \text{block diag}(B_{t_1}, B_{t_2}, \ldots, B_{t_k}) \\ C_{N_T} &\triangleq \text{block diag}(C_{t_1}, C_{t_2}, \ldots, C_{t_k}) \\ C^m_{N_T} &\triangleq \text{block diag}\left(C^m_{t_1}, C^m_{t_2}, \ldots, C^m_{t_k}\right) \end{aligned} \tag{28}$$

Definition. A *strongly connected graph* is a directed graph in which every pair of nodes is mutually reachable, i.e., for every pair of nodes i, j there exists a path from node i to node j and a path from node j to node i.

The following definition is now made to describe the class of perturbations which is assumed may occur in (26).

Class of Structural Perturbations Allowed. Given the system (26), assume that any nonzero interconnection matrix A_{ij}, $i \neq j$, or groups of nonzero interconnection matrices may suddenly take on the value of zero. This will be called a *structural perturbation* [14] of the original interconnected system (26). This implies that, given a directed graph G = (N, L) representing the composite system (26), then a subgraph G_T of F is obtained if one or more interconnections from the original system are dropped.

The following definition is now made for the interconnected system (26).

Definition. The interconnected system (26) is called *decentrally retunable under structural perturbations* if after any structural perturbation imposed on the system, the ν control agents of (26) can always readjust their controllers, using local models of the resultant perturbed system, so as to solve the robust decentralized servomechanism problem for the resultant perturbed system.

The following result is now obtained:

Theorem 7. Given the interconnected system (26), assume that $m_i = r_i$, $i = 1, 2, \ldots, \nu$; then the system (26) is decentrally retunable under structural perturbations if and only if the following three conditions are all satisfied:

(i) The systems $\left\{C^m_{N_T}, A_{N_T}, B_{N_T}\right\}$ have no unstable decentralized fixed modes for every strongly connected subgraph $G_T = \{N_T, L_T\}$.

(ii) The systems $\{C_{N_T}, A_{N_T}, B_{N_T}\}$ have no transmission zeros [13] at $\lambda_1, \lambda_2, \ldots, \lambda_q$ for every strongly connected subgraph $G_T = \{N_T, L_T\}$.

(iii) $y_i \subset y^m_i$, $i = 1, 2, \ldots, \nu$, i.e., the output y_i is measurable.

Controller Synthesis. Given the system (26), assume that Theorem 7 holds; then the controllers can always readjust their controllers (using local models), after a structural perturbation, by using Algorithm I.

Remark 9. If the resulting perturbed system remains asymptotically stable, then the control agents can always readjust their controllers so as to satisfy the sequential stability constraint condition.

Corollary 1. If $m_i \geq r_i$, $i = 1, 2, \ldots, \nu$ in (26), then necessary conditions that the system (26) be decentrally retunable under structural perturbation are that conditions (i), (ii), (iii) of Theorem 7 all be satisfied.

Theorem 8. Given the interconnected system (26), assume that $C_i^m = I_{n_i}$, $i = 1, 2, \ldots, \nu$ (i.e., local state feedback of each subsystem is available) and that $m_i \geq r_i$, $i = 1, 2, \ldots, \nu$; then necessary and sufficient conditions for the system (26) to be decentrally retunable under structural perturbation are that the three conditions (i), (ii), (iii) of Theorem 7 all be satisfied.

Corollary 2. In (26), assume that $C_i^m = I_{n_i}$, $i = 1, 2, \ldots, \nu$; then a sufficient condition for (i) of Theorem 7 to be satisfied is that for every strongly connected subgraph $G_T = \{N_T, L_T\}$, the matrix pairs (A_{N_T}, B_{N_T}) be stabilizable.

To prove the above results, the following three lemmas are required:

Lemma 1. Given the system (26) with $C_i^m = I_{n_i}$, $i = 1, 2, \ldots, \nu$, assume that for every strongly connected subgraph $G_T = \{N_T, L_T\}$, the matrix pairs $\{A_{N_T}, B_{N_T}\}$ are stabilizable; then this implies that the system (26) has no unstable decentralized fixed modes.

Proof. The proof of this result follows directly on using the same development given in [15].

The following result is obtained which is an extension of Remark 5 obtained in [1], which deals with the case when $s = 0$.

Lemma 2. Given the system (1), assume that $m_i = r_i$, $i = 1, 2, \ldots, \nu$; then condition (2) of Theorem 1 will be satisfied if, and only if, the decentralized fixed modes of the q systems

$$\left\{\hat{C}_m^*, \begin{pmatrix} A & B \\ C & D + \lambda_j I \end{pmatrix}, \begin{pmatrix} \hat{B} \\ 0 \end{pmatrix}\right\}, \qquad j = 1, 2, \ldots, q,$$

do not contain λ_j, $j = 1, 2, \ldots, q$, respectively. If $m_i \geq r_i$, $i = 1, 2, \ldots, \nu$, then the above condition is necessary in order to satisfy condition (2) of Theorem 1.

Proof. The proof of this result follows by applying the same development as given in [1] to the system (1).

Remark 10. If $s = 0$ in (1), then the condition obtained in Lemma 2 is equivalent to the condition that the system (C, A, B, D) have no transmission zeros at λ_j, $j = 1, 2, \ldots, q$.

Lemma 3. Given (26), assume that $C_i^m = I_{n_i}$, $i = 1, 2, \ldots, \nu$, that $m_i \geq r_i$, and that the system $(C_{N_T}, A_{N_T}, B_{N_T})$ has no transmission zeros [13] at $\lambda_1, \lambda_2, \ldots, \lambda_q$ for every strongly connected subgraph $G_T = (N_T, L_T)$; then this implies that the q systems

$$\left\{\left[\begin{array}{c|c|c|c|c} I_{n_1+r_1} & 0 & 0 & \cdots & 0 \\ \hline 0 & I_{n_2+r_2} & 0 & \cdots & 0 \\ \hline \vdots & \vdots & \vdots & & \vdots \\ \hline 0 & 0 & 0 & \cdots & I_{n_\nu+r_\nu} \end{array}\right],\right.$$

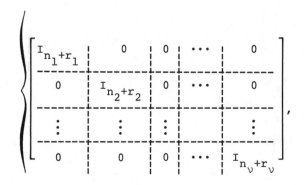

$$\left\{\left[\begin{array}{cc|cc|c|cc} A_{11} & 0 & A_{12} & 0 & & A_{1\nu} & 0 \\ C_1 & \lambda_j I & 0 & 0 & \cdots & 0 & 0 \\ \hline A_{21} & 0 & A_{22} & 0 & & A_{2\nu} & 0 \\ 0 & 0 & C_2 & \lambda_j I & \cdots & 0 & 0 \\ \hline \vdots & & \vdots & & & \vdots & \\ \hline A_{\nu 1} & 0 & A_{\nu 2} & 0 & & A_{\nu\nu} & 0 \\ 0 & 0 & 0 & 0 & \cdots & C_\nu & \lambda_j I \end{array}\right], \left[\begin{array}{c|c|c|c} B_1 & 0 & \cdots & 0 \\ 0 & 0 & \cdots & 0 \\ 0 & B_2 & \cdots & 0 \\ 0 & 0 & \cdots & 0 \\ \vdots & \vdots & & \\ 0 & 0 & \cdots & B_\nu \\ 0 & 0 & \cdots & 0 \end{array}\right]\right\}, \quad j = 1, 2, \ldots, q \tag{29}$$

have no decentralized fixed mode at λ_j, $j = 1, 2, \ldots, q$, respectively, and that all subsystems corresponding to the strongly connected subgraphs of (29) have no decentralized fixed mode at λ_j, $j = 1, 2, \ldots, q$, respectively.

Proof. It is assumed that:

$$\text{rank}\begin{bmatrix} A_{N_T} & -\lambda_j I & B_{N_T} \\ C_{N_T} & & 0 \end{bmatrix} = \sum_{i \in N_T} (n_i + r_i), \quad \forall N_T \in N,$$

which implies that $\forall N_T \in N$, λ_j is a controllable mode for the pairs:

$$\left\{\begin{pmatrix} A_{N_T} & 0 \\ C_{N_T} & \lambda_j I \end{pmatrix}, \begin{pmatrix} B_{N_T} \\ 0 \end{pmatrix}\right\}.$$

This immediately implies from Lemma 1, that λ_j is not a decentralized fixed mode for the system (29).

Proof of Theorem 7. The proof of necessity of Theorem 7 now immediately follows from Lemma 2, Remark 10, on noting that the requirement that (26) should satisfy the conditions of Theorem 1 for any structural perturbation requires that the resultant systems corresponding to the strongly connected subgraphs $G_T = (N_T, L_T)$ must all satisfy Theorem 1. The proof of sufficiency of Theorem 7 follows from Lemma 2, Remark 10 on noting that if conditions (i)-(iii) of Theorem 7 all hold, then this implies that Theorem 1 is satisfied for all structural perturbations of (26), and that Algorithm I can then be used to retune the controllers for the controllers for the system using local models.

The proof of Corollary 1, follows directly from Theorem 1 and from Lemma 2 applied to (26).

Proof of Theorem 8. The proof of necessity of Theorem 8 follows directly from Theorem 1 and Remark 10 applied to (26). The proof of sufficiency follows from Theorem 1, on noting that Lemma 3 implies that condition (2) of Theorem 1 is satisfied for all subsystems corresponding to the strongly connected subgraphs $G_T = (N_T, L_T)$ of (26).

The proof of Corollary 2 follows directly from Lemma 1 applied to condition (i) of Theorem 7.

VII. CONCLUSIONS

An overview of some results obtained for the decentralized control problem *using only local models* is made in this chapter. The motivation for examining this class of problems is that in large-scale systems it is often unrealistic to assume that a complete knowledge of the overall system is available to the control agents. A number of problems are considered in this context: (i) the *decentralized robust servomechanism problem with sequential stability* (in Section IV), (ii) the *expanding system problem* (in Section V), and the *retunability problem* (in Section VI).

The sequential stability constraint deals with the practical constraint of decentralized controller synthesis in which it is recognized that the decentralized controllers of a system cannot, in general, be applied to a system simultaneously. The expanding system problem deals with the case of determining under what type of conditions a new subsystem can be added to an existing controlled system, so that no retuning of the previous controllers obtained in the system is necessary. The retunability problem has considered the question of determining when control agents in an interconnected system can retune their controllers to solve the robust decentralized servomechanism problem, when the system is subject to structural perturbations. Clearly, if it is known that under certain structural perturbations, a system may result for which there is no solution, certain precautions may have to be taken; the identification of such cases is therefore important.

ACKNOWLEDGMENTS

This work has been supported by the National Sciences and Engineering Research Council, Canada under Grant No. A4396, and by NSF Grant ECS-8203877.

REFERENCES

1. E. J. DAVISON, "The robust decentralized control of a general servomechanism problem," *IEEE Trans. Automat. Control AC-21*, 16-24 (1976).

2. E. J. DAVISON, "The robust decentralized servomechanism problem with extra stabilizing control agents," *IEEE Trans. Atuomat. Control AC-22*, 256-258 (1977).

3. S. H. WANG, and E. J. DAVISON, "On the stabilization of decentralized control systems," *IEEE Trans. Automat. Control AC-18*, 473-478 (1973).

4. E. J. DAVISON and W. GESING, "Sequential stability and optimization of large scale decentralized systems," *Automatica 15*, 307-324 (1979).

5. E. J. DAVISON and Ü. ÖZGÜNER, "Synthesis of the decentralized robust servomechanism problem using local models," *IEEE Trans. Automat. Control AC-27* (3), 583-599 (1982).

6. E. J. DAVISON and A. GOLDENBERG, "The robust control of a general servomechanism problem: The servo-compensator," *Automatica 11*, 461-471 (1975).

7. E. J. DAVISON, "Robust control of a servomechanism problem for linear time-invariant multivariable systems," *IEEE Trans. Automat. Control AC-21*, 25-34 (1976).

8. E. J. DAVISON and I. FERGUSON, "The design of controllers for the multivariable robust servomechanism problem using parameter optimization methods," *IEEE Trans. Automat. Control AC-26*, 93-110 (1981).

9. E. J. DAVISON, W. GESING, and S. H. WANG, "An algorithm for obtaining the minimal realization of a linear time-invariant system and determining if a system is stabilizable-detectable," *IEEE Trans. Automat. Control AC-23*, 1048-1054 (1978).

10. E. J. DAVISON and S. H. WANG, "Properties of linear time-invariant multivariable systems subject to arbitrary output and state feedback," *IEEE Trans. Automat. Control AC-18*, 24-32 (1973).

11. H. H. ROSENBROCK, "Computer-Aided Design of Control Systems," New York, Academic Press, 1974.

12. E. J. DAVISON and Ü. ÖZGÜNER, "The expanding system problem," *Systems Control Lett. 1*, 255-260 (1982).

13. E. J. DAVISON and S. H. WANG, "Properties and calculation of transmission zeros of linear multivariable systems," *Automatica 10*, 643-658 (1974).

14. D. D. SILJAK, "Connective Stability of Competitive Equilibrium," *Automatica 11* (4), 389-400 (1975).

15. E. J. DAVISON and U. OZGUNER, "Characterizations of Decentralized Fixed Modes for Interconnected Systems," *Automatica 19* (2), 169-182 (1983).

Learning Automata in Distributed Control Systems

YOUSRI M. EL-FATTAH

Faculty of Sciences
University Mohamed V
Rabat, Morocco

I. INTRODUCTION

The simplest model of a learning system is that of the behavior of a finite sutomaton in a stationary random environment, simulating "a small animal in a big world" [1]. The automaton has a finite number, say $r \geq 2$, of actions available. For each

ISBN 0-12-012722-9

action used by the automaton, the environment responds with a reward or penalty. The penalty probability for each action is unknown a priori. The behavior of an automaton is called expedient if the average penalty is less than the value corresponding to the choice of all possible actions with equal probabilities. The behavior is called optimal or ϵ-optimal if the average penalty is equal or arbitrarily close, respectively, to the minimum value. Vershavskii and Vorontsova [2] demonstrated that the basic concepts and results for finite automata derived previously in Tsetlin's [1] work carry over to stochastic automata. They indicated that the functioning process of a stochastic automaton with variable structure (learning automaton) can be treated as the synthesis of a finite automaton according to a certain criterion; specifically, minimum expected average penalty. "The synthesis of a finite automaton" means the determination of the updating mechanism of the automaton's action (output) probabilities. That mechanism is usually called a "reinforcement scheme."

Since the aforementioned works, a growing interest in the theory and applications of learning automata has been taking place. For surveys on the subject, see Narendra and Thathachar [3] and Narendra and Lakshmivarahan [4].

A learning automaton can be employed as a basic instrument for distributed control systems. A distributed control system consists of a collective of interacting decision-making elements (automata) functioning in a common environment and cooperating more or less to achieve a global objective. The information exchange between the automata is generally limited; for example, an automaton is supposed to communicate only with its neighbors.

In other words, the information structure is generally non-classical; that is, each decision-making element has partial information about the environment.

Interesting applications for distributed control systems are adaptive routing in communication networks (telephone or data networks) and task scheduling in multiple-processor distributed computer systems (cf. Glorioso and Colon Osorio [5]). Extended study on application of learning automata for routing in communication networks has been carried out by Narendra, Mars, and co-workers [6-11].

In the present paper the distributed control problem is modeled as a problem of collective behavior of learning automata in a random environment. Analytical results are given concerning the collective behavior of automata, specifically the characterization of the equilibrium situation, convergence, and rate of convergence. Applications of the results to adaptive routing in telephone and store-and-forward networks are outlined.

II. LEARNING AUTOMATA MODELS

A. LEARNING AUTOMATON

A learning automaton A is modeled as a stochastic automaton with variable structure characterized by the six-tuple

$$A = \langle U, X, Y, F, G, T \rangle$$

where

(1) U is the input set that characterizes the automaton models as follows:

(i) If the input set U is binary, {0, 1}, the automata model is classified as a *P model*.

(ii) If U belongs to the finite set $\{u_1, u_2, \ldots, u_q\}$ with elements in the interval [0, 1], the automaton is classified as a *Q model*.

(iii) If U is a real number in the interval [0, 1], the automaton is classified as an *S model*.

(2) X is the set of s internal states $\{x_1, x_2, \ldots, x_s\}$ where $s < \infty$ corresponds in some sense to the memory capacity of a finite automaton.

(3) $Y = \{y_1, y_2, \ldots, y_r\}$ is the output or action set with $r \leq s$.

(4) F is the transition function providing a means of determining the next state of the automaton $x(n + 1)$, given the input $u(n)$ and the current state $x(n)$:

$$x(n + 1) = F(x(n), u(n));$$

n denotes the time step, considered to be a discrete variable taking on the values 1, 2, ... F is a stochastic function, that is, for each pair $x(n)$ and $u(n)$ a probability distribution is associated on the state set.

(5) G is the output function that defines the value of the output variable y in each state $y(n) = G(x(n))$. G may be stochastic or deterministic.

(6) T is the mechanism, also called an updating or *reinforcement scheme*, that changes the structure of the automaton (i.e., the transition function F). It can be seen that T may be equivalently described as the mechanism for changing the action probability vector

$$P(n) = (p_1(n), p_2(n), \ldots, p_r(n))$$

where $p_i(n)$ denotes the probability of taking the ith action at time n. Note that P(n) must belong to the simplex

$$S_r = \left\{ P \in R^r : p_i \geq 0, \sum_{i=1}^{r} p_i = 1 \right\}. \tag{1}$$

The role of the updating operation is to modify the automaton state so as to reflect the experience gained through the received response. For our purposes, the reinforcement scheme T is the function

$$P(n + 1) = T(n, u(n), y(n), P(n)), \quad n = 1, 2, \ldots .$$

In other words, based on the latest action taken y(n), and the response u(n) to it, the learning automaton modifies its action probability vector at the next time step according to the reinforcement scheme T.

B. ENVIRONMENT

A learning automaton operates in a random environment with random response characteristics. The environment accepts inputs from a set $Y = \{y_1, \ldots, y_r\}$ and produces outputs belonging to the set U.

Corresponding to every input set Y there is an associated probability set C, called the *penalty probability set*, where

$$C = \{C_1, \ldots, C_r\}$$

and

$$C_i = \text{Prob}(u = 1 \mid y = y_i)$$

for P models, and

$$C = \{C_{ij}, i = 1, 2, \ldots, r; j = 1, 2, \ldots, q\}$$

where

$$C_{ij} = \text{Prob}(u = u_j \mid y = y_i)$$

for Q models, and

$$C = \{C_1(\xi), C_2(\xi), \ldots, C_r(\xi)\}$$

$$C_i(\xi) = \text{Prob}(u \leq \xi \mid y = y_i), \quad \xi \in [0, 1]$$

for S models. If the set C is constant and independent of time, the environment is said to be *stationary*.

Figure 1A indicates the features of a learning automaton, Fig. 1B that of a random environment, while Fig. 1C shows a learning automaton and a random environment in a feedback configuration.

To analyze the behavior of a learning automaton in a random environment, it is necessary to devise a criterion for evaluating the automaton's performance at consecutive epochs. The most widely used measures have been (i) the *average penalty*, also called the Tsetlin function [12], received by the automaton at consecutive times

$$M(n) = E(u(n)/P(n)) \tag{2}$$

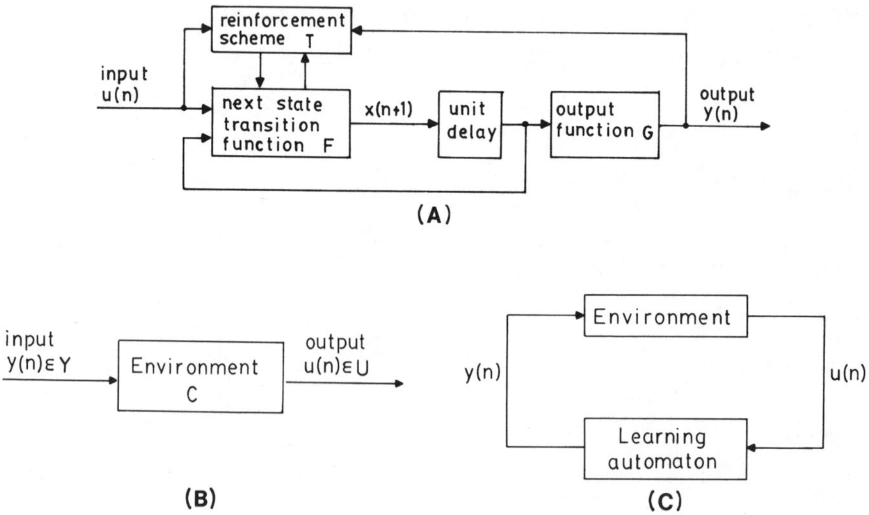

Fig. 1. (A) Learning automaton. (B) Random environment. (C) Feedback configuration.

and (ii) the *Liapunov criterion* measuring the distance between the current action probability and the optimal one

$$V(P(n)) = \sum_{i=1}^{r} \left(p_i(n) - \overset{*}{p}_i\right)^2 \quad (3)$$

where $P^* = \left(\overset{*}{p}_1, \overset{*}{p}_2, \ldots, \overset{*}{p}_r\right)$ denotes the optimal action probability. While the average penalty criterion is very suitable for physical description, the Liapunov criterion is more suitable for analytical purposes.

C. BEHAVIOR CLASSIFICATION

Let us for now concern ourselves with the case of a P model and stationary random environment. It is customary to classify a learning automaton's behavior as follows:

Careless: A learning automaton is called careless if it chooses all actions with equal probability, which yields the average penalty

$$M_0 = (C_1 + C_2 + \cdots + C_r)/r.$$

Expedient: A learning automaton is called expedient if it asymptotically "behaves" better than a careless automaton, i.e.,

$$\lim_{n\to\infty} EM(n) < M_0.$$

Optimal: A learning automaton is called optimal if

$$\lim_{n\to\infty} EM(n) = C_\ell$$

where

$$C_\ell = \min(C_1, C_2, \ldots, C_r).$$

Therefore, optimality means that asymptotically M(n), the average penalty, achieves its minimum value.

ϵ-optimal: A learning automaton is called ϵ-optimal if for each $\epsilon > 0$ it is possible to adjust a reinforcement scheme

parameter δ so that

$$\lim_{n\to\infty} EM(n) \leq C_\ell + \epsilon.$$

ϵ-Optimality means that the performance of the automaton can be made as close to optimal as desired.

D. REINFORCEMENT SCHEMES

The basic idea behind any reinforcement scheme is rather simple. If a learning automaton selects an action y_i at time n and a nonpenalty input occurs, the action probability $p_i(n)$ is increased and all other components of P(n) are decreased. For a penalty input, $p_i(n)$ is decreased and the other components are increased. The changes in $p_i(n)$ are known for P models as reward (u = 0) and penalty (u = 1), respectively. In some models, the action probabilities do not change; for these cases, the term "inaction" has been coined. If the inaction takes place in case of a reward response, the automaton is called "severe." If the inaction corresponds to a penalty response, the automaton is called "benevolent."

For P models a reinforcement scheme can be expressed in the following general form:

If $y(n) = i$ and $u(n) = 0$, then

$$p_i(n + 1) = p_i(n) + \sum_{j\neq i} \psi_j(P(n))$$

$$p_j(n + 1) = p_j(n) - \psi_j(P(n)), \quad j \neq i.$$

If $y(n) = i$ and $u(n) = 1$, then

$$p_i(n + 1) = p_i(n) - \sum_{j\neq i} \varphi_j(P(n))$$

$$p_j(n + 1) = p_j(n) + \varphi_j(P(n)), \quad j \neq i,$$

where ψ_j and φ_j are nonnegative continuous functions. Furthermore, the restriction that $P(n) \in S_r$ is required.

If ψ_j and φ_j are linear functions of $P(n)$, the reinforcement scheme is called linear. In contrast, schemes involving higher orders of $P(n)$ are described as nonlinear. Examples of nonlinear schemes are the benevolent automaton of Lakshmivarahan and Thathacher [13] and the reward-penalty automaton of Varshavskii and Vorontsova [2]. In the majority of applications, the linear schemes are of the greatest interest due to their simplicity.

An example of a class of commonly used linear automata (P model) are given by the following reinforcement scheme:

If $y(n) = i$ and $u(n) = 0$, then

$$\begin{aligned} p_i(n+1) &= p_i(n) + a(1 - p_i(n)) \\ p_j(n+1) &= (1 - a)p_j(n), \quad \text{all } j \neq i \end{aligned} \tag{4a}$$

If $y(n) = i$ and $u(n) = 1$, then

$$\begin{aligned} p_i(n+1) &= (1 - b)p_i(n) \\ p_j(n+1) &= p_j(n) + \frac{b}{r-1} p_i(n), \quad \text{all } j \neq i \end{aligned} \tag{4b}$$

where a and b are some constants: $0 < a, b < 1$.

If $0 < a < 1$ and $b = 1 - a$, the above scheme becomes the scheme of Bush and Mosteller [14] (Tsypkin and Poznyak [15]). In the symmetric case when $a = b$ the above scheme is called the L_{R-P} algorithm [10]. When $b = o(a)$, where $o(a)$ implies $o(a)/a \to 0$ as $a \to 0$, the resulting scheme is called the $L_{R-\epsilon P}$ algorithm (cf. [10]).

The L_{R-I} automaton (reward-inaction) corresponding to the P model is a particular case of the scheme (4) when the punishment coefficient is set to zero, i.e., $b = 0$, (cf. [16]).

For the S model the L_{R-I} automaton corresponds to the following reinforcement scheme:

$$\begin{aligned} &\text{If } y(n) = i \text{ and } u(n) = u \ (0 \le u \le 1), \text{ then} \\ &p_i(n+1) = p_i(n) + a(1-u)(1-p_i(n)) \\ &p_j(n+1) = p_j(n) - a(1-u)p_j(n) \quad \text{all} \quad j \neq i, \end{aligned} \tag{5}$$

where a is some constant, $0 < a < 1$.

Another class of sutomata, called "estimating automata" or "stochastic approximation automata," has the characteristics that the "forcing term" in the reinforcement scheme explicitly depends on an estimate of a "penalty indicator index," which is a time-varying function of P(n), the automaton's action, and the environment's response [17-19]. In its general form, the reinforcement scheme of an estimating automaton can be written as

$$\begin{aligned} &\text{If } y(n) = i \text{ and } u(n) = u \ (0 \le u \le 1), \text{ then} \\ &p_i(n+1) = p_i(n) - \min(\nu(n)\theta(n, i, u, P(n)), \Delta_i) \\ &p_j(n+1) = p_j(n) + \frac{1}{r-1} \min(\nu(n)\theta(n, i, u, P(n)), \Delta_i) \\ &\qquad\qquad \text{all} \quad j \neq i. \end{aligned} \tag{6}$$

where θ denotes the penalty indicator index, in general time varying, and Δ_i is the upper bound on the "step length" so that $P(n+1)$ still remains in the simplex S_r. Δ_i is given by

$$\Delta_i = \min(p_i, (r-1)(1 - \max_{j \neq i} p_j)). \tag{7}$$

The sequence $\nu(n)$ is in general time varying and satisfies the conditions

$$\nu(n) \ge 0, \qquad \sum_{n=1}^{\infty} \nu(n) = \infty. \tag{8}$$

The penalty indicator index θ may be thought of as the realization of the gradient of some "cost function" (cf. [15]).

An example for an estimating automaton is given by the following scheme for the P model (cf. [20]):

If $y(n) = i$ and $u(n) = 0$, then

$$P(n + 1) = P(n) \tag{9a}$$

If $y(n) = i$ and $u(n) = 1$, then

$$\begin{aligned} p_i(n + 1) &= p_i(n) - \min\left(\frac{\nu_0}{n}, \Delta_i\right) \\ p_j(n + 1) &= p_j(n) + \frac{1}{r - 1} \min\left(\frac{\nu_0}{n}, \Delta_i\right) \quad \text{all} \quad j \neq i, \end{aligned} \tag{9b}$$

where $\nu_0 > 0$.

The automaton corresponding to the above scheme is called E_{I-P} (estimating inaction penalty). In contradistinction with the automaton L_{R-I}, the automaton E_{I-P} does not respond to reward. E_{I-P} is a "severe" automaton as it responds only to "negative outcomes."

For the S model, the E_{I-P} automaton corresponds to the following reinforcement scheme:

If $y(n) = i$ and $u(n) = u$ $(0 \leq u \leq 1)$, then

$$\begin{aligned} p_i(n + 1) &= p_i(n) - \min\left(\frac{\nu_0}{n} u, \Delta_i\right) \\ p_j(n + 1) &= p_j(n) + \frac{1}{r - 1} \min\left(\frac{\nu_0}{n} u, \Delta_i\right) \quad \text{all} \quad j \neq i. \end{aligned} \tag{10}$$

E. NONSTATIONARY ENVIRONMENT

So far, the environment is assumed to be stationary, memoryless, and its characteristics unaffected by the automaton's behavior. Indeed, the optimal action probability P^* in that case is a Dirac measure. For example, for the P model, P^* is given by

$$\overset{*}{P}_i = \delta_\ell = \begin{cases} 1 & \text{if } i = \ell, \\ 0 & \text{if } i \neq \ell, \end{cases} \tag{11}$$

where

$$\ell = \min_i(\min_{C_i}(C_1, C_2, \ldots, C_r)).$$

Learning is, however, essentially valuable when the environment is either nonstationary and/or its characteristics, like the automaton, self-adjusts as a function of the automaton's behavior.

Narendra and his co-workers [9,10] have proposed two mathematical models to describe the behavior of learning automata in nonstationary environments. In the first model, the environment's response characteristics are affected by the action of the automaton. The second model assumes that the penalty probabilities characterizing the environment C are a function of the probabilities P with which such actions are selected. The latter environment model is called the class of *nonautonomous environments*. In the routing problem in telephone or computer communication networks, the network represents a nonautonomous environment when an automaton routing controller is used to select an outgoing link. By choosing a certain link with a high probability, that channel obviously becomes less attractive due to increased delay or call or data blocking caused by the higher traffic rate. On the other hand, the alternative channel which is not used for an interval of time is handling less traffic and therefore produces a better response. In general, for a nonautonomous environment the "optimal" action probability is an interior point of the simplex S_r, and not a boundary point as in the case of autonomous environments, Eq. (11).

III. DISTRIBUTED CONTROL SYSTEMS

A distributed control system may be modeled as a game of collective behavior of N automata in a random environment. Let I denote the set of all automata players. Each automaton will be assigned a number so that I = {1, 2, ..., N}. Let each automaton have at its disposal a certain set Y^i of available actions which are referred to in the theory of games as (pure) strategies. Y^i is assumed to consist of r^i strategies numbered 1 through r^i. At the beginning of each time epoch n (=0, 1, 2, ...) of the game, each player chooses a mixed strategy $P^i(n)$ which is a probability on Y^i, and holds it fixed throughout that time epoch. P^i will be specified as the r^i row vector $\left(p_1^i, p_2^i, \ldots, p_{r^i}^i\right)$, where $p_k^i = P^i(y^i = k)$, and thus belongs to the $r^i - 1$ dimensional simplex S_{r^i}. The probability of arriving at a collective play $y = (y^1, y^2, \ldots, y^N)$ is assumed to be the *product* of probabilities of choosing its components: $P^1(y^1)p^2 \times (y^2) \cdots p^N(y^N)$. Thus we arrive at the probability distribution P on the set of all plays $Y = \prod_{i\in I} Y^i$ defined by

$$P(y) = \prod_{i\in I} P^i(y^i)$$

for all collective plays y in the game. These types of probability distributions P are called *situations in mixed strategies*. Note that P belongs to the product simplex $S = \prod_{i\in I} S_{r^i}$.

A time epoch n denotes the time interval $n\Delta \leq t < (n + 1)\Delta$. At the start of each epoch each ith automaton generates a strategy $y^i(n) \in Y^i$ according to the probability distribution $P^i(n)$. Thus, during each epoch a collective play y(n) is formed. Following that play, each ith automaton observes the environment response in continuous time and evaluates at the end of the nth epoch that response by the loss-indicator index $u^i(n+1)$. The loss-indicator index is assumed to be a random variable taking values in the set of real numbers [0, 1] and having finite first and second moments. Furthermore, for each n the first and second moments of $u^i(n+1)$ (all $i \in I$) are entirely determined by the situation P(n) in mixed strategies. That is,

$$E(u^i(n+1) \mid y^i(n) = j;\ P(n)) = C^i_j(P(n)) \tag{12a}$$

$$E((u^i(n+1))^2 \mid y^i(n) = j;\ P(n)) = D^i_j(P(n)). \tag{12b}$$

The loss-rate from the jth strategy for the ith automaton at epoch n is given by the function

$$\begin{aligned} f^i_j(P(n)) &= E(u^i(n+1)1(y^i(n) = j) \mid P(n)) \\ &= C^i_j(P(n))p^i_j(n). \end{aligned} \tag{13}$$

Here $1(\cdot)$ denotes the indicator function of $(\cdot)$.

Henceforth, we make use of the following assumptions:

A.1. $0 < C^i_j(P) < 1$ and $C^i_j(P)$ is a continuous function on the simplex S.

A.2. The derivatives $\partial C^i_j(P)/\partial p^i_j$ exist and satisfy the condition

$$\partial C^i_j(P)/\partial p^i_k \begin{cases} \geq 0 & \text{if } k = j, \\ = 0 & \text{if } k \neq j. \end{cases}$$

The above assumption has the following interpretation: the environment increases the penalty (loss) probability corresponding to an action as the frequency of using that action (strategy) by the automaton increases. The aim of the automata collective is to behave in the environment in a way that asymptotically yields expediency for each member of the collective. Expediency may be defined as a situation where the loss rate is equalized on the set of strategies for every automaton. That is, for each automaton $i \in I$ an expedient (mixed) strategy at a situation P is the strategy $\hat{p}^i$ which yields the system of equalities:

$$\hat{p}_1^i c_1^i(P) = \hat{p}_2^i c_2^i(P) = \cdots \hat{p}_{r^i}^i c_{r^i}^i(P). \tag{14}$$

Let us now show that there exists a solution for the above equation. First, let us define for every system of "foreign" strategies P^j, $j \neq i$, the vector function $g^i: S_{r^i} \to S_{r^i}$ given by

$$g^i(P^i) = \left(g_1^i(P),\ g_2^i(P),\ \ldots,\ g_{r^i}^i(P)\right)$$

where

$$g_j^i(P) = \left(c_j^i(P)\right)^{-1} \Bigg/ \sum_{k=1}^{r^i} \left(c_k^i(P)\right)^{-1}.$$

Under A.1 it is obvious that $g^i(P^i)$ is a continuous mapping of S_{r^i} into itself. Second, since S_{r^i} is a closed simplex, it follows from the Brouwer fixed-point theorem (cf. [21]) that a $\hat{P}^i$ exists such that $\hat{P}^i = g^i(\hat{P}^i)$. It is possible to show that $\hat{P}^i(P)$ is unique. Assume that this is not so; that is, there exist two values for $\hat{P}^i$, say $\hat{P}^{i(1)}$ and $\hat{P}^{i(2)}$. If $\hat{P}^{i(1)} \neq \hat{P}^{i(2)}$, then it is possible to decompose Y^i into two disjoint nonvoid sets

$$Y^{i+} = \left\{j : p_j^{i(2)} > p_j^{i(1)}\right\}$$

$$Y^{i-} = \left\{j : p_j^{i(2)} > p_j^{i(1)}\right\}.$$

Since c_j^i is monotonically nondecreasing with respect to p_j^i (assumption A.2) and $0 < c_j^i < 1$, it then follows that $p_j^i c_j^i$ takes strictly higher values on the set $j \in Y^{i+}$ than on the set

$j \in Y^{i-}$. Hence, there can be no admissible variation from $\hat{P}^{i(1)}$ which satisfies the system of equalities (14). Hence, $\hat{P}^{i(2)} = \hat{P}^{i(1)}$. We state the above results in the following theorem:

Theorem 1. If assumptions A.1 and A.2 hold, then for every system of foreign strategies P^j, $j \neq i$, there exists a unique expedient strategy $\hat{P}^i(P)$ satisfying the system of equalities (14).

Since S is a closed simplex and

$$\hat{P}(P) = (\hat{P}^1(P), \hat{P}^2(P), \ldots, \hat{P}^N(P))$$

is a continuous mapping of S into itself, it follows again from the Brouwer fixed-point theorem (cf. [21]) that a $\overline{P}$ exists satisfying the system of equations

$$\overline{P} = \hat{P}(\overline{P}).$$

Alternatively stated, at $\overline{P}$ we have the system of equations

$$\overline{P}_1^i C_1^i(\overline{P}) = \overline{P}_2^i C_2^i(\overline{P}) = \cdots = \overline{P}_{r^i}^i C_{r^i}^i(\overline{P}), \quad \text{all} \quad i \in I. \tag{15}$$

$\overline{P}$ is called a *collective expedient equilibrium* since at $\overline{P}$ expediency is attained for *all* the automata. The expedient value of the average loss rate for each ith automaton is given by

$$f^i(\overline{P}) = r^i \Bigg/ \left(\sum_{j=1}^{r^i} \left(C_j^i(\overline{P}) \right)^{-1} \right), \quad \text{all} \quad i \in I. \tag{16}$$

IV. ANALYSIS OF COLLECTIVE BEHAVIOR

A. CONVERGENCE

Let us study the collective behavior of NE_{I-P} automata. First, let us determine the equilibrium situation for those automata in its S-model version (10) in the nonautonomous environment characterized by (12). To do so, we determine the expected value of the forcing term of each ith automaton in an arbitrary situation P(n). Following (10) and (12a), we have for sufficiently small values of $\Delta p_j^i(n)$,

$$E\left(\Delta p_j^i(n) \mid P(n)\right) = -\frac{\nu_0}{n}\Bigg(E(u^i(n+1)1(y^i(n)=j) \mid P(n)) - \frac{1}{r^i-1}\sum_{k\neq j} E(u^i(n+1)1(y^i(n)=k) \mid P(n))\Bigg)$$

$$= -\frac{\nu_0}{n}\left(\frac{r^i}{r^i-1}\left(c_j^i(P(n))p_j^i(n) - \frac{1}{r^i}\sum_{k=1}^{r^i} c_k^i(P(n))p_k^i(n)\right)\right). \tag{17}$$

The equilibrium corresponds to the situation where

$$E\left(\Delta p_j^i(n) \mid P(n)\right) = 0. \tag{18}$$

Hence, the equilibrium is defined by the system of equations

$$c_j^i(P)p_j^i - \frac{1}{r^i}\sum_{k=1}^{r^i} c_k^i(P)p_k^i = 0 \quad \text{all} \quad i,\ j. \tag{19}$$

The above is equivalent to the condition of collective expediency stated in (15). In other words, the equilibrium of the collective of the E_{I-P} automata is attained at the expedient strategy $\overline{P}$. At $\overline{P}$ the behavior of the automata corresponds to the martingale equation (18). This means that at equilibrium each ith automaton does not change on the average its mixed strategy $P^i(n)$, i.e., $EP^i(n)$ becomes independent of n.

It can also be shown that the second moment of the jth component of the forcing term for each ith automaton, provided that ΔP_j^i is sufficiently small, can be written as

$$E\left(\Delta p_j^i(n)^2 \mid P(n)\right)$$

$$= \left(\frac{\nu_0}{n}\right)^2 \left(p_j^i(n) D_j^i(P(n)) + \left(\frac{1}{r^i - 1}\right)^2 \sum_{k \neq j} p_k^i(n) D_k^i(P(n))\right)$$

$$= \left(\frac{\nu_0}{n}\right)^2 F_j^i(P(n)). \tag{20}$$

Let us now examine the convergence of the automata situation in mixed strategies toward the expedient equilibrium $\overline{P}$. Let us introduce the Liapunov function

$$V(P) = \sum_{i \in I} \sum_{j \in Y^i} \left(p_j^i - \overline{p}_j^i\right)^2. \tag{21}$$

In view of the reinforcement scheme (10) we can write

$$E(V(P(n + 1)) \mid P(n))$$

$$= \sum_{i \in I} \sum_{j \in Y^i} E\left(\left(p_j^i(n) + \Delta p_j^i(n) - \overline{p}_j^i\right)^2 \mid P(n)\right)$$

$$= V(P(n)) + 2 \sum_{i \in I} \sum_{j \in Y^i} \left(p_j^i(n) - \overline{p}_j^i\right) E\left(\Delta p_j^i(n) \mid P(n)\right)$$

$$+ \sum_{i \in I} \sum_{j \in Y^i} E\left(\left(\Delta p_j^i(n)\right)^2 \mid P(n)\right). \tag{22}$$

Substituting (17) and (20) into the above and making use of the contraction property of the projection operator implied in (10), yields

$$E(V(P(n + 1)) \mid P(n))$$

$$= V(P(n)) - 2\frac{\nu_0}{n} \sum_{i \in I} \frac{r^i}{r^i - 1} \sum_{j \in Y^i} \left(p_j^i(n) - \overline{p}_j^i\right)$$

$$\times\ p_j^i(n)c_j^i(P(n)) + \left(\frac{\nu_0}{n}\right)^2 \sum_{i\in I} \sum_{j\in Y^i} F_j^i(P(n)). \tag{23}$$

It is shown in Appendix C that there exists a strictly positive number $\rho > 0$ so that

$$\sum_{i\in I} \sum_{j\in Y^i} \left(p_j^i - \bar{p}_j^i\right) p_j^i c_j^i(P) \geq \rho V(P) \tag{24}$$

holds for all $P \in S$. The above implies a collective monotonicity property: a variant of the concept of a monotonically increasing function, generalized to the case of the collection of functions $p_j^i c_j^i(P)$, $i \in I$, $j \in Y^i$. Substituting (24) into (23) yields

$$\begin{aligned} &E(V(P(n+1)) \mid P(n)) \\ &\quad \leq V(P(n)) - \frac{\nu_0}{n}\rho_1 V(P(n)) \\ &\qquad + \left(\frac{\nu_0}{n}\right)^2 \sum_{i\in I} \sum_{j\in Y^i} F_j^i(P(n)), \end{aligned} \tag{25}$$

where

$$\rho_1 = 2\rho \min_i r^i/(r^i - 1).$$

It follows from (25) that $V(n)$ is a nonnegative almost supermartingale and we can apply the convergence theorem of Robbins and Siegmund; see Appendix A. First, note that the functions $F_j^i(\cdot)$ are continuous functions on the closed simplex S and consequently are uniformly bounded,

$$F_j^i(P(n)) \leq L_{ij} \quad \text{all} \quad i, j. \tag{26}$$

Hence, the convergence of the series

$$\sum_{n=1}^{\infty} \sum_{i\in I} \left(\frac{\nu_0}{n}\right)^2 \sum_{j\in Y^i} F_j^i(P(n))$$

is ensured. Second, the Robbins-Siegmund theorem yields that $V(P(n))$ converges almost surely to a random variable, and

$$\sum_{n=1}^{\infty} \frac{\nu_0}{n} V(P(n)) < \infty \text{ almost surely.} \tag{27}$$

The above, and the positivity property of the function V, automatically imply that $V(P(n))$ converges to 0 almost surely. Hence, the following theorem:

Theorem 2. Under the underlying assumptions the collective behavior of the automata E_{I-P} converges to the expedient collective strategy $\overline{P}$ given by (15) with probability 1.

B. RATE OF CONVERGENCE

Taking the expectation of (25) on both sides and making use of (26) yields the inequality

$$\lambda(n+1) \leq \lambda(n) - \frac{\nu_0}{n} \rho_1 \lambda(n) + \left(\frac{\nu_0}{n}\right)^2 L \tag{28}$$

where

$$\lambda(n) = EV(P(n))$$

and

$$L = \sum_{i \in I} \sum_{j \in Y^i} L_{ij}.$$

If follows from Theorem 1 of Al'ber and Shil'man (see Appendix B) that

$$\lim_{n \to \infty} \lambda(n) = 0. \tag{29}$$

The rate of convergence of $\lambda(n)$ can be determined from Theorem 2 of Al'ber and Shil'man (see Appendix B). Using the notation in the appendix we can write

$$s = 2, \quad b = \nu_0\rho_1, \quad d = \nu_0^2 L, \quad c = \nu_0^2 L(c_0/b + 1),$$
$$\overline{C} = 1. \tag{30}$$

We can then readily obtain the following result:

Theorem 3. Under the underlying assumptions we have $\lambda(n) \to 0$ and

(1) If $1 < \nu_0\rho_1$, then for any $c_0 \geq \nu_0\rho_1/(\nu_0\rho_1 - 1)$ (or $a = (c_0 - 1)/c_0$) and for $\lambda(1) > c$, we have the bounds

$$\lambda(n) \leq \lambda(1)(1/(n - 1))^{ab}, \quad 2 \leq n < \overline{x} = (\lambda(1)/c)^{1/(ab-1)} + 1 \tag{31a}$$

$$\lambda(n) \leq c(1/(n - 1)), \quad n > \overline{x} \tag{31b}$$

(2) If $1 < \nu_0\rho_1$ and $1 < c_0 < \nu_0\rho_1/(\nu_0\rho_1 - 1)$, or $1 \geq b$ and $c_0 > 1$, then we have for any $n \geq 2$ the bound

$$\lambda(n) \leq (1/(n - 1))^{ab} \max(\lambda(1), c). \tag{32}$$

V. ADAPTIVE ROUTING IN COMMUNICATION NETWRKS

A communication network consists of a number of channels and switching equipment to enable the channels of the network to be employed in various ways according to the need of its users [22]. A network that can connect its channels in such a way as to establish a single continuous channel for the transmission of signals between two terminals is called a *circuit switching* network. A network in which signals are switched from the transmitter toward their destination using channels as they become available, and in which they are stored at an intermediate point when no channel is available, is called a *message switching* network. The classic example of a network using circuit switching is the telephone network. The switching is performed at exchanges. The public telegraph network uses message switching.

A recent development is *packet-switching* networks that are suitable for such applications as real-time and interactive communication between any pair of computers of a set connected to a network [23,24]. Neither circuit- nor message-switching networks are entirely suitable for this purpose: in the former, there is always some probability of not being able to communicate because a continuous channel cannot be established, while the latter is suitable for one-way communication only.

Packet-switching networks use *store-and-forward* methods. The shortcomings of message switching are overcome by dividing messages into comparatively short fixed-length segments called "packets" which are then transmitted over the network. A packet can be handled in a short known time by a switching center. The long delays that a lengthy message can cause while using a channel or a center in message-switching networks are eliminated.

A. CIRCUIT-SWITCHING NETWORKS

Communication is established between two terminals attached to a circuit-switching network by causing the switching centers in the network to operate switches that physically connect channels in the network and to create a single continuous channel between them. Each terminal of the network is connected to an exchange called its *local exchange* where switching equipment is located. However, the geographical distribution of the locations of the terminals may make it more economical for a network to have a number of local exchanges than it is to connect all the terminals to one exchange. In this case, the local exchanges must themselves be connected by exchanges, which in the telephone network are called *trunk exchanges*. A two-level network of this kind is illustrated in Fig. 2A. To establish communication between two terminals not attached to the same local exchange, at least three switching operations are necessary: one at the local exchange of the transmitter, one at the local exchange of the receiver, and one at a trunk exchange.

A hierarchy of switching centers is created in a circuit-switching network in an attemp to reach the optimum balance between transmission and switching for a particular network. The AT&T network has five levels of switching: it has local exchanges and four levels of trunk exchanges (see Fig. 2B). In general, the network has N nodes labeled 1, 2, ..., N and r_i, i = 1, 2, ..., N, trunk groups connected to the ith node. Thus, each node may be able to communicate directly with up to N - 1 other nodes. A call of class i, j is a session of communication between the calling node i and some node j. A route R_{ij}, from node i to j, is an ordered sequence of trunk groups (T_{ia}, T_{ab}, ..., T_{fj}) connected to provide a path for a call of class i, j. Using learning automata, the establishment of a route R_{ij} for a call of class i, j requires a chain of distributed routing decisions, each carried out by an independent automaton (A^i, A^a, A^b, ..., A^f). The automaton A^i for the ith node can be thought of as a collection of automata

$$A^i = \left(A^i_1, A^i_2, \ldots, A^i_N\right)$$

where the A^i_j automaton, $j \neq i$, serves as trunk selector for calls of destination j. The action set of automaton A^i_j corresponds to the outgoing trunk groups of the ith node.

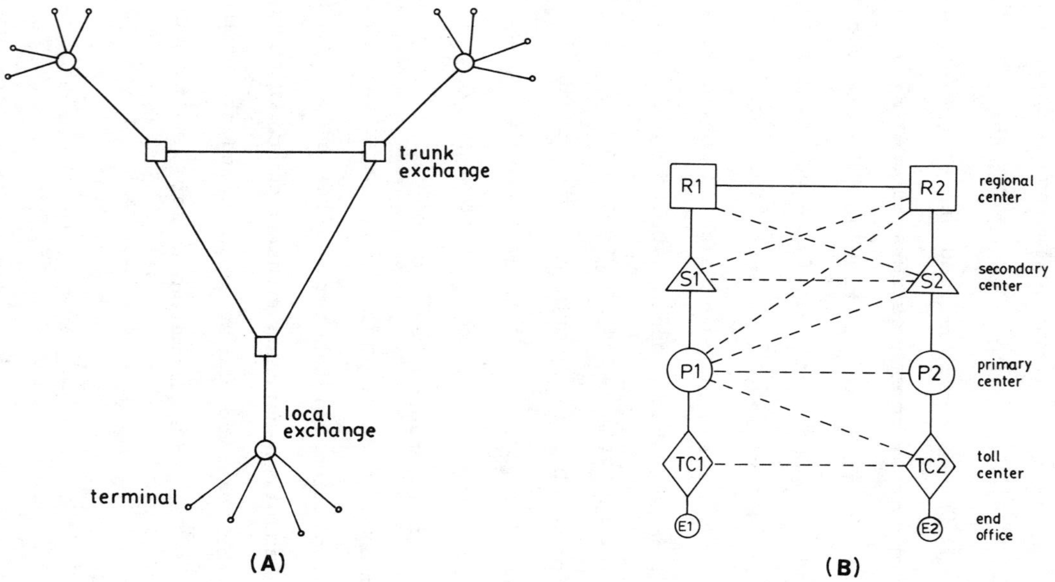

Fig. 2. (A) Two-level network. (B) AT&T network hierarchy.

If a call originating at node i and destined for node j is at node k, and there are r_k allowable trunk groups at node k, the call will be offered to one of these trunk groups using a routing scheme. If this trunk group is busy, the call is offered to an alternative link and the process is repeated until either a free link is found or the call is rejected.

If a fixed rule [25] which is currently used in the AT&T network is employed, the call is offered to the r_k links in a specific order (the most direct path first and then the backbone routes). If a learning automaton is used, the order in which the links are chosen is altered using feedback information regarding call completion or rejection. Call completion (termed win) and call rejection (termed loss) are used to update the automata actions.

As mentioned earlier, in a learning routing scheme independent automata at each node select a suitable trunk group from an allowable set. A complete routing operation is therefore a chain of decisions, the route taking one of several paths. Feedback in such schemes is quite simple, a blocked call producing a loss to *all* automata in the chain, the successful call giving a corresponding sequence of wins.

The principal reason for using learning rules for routing calls is to minimize the blocking probability of the network. Using the Erlang formula, it can be demonstrated that the loss (blocking) probability set for the automata satisfy Assumption 1 (see [26,10]). Furthermore, at least for the simple four node network (cf. [26]), the minimum average blocking probability is attained at the expedient equilibrium defined by (15).

The measures that are important to the evaluation of network behavior are usually

(i) the percentage of calls completed with respect to calls attempted over some time interval, called the grade of service;

(ii) the average path length needed to process calls through the network;

(iii) the system entropy, measuring the order or structure of the routing scheme, given by

$$H = \sum_{i \in I} \sum_{\substack{j \in I \\ j \neq i}} \sum_{k \in Y^i} p^i_{jk} \log p^i_{jk} \quad \text{bits,} \tag{33}$$

where I is the set of N nodes and Y^i is the set of available actions for the ith node, and p^i_{jk} is the probability of routing calls at i destined to j through the kth trunk group.

Extensive simulation experience [6-8,26] using the L_{R-P} automata demonstrated that the above performance measures are all successfully met while the automata achieve the expediency state corresponding to a uniform loss rate for each automaton, or what amounts to the same, equality of service to the individual call sources. Analogous results can be expected using the E_{I-P} automata.

B. *PACKET-SWTICHING NETWORKS*

A computer network consists of a collection of machines (*hosts*) connected by a *communication subnet* [23]. The job of the subnet is to carry messages from host to host. The subnet consists of two basic components: switching elements and transmission lines. The switching elements are generally specialized computers, called *IMPs* (interface message processors). Transmission lines are often called *circuits* or *channels*.

Adaptive routing is an important contender for routing in packet-switched networks, be they civil or military. Existing adaptive routing algorithms may be classified into the following categories:

Centralized. When centralized routing is used, somewhere within the network there is a *routing decision center* (RDC). Periodically, each IMP sends status information to the RDC (a list of its neighbors that are up, current queue lengths, amount of traffic processed per line since the last report, etc.). The RDC collects all this information, and then based upon its global knowledge of the entire network, computes the optimal routes from every IMP to every other IMP. Centralized routing has the potential for optimal routing, but unfortunately this is only achieved at the expense of heavy control overheads and an undesirable reliance on a common processing component. It has also the serious drawback that if the subnet is to adapt to changing traffic, the routing calculation will have to be performed fairly often. For a large network, the calculation will take many seconds, even on a substantial CPU.

Isolated. All the problems with centralized routing suggest that decentralized algorithms might have something to offer. In isolated routing each IMP makes routing decisions based on purely local information. One simple isolated algorithm is Baran's *hot potato* algorithm [27]. When a packet comes in, the IMP tries to get rid of it as fast as it can by putting it on the shortest output queue.

Hybrid. Rudin has described an interesting hybrid between centralized routing and isolated routing, which he calls *delta routing* [28]. In this algorithm the functions of isolated and centralized routing are integrated to provide global optimization while still maintaining the ability to react to minor local disturbances. The French public packet-switching network, Transpac (cf. [29]) uses delta routing.

Distributed. The most practical form of adaptive routing are the distributed schemes, where routing decisions are made locally; but unlike the isolated doctrine, these are supported by global feedback from the network, gathered in cooperation with other IMPs. A further distinction can be drawn between distributed schemes which employ a single path between source/destination pairs and others which operate using several paths. In the first category the ARPANET [30] schemes are included. In the second category Gallager's scheme [31] and learning automata [11] are included.

In the following, two approaches for adaptive routing by learning automata are presented.

A simple network/learning automaton combination is now proposed with a view to establishing an understanding of the basic routing behavior in a packet-switched network. Consider the four-node arrangement shown in Fig. 3. Let r_{ij} be the average flow rate in packets/second between source i and destination j, $1/\mu$ the mean packet length in bits, and C_{ik} be the capacity of the link i, k in bits/second. An automaton at node 1 is used to select a suitable path for a packet, the path options being performed with probabilities p_1 and p_2.

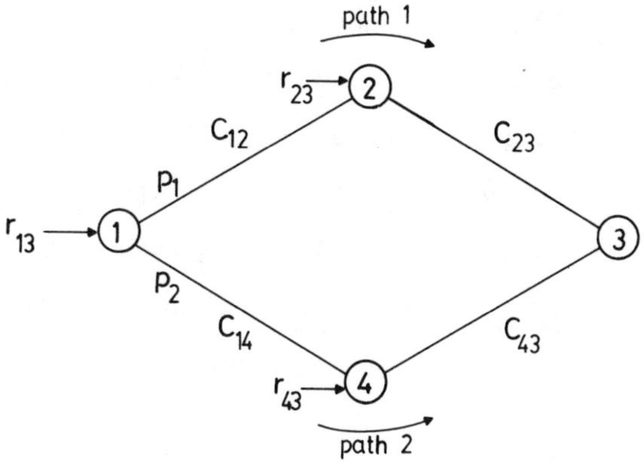

Fig. 3. Four-node network.

Two expediency criteria may be conceived for the operation of the automaton:

(1) equalization of the accumulated path delays;

(2) equalization of the blocking rates on the optimal paths.

Assuming Poisson/exponential flow statistics, the independence assumption (cf. [32]), we can express the average time delay on the optional paths as follows:

$$T_1 = 1/(C_{12} - f_{12}) + 1/(C_{23} - f_{23})$$
$$T_2 = 1/(C_{14} - f_{14}) + 1/(C_{43} - f_{43}) \tag{34}$$

where

$$f_{12} = p_1 r_{13}/\mu, \quad f_{23} = f_{12} + r_{23}/\mu$$
$$f_{14} = p_2 r_{13}/\mu, \quad f_{43} = f_{14} + r_{43}/\mu.$$

In the above the effect of a finite buffering size for the input and output queues of the IMPs is neglected. The first expediency criterion then amounts to the condition

$$p_1 T_1 = p_2 T_2. \tag{35}$$

While the first expediency criterion is suitable for a low-intensity traffic, the second expediency criterion focuses on the situation of a high-intensity traffic taking into effect the likely buffers overflow and higher rejection probability.

Let the IMPs buffers be all of the same size, say Q. Again, using the independence assumption we can write the probability that packets be blocked on the optional paths as follows:

$$P_1^B(1) = P_{12}^B P_{23}^B$$

$$P_2^B(1) = P_{14}^B P_{43}^B .$$

$P_1^B(1)$, $P_2^B(1)$ denote the probability of a blocking at node 1 conditioned on the choice of paths 1 and 2, respectively. P_{ij}^B denotes the blocking probability on the link (ij) given by [33]

$$P_{ij}^B = \frac{(1 - \rho_{ij})\rho_{ij}^Q}{1 - \rho_{ij}^{Q+1}}, \tag{36}$$

where ρ_{ij} is the link utilization, viz., f_{ij}/C_{ij}. The expediency criterion for equalizing the blocking rates on the optional paths will then amount to

$$p_1 P_1^B(1) = p_2 P_2^B(1)$$

or (37)

$$p_1 P_{12}^B / p_2 P_{14}^B = P_{43}^B / P_{23}^B .$$

The above means that expediency is attained when the flow at node 1 is split in such a way that the rate of blocking on each link is inversely proportional to the blocking probability of the neighboring node.

Let us consider the following numerical values for the four-node network of Fig. 3:

$$r_{13} = 1000 \text{ pack/sec} \qquad r_{23} = 600 \text{ pack/sec}$$
$$r_{43} = 800 \text{ pack/sec} \qquad 1/\mu = 350 \text{ bits/pack}$$
$$C_{12} = 350 \text{ Kbits/sec} \qquad C_{23} = 550 \text{ Kbits/sec}$$
$$C_{14} = 230 \text{ Kbits/sec} \qquad C_{43} = 525 \text{ Kbits/sec}$$

It is easy to see that

$$\rho_{12} = \rho_{14} = 0.6 \quad \rho_{23} = 0.7 \quad \rho_{43} = 0.8.$$

Hence, Eq. (37) yields

$$p_1 = 0.6 \quad p_2 = 0.4.$$

The resulting flow splitting yields also minimum average time delay:

$$\overline{T} = \frac{1}{r_{13} + r_{23} + r_{43}}\left(\frac{p_1 r_{13}}{C_{12} - f_{12}} + \frac{(r_{23} + p_1 r_{13})}{C_{23} - f_{23}} + \frac{p_2 r_{13}}{C_{14} - f_{14}} + \frac{r_{43} + p_2 r_{13}}{C_{43} - f_{43}}\right). \tag{38}$$

$\overline{T}$ versus p_1 is shown in Table I.

TABLE I. Average Delay Versus Routing Decision

Routing decision p_1	Average delay $\overline{T}$ (msec)
0.4	19.2
0.5	10.0
0.6	8.7
0.7	9.5
0.8	12.6
0.9	22.4

The operational details of learning automata based on the criterion of equalizing the path delays are given in Chrystall [26] and in Chrystall and Mars [11].

For the implementation of learning automata for equalizing the rate of blocking, the following mechanism may be proposed.

Let $\mathcal{N}$ denote the collection of the IMPs {1, 2, ..., N} in the network. Let $\mathcal{L}$ be the collection of all links in the network (all lines are taken to be unidirectional): $\mathcal{L} = \{(i, k)$, such that $i, k \in \mathcal{N}$ and there is a direct link connecting i to $k\}$, and for every $i \in \mathcal{N}$, denote

$E(i)$ = collection of nodes k such that $(i, k) \in \mathcal{L}$

$I(i)$ = collection of nodes ℓ such that $(\ell, i) \in \mathcal{L}$.

Let us consider the routing mechanism at the ith IMP performed by the automaton A^i. The automaton receives estimates of the blocking probabilities from all nodes $k \in E(i)$. Let the present epoch be n, and suppose that the A^i have chosen actions $k^i \in E(i)$. At the end of the nth epoch the automaton determines the blocking frequency on the link (i, k^i) given by

$$\eta_{k^i}^{i}(n) = \frac{\text{number of blocked packets for link } (i, k^i) \text{ during the nth epoch}}{\text{number of packets arriving on the link } (i, k^i) \text{ during the nth epoch}}. \tag{39}$$

The blocking frequency is weighed inversely proportional to the blocking probability of the node k^i, so that a penalty index $0 \leq u^i(n) \leq 1$ is formed:

$$u^i(n) = \frac{1/\hat{P}^B_{k^i}(n)}{\sum_{k \in E(i)} 1/\hat{P}^B_k(n)} \eta^i_{k^i}(n). \tag{40}$$

The reinforcement scheme is given by (10) for the E_{I-P} automata. The blocking probability estimate at IMP k is determined with the widely used exponential smoothing technique

$$P_k^B(n) = \epsilon P_k^B(n - 1) + (1 - \epsilon) p_{lk}^{k}(n - 1) \eta_{lk}^{k}(n),$$

$$0 < \epsilon < 1. \tag{41}$$

The IMP i estimates likewise its blocking probability and broadcasts it to the neighboring nodes.

VI. CONCLUDING REMARKS

Learning automata offer a versatile tool for organizing solutions to complex decision-making problems. The basic model of an automaton interacting with a random environment in a feedback configuration can be generalized to situations where the environment is influenced by a group of automata. This is relevant when the decision-making process is shared by a number of automata giving rise to distributed control systems. Concepts like "expediency" can be extended to collective behavior of automata in a random medium. The paper gives a definition of expediency of collective behavior and stipulates conditions ensuring existence and uniqueness of an expedient collective mixed strategy. New automata, called E_{I-P}, as well as previously known automata like L_{R-I} possess an expedient equilibrium strategy in the present sense.

Convergence and rate of convergence of collective behavior of the E_{I-P} automata are examined. Application of learning automata models to adaptive routing in communication networks (circuit or packet switching) is discussed. Previous work related to that application is reported and new ideas are also outlined.

APPENDIX A. ROBBINS AND SIEGMUND THEORY

Theorem [34]. Let $(\Omega, \mathscr{F}, P)$ be a probability space and $\mathscr{F}_1 \subset \mathscr{F}_2 \subset \cdots$ be a sequence of sub σ-algebra of $\mathscr{F}$. Let U_n, β_n, ξ_n, and ζ_n, $n = 1, 2, \ldots$ be nonnegative $\mathscr{F}_n$-measurable random variables such that

$$E(U_{n+1}/\mathscr{F}_n) \leq (1 + \beta_n)U_n + \xi_n - \zeta_n, \quad n = 1, 2, \ldots. \tag{A.1}$$

Then, on the set $\left\{\Sigma_{n=1}^{\infty} \beta_n < \infty, \Sigma_{n=1}^{\infty} \xi_n < \infty\right\}$ U_n converges almost surely to a random variable and $\Sigma_{n=1}^{\infty} \zeta_n < \infty$ almost surely.

APPENDIX B. AL'BER AND SHIL'MAN THEOREMS

Theorem 1 [35]. Suppose that for an iterative process we can obtain an inequality

$$\lambda_{n+1} \leq (1 + \beta_n)\lambda_n - \alpha_n\theta_n\lambda_n + \alpha_n x_n \tag{B.1}$$

where $\beta_n \geq 0$, $\theta_n > 0$, $x_n \geq 0$. Then, we have the convergence $\lim_{n\to\infty} \lambda_n = 0$ if

$$\lim_{n\to\infty} \alpha_n\theta_n = 0, \qquad \sum_{n=1}^{\infty} \alpha_n\theta_n = \infty, \qquad \lim_{n\to\infty} \frac{x_n}{\theta_n} = 0,$$

$$\prod_{n=1}^{\infty} (1 + \beta_n) \leq \overline{C} < \infty. \tag{B.2}$$

Theorem 2 [35]. Let $c = d(c_0/b + 1)$, $\alpha_n\theta_n(1 + \beta_n)^{-1} \geq bn^{-1}$, $b > 0$, $\alpha_n x_n \leq dn^{-s}$, $d > 0$, $s > 1$.

(1) If $s - 1 < b$, then for any $c_0 \geq b/(b - s + 1)$ (or $ab > s - 1$, $a = (c_0 - 1)/c_0$) and for $\lambda_1 > c$ we have the bounds

$$\lambda_n \leq \lambda_1\overline{C}\left(\frac{1}{n-1}\right)^{ab}, \qquad 2 \leq n < \overline{x} = \left(\frac{\lambda_1}{c}\right)^{1/(ab-s+1)} + 1 \tag{B.3}$$

$$\lambda_n \leq \bar{C}c\left(\frac{1}{n-1}\right)^{s-1}, \qquad n > \bar{x} \tag{B.4}$$

and for $\lambda_1 \leq c$ the bound (B.4) holds for any $n \geq 2$.

(2) If $s - 1 < b$ and $1 < c_0 < b/(b - s + 1)$, or $s - 1 \geq b$ and $c_0 > 1$, then we have for any $n \geq 2$ the bound

$$\lambda_n \leq \bar{C}\left(\frac{1}{n-1}\right)^{ab} \max(\lambda_1, c). \tag{B.5}$$

APPENDIX C. PROOF OF COLLECTIVE MONOTONICITY

Let us consider the function

$$W(P) = \sum_{i \in I} \sum_{j \in Y^i} \left(p^i_j - \bar{p}^i_j\right) p^i_j C^i_j(P). \tag{C.1}$$

Note that

$$W(\bar{P}) = 0 \tag{C.2}$$

Let us introduce the variation $\delta^i_{k^i}(\Delta)$ of a situation P as follows:

$$P + \delta^i_{k^i}(\Delta) = \begin{cases} \text{change the probability } P^i \text{ into } P^i + \Delta z^i_{k^i}; \\ \text{let the remaining probabilities be the same.} \end{cases} \tag{C.3}$$

where

$$z^i_{k^i} = \Big(\underbrace{-\frac{1}{r^i - 1}, \ldots, -\frac{1}{r^i - 1}}_{k^i - 1}, 1, -\frac{1}{r^i - 1}, \ldots, -\frac{1}{r^i - 1}\Big). \tag{C.4}$$

A variation $\delta^i_{k^i}(\Delta)$ of the situation P leads to a corresponding variation $\delta^i_{k^i}W(P; \Delta)$ of the function (C.1). This variation can be written as

$$\delta^{i}_{k^i} W(P;\ \Delta) = W\left(P + \delta^{i}_{k^i}(\Delta)\right) - W(P)$$

$$= \Delta^2 h^{i}_{k^i}(P^0) + \Delta^2\left(\frac{1}{r^i - 1}\right)^2 \sum_{j \neq k^i} h^{i}_{j}(P^0) \tag{C.5}$$

where

$$h^i_j(P^0) = \frac{\partial}{\partial p^i_j}\left(p^i_j c^i_j(P)\right)\Big|_{P^0}$$

$$= c^i_j(P^0) + p^{i0}_j \frac{\partial c^i_j}{\partial p^i_j}(P^0) \tag{C.6}$$

and P^0 lies on the segment connecting P to $P + \delta^{i}_{k^i}(\Delta)$. It can be easily varified that any two arbitrary situations P and P' satisfy the relationship

$$P^i - P^{i'} = \sum_{j=1}^{r^i} \Delta^i_j z^i_j \tag{C.7}$$

where

$$\Delta^i_j = \frac{r^i - 1}{r^i}\left(p^i_j - p^{i'}_j\right).$$

Equation (C.7) means that one can construct any situation P from another situation P' by means of successive variations $\delta^{i}_{k^i}(\Delta^{i}_{k^i})$. Successive application of Eq. (C.5) yields the following formula for the total variation in the function W(P):

$$\begin{aligned} W(P) &= \delta^1_1 W\left(\overline{P};\ \Delta^1_1\right) + \delta^1_2 W\left(\overline{P} + \delta^1_1\left(\Delta^1_1\right);\ \Delta^1_2\right) + \cdots \\ &\quad + \delta^1_{r^1} W\left(\overline{P} + \delta^1_1\left(\Delta^1_1\right) + \cdots + \delta^1_{r^1-1}\left(\Delta^1_{r^1-1}\right);\ \Delta^1_{r^1}\right) + \cdots \\ &\quad + \delta^i_{k^i} W\left(\overline{P} + \sum_{\substack{i'<i,k^{i'} \\ i'=i,k^{i'}<k^i}} \delta^{i'}_{k^{i'}}\left(\Delta^{i'}_{k^{i'}}\right);\ \Delta^i_{k^i}\right) + \cdots . \end{aligned} \tag{C.8}$$

By virtue of Assumption A the functions h_k^i given by (C.6) are all positive quantities and we deduce from (C.5) and (C.8) that

$$W(P) \geq \rho \sum_{i \in I} \sum_{j \in Y^i} \left(p_j^i - \bar{p}_j^i\right)^2$$

$$\geq \rho V(P), \tag{C.9}$$

where

$$\rho = \min_{i,j} \inf_{P \in S} \left(1 + \frac{1}{(r^i - 1)^2}\right) c_j^i(P). \tag{C.10}$$

REFERENCES

1. M. L. TSETLIN, *Automat. Remote Control 22*, 1210 (1961).
2. V. I. VARSHAVSKII and I. P. VORONTSOVA, *Automat. Remote Control 24*, 327 (1963).
3. K. S. NARENDRA and M. A. L. THATHACHAR, *IEEE Trans. Systems, Man, and Cybernet. SMC-4*, 323 (1974).
4. K. S. NARENDRA and S. LAKSHMIVARAHAN, *J. Cybernet. Inform. Sci. 1*, 53 (1978).
5. R. M. GLORIOSO and F. C. COLON OSORIO, "Engineering Intelligent Systems," Digital Press, Bedford, Massachusetts, 1980.
6. K. S. NARENDRA and D. McKENNA, "Simulation Study of Telephone Traffic Routing Using Learning Algorithms — Part I," S&IS Report No. 7806, Yale University, 1978.
7. K. S. NARENDRA, P. MARS, and M. S. CHRYSTALL, "Simulation Study of Telephone Traffic Routing Using Learning Algorithms — Part II," S&IS Report No. 7907, Yale University, 1979.
8. P. MARS and M. S. CHRYSTALL, "Real-Time Telephone Traffic Simulation Using Learning Automata Routing," S&IS Report No. 7909, Yale University, 1979.
9. K. S. NARENDRA and M. A. L. THATHACHAR, "On the Behavior of a Learning Automaton in a Changing Environment with Application to Telephone Traffic Routing," S&IS Report No. 7803, Yale University, 1978.
10. P. R. SRIKANTA-KUMAR and K. S. NARENDRA, *SIAM J. Control Optim. 25*, 34 (1982).

11. M. S. CHRYSTALL and P. MARS, "Learning Automata Adaptive Routing for Datagram and Virtual Call Packet-Switched Networks," Technical Report 8103, R.G.I.T., Aberdeen, Scotland, 1981.

12. A. S. POZNYAK, *Automat. Remote Control 36*, 77 (1975).

13. S. LAKSHMIVARAHAN and M. A. L. THATHACHAR, *Inform. Sci. 4*, 121 (1972).

14. R. R. BUSH and F. MOSTELLER, "Stochastic Models for Learning," Wiley, New York, 1955.

15. YA. Z. TSYPKIN and A. S. POZNYAK, *Engrg. Cybernet. 10*, 478 (1972).

16. I. J. SHAPIRO and K. S. NARENDRA, *IEEE Trans. Systems, Sci. Cybernet. SSC-5*, 352 (1969).

17. Y. M. EL-FATTAH, *IEEE Trans. Systems, Man, Cybernet. SMC-10*, 304 (1980).

18. Y. M. EL-FATTAH, *IEEE Trans. Systems, Man, Cybernet. SMC-11*, 135 (1981).

19. YU. A. FLEROV, *J. Cybernet. 2*, 112 (1972).

20. Y. M. EL-FATTAH, *Systems Control Lett. 1*, 332 (1982).

21. S. KARLIN, "Mathematical Methods in Game Theory, Programming, and Economics," Addison-Wesley, Reading, Massachusetts, 1959.

22. G. J. MARSHALL, "Principles of Digital Communications," McGraw-Hill, London, 1980.

23. A. S. TANENBAUM, "Computer Networks," Prentice-Hall, Englewood Cliffs, New Jersey, 1981.

24. D. W. DAVIES, D. L. A. BARBER, W. L. PRICE, and C. M. SOLOMONIDES, "Computer Networkds and their Protocols," Wiley, Chichester, 1979.

25. M. T. HILL, "Telecommunications Switching Principles," Allen and Unwin, London, 1979.

26. M. S. CHRYSTALL, "Adaptive Control of Communication Networks Using Learning Automata," Ph.D. thesis, School of Electronic and Electrical Engineering, R.G.I.T., Aberdeen, Scotland, 1982.

27. P. BARAN, *IEEE Trans. Comm. Systems CS-12*, 1 (1964).

28. H. RUDIN, *IEEE Trans. Comm. COM-24*, 43 (1976).

29. J. M. SIMON and A. DANET, *in* "Flow Control in Computer Networks" (J. L. Grangé and M. Gien, eds.), p. 33, North-Holland, Amsterdam, 1979.

30. J. M. McQUILLAN, I. RICHER, and R. C. ROSEN, *IEEE Trans. Comm. COM-28*, 711 (1980).

31. R. G. GALLAGER, *IEEE Trans. Comm. COM-25*, 73 (1977).

32. L. KLEINROCK, "Communication Nets: Stochastic Message Flow and Delays," McGraw-Hill, New York, 1964.

33. M. SCHWARTZ, "Computer Communication Network Design and Analysis," Prentice-Hall, Englewood Cliffs, New Jersey, 1977.

34. H. ROBBINS and D. SIEGMUND, *in* "Optimization Methods in Statistics" (J. S. Rustagi, ed.), p. 233, Academic, New York and London, 1971.

35. YA. I. AL'BER and S. V. SHIL'MAN, *Automat. Remote Control 42*, 32 (1981).

Covariance Equivalent Realizations with Application to Model Reduction of Large-Scale Systems

A. YOUSUFF

R. E. SKELTON

School of Aeronautics and Astronautics
Purdue University
West Lafayette, Indiana

I. INTRODUCTION

The controller design for distributed systems typically involves two steps: (1) model reduction and (2) control design, although not necessarily in that order. The direct application of the linear-quadratic-Gaussian (LQG) theory becomes infeasible since the plant models which are accurate enough to serve

ISBN 0-12-012722-9

in the evaluation of candidate controllers are often too complex for direct LQG computations (beyond "Riccati-solvable" dimension).

A traditional approach to synthesize a controller of a specified order n_c follows these steps:

(1) Apply (one's favorite) model reduction theory to obtain a low-order model of "Riccati-solvable" dimension r.

(2) Solve for the optimal LQG controller for this reduced model. This yields a controller of order r.

(3) If the required dimension of the controller n_c is less than r, then apply (again one's favorite) controller reduction theory to reduce the controller from order r to n_c.

Finally, one evaluates the resulting controller by driving the full model of order $n > r$.

Although these three steps are accomplished sequentially, the methods (theories) used in each step should not be independent. Since the subsequent goal is to minimize the performance objective, every step in the above strategy should be aimed at minimizing the same performance objective. This is to say, for example, that the model reduction theory used in step 1 should produce a reduced model which represents the performance objective accurately so that the controller of step 2 can be expected to reduce (if not minimize) the *actual* performance objective.

Both steps 1 and 3 require approximations (reductions). Yet, it is emphasized that, the model reduction (step 1) and the controller reduction (step 3) are *different* mathematical procedures. Moreover, due to the approximations involved there are inevitable errors introduced in these steps and these errors should be minimal so that the results of the subsequent steps would be more reliable.

Thus one needs a unifying theory which integrates steps 1-3 and yet be flexible enough to incorporate the different mathematical requirements of steps 1 and 3.

Component cost analysis (CCA) [1-4] was introduced as an attempt to unify the model reduction and control design problems, steps 1-3. In the open-loop model reduction versions of CCA theory, the state dependent term in the quadratic performance objective (which is intended for later controller design in steps 2 and 3) is used in the model reduction decisions. In this way, the modeling and control problems were "integrated" in [1-3].

The purpose of this chapter is to use CCA to present a theory of *covariance equivalent realizations* (COVERs) as a likely candidate for the above-mentioned unifying theory. The COVER theory is equally applicable to both model and controller reduction problems, though only the model reduction problem is treated herein. The flexibility offered by the COVER theory is used in the model reduction problem to minimize the error introduced in step 1 above.

II. BRIEF REVIEW OF COMPONENT COST ANALYSIS

The references pertaining to this section are [1-4]. Readers familiar with these references may skip this section.

Basically, component cost analysis considers any systems as an interaction of different "components[1]" constituting the

[1]*In this chapter, these "components" are the individual* states *representing the system dynamics.*

system. The definition of these components is up to the analyst; they may have physical significance, or they may be defined for mathematical convenience. For *any* choice of the components, the CCA assigns a metric called *component cost* to each component. These component costs measure the significance (contribution) of each component to a predefined quadratic cost function. Then a partial realization of the given system is obtained by deleting those components that have the smallest component costs.

Mathematically, the concepts of CCA are explained as follows. Let a state space description of a time-invariant system be given as

$$\mathscr{S}(n;\ A,\ D,\ C):\quad \begin{aligned} \dot{x}(t) &= Ax(t) + Dw(t) \\ y(t) &= Cx(t) \end{aligned} \tag{1}$$

where the states $x(t) \in \mathscr{R}^n$, the outputs $y(t) \in \mathscr{R}^k$ and the process noise vector $w(t) \in \mathscr{R}^q$. The following assumptions (though not all necessary for the implementation of CCA) are made with respect to (1).

(A.1) The model (1) is controllable, observable and asymptotically stable.

(A.2) The initial condition x(0) is a zero mean Gaussian white noise process with covariance X_0, i.e.,

$$\mathscr{E}\{x(0)\} = 0, \quad \mathscr{E}\{x(0)x^T(0)\} = X_0,$$

where $\mathscr{E}$ denotes the expectation operator.

(A.3) w(t) is a zero mean Gaussian white noise process with a positive definite intensity W and is uncorrelated with the states:

$$\mathscr{E}\{w(t)\} = 0, \quad \mathscr{E}\{w(t)w^T(\tau)\} = W\delta(t - \tau)$$

$$\mathscr{E}\{x(t)w^T(\tau)\} = 0, \quad \tau > t \geq 0$$

$$\mathscr{E}\{x(0)w^T(t)\} = 0, \quad t \geq 0,$$

where δ is the Dirac delta function.

(A.4) There are k independent outputs, i.e., rank[C] = k and q independent inputs, i.e., rank[D] = q.

We will use the notation $\mathscr{S}(n; A, D, C)$ to denote the system realization in the form (1). When it is not necessary to explicitly indicate the parameters {A, D, C} we shall simply use the notation $\mathscr{S}(n)$ for $\mathscr{S}(n; A, D, C)$.

Let a quadratic cost function associated with $\mathscr{S}(n)$ be given as

$$\mathscr{V} = \lim_{t\to\infty} \mathscr{E}\{\mathscr{V}(t)\}, \quad \mathscr{V}(t) \triangleq \frac{1}{t}\int_0^t \|y(\tau)\|_Q^2 \, d\tau, \tag{2}$$

where $\|\cdot\|_Q$ is the weighted Euclidean norm, i.e., $\|y\|_Q^2 = y^TQy$, and where Q is a symmetric positive definite weighting matrix.

Now, partitioning the state vector x(t) as $x(t) = [x_1(t), x_2(t), \ldots, x_n(t)]^T$ for the simplicity of presentation, the "components" of $\mathscr{S}(n)$ are defined to be the individual states x_i (there are therefore n components). The component costs $\hat{\mathscr{V}}_i$ associated with each component x_i is defined by [3]

$$\hat{\mathscr{V}}_i \triangleq \frac{1}{2} \lim_{t\to\infty} \mathscr{E}\{(\partial\mathscr{V}(t)/\partial x_i)x_i\}, \quad i = 1, 2, \ldots, n, \tag{3}$$

and are calculated according to the following component cost formula.

Component Cost Formula

$$\hat{\mathcal{V}}_i = [C^TQCX]_{ii}, \quad i = 1, 2, \ldots, n, \tag{4a}$$

where $[\cdot]_{ii}$ denotes the (i, i) element of $[\cdot]$ and where X, the steady-state covariance of the states, defined by

$$X \triangleq \lim_{t\to\infty} \mathscr{E}\{x(t)x^T(t)\} \tag{4b}$$

satisfies [5]

$$XA^T + AX + DWD^T = 0. \tag{4c}$$

Clearly, since $\mathcal{V} = \mathrm{Tr}[C^TQCX]$ the component costs satisfy the *cost-decomposition* property

$$\mathcal{V} = \sum_{i=1}^{n} \hat{\mathcal{V}}_i. \tag{5}$$

In some choices of coordinates, it is possible for a component cost $\hat{\mathcal{V}}_i$ to be negative [2]. However, for the choice of coordinates used herein and in [3], these component costs are nonnegative, $\hat{\mathcal{V}}_i \geq 0$, i = 1, 2, ..., n.

Based upon the definition of component costs, the CCA algorithm for constructing partial realizations from a given set of coordinates is therefore characterized by these two steps.

The Basic CCA Partial Realization Algorithm

I. Compute the component costs $\hat{\mathcal{V}}_i$ by (4) and reorder the states x_i so that

$$\hat{\mathcal{V}}_1 \geq \hat{\mathcal{V}}_2 \geq \cdots \geq \hat{\mathcal{V}}_n. \tag{6}$$

II. To obtain a partial realization of order r, partition the "reordered model" as

$$\begin{aligned} \dot{x}_R(t) &= A_R x_R(t) + A_{RT} x_T(t) + D_R w(t) \\ \dot{x}_T(t) &= A_{TR} x_R(t) + A_T x_T(t) + D_T w(t) \\ y(t) &= C_R x_R(t) + C_T x_T(t), \end{aligned} \tag{7}$$

$$\mathscr{E}\{x_R(0)\} = 0, \qquad \mathscr{E}\{x_T(0)\} = 0,$$

$$\mathscr{E}\left\{x_R(0)x_R^T(0)\right\} = X_{R_0}, \quad \mathscr{E}\left\{x_R(0)x_T^T(0)\right\} = X_{RT_0},$$

$$\mathscr{E}\left\{x_T(0)x_T^T(0)\right\} = X_{T_0},$$

where $x_R(t) \in \mathscr{R}^r$ and $x_T(t) \in \mathscr{R}^{n-r}$. The matrices are compatibly dimensioned. The partial realization $\mathscr{S}(r;\, A_R,\, D_R,\, C_R)$ is then given by

$$\mathscr{S}(r;\, A_R,\, D_R,\, C_R): \quad \begin{aligned} \dot{\hat{x}}_R(t) &= A_R\hat{x}_R(t) + D_R w(t) \\ \hat{y}(t) &= C_R\hat{x}_R(t) \end{aligned} \tag{8}$$

$$\mathscr{E}\left\{\hat{x}_R(0)\right\} = 0, \quad \mathscr{E}\left\{\hat{x}_R(0)\hat{x}_R^T(0)\right\} = X_{R_0},$$

with a corresponding cost function $\mathscr{V}_R$ defined as

$$\mathscr{V}_R = \lim_{t\to\infty} \mathscr{E}\{\mathscr{V}_R(t)\}, \quad \mathscr{V}_R(t) \triangleq \frac{1}{t}\int_0^t \|\hat{y}(\tau)\|_Q^2 \, d\tau. \tag{9}$$

Now, the *predicted* value of $\mathscr{V}_R$ is based upon the a priori knowledge of $\mathscr{S}(n)$ and its component costs $\hat{\mathscr{V}}_i$. This is denoted by $\hat{\mathscr{V}}_R$ and is defined by

$$\hat{\mathscr{V}}_R \triangleq \sum_{i=1}^{r} \hat{\mathscr{V}}_i. \tag{10}$$

But the *actual* value of $\mathscr{V}_R$ (available *after* $\mathscr{S}(r)$ is obtained) is given by

$$\mathscr{V}_R = \mathrm{Tr}\left[C_R^T Q C_R X_R\right], \tag{11a}$$

where X_R satisfies

$$X_R A_R^T + A_R X_R + D_R W D_R^T = 0. \tag{11b}$$

In general, $\mathscr{V}_R \neq \hat{\mathscr{V}}_R$ and the partial realization $\mathscr{S}(r)$ may not be asymptotically stable. This is due to the fact that this method computes only the *in situ* component cost (while all components are in place and interacting), which does not precisely correspond to the a posteriori component cost (the amount the total cost is perturbed after the deletion of the component). The "cost-decoupled" coordinates developed in [3] are defined by the property $\mathcal{V}_i = \hat{\mathcal{V}}_i$, i = 1, 2, ..., r. The cost-decoupled coordinates of [3] have these properties:

$$\text{(a)} \quad X = I_n \ (I_n \text{ denotes the } (n \times n) \text{ identity matrix}) \tag{12}$$

and

$$\text{(b)} \quad C^TQC = \text{diag}\left\{\alpha_1^2, \alpha_2^2, \ldots, \alpha_k^2, 0, \ldots, 0\right\}, \tag{13}$$

$$\alpha_1^2 \geq \alpha_2^2 \geq \cdots \geq \alpha_k^2 > 0.$$

Furthermore, in these coordinates we have

$$\mathcal{V}_i = \hat{\mathcal{V}}_i = \alpha_i^2 \geq 0, \quad i = 1, 2, \ldots, r, \tag{14a}$$

and

$$\mathcal{V}_R = \hat{\mathcal{V}}_R. \tag{14b}$$

It is shown in [3] that a transformation

$$x(t) = T\chi(t) \tag{15}$$

which takes $\mathcal{S}(n; A, D, C)$ to the cost-decoupled coordinates can always be found and an algorithm to obtain such a transformation (15) is also presented in [3]. A partial realization $\mathcal{S}(r)$ of $\mathcal{S}(n)$ which has the property

$$\mathcal{V}_R = \mathcal{V} \tag{16}$$

is called *cost-equivalent realization* (CER) in [3]. CERs are obtained by the CCA algorithm in cost-decoupled coordinates.

III. DEFINITION AND PROPERTIES OF COVERs

A. *DEFINITION AND MOTIVATION*

The CCA offers a convenient means of pricing the components via component cost which can then be used to identify the least significant components from the full-order realization $\mathscr{S}(n)$ and delete them to obtain a partial realization $\mathscr{S}(r)$.

Now, note from the definitions of the cost functions $\mathscr{V}$ in (2) and $\mathscr{V}_R$ in (9) and from the definition of a cost-equivalent realization (16) that the CERs satisfy

$$\lim_{t\to\infty} \frac{1}{t}\mathscr{E}\int_0^t \|\hat{y}(\tau)\|_Q^2 \, d\tau = \lim_{t\to\infty} \frac{1}{t}\mathscr{E}\int_0^t \|y(\tau)\|_Q^2 \, d\tau. \tag{17}$$

This shows that the CERs match the *average* mean-squared value of the output vector y of $\mathscr{S}(n)$. However, this does not imply that the RMS values of every output y_i, i = 1, 2, ..., k are matched, where the RMS value $\hat{\mathscr{V}}_{y_i}$ of each output is defined by

$$\hat{\mathscr{V}}_{y_i} \triangleq \left\{\lim_{t\to\infty} \frac{1}{t}\mathscr{E}\int_0^t y_i^2(\tau) \, d\tau\right\}^{1/2}, \quad i = 1, 2, \ldots, k, \tag{18a}$$

and where y_i is the ith output, i.e.,

$$y = [y_1, y_2, \ldots, y_k]^T. \tag{18b}$$

The $\hat{\mathscr{V}}_{y_i}$ is a fundamental input-output property of a system and is independent of any coordinate transformation. Furthermore, in general, mission requirements are given only in terms of the RMS values of the outputs. Hence, it is desirable for a partial realization to preserve these quantities. With this in view the following definitions are presented.

Definition 1. The realizations (8) are called *covariance equivalent realizations* (COVERs) if

$$\lim_{t\to\infty} \mathscr{E}\{\hat{y}(t)\hat{y}^T(t)\} = \lim_{t\to\infty} \mathscr{E}\{y(t)y^T(t)\}. \tag{19}$$

Definition 2. A *minimal COVER* is defined to be a COVER $\mathscr{S}(r)$ whose order r is the smallest.

Remarks. (1) Since $\mathscr{S}(n)$ is asymptotically stable and time invariant, the process y(t), t > 0 is ergodic [5], and as a consequence (18a) can be expressed as

$$\hat{\mathscr{V}}^2_{y_i} = \lim_{t\to\infty} \mathscr{E}\left\{y_i^2(t)\right\} = [\lim_{t\to\infty} \mathscr{E}\{y(t)y^T(t)\}]_{ii},$$

$$i = 1, \ldots, k. \tag{20}$$

It then follows from Definition 1 that the COVERs preserve the RMS values of each output. Moreover, since $\mathscr{V}_R = \Sigma_{i=1}^k \hat{\mathscr{V}}^2_{y_i} = \mathscr{V}$, all COVERs are cost equivalent.

(2) Note that by definition the COVERs match the output covariance at steady state ($t \to \infty$) unlike the realizations discussed by Anderson [6] which match the output autocorrelation function $\mathscr{E}y(t + \tau)y^T(\tau)$ for *all* time, $\tau \in [0, \infty)$, $t \to \infty$. As will be shown in Proposition 7, under certain conditions the COVERs also match the autocorrelation at all times.

It is clear that the order of the minimal COVER must be greater than or equal to the number of independent outputs k. This fact is formally established in the following proposition.

Proposition 1 (Order of the minimal COVER). The order, denoted by r^*, of the minimal COVER satisfies

$$r^* \geq k. \tag{21}$$

Proof. Since,

$$\lim_{t\to\infty} \mathscr{E}\{y(t)y^T(t)\} = \lim_{t\to\infty} \mathscr{E}\{Cx(t)x^T(t)C^T\} = CXC^T \tag{22a}$$

and

$$\lim_{t\to\infty} \mathscr{E}\{\hat{y}(t)\hat{y}^T(t)\} = \lim_{t\to\infty} \mathscr{E}\left\{C_R\hat{x}_R(t)\hat{x}_R^T(t)C_R^T\right\} = C_RX_RC_R^T, \tag{22b}$$

for $\mathscr{S}(r)$ to be a COVER the following equation must be satisfied

$$C_RX_RC_R^T = CXC^T. \tag{23a}$$

Imposing rank condition on (23a) yields

$$\text{rank}\left[C_R X_R C_R^T\right] = \text{rank}[CXC^T] = k \tag{23b}$$

where the last equality arises from the assumptions[2] that the matrix pair (A, D) is controllable (A.1), i.e., $X > 0$ [5], and that rank [C] = k (A.4). Observing that $\text{rank}\left[C_R X_R C_R^T\right] \leq r$, where r is the order of $\mathscr{S}(r)$ completes the proof.

Remark. It is called to the reader's attention that there is no feedforward present in the output equation of (1), i.e., w(t) does not explicitly appear in y(t). If such a feedforward exists, then the order of the minimal COVER can be less than k. However, since the presence of feedforward in the output causes the cost function $\mathscr{V}$ to grow unbounded, only systems without feedforward are considered herein.

B. *CONSTRUCTION OF COVERs BY CCA*

Recall that all COVERs are also cost equivalent realizations, but the reverse is not true in general. However, the CERs produced in [3] are COVERs, as will be shown subsequently in this section. The CERs in [3] are produced from the cost-decoupled coordinates which satisfy properties (12) and (13). We shall first establish some properties of these coordinates. The cost-decoupled coordinates are nonunique as shown by the following proposition.

Proposition 2 (Nonuniqueness of cost-decoupled coordinates). Under the assumption of distinct α_i,[3] $i = 1, 2, \ldots, k$, in (13) the cost-decoupled coordinates are unique to within a similarity

[2] *The output controllability of $\mathscr{S}(n)$ is the necessary and sufficient condition for $\text{rank}[CXC^T] = k$ [5].*

[3] *If there are repeated α_i^2 such as $\alpha_1^2 > \cdots > \alpha_{p+1}^2 = \cdots = \alpha_{p+j}^2 > \cdots > \alpha_k^2$, then the proposition holds for a more general matrix T_{11} of the form $T_{11} = \text{diag}\{\pm 1, \ldots, \pm 1, T_{jj}, \pm 1, \ldots, \pm 1\}$ where T_{jj} is any $(j \times j)$ orthonormal matrix.*

transformation of the form

$$T = \text{diag}\{T_{11}, T_{22}\} \tag{24a}$$

where

$$T_{11} \triangleq \text{diag}\{\pm 1, \pm 1, \ldots, \pm 1\} \in \mathscr{R}^{k\times k} \tag{24b}$$

and

$$T_{22} \in \mathscr{R}^{(n-k)\times(n-k)} \tag{24c}$$

is any orthonormal matrix.

Proof. Let T be any nonsingular matrix and consider the transformation $x(t) = T\eta(t)$. Since the covariance of the transformed coordinates is given by

$$\mathscr{E}\{\eta(t)\eta^T(t)\} = T^{-1}\mathscr{E}\{x(t)x^T(t)\}T^{-T},$$

the matrix T must be orthonormal to satisfy (12). The state weighting matrix C^TQC in the transformed coordinates is T^TC^TQCT, which should satisfy (13), i.e.,

$$T^TC^TQCT = \text{diag}\left\{\alpha_1^2, \alpha_2^2, \ldots \alpha_k^2, 0, \ldots, 0\right\}. \tag{25a}$$

Now, since $Q > 0$, (13) implies that

$$C = [C_1, 0], \quad C_1 \in \mathscr{R}^{k\times k}, \quad \text{rank}[C_1] = k, \tag{25b}$$

and

$$C_1^TQC_1 = \underline{\alpha}^2 \triangleq \text{diag}\left\{\alpha_1^2, \alpha_2^2, \ldots, \alpha_k^2\right\}. \tag{25c}$$

Hence, partitioning T as

$$T = \begin{bmatrix} T_{11} & T_{12} \\ T_{21} & T_{22} \end{bmatrix}$$

rewrite (25a) as

$$\begin{bmatrix} T_{11}^T & T_{21}^T \\ T_{12}^T & T_{22}^T \end{bmatrix}\begin{bmatrix} C_1^TQC_1 & 0 \\ 0 & 0 \end{bmatrix}\begin{bmatrix} T_{11} & T_{12} \\ T_{21} & T_{22} \end{bmatrix} = \begin{bmatrix} \underline{\alpha}^2 & 0 \\ 0 & 0 \end{bmatrix}. \tag{25d}$$

Two of the equations resulting from (25d) are

$$T_{11}^T C_1^T Q C_1 T_{11} = T_{11}^T \underline{\alpha}^2 T_{11} = \underline{\alpha}^2$$

and

$$T_{12}^T C_1^T Q C_1 T_{12} = T_{12}^T \underline{\alpha}^2 T_{12} = 0,$$

which can be satisfied if and only if $T_{12} = 0$ and T_{11} satisfies (24b). Furthermore, since T must be orthonormal $T_{21} = 0$.

Remark. The implication of Proposition 2 is that there exists considerable flexibility in the cost-decoupled coordinates (of course, if $k = n$ or $n - 1$ this flexibility is lost). From the structure of the transformation (24) and from (25b) notice that these coordinates are not uniquely defined within the null space of the output matrix C. This nonuniqueness will be used in the next section to improve the "quality" of the COVERs as reduced model.

The following proposition which presents additional properties of cost-decoupled coordinates is proved in [3].

Proposition 3 (Properties of cost-decoupled coordinates) [3]. In cost-decoupled coordinates $\mathscr{S}(n;\ A,\ D,\ C)$ has the following properties, in addition to (12) and (13)

(1) $$\hat{\mathscr{V}}_i = \begin{cases} \alpha_i^2, & i \leq k, \\ 0, & i > k. \end{cases}$$

For any $r \leq n$,

(2) $\text{Re}\{\lambda_i(A_R)\} \leq 0, \quad i = 1, 2, \ldots, r,$

where Re $\{\cdot\}$ denotes the real part of $\{\cdot\}$ and $\lambda_i(A_R)$ denotes the ith eigenvalue of A_R.

(3) $\text{Re}\{\lambda_i(A_R)\} < 0$ for all $i = 1, 2, \ldots, r$, if and only if the matrix pair (A_R, D_R) is controllable.

(4) $\mathrm{Re}\{\lambda_i(A_T)\} \leq 0, \quad i = 1, 2, \ldots, n - r,$

$\mathrm{Re}\{\lambda_i(A_T)\} < 0$ for all $i = 1, 2, \ldots, n - r$, if and only if the matrix pair (A_T, D_T) is controllable.

As a consequence of claim (1) of Proposition 3 the following corollary results.

Corollary 1 (Minimal sensitivity of the component costs). The component costs associated with the cost-decoupled coordinates are minimally sensitive to the perturbations in the state weighting matrix C^TQC.

Proof. The proof relies on a result derived by Skelton and Wagie [8] which is restated here.

Lemma 1 (Minimal root sensitivity) [8]. Let λ_i be an eigenvalue of a real matrix A with linearly independent eigenvectors. Then the sensitivity of λ_i to the perturbations in A, measured by

$$\mathscr{S}_i \triangleq \left\|\frac{\partial \lambda_i}{\partial A}\right\|^2, \qquad \|[\cdot]\|^2 \triangleq \mathrm{Tr}\{[\cdot]^T[\cdot]\}$$

is minimal if and only if A is normal (i.e., $AA^T = A^TA$). Now note from Proposition 3 and from (13) that the component costs are the eigenvalues of C^TQC, i.e.,

$$\hat{\mathscr{V}}_i = \lambda_i(C^TQC), \qquad i = 1, 2, \ldots, n.$$

Since C^TQC is symmetric (hence, it is normal), the proof of Corollary 1 follows from Lemma 1.

Remark. Consider the case when the *state* weighting matrix C^TQC in the cost function is subject to perturbations; this may happen, for example, when the output matrix C is not known exactly, or when the realization is used for subsequent modification of the output weighting matrix Q, as in [9]. In this situation, Corollary 1 shows that the choice of the partial realization $\mathscr{S}(r)$ is least sensitive to these perturbations.

Since any model which is asymptotically stable and controllable can be transformed[4] to the cost-decoupled coordinates, it will be assumed without loss of generality that $\mathscr{S}(n;\ A,\ D,\ C)$ is in cost-decoupled coordinates, i.e., properties (12) and (13) are satisfied. With this assumption, the conditions under which the CCA algorithm produces COVERs are now presented.

Proposition 4 (Generation of COVERs by the CCA algorithm). The realization $\mathscr{S}(r;\ A_R,\ D_R,\ C_R)$ is a COVER if and only if both the following conditions hold simultaneously.

(1) $r \geq k$;

(2) the uncontrollable subspace of $\mathscr{S}(r)$ is also unobservable.

Proof. Claim (1) follows from Proposition 1.

To prove claim (2) proceed as follows. First, substitute (12) in (4c) and write the resulting equation in its partitioned form as

$$A_R^T + A_R + D_R W D_R^T = 0, \tag{26a}$$

$$A_{TR}^T + A_{RT} + D_R W D_T^T = 0, \tag{26b}$$

$$A_T^T + A_T + D_T W D_T^T = 0. \tag{26c}$$

Now, consider $\mathscr{S}(r;\ A_R,\ D_R,\ C_R)$. If it is not controllable then there exists an *orthonormal* transformation [10]

$$\eta(t) = \begin{bmatrix} \eta_1(t) \\ \\ \eta_2(t) \end{bmatrix} = T^T \hat{x}_R(t) = \begin{bmatrix} T_1^T \\ \\ T_2^T \end{bmatrix} \hat{x}_R(t) \tag{27a}$$

[4] *The algorithm to obtain such a transformation can be found in [3].*

to transform $\mathscr{S}(r;\ A_R,\ D_R,\ C_R)$ to its controllable canonical form

$$\begin{aligned}\dot{\eta}_1(t) &= \mathscr{A}_{11}\eta_1(t) + \mathscr{A}_{12}\eta_2(t) + \mathscr{D}_1 w(t)\\ \dot{\eta}_2(t) &= \mathscr{A}_{22}\eta_2(t)\\ \hat{y}(t) &= \mathscr{C}_1\eta_1(t) + \mathscr{C}_2\eta_2(t)\end{aligned} \tag{27b}$$

where $\eta_1(t) \in \mathscr{R}^{n_1}$, with n_1 being the dimension of the controllable subspace. Now, (26a) becomes

$$\mathscr{A}_{11}^T + \mathscr{A}_{11} + \mathscr{D}_1 W \mathscr{D}_1^T = 0, \tag{28a}$$

$$\mathscr{A}_{12} = 0, \tag{28b}$$

$$\mathscr{A}_{22}^T + \mathscr{A}_{22} = 0. \tag{28c}$$

Since the matrix pair $(\mathscr{A}_{11},\ \mathscr{D}_1)$ is controllable and (28a) holds, $\mathscr{A}_{11}$ is asymptotically stable [10]. In view of (28c) $\mathscr{A}_{22}$ is skew-symmetric and hence is not asymptotically stable.

Now, express the steady state output covariance of $\mathscr{S}(r;\ A_R,\ D_R,\ C_R)$ as

$$\begin{aligned}\hat{Y} &\triangleq \lim_{t\to\infty} \mathscr{E}\{\hat{y}(t)\hat{y}^T(t)\}\\ &= [\mathscr{C}_1 \mathscr{C}_2] \lim_{t\to\infty} \mathscr{E}\{\eta(t)\eta^T(t)\} [\mathscr{C}_1 \mathscr{C}_2]^T\\ &= \mathscr{C}_1 \underline{\eta}_{11} \mathscr{C}_1^T + \mathscr{C}_1 \underline{\eta}_{12} \mathscr{C}_2^T + \mathscr{C}_2 \underline{\eta}_{12}^T \mathscr{C}_1^T + \mathscr{C}_2 \underline{\eta}_{22} \mathscr{C}_2^T,\end{aligned} \tag{29}$$

where

$$\underline{\eta}_{ij} \triangleq \lim_{t\to\infty} \underline{\eta}_{ij}(t); \quad \underline{\eta}_{ij}(t) \triangleq \mathscr{E}\left\{\eta_i(t)\eta_j^T(t)\right\},$$
$$i,\ j = 1,\ 2.$$

The covariance of $\eta(t)$ is given by [5]

$$\mathscr{E}\{\eta(t)\eta^T(t)\} = e^{\mathscr{A}t}\underline{\eta}(0)e^{\mathscr{A}^T t} + \int_0^t e^{\mathscr{A}(t-\tau)}\mathscr{D}W\mathscr{D}^T e^{\mathscr{A}^T(t-\tau)}\, d\tau, \tag{30}$$

where

$$\mathscr{A} \triangleq T^T A_R T, \quad \mathscr{D} \triangleq T^T D_R, \quad \underline{\eta}(0) \triangleq T^T X_{R_0} T.$$

From (30) and from (27) obtain the following expressions for $\underline{\eta}_{ij}(t)$, i, j = 1, 2,

$$\underline{\eta}_{11}(t) = e^{\mathscr{A}_{11}t}\underline{\eta}_{11}(0)\, e^{\mathscr{A}_{11}^T t} + \int_0^t e^{\mathscr{A}_{11}(t-\tau)} \mathscr{D}_1 W \mathscr{D}_1^T \times e^{\mathscr{A}_{11}^T(t-\tau)}\, d\tau, \tag{31a}$$

$$\underline{\eta}_{12}(t) = e^{\mathscr{A}_{11}t}\underline{\eta}_{12}(0)\, e^{\mathscr{A}_{22}^T t} \tag{31b}$$

$$\underline{\eta}_{22}(t) = e^{\mathscr{A}_{22}t}\underline{\eta}_{22}(0)\, e^{\mathscr{A}_{22}^T t}. \tag{31c}$$

Now, since $\mathscr{A}_{11}$ is asymptotically stable, in the limit as $t \to \infty$ Eqs. (31a)-(31c) result in

$$\underline{\eta}_{11} = \int_0^\infty e^{\mathscr{A}_{11}(t-\tau)} \mathscr{D}_1 W \mathscr{D}_1^T e^{\mathscr{A}_{11}^T(t-\tau)}\, d\tau, \tag{32a}$$

$$\underline{\eta}_{12} = 0, \tag{32b}$$

$$\underline{\eta}_{22} = \lim_{t\to\infty} e^{\mathscr{A}_{22}t}\underline{\eta}_{22}(0)\, e^{\mathscr{A}_{22}^T t}, \tag{32c}$$

where in (32c) it suffices to realize that $e^{\mathscr{A}_{22}t}$ does not converge to zero as $t \to \infty$ since $\mathscr{A}_{22}$ is not asymptotically stable.

Note from (32a) that $\underline{\eta}_{11}$ is the solution to [5]

$$\underline{\eta}_{11}\mathscr{A}_{11}^T + \mathscr{A}_{11}\underline{\eta}_{11} + \mathscr{D}_1 W \mathscr{D}_1^T = 0. \tag{33}$$

Since $\mathscr{A}_{11}$ is asymptotically stable, comparison of Eqs. (33) and (28a) reveals that

$$\underline{\eta}_{11} = I_{n_1}. \tag{34}$$

Hence in view of (34) and (32), the expression (29) for $\hat{Y}$ becomes

$$\hat{Y} = \mathscr{C}_1\mathscr{C}_1^T + \mathscr{C}_2\underline{n}_{22}\mathscr{C}_2^T. \tag{35}$$

It therefore follows from (32c) that $\hat{Y}$ depends on the initial conditions and may even be unbounded.

Now, the steady-state output covariance of $\mathscr{S}(n;\ A,\ D,\ C)$ is given by

$$Y \triangleq \lim_{t\to\infty} \mathscr{E}\{y(t)y^T(t)\} = CXC^T = C_RC_R^T, \tag{36a}$$

where (12), (25b), and the condition that $r \geq k$ have been used. Using the transformation matrix in (27a), rewrite (36a) as

$$Y = C_RTT^TC_R^T = \mathscr{C}_1\mathscr{C}_1^T + \mathscr{C}_2\mathscr{C}_2^T, \tag{36b}$$

which is independent of the initial conditions. Thus, for $\mathscr{S}(r)$ to be a COVER, i.e., for the equality $\hat{Y} = Y$ to hold for all initial conditions, it is necessary and sufficient that $\mathscr{C}_2 = 0$.

Now, since $\mathscr{A}_{12} = 0$ and the columns of T_2 span the uncontrollable subspace of $\mathscr{S}(r)$ [10], $\mathscr{C}_2 = 0$ if and only if condition (2) of the proposition holds. This completes the proof.

Remark. The unobservable and uncontrollable subspace of any system can be factored out without affecting the input-output properties of the system [5]. Hence, if a COVER $\mathscr{S}(r;\ A_R,\ D_R,\ C_R)$ generated by the CCA algorithm contains an uncontrollable subspace (this subspace is also unstable and unobservable by Propositions 3 and 4), then it can be further reduced to yield an asymptotically stable COVER, namely $\mathscr{S}(n_1;\ \mathscr{A}_{11},\ \mathscr{D}_1,\ \mathscr{C}_1)$.

Thus the CCA algorithm when applied in the cost-decoupled coordinates produces COVERs subject to the conditions presented in Proposition 4. The properties of the COVERs thus generated are presented in the sequel.

C. PROPERTIES OF COVERs

The COVERs by Definition 1 match the steady state covariance of the output. The following corollary which presents an additional property of the COVER assumes[5] that the COVER generated by the CCA algorithm is asymptotically stable.

Corollary 2 (An additional property of the COVER). The COVERs satisfy

$$\lim_{t\to\infty} \mathscr{E}\{\dot{\hat{y}}(t)\hat{y}^T(t)\} = \lim_{t\to\infty} \mathscr{E}\{\dot{y}(t)y^T(t)\} \tag{37}$$

Proof.

$$\begin{aligned}\lim_{t\to\infty} \mathscr{E}\{\dot{y}(t)y^T(t)\} &= \lim_{t\to\infty} \mathscr{E}\{C\dot{x}(t)x^T(t)C^T\}\\ &= \lim_{t\to\infty} \mathscr{E}\{C[Ax(t) + Dw(t)]x^T(t)C^T\}\\ &= \lim_{t\to\infty} CA\mathscr{E}\{x(t)x^T(t)\}C^T\\ &\quad + \lim_{t\to\infty} CD\mathscr{E}\{w(t)x^T(t)\}C^T. \end{aligned} \tag{38a}$$

Since the trajectory x(t) is given by

$$x(t) = e^{At}x(0) + \int_0^t e^{A(t-\tau)}Dw(\tau)\, d\tau,$$

the last term of (38a) can be simplified as

$$\begin{aligned}&\lim_{t\to\infty} CD\mathscr{E}\{w(t)x^T(t)\}C^T\\ &\quad = \lim_{t\to\infty} CD\mathscr{E}\{w(t)x^T(0)\}\, e^{A^Tt}\\ &\quad\quad + \lim_{t\to\infty} CD\mathscr{E}\int_0^t w(t)w^T(\tau)D^T\, e^{A^T(t-\tau)}\, d\tau\\ &\quad = \frac{1}{2}\, CDWD^TC^T, \end{aligned} \tag{38b}$$

[5] *See the remark following the proof of the corollary.*

where

$$\mathscr{E}\{x(0)w^T(t)\} = 0, \quad t \geq 0$$

and the screening property of the Dirac delta function, i.e.,

$$\mathscr{E} \int_0^t w(t)w^T(\tau)\ e^{A^T(t-\tau)}\ d\tau = \int_0^t W\delta(t - \tau)\ e^{A^T(t-\tau)}\ d\tau$$

$$= \frac{1}{2} W$$

have been used. Hence using (12) and (38b), (38a) becomes

$$\lim_{t\to\infty} \mathscr{E}\{\dot{y}(t)y^T(t)\} = CAC^T + \frac{1}{2} CDWD^TC^T$$

$$= C_RA_RC_R^T + \frac{1}{2} C_RD_RWD_R^TC_R^T, \tag{38c}$$

where the structure of C in the cost-decoupled coordinates, i.e., $C = [C_R\ 0]$ for $r \geq k$, has been used. Proceeding similarly and using the assumption of the asymptotic stability of the COVER, it can be shown that

$$\lim_{t\to\infty} \mathscr{E}\{\dot{\hat{y}}(t)\hat{y}^T(t)\} = C_RA_RC_R^T + \frac{1}{2} C_RD_RWD_RC_R^T. \tag{38d}$$

Comparison of (38c) and (38d) completes the proof.

Remark. A similar proof can also be provided for the case when the COVER is not asymptotically stable (the reader is reminded that the subspace of a COVER that is not asymptotically stable is neither controllable nor observable). However, besides introducing additional mathematical steps such a proof does not offer any further insight. Hence for simplicity the assumption of asymptotic stability has been made.

Now, since the order r^* of the minimal COVER satisfies $r^* \geq k$, it is of interest to study the conditions under which the CCA algorithm yields a COVER of order k. The conditions that dictate the order of the minimal COVER is provided in the following proposition.

Proposition 5 (First Markov parameter and the order of the minimal COVER). The order r^* of the minimal COVER produced by the CCA algorithm satisfies the following:

(1) if $\mathcal{T}_1(n) = 0$, then $r^* > k$;

(2) if $\text{rank}[\mathcal{T}_1(n)] = k$, then $r^* = k$, where $\mathcal{T}_i(n) \triangleq CA^{i-1}D$, $i = 1, 2, \ldots$ is the ith Markov parameter of $\mathcal{S}(n; A, D, C)$.

Proof. Let $r = k$ so that $C_R = C_1$ and $r = k = \text{rank}[C_1]$. Now, since the Markov parameters are invariant under similarity transformations,

$$\mathcal{T}_1(n) = CD = [C_1 \quad 0]\begin{bmatrix} D_1 \\ D_2' \end{bmatrix} = C_1 D_1, \tag{39}$$

where (25b) has been used, and where $D_1 \in \mathcal{R}^{k\times q}$. Thus, since C_1 is square and of full rank, $\mathcal{T}_1(n) = 0$ if and only if $D_1 = 0$. Hence, $\mathcal{S}(k; A_R, D_1, C_1)$ is uncontrollable but is completely observable since $\text{rank}[C_1] = k = r$. Therefore by Proposition 4 it cannot be a COVER, which in view of Proposition 1 proves claim (1).

To prove claim (2) note from (39) that $\text{rank}[\mathcal{T}_1(n)] = k$ if and only if $\text{rank}[D_1] = k$. Therefore $\mathcal{S}(k; A_R, D_1, C_1)$ is controllable and hence is the minimal COVER by Propositions 1 and 4.

Remark. Observe that the first Markov parameter dictates the asymptotic stability of $\mathcal{S}(k)$. For single input-single output systems, the same observation can be made in the original version of model reduction by Routh approximations [11].

In many situations such as optimal sensor selection [9],[6] the number of independent outputs k may be quite large and the analyst is then forced to use a partial realization of order

[6] *Another such situation is when one is interested in controlling the total energy (kinetic and potential) of a flexible structure where the number of outputs equals the number of states.*

$r < k$. The following proposition presents the property of $\mathscr{S}(r < k)$ assuming it is asymptotically stable.

Proposition 6 (Perturbation in the covariance of $\mathscr{S}(r)$). If $Q = I_k$, then the perturbation in the output covariance satisfies

$$\|Y - \hat{Y}\|_2 = \alpha_{r+1}^2 \tag{40}$$

where Y and Y are the output covariances of $\mathscr{S}(n)$ and $\mathscr{S}(r)$, respectively [defined in (36a) and (29)], and $\|\cdot\|_2$ is the spectral radius of $[\cdot]$, i.e., $\|\cdot\|_2 = \lambda_{max}(\cdot)$.

Proof. Since $\mathscr{S}(r)$ is assumed to be asymptotically stable, it follows from the proof of Proposition 4, and (34) in particular, that

$$X_R = I_r. \tag{41a}$$

Therefore,

$$\hat{Y} = C_R X_R C_R^T = C_R C_R^T. \tag{41b}$$

Now, in view of (12) and by partitioning C as $C = [C_R, C_T]$, $C_R \in \mathscr{R}^{k \times r}$ we get

$$Y = CC^T = C_R C_R^T + C_T C_T^T. \tag{41c}$$

Therefore, from (41b) and (41c)

$$\|Y - \hat{Y}\|_2 = \lambda_{Max}(Y - \hat{Y}) = \lambda_{Max}\left(C_T C_T^T\right) = \alpha_{r+1}^2$$

which follows from (13) and from the hypothesis $Q = I_k$.

Remark. If there exists a $r < k$ such that $\alpha_r^2 \gg \alpha_{r+1}^2$, then by Proposition 6 the realization $\mathscr{S}(r)$ is a relatively "good" approximation to the COVER.

Recall that the COVERs match the output covariance at steady state, $t \to \infty$. On the other hand, the partial realizations of Anderson [6] match the autocorrelation function for *all* time,

$\tau \in [0, \infty)$, $t \to \infty$. The realizations of [6] are called herein stochastic equivalent realizations (SERs). The SERs are obtained in [6] by enforcing the following property on the partial realizations. Let G(s) and $G_R(s)$ be the transfer functions of $\mathscr{S}(n; A, D, C)$ and $\mathscr{S}(r; A_R, D_R, C_R)$, respectively, i.e.,

$$y(s) = G(s)w(s) \tag{42a}$$

$$\hat{y}(s) = G_R(s)w(s) \tag{42b}$$

where

$$G(s) \triangleq C(sI - A)^{-1}D. \tag{42c}$$

$$G_R(s) \triangleq C_R(sI - A_R)^{-1}D_R. \tag{42d}$$

Now, the spectral densities of y(s) and $\hat{y}(s)$ are given, respectively, by [6]

$$\Phi(s) = G(s)WG^T(-s), \tag{43a}$$

$$\Phi_R(s) = G_R(s)WG_R^T(-s). \tag{43b}$$

Then,

$$\mathscr{E}\{\hat{y}(t + \tau)\hat{y}^T(t)\} = \mathscr{E}\{y(t + \tau)y^T(t)\}, \quad \tau \in [0, \infty], \ t \to \infty \tag{44a}$$

is achieved by matching the spectral densities, i.e., by enforcing

$$\Phi_R(s) = \Phi(s). \tag{44b}$$

Anderson [6] has characterized all SERs as follows.

Lemma 2 (Characterization of the SERs) [6]. The realization $\mathscr{S}(r)$ is an SER if the transfer function G(s) of $\mathscr{S}(n)$ is as follows.

$$G(s) = G_R(s)U(s) \tag{45a}$$

where U(s) is any stable "all-pass" network [12] with the property

$$U(s)WU^T(-s) = W. \tag{45b}$$

Note that the transfer function G(s) in (44) may be minimal in the sense of Kalman [13], i.e., $\mathscr{S}(n)$ is controllable and observable, in which case the order of the Kalman minimal realizations [13] is n. On the other hand, the minimal order of an SER is dictated by the all-pass network present in G(s). Thus, the minimal SER can be of order less than the Kalman minimal realization.

Now, from Propositions 1 and 5 the minimal COVER can be of order still less than the minimal SER. Furthermore, there exists a situation in which the COVERs produced by the CCA algorithm are also SERs, i.e., these COVERs satisfy (44) as shown by the following proposition.

Proposition 7 (Condition for the COVER to be an SER). In cost-decoupled coordinates if $A_{TR} = 0$ for some $r \geq k$, then the realization $\mathscr{S}(r;\ A_R,\ D_R,\ C_R)$ is also an SER.

Proof. Let $A_{TR} = 0$ and consider the transfer function

$$G(s) = C(sI - A)^{-1}D. \tag{46a}$$

Since for $r \geq k$, $C = [C_R\ \ 0]$ in cost-decoupled coordinates, and since $A_{TR} = 0$, (46a) simplifies to

$$\begin{aligned} G(s) &= C_R(sI - A_R)^{-1}D_R + C_R(sI - A_R)^{-1}A_{RT}(sI - A_T)^{-1}D_T \\ &= C_R(sI - A_R)^{-1}\Big[D_R + A_{RT}(sI - A_T)^{-1}D_T\Big], \end{aligned} \tag{46b}$$

which in view of (26b) $\Big($i.e., $A_{RT} = -D_R W D_T^T - A_{TR}^T = -D_R W D_T^T\Big)$, is written as

$$G(s) = G_R(s)\Big[I - WD_T^T(sI - A_T)^{-1}D_T\Big], \tag{46c}$$

where

$$G_R(s) = C_R(sI - A_R)^{-1}D_R \tag{46d}$$

is the transfer function of $\mathscr{S}(r;\ A_R,\ D_R,\ C_R)$. Hence, in view of Lemma 2 to prove the proposition it suffices to show that

$$G_T(s) \triangleq \left[I - WD_T^T(sI - A_T)^{-1}D_T\right] \tag{47}$$

is an all-pass network satisfying $G_T(s)WG_T^T(-s) = W$.

To show this consider

$$G_T(s)WG_T^T(-s) = W - WD_T^T(sI - A_T)^{-1}D_TW - WD_T^T(-sI - A_T)^{-T}D_TW$$
$$+ WD_T^T(sI - A_T)^{-1}D_TWD_T^T(-sI - A_T)^{-T}D_TW. \tag{48a}$$

Since $D_TWD_T^T = -\left(A_T + A_T^T\right)$ from (26c), (48a) becomes

$$G_T(s)WG_T^T(-s) = W - WD_T^T\overline{\Psi}(s)D_TW, \tag{48b}$$

where

$$\overline{\Psi}(s) \triangleq (sI - A_T)^{-1} + (-sI - A_T)^{-T}$$
$$+ (sI - A_T)^{-1}\left(A_T + A_T^T\right)(-sI - A_T)^{-T},$$

which after some algebraic manipulation becomes

$$\overline{\Psi}(s) = (sI - A_T)^{-1}\left[I - \left(sA_T^{-1} + I\right)^{-T}\right]$$
$$+ \left[I - \left(-sA_T^{-1} + I\right)^{-1}\right](-sI - A_T)^{-T}. \tag{48c}$$

The fact that A_T^{-1} exists in (48c) follows from $A_{TR} = 0$ and from the asymptotic stability of $\mathscr{S}(n)$. Now, use the following identity [14],

$$(A + BDC)^{-1} = A^{-1} - A^{-1}B(D^{-1} + CA^{-1}B)^{-1}CA^{-1};$$
$$|A| \neq 0, \quad |D| \neq 0,$$

to establish

$$(sI - A_T)^{-1} = (1/s)\left[I - \left(-sA_T^{-1} + I\right)^{-1}\right], \tag{49a}$$

$$(-sI - A_T)^{-1} = -(1/s)\left[I - \left(sA_T^{-1} + I\right)^{-1}\right] \tag{49b}$$

from which obtain

$$\left(-sA_T^{-1} + I\right)^{-1} = I - s(sI - A_T)^{-1}, \tag{49c}$$

$$\left(sA_T^{-1} + I\right)^{-1} = I + s(-sI - A_T)^{-1}. \tag{49d}$$

Substituting (49c) and (49d) in (48c) results in

$$\overline{\Psi}(s) = 0.$$

Hence, from (48b) we get

$$G_T(s)WG_T^T(-s) = W,$$

thus completing the proof.

Now, assuming $W = I_q$, it follows from the proof that under the hypothesis of Proposition 7 the transfer function G(s) of $\mathscr{S}(n)$ is of the form

$$G(s) = G_R(s)G_T(s)$$

where $G_T(s)$ is an all-pass network. Furthermore, with some block-diagram manipulation [15] it is possible to represent $\mathscr{S}(n)$ as

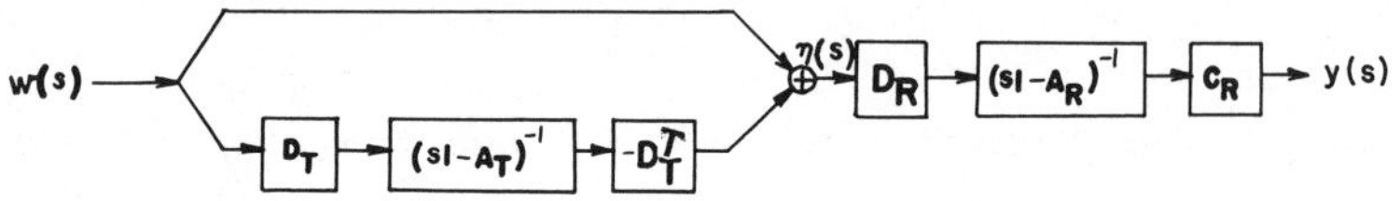

where

$$\eta(s) = \left[I - D_T^T(sI - A_T)^{-1}D_T\right]w(s) = G_T(s)w(s)$$

and

$$y(s) = C_R(sI - A_R)^{-1}D_R\eta(s) = G_R(s)\eta(s).$$

Recalling that in cost-decoupled coordinates the relation (26c) holds between A_T and D_T, it then follows that for all systems

of the form

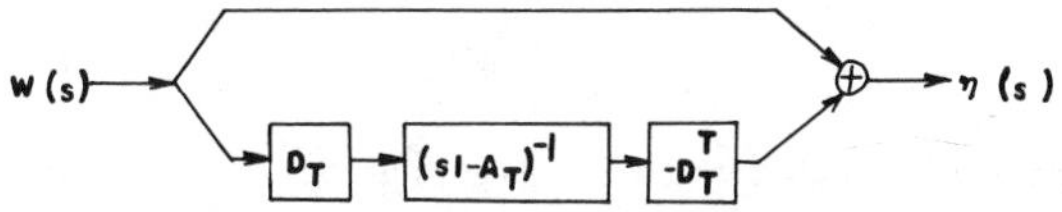

with $A_T^T + A_T + D_T D_T^T = 0$, its SER is given by

$$w(s) \longrightarrow \boxed{1} \longrightarrow \hat{\eta}(s).$$

In state space representation the above claim can be restated as follows. The SER for the system

$$\begin{aligned} \dot{x}_T(t) &= A_T x_T(t) + D_T w(t) \\ \eta(t) &= -D_T^T x_T(t) + w(t) \end{aligned} \tag{50a}$$

with $A_T^T + A_T + D_T D_T^T = 0$, is given by

$$\hat{\eta}(t) = w(t), \tag{50b}$$

and therefore,

$$\mathscr{E}\{\hat{\eta}(t+\tau)\hat{\eta}^T(t)\} = \mathscr{E}\{\eta(t+\tau)\eta^T(t)\}, \qquad \tau \in [0, \infty),\ t \to \infty.$$

This offers an apparent contradiction to Proposition 1 which says that the minimal COVER of (50a) cannot be of order less than the dimension of η, whereas the SER (50b) which is of order zero is a COVER. This paradox is settled by recognizing that the COVER theory developed herein assumes that there is no feed-forward present in the output η.

Also note that Proposition 7 seems to suggest a means of selecting the arbitrary orthonormal matrix T_{22} of Proposition 2, which is to compute T_{22} so as to make $A_{TR} = 0$ for some r if possible. One way of obtaining such a matrix T_{22} is to use the orthonormal transformations suggested by Patel [16]. However, in the following section it will be shown that the model reduction problem imposes a different requirement on T_{22}.

IV. APPLICATION OF COVER THEORY TO MODEL REDUCTION

A. *PREAMBLE*

The covariance equivalent realizations match the steady-state output covariance (19). And as a consequence they are also cost-equivalent realizations [3], i.e., they satisfy (16). However, for the purposes of designing a controller based upon the reduced order models one would desire the *tracking error index* μ,

$$\mu \triangleq \frac{1}{\mathscr{V}} \lim_{t\to\infty} \frac{1}{t} \mathscr{E} \int_0^t \|y(\tau) - \hat{y}(\tau)\|_Q^2 \, d\tau$$

to be minimized. Hence the natural question that arises is "how well do the COVERs 'measure up' with respect to μ?"

Recall that the partial realizations[7] of order $r \leq k$ generated by the CCA algorithm in cost-decoupled coordinates are essentially unique, except for the change of direction of the basis vectors (as indicated by the ± 1 entries in (24b)). However, for $r > k$ they are not unique — this nonuniqueness is reflected by the arbitrariness of the orthonormal matrix T_{22} of Proposition 2. This leads to another question: How can one make use of this nonuniqueness to advantage so that the tracking error index is reduced?

We will first establish an expression for μ in Lemma 3 and answer the above questions in the sequel.

Lemma 3 (Formula for μ*).* Let $\mathscr{S}(n;\, A,\, D,\, C)$ and $\mathscr{S}(r;\, A_R,\, D_R,\, C_R)$ be a full model and its stable reduced model, respectively. Then the tracking error index associated with $\mathscr{S}(r;\, A_R,\, D_R,\, C_R)$

[7] *For* $r < k$*, these realizations are not COVERs by Proposition 1.*

is given by

$$\mu = (1/\mathscr{V})\Big\{\mathrm{Tr}\,[C^TQCX] + \mathrm{Tr}\Big[C_R^TQC_RX_R\Big] - 2\mathrm{Tr}\Big[C^TQC_RX_{12}^T\Big]\Big\}, \tag{52a}$$

where X and X_R are the steady state covariance matrices of x(t) and $\hat{x}_R(t)$, respectively, and

$$X_{12} \triangleq \lim_{t\to\infty} \mathscr{E}\Big\{x(t)\,\hat{x}_R^T(t)\Big\}. \tag{52b}$$

Proof. Rewrite (51) as

$$\begin{aligned}\mathscr{V}\mu &= \lim_{t\to\infty} \frac{1}{t}\mathscr{E}\int_0^t \Big\{\|y(\tau)\|_Q^2 - 2y^T(\tau)Q\hat{y}(\tau) + \|\hat{y}(\tau)\|_Q^2\Big\}\,d\tau \\ &= \lim_{t\to\infty} \frac{1}{t}\mathscr{E}\int_0^t \Big\{\|x(\tau)\|^2_{C^TQC} - 2x^T(\tau)C^TQC_R\hat{x}_R(\tau) \\ &\qquad + \|\hat{x}_R(\tau)\|^2_{C_R^TQC_R}\Big\}\,d\tau. \end{aligned} \tag{53}$$

Now, use the following properties

$$\|\eta\|_Q^2 = \eta^TQ\eta = \mathrm{Tr}\,[Q\eta\eta^T] \quad \text{for any vector } \eta$$

and

$$\lim_{t\to\infty} \frac{1}{t}\mathscr{E}\int_0^t \|\eta(\tau)\|_Q^2\,d\tau = \lim_{t\to\infty} \mathscr{E}\|\eta(t)\|_Q^2$$

for any ergodic process $\eta(t)$ [5] to rewrite (53) as

$$\mathscr{V}\mu = \lim_{t\to\infty} \mathscr{E}\Big\{\mathrm{Tr}\,[C^TQCx(t)x^T(t)] - 2\mathrm{Tr}\Big[C^TQC_R\hat{x}_R(t)x^T(t)\Big] + \mathrm{Tr}\Big[C_R^TQC_R\hat{x}_R(t)\hat{x}_R^T(t)\Big]\Big\},$$

to yield (52a) with the substitution of the definitions of X, X_R, and X_{12}.

B. MODEL REDUCTION BY COVER THEORY

Now, when $\mathscr{S}(n; A, D, C)$ is in cost-decoupled coordinates and $\mathscr{S}(r; A_R, D_R, C_R)$ for any r is obtained by the CCA algorithm considerable simplification of Lemma 3 results.

Proposition 8 (μ of COVERs). If $\mathscr{S}(n; A, D, C)$ is in cost-decoupled coordinates, then the tracking error index μ associated with the asymptotically stable reduced model $\mathscr{S}(r; A_R, D_R, C_R)$ produced by the CCA algorithm satisfies the following:

$$(1) \quad \mu = 1 + \sum_{i=1}^{r} \hat{\upsilon}_i (1 - 2x_{ii}) \tag{54a}$$

$$(2a) \quad \sum_{i=r+1}^{k} \hat{\upsilon}_i \leq \mu \leq 4 \sum_{i=1}^{r} \hat{\upsilon}_i + \sum_{i=r+1}^{k} \hat{\upsilon}_i \quad \text{for } r < k \tag{54b}$$

$$(2b) \quad 0 \leq \mu \leq 4 \quad \text{for } r \geq k, \tag{54c}$$

where the *normalized* component costs $\hat{\upsilon}_i$ are defined by

$$\hat{\upsilon}_i \triangleq \hat{\mathscr{V}}_i/\mathscr{V}, \qquad i = 1, 2, \ldots, n, \tag{54d}$$

and where

$$x_{ii} \triangleq \lim_{t\to\infty} \mathscr{E}\{x_i(t)\hat{x}_{R_i}(t)\} = [X_{12}]_{ii}. \tag{54e}$$

Proof. Due to the hypothesis of the proposition, it follows from (12) and (40a) that $X = I_n$ and $X_R = I_r$. Hence (52a) simplifies to

$$\mu = \frac{1}{\mathscr{V}}\left\{\mathrm{Tr}[C^TQC] + \mathrm{Tr}\left[C_R^TQC_R\right] - 2\mathrm{Tr}\left[C^TQC_RX_{12}^T\right]\right\}. \tag{55}$$

Now, in view of (13), partitioning C as $C = [C_R, C_T]$ with $C_R \in \mathscr{R}^{k\times r}$ we get

$$\mathrm{Tr}[C^TQC] = \sum_{i=1}^{k} \alpha_i^2 \tag{56a}$$

$$\mathrm{Tr}\left[C_R^T Q C_R\right] = \sum_{i=1}^{r} \alpha_i^2, \tag{56b}$$

and

$$\mathrm{Tr}\left[C^T Q C_R X_{12}^T\right] = \mathrm{Tr}\left[C_R^T Q C_R X_1^T\right], \tag{56c}$$

where $X_1 \in \mathscr{R}^{r\times r}$ is obtained from partitioning X_{12} as

$$X_{12}^T = \left[X_1^T,\ X_2^T\right]. \tag{56d}$$

Then, substituting (56a)-(56d) into (55) and using claim 1 of Proposition 3 $\left(\text{i.e., } \hat{\mathscr{V}}_i = \alpha_i^2\right)$, (55) is rewritten as

$$\mu = \frac{1}{\mathscr{V}} \sum_{i=1}^{k} \hat{\mathscr{V}}_i + \frac{1}{\mathscr{V}} \sum_{i=1}^{r} \hat{\mathscr{V}}_i - \frac{2}{\mathscr{V}} \mathrm{Tr}\left[C_R^T Q C_R X_1^T\right]$$

$$= \sum_{i=1}^{k} \hat{\upsilon}_i + \sum_{i=1}^{r} \hat{\upsilon}_i - \frac{2}{\mathscr{V}} \mathrm{Tr}\left[C_R^T Q C_R X_1^T\right], \tag{57}$$

where the definition (54d) has been used. Since there are only k nonzero component costs in cost-decoupled coordinates (by Proposition 3) and since $C_R^T Q C_R = \mathrm{diag}\left\{\alpha_1^2,\ \alpha_2^2,\ \ldots,\ \alpha_r^2\right\}$ from (13), (57) simplifies to (54a).

Now, since both $x(t)$ and $\hat{x}_R(t)$ are covariance normalized, i.e., $X = I_n$ and $X_R = I_r$, from the Cauchy-Schwartz inequality [17] it follows that

$$-1 \le x_{ij} = \lim_{t\to\infty} \mathscr{E}\left\{x_i(t)\hat{x}_{R_j}(t)\right\}$$

$$\le 1; \quad i,\ j = 1,\ 2,\ \ldots,\ r. \tag{58}$$

Using the upper and the lower bounds of (58) in (54a), respectively, yields

$$\mu \ge 1 + \sum_{i=1}^{r} \hat{\upsilon}_i - 2\sum_{i=1}^{r} \hat{\upsilon}_i = 1 - \sum_{i=1}^{r} \hat{\upsilon}_i \tag{59a}$$

and

$$\mu \leq 1 + \sum_{i=1}^{r} \hat{\upsilon}_i + 2 \sum_{i=1}^{r} \hat{\upsilon}_i = 1 + 3 \sum_{i=1}^{r} \hat{\upsilon}_i. \tag{59b}$$

Now, using the fact that for $r < k$

$$1 = \sum_{i=1}^{k} \hat{\upsilon}_i = \sum_{i=1}^{r} \hat{\upsilon}_i + \sum_{i=r+1}^{k} \hat{\upsilon}_i$$

in (59) proves (54b). (54c) readily follows from (54b) by recognizing that $\hat{\upsilon}_i = 0$, $i > k$.

From (54a) the tracking error index associated with COVERs ($r \geq k$) is given by

$$\mu = 2 \sum_{i-1}^{k} (1 - x_{ii})\hat{\upsilon}_i. \tag{60}$$

This establishes the relationship between tracking error μ and component costs.

How can the tracking error index μ be reduced? To answer this question observe from (60) that if $x_{ii} = 1$, $i = 1, 2, \ldots, k$, then $\mu = 0$. But when $\mathscr{S}(n)$ is observable and controllable there exists no reduced model which yields $\mu = 0$ [13]. Hence, $x_{ii} = 1$, $i = 1, 2, \ldots, k$, cannot be achieved. One may therefore opt to minimize $1 - x_{ii}$, $i = 1, 2, \ldots, k$. The nonuniqueness of the cost-decoupled coordinates offers a means of achieving this. The following lemma aids in this task.

Lemma 4 (Alternative formula for μ of COVERs). The tracking error index associated with the COVERs can be expressed as

$$\mu = \frac{2}{\mathscr{V}} \operatorname{Tr}\left[\underline{\alpha}^2 \tilde{X}_{11}\right] \tag{61a}$$

where $\underline{\alpha}^2$ is defined in (25c) and $\tilde{X}_{11}$ is the leading $(k \times k)$

submatrix of $\tilde{X}_1 \triangleq I_r - X_1$ which satisfies

$$\begin{bmatrix} \tilde{X}_1 \\ -X_2 \end{bmatrix} A_R^T + \begin{bmatrix} A_R & A_{RT} \\ A_{TR} & A_T \end{bmatrix} \begin{bmatrix} \tilde{X}_1 \\ -X_2 \end{bmatrix} + \begin{bmatrix} 0 \\ A_{RT}^T \end{bmatrix} = 0 \tag{61b}$$

Proof. (61a) results from using (25c) and the definition of $\tilde{X}_{11}$ in (60). Now, since A and A_R are asymptotically stable, the matrix X_{12} defined in (52b) satisfies

$$X_{12}A_R^T + AX_{12} + DWD_R^T = 0. \tag{62a}$$

Partitioning X_{12} as in (56d), Eq. (62a) is written as

$$X_1A_R^T + A_RX_1 + A_{RT}X_2 + D_RWD_R^T = 0 \tag{62b}$$

$$X_2A_R^T + A_{TR}X_1 + A_TX_2 + D_TWD_R^T = 0. \tag{62c}$$

Using (26a) and (26b) rewrite (62b) and (62c) as

$$(X_1 - I_r)A_R^T + A_R(X_1 - I_r) + A_{RT}X_2 = 0 \tag{62d}$$

$$X_2A_R^T + A_{TR}(X_1 - I_r) + A_TX_2 - A_{RT}^T = 0. \tag{62e}$$

In view of $\tilde{X}_1 = I_r - X_1$ recognizing that Eqs. (62d) and (62e) are written compactly in (61b) completes the proof.

Corollary 3 (μ of MISO systems). For multi-input single-output systems (i.e., k = 1) the tracking error index is given by

$$\mu = 2\tilde{x}_{11} \tag{63}$$

Proof. The proof follows from Lemma 4, since now $\underline{\alpha}^2 = \alpha_1^2 = \hat{\mathcal{V}}_1 = \mathcal{V}$ due to k = 1. Therefore,

$$\hat{\upsilon}_1 = \alpha_1^2/\mathcal{V} = 1$$

and thus (61a) reduces to (63).

Now, note from (61b) that if $A_{RT} = 0$, then both $\tilde{X}_1 = 0$ and $X_2 = 0$, since A and A_R are asymptotically stable matrices. Also observe from the structure (25b) of the output matrix C in cost-decoupled coordinates that for $r \geq k$, $A_{RT} = 0$ if and only if the states x_i, $i > k$, are unobservable [5]. In this case obviously $\mu = 0$ since the CCA algorithm truncates these states producing the reduced model $\mathcal{S}(r)$. But, when $\mathcal{S}(n)$ is observable A_{RT} cannot be zero. Nevertheless, it is reasonable to expect that if there exists some $r > k$ for which the states x_i, $i > r$ are "nearly" unobservable (indicated by "small" A_{RT}),[8] then a truncation of these states would yield a reduced model with "small " μ. To identify such "nearly" unobservable states, the nonuniqueness of the cost-decoupled coordinates (equivalently, the arbitrary but orthonormal matrix T_{22}) can be used to obtain the following special case of cost-decoupled coordinates.

Definition 3. The *cost-decoupled Hessenberg* (CODH) coordinates are defined as those cost-decoupled coordinates that in addition to satisfying (12) and (13) yield the following form to $\mathcal{S}(n;\ A,\ D,\ C)$.

$$\begin{bmatrix} \dot{\underline{x}}_1 \\ \dot{\underline{x}}_2 \\ \dot{\underline{x}}_3 \\ \dot{\underline{x}}_4 \\ \vdots \\ \dot{\underline{x}}_{p-1} \\ \dot{\underline{x}}_p \end{bmatrix} = \begin{bmatrix} A_{11} & A_{12} & 0 & 0 & \cdots & 0 \\ A_{21} & A_{22} & A_{23} & 0 & & 0 \\ A_{31} & A_{32} & A_{33} & A_{34} & & 0 \\ A_{41} & A_{42} & A_{43} & A_{44} & & 0 \\ \vdots & & & & & \vdots \\ A_{p-1,1} & A_{p-1,2} & A_{p-1,3} & A_{p-1,4} & & A_{p-1,p} \\ A_{p1} & A_{p2} & A_{p3} & A_{p4} & \cdots & A_{pp} \end{bmatrix} \begin{bmatrix} \underline{x}_1 \\ \underline{x}_2 \\ \underline{x}_3 \\ \underline{x}_4 \\ \vdots \\ \underline{x}_{p-1} \\ \underline{x}_p \end{bmatrix} + \begin{bmatrix} D_1 \\ D_2 \\ D_3 \\ D_4 \\ \vdots \\ D_{p-1} \\ D_p \end{bmatrix} w \tag{64a}$$

[8] *Recall Proposition 7 which requires $A_{TR} = 0$ for the COVERs to be stochastically equivalent [6]. However, to minimize μ it is A_{RT} that needs to be minimized (by a proper choice of T_{22} in Proposition 2) and not A_{TR}. Thus, SERs are not the most desirable* reduced *models from the tracking error criterion.*

$$y = [C_1 \quad 0 \quad 0 \quad 0 \cdots 0]x, \tag{64b}$$

where $\underline{x}_i \in \mathscr{R}^{n_i}$, $\Sigma_{i=1}^{p} n_i = n$ and where $n_{i+1} = \text{rank}[A_{i,i+1}]$, $i = 1, 2, \ldots, p-1$ with $n_1 = k$. The matrices are compatibly dimensioned.

Representations of systems in the form (64) *without* the constraints (12) and (13) have been used in connection with different applications by several researchers — see [18] for a comprehensive exposure to such a representation. It should be pointed out that the representation (64), in the absence of (12) and (13), is not unique although as mentioned in [18] there are certain invariant and, therefore, unique features relating to this representation. Some of these features are highlighted in the following lemma.

Lemma 5 (Invariant properties of (64)).

(1) $n_{i+1} \leq n_i$, $i = 1, 2, \ldots, p-1$, (65a)

(2) $$r_i \triangleq \text{rank}[\mathscr{O}_i] = \sum_{j=1}^{i} n_j, \tag{65b}$$

where $\mathscr{O}_i$, the ith observability matrix is defined as

$$\mathscr{O}_i^T \triangleq [C^T, A^T C^T, \ldots, A^{T^{i-1}} C^T] \tag{65c}$$

and r_i is invariant under any similarity transformation.

Of interest to this chapter are the references [19-21][9] in which the representation (64) is used in the context of model reduction. In particular in [21] Kwong has suggested that if for some i and for some suitable norm, $||A_{i,i+1}||$ is "small"

[9] *The motivation for such a representation in these references follows the same line of argument presented herein. However, they do not consider any controllability information which is taken into account herein via condition (12).*

compared to $||A_i||$ where

$$A_i \triangleq \begin{bmatrix} A_{11} & A_{12} & \cdots & 0 \\ A_{21} & A_{22} & & 0 \\ \vdots & & & \vdots \\ A_{i1} & A_{i2} & \cdots & A_{ii} \end{bmatrix}, \tag{66a}$$

then the coordinates $\underline{x}_j$, $j > i$, can be deleted to yield a "good" reduced model. However, by nonorthonormal transformations one can reduce $||A_{i,i+1}||$ without altering $||A_i||$. To eliminate this arbitrariness one therefore requires some normalization. The natural normalization used in this chapter is condition (12). To maintain this normalization, only orthonormal transformations (as in Proposition 2) must be used to obtain (64) from the cost-decoupled coordinates. Reference [16] offers a suitable algorithm for this task.

Now, the application of the CCA algorithm in the CODH coordinates yields the following structure to the parameters $\{A_R, D_R, C_R\}$ of $\mathscr{S}(r;\ A_R, D_R, C_R)$, $r = r_i \geq k$ for some i.

$$A_R = A_i, \quad \text{defined in (66a)}$$

$$D_R^T = \left[D_1^T,\ D_2^T,\ \ldots,\ D_i^T\right] \tag{66b}$$

$$C_R = [C_1,\ 0,\ \ldots,\ 0]. \tag{66c}$$

Thus $\mathscr{S}(r;\ A_R, D_R, C_R)$ is a COVER if it satisfies condition (2) of Proposition 4. The following proposition presents the observability properties of these reduced models.

Proposition 9 (Observability of S(r), r ≥ k). The reduced models $\mathscr{S}(r)$ are completely observable for $r = r_i$ for any $i = 1, 2, \ldots, p$ where r_i is defined in (65b).

Proof. Define $\mathcal{O}^T_{R,r_i}$ the observability matrix of $\mathcal{S}(r_i)$ as

$$\mathcal{O}^T_{R,r_i} = \left[C^T_R,\ A^T_R C^T_R,\ \ldots,\ A^{T^{r_i-1}} C^T_R\right], \tag{67}$$

and consider i = 1, so that $r = r_1 = n_1 = k$ and $C_R = C_1$, $A_R = A_{11}$. Then

$$\operatorname{rank}[\mathcal{O}_{R,r_1}] = \operatorname{rank}\begin{bmatrix} C_R \\ C_R A_R \\ C_R A_R^{k-1} \end{bmatrix} = \operatorname{rank}\begin{bmatrix} C_1 \\ C_1 A_{11} \\ C_1 A_{11}^{k-1} \end{bmatrix} \tag{68a}$$

$$= k = r_1 = \operatorname{rank}[\mathcal{O}_1].$$

Since r_1 is the dimension of the state space of $\mathcal{S}(r_1)$, the reduced model $\mathcal{S}(r_1)$ is observable. Now let i = 2 so that $r_2 = n_1 + n_2$. Then

$$\operatorname{rank}[\mathcal{O}_{R,r_2}] = \operatorname{rank}\begin{bmatrix} C_R \\ C_R A_R \\ C_R A_R^{r_2-1} \end{bmatrix} \geq \operatorname{rank}\begin{bmatrix} C_R \\ C_R A_R \end{bmatrix}$$

$$= \operatorname{rank}\begin{bmatrix} C_1 & 0 \\ C_1 A_{11} & C_1 A_{12} \end{bmatrix}$$

$$= n_1 + n_2 = r_2 = \operatorname{rank}[\mathcal{O}_2] \tag{68b}$$

where the structure of the matrices A_R and C_R and the facts that $\operatorname{rank}[C_1] = k = n_1$ and $\operatorname{rank}[A_{12}] = n_2$ have been used. Since $\operatorname{rank}[\mathcal{O}_{R,r_2}] \leq r_2$, this proves that $\operatorname{rank}[\mathcal{O}_{R,r_2}] = r_2$ and hence $\mathcal{S}(r_2)$ is observable. Thus, extending this argument we get

$$\operatorname{rank}[\mathcal{O}_{R,r_i}] = r_i = \operatorname{rank}[\mathcal{O}_i], \tag{68c}$$

thus completing the proof.

Remark. A similar proof can be used to prove the observability of $\mathscr{S}(r)$ for *any* r (r need not be constrained to be $r = r_i$). It thus follows from Proposition 4 that the reduced models $\mathscr{S}(r)$ with $r \geq k$ are COVERs if and only if they are controllable.

The following proposition extends the above remark to present the conditions which dictate the order of the minimal COVER.

Proposition 10 (Markov parameters and the order of the minimal COVER). If $\mathscr{T}_l(n) = 0$ for all $l = 1, 2, \ldots, i$ for some i, then the order r^* of the minimal COVER satisfies

$$r^* > r_i = \sum_{j=1}^{i} n_j, \tag{69}$$

where $\mathscr{T}_l(n)$ is the lth Markov Parameter of $\mathscr{S}(n)$.

Before the proof of this proposition is presented the following lemma is established.

Lemma 6.

(1) *(Stability of $\mathscr{S}(r)$)* If $\mathscr{T}_l(n) = 0$ for all $l = 1, 2, \ldots, i$ for some i, then for any $r \leq r_i = \Sigma_{j=1}^{i} n_j$, $\mathscr{S}(r)$ is not asymptotically stable.

(2) *(Markov Parameters of $S(r)$)* If $r = r_i$, then

$$\mathscr{T}_l(r_i) = \mathscr{T}_l(n), \quad l = 1, 2, \ldots, i \tag{70}$$

where $\mathscr{T}_l(r_i) \triangleq C_R A_R^{l-1} D_R$ is the lth Markov Parameter of $\mathscr{S}(r_i)$.

Proof. Let $\mathscr{T}_l(n) = 0$, $l = 1, 2, \ldots, i$. Then

$$\mathscr{T}_1(n) = CD = C_1 D_1 = 0,$$

where the structures in (66b) and (66c) have been used. From (25b) it then follows that $C_1 D_1 = 0$ if and only if $D_1 = 0$.

Hence,

$$\mathcal{T}_2(n) = CAD = C_1A_{11}D_1 + C_1A_{12}D_2 = C_1A_{12}D_2 = 0.$$

Now, since $|C_1| \neq 0$ and $\text{rank}[A_{12}] = n_2 \leq n_1$, $C_1A_{12}D_2 = 0$ if and only if $D_2 = 0$. Proceeding similarly yields $\mathcal{T}_l(n) = 0$, $l = 1, 2, \ldots i$ if and only if $D_l = 0$, $l = 1, 2, \ldots, i$. Therefore from the definition of D_R in (66b) it follows that

$$D_R = 0 \quad \text{for all} \quad r \leq r_i = \sum_{j=1}^{i} n_j.$$

Hence by Proposition 4 $\mathcal{S}(r)$ is not asymptotically stable for all $r \leq r_i$, thus proving claim (1).

Now, by using the structures of $\{A_R, D_R, D_R\}$ it follows that

$$\mathcal{T}_1(r_i) = C_RD_R = C_1D_1 = \mathcal{T}_1(n) \quad \text{for all} \quad i = 1, 2, \ldots, p$$

and

$$\mathcal{T}_2(r_i) = C_RD_R = C_1A_{11}D_1 + C_1A_{12}D_2$$
$$= \mathcal{T}_2(n), \quad \text{for all} \quad i = 2, 3, 4, \ldots, p.$$

Claim (2) is thus proved by extending this argument.

Proof of Proposition 10. The proof now follows from Lemma 6 and the remark following Proposition 9.

Corollary 4 (Order of the minimal COVER of MISO systems). For multi-input single-output systems the order of the minimal COVER is $r^* = i_0$ where $\mathcal{T}_{i_0}(n)$ is the first nonzero Markov Parameter of $\mathcal{S}(n)$.

Proof. Since $\mathcal{T}_{i_0}(n)$ is the first nonzero Markov Parameter of $\mathcal{S}(n)$ it follows from Lemma 6 that $r^* > i_0 - 1$. To prove that $r^* = i_0$, it remains to be shown that $\mathcal{S}(i_0)$ is controllable. To show this consider the matrices A_R and D_R with $r = i_0$, which have the structures given in (66). In particular, since $n_1 = k = 1$ and since $\mathscr{S}(n)$ is observable, it follows that $p = n$ and $n_i = 1$ with $A_{i,i+1} \neq 0$, $i = 1, 2, \ldots, n$. Furthermore $A_{i,i+1}$, $i = 1, 2, \ldots, n$ and C_1 are scalars and $D_i \in \mathscr{R}^{1\times q}$, $i = 1, 2, \ldots, n$ are row vectors.

Now, since $\mathscr{T}_l(n) = 0$, $l = 1, 2, \ldots, i_0 - 1$ it follows from the proof of Lemma 6 that

$$D_l = 0, \quad l = 1, 2, \ldots, i_0 - 1. \tag{71a}$$

Thus,

$$\mathscr{T}_{i_0}(n) = CA^{i_0-1}D = C_1 \prod_{j=1}^{i_0-1} A_{j,j+1}D_{i_0} \tag{71b}$$

Therefore, $\mathscr{T}_{i_0}(n) \neq 0$ if and only if $D_{i_0} \neq 0$. Hence, substitution of the structure of A_R (66a) in the controllability matrix Γ_R of $\mathscr{S}(i_0)$ gives

$$\Gamma_R \triangleq \left[D_R, A_R D_R, \ldots, A_R^{i_0-1} D_R\right]$$
$$= \begin{bmatrix} 0 & 0 & \cdots & 0 & \omega_1 \\ 0 & 0 & & \omega_2 & * \\ 0 & 0 & & * & * \\ 0 & \omega_{i_0-1} & & * & * \\ D_{i_0} & & \cdots & * & * \end{bmatrix}, \tag{71c}$$

where asterisks indicate possibly nonzero entries and

$$\omega_j \triangleq D_{i_0} \prod_{l=j}^{i_0} A_{l,l+1}. \tag{71d}$$

Since $A_{l,l+1} \neq 0$, $l = 1, 2, \ldots, n$, and $D_{i_0} \neq 0$, it follows from the structure of Γ_R in (71c) that $\text{rank}[\Gamma_R] = i_0$. Hence $\mathscr{S}(i_0)$ is controllable and is therefore asymptotically stable by Proposition 3. This completes the proof.

Remarks. (1) By retaining the states $\underline{x}_j$, j = 1, 2, ..., i in $\mathscr{S}(r)$ one therefore, by Lemma 6, matches the first i Markov parameters of $\mathscr{S}(n)$. Since matching of the Markov parameters reflects the matching of the transient response between y(t) and $\hat{y}(t)$ [22] Lemma 6 implies that by increasing the order of $\mathscr{S}(r)$ better matching of the transient response can be achieved.

(2) When the description of a MISO system is available in the frequency domain as

$$y(s) = G(s)w(s), \tag{72a}$$

where

$$G(s) = \sum_{i=1}^{n} D_i s^{n-i} \Bigg/ \left(s^n + \sum_{i=1}^{n} a_i s^{n-1}\right), \tag{72b}$$

the Markov parameters are dictated by D_i and a_i, i = 1, 2, ..., n. In particular, it can be verified that, if $D_i = 0$, i = 1, 2, ..., $i_0 - 1$, then the first $i_0 - 1$ Markov parameters of $\mathscr{S}(n)$ are zero. Hence, due to Corollary 4, by inspection of the numerator polynomial of the transfer function G(s) one can determine the order of the minimal COVER. Alternatively if j_0 is the number of finite zeros of G(s) then the order of the minimal COVER if $n - j_0$. It is interesting to observe that in the original work of Hutton and Friedland [11] the order of the smallest reduced model that is asymptotically stable is also $n - j_0$.

C. THE COVER ALGORITHM

The CCA algorithm applied in the CODH coordinates produces COVERs under the conditions mentioned above. It is in order now to point out the computations involved in generating the COVERs in this way — the computations include the "CER algorithm" of [3] and the orthonormal transformations of [16]. Thus, the algorithm needed to obtain CODH coordinates essentially uses the following steps:

(1) Transform the given system to "covariance normalized" coordinates (i.e., $X = I_n$). (This requires an $n \times n$ matrix square-root computation and an $n \times n$ matrix inversion [3].)

(2) Compute the orthonormal modal matrix of the transformed system's (of step 1) state-weighting matrix C^TQC in the cost function to obtain the cost-decoupled coordinates. (This requires a singular value decomposition or a spectral decomposition of the symmetric matrix C^TQC [3].)

(3) Finally, transform the system to the CODH coordinates. (This requires $p - 1$ singular value decompositions of matrices of decreasing dimensions [16].)

Note that the transformations involved in steps 2 and 3 are orthonormal, and efficient algorithms [23] exist for this task. Yet, to obtain a COVER of order r_i there are i such computations required (one in step 2 and $i - 1$ in step 3, in addition to the computations involved in step 1). Even though efficient algorithms do exist for square-root computations [24] and matrix inversions [23], this task becomes formidable when n is large as is normally the case with large-scale systems.

Thus, even though the CODH coordinates have served to clarify the process of the model reduction involved (such as component costs and observability and controllability of the truncated and the retained states) in obtaining the COVERs, the computations involved discourage the use of CODH coordinates. To overcome this obstacle, we shall now present a much simpler algorithm. The COVERs generated by this algorithm will be shown to be related by a similarity transformation to those produced from the CODH coordinates.

The COVER Algorithm

I. Read the system parameters {A, D, C, W} and i the number of Markov parameters to be matched by the COVER.[10]

II. (a) Construct the ith observability matrix $\mathcal{O}_i$ as

$$\mathcal{O}_i^T = [C^T, A^TC^T, \ldots, A^{T^{i-1}}C^T] \in \mathcal{R}^{n\times ik} \tag{73}$$

(b) Obtain the singular value decomposition (SVD) of $\mathcal{O}_i$ as

$$\mathcal{O}_i = [U_1 \quad U_2]\begin{bmatrix} \Sigma & 0 \\ 0 & 0 \end{bmatrix} V^T \tag{74a}$$

where

$$\Sigma = \text{diag}\left\{\sigma_1^2, \sigma_2^2, \ldots, \sigma_{r_i}^2\right\} \tag{74b}$$

$$\begin{bmatrix} U_1^T \\ U_2^T \end{bmatrix} [U_1 \quad U_2] = I_{ik}; \qquad U_1 \in \mathcal{R}^{ik\times r_i}. \tag{74c}$$

III. Solve for X from

$$XA^T + AX + DWD^T = 0. \tag{75}$$

IV. Construct the reduced model of order r_i as follows

$$\dot{\chi}_R(t) = \mathcal{A}_R\chi_R(t) + \mathcal{D}_R w(t); \qquad \chi_R \in \mathcal{R}^{r_i} \tag{76a}$$

$$\hat{y}(t) = \mathcal{C}_R\chi_R(t)$$

$$\mathcal{E}\{\chi_R(0)\} = 0; \qquad \mathcal{E}\left\{\chi_R(0)\chi_R^T(0)\right\} = \mathcal{X}(0)$$

where

$$\mathcal{A}_R \triangleq U_1^T\mathcal{O}_i AX\mathcal{O}_i^T U_1\left(U_1^T\mathcal{O}_i X\mathcal{O}_i^T U_1\right)^{-1} \tag{76b}$$

$$\mathcal{D}_R \triangleq U_1^T\mathcal{O}_i D \tag{76c}$$

[10] *Note that the output weighting matrix Q is not required. But i needs to be specified.*

$$\mathscr{C}_R \triangleq [I_k \quad 0]U_1 \tag{76d}$$

$$\mathscr{X}(0) \triangleq U_1^T \mathscr{O}_i X_0 \mathscr{O}_i^T U_1 \tag{76e}$$

Proposition 11 (Proof of the COVER algorithm). The reduced model $\mathscr{S}(r_i; \mathscr{A}_R, \mathscr{D}_R, \mathscr{C}_R)$ is related by a similarity transformation to the reduced model of order r_i generated from the CODH coordinates.

Proof. Observe from (76b)-(76d) that the parameters $\{\mathscr{A}_R, \mathscr{D}_R, \mathscr{C}_R\}$ are independent of the choice of coordinates for $\mathscr{S}(n)$. Hence we shall assume without loss of generality that $\mathscr{S}(n)$ is in CODH coordinates and show that there exists a similarity transformation relating (76) and (66) as follows.

Substituting the structure of the matrices A and C from (64) in the ith observability matrix (73) yields

$$\mathscr{O}_i = \begin{bmatrix} C_1 & 0 & 0 & \cdots & 0 \\ C_1A_{11} & C_1A_{12} & 0 & & 0 \\ * & * & * & \cdots & 0 \end{bmatrix} \tag{77a}$$

where asterisks denote possibly nonzero entries. It suffices to realize that $\mathscr{O}_i$ takes the form

$$\mathscr{O}_i = [\mathscr{O}_{i_1}, 0], \qquad \mathscr{O}_{i_1} \in \mathscr{R}^{ik \times r_i} \tag{77b}$$

with $\operatorname{rank}[\mathscr{O}_i] = \operatorname{rank}[\mathscr{O}_{i_1}] = r_i$. Also note that

$$U_1^T\mathscr{O}_i = \left[U_1^T\mathscr{O}_{i_1}, 0\right]; \qquad U_1^T\mathscr{O}_{i_1} \in \mathscr{R}^{r_i \times r_i} \tag{77c}$$

and is of full rank $|U_1^T\mathscr{O}_{i_1}| \neq 0$. Thus, substituting (12), (64), and (77c) in (76b)-(76d) yields

$$\mathscr{A}_R = \left(U_1^T\mathscr{O}_{i_1}\right)A_R\left(\mathscr{O}_{i_1}^T U_1\right)\left(U_1^T\mathscr{O}_{i_1}\mathscr{O}_{i_1}^T U_1\right)^{-1}$$

$$= \left(U_1^T\mathscr{O}_{i_1}\right)A_R\left(U_1^T\mathscr{O}_{i_1}\right)^{-1}$$

$$\mathscr{D}_R = \left(U_1^T \mathscr{O}_{i_1}\right) D \tag{78a}$$

$$\mathscr{C}_R = [I_k, 0] U_1.$$

Then, since

$$\begin{aligned}\mathscr{C}_R\left(U_1^T \mathscr{O}_{i_1}\right) &= [I_k \ 0] U_1 U_1^T \mathscr{O}_{i_1} \\ &= [I_k \ 0]\left(I_{ik} - U_2 U_2^T\right)\mathscr{O}_{i_1} \\ &= [I_k \ 0]\mathscr{O}_{i_1} = [C_1 \ 0] = C_R,\end{aligned} \tag{78b}$$

where (74c), (74a), and (73) have been used, the triplet $\{\mathscr{A}_R, \mathscr{D}_R, \mathscr{C}_R\}$ is clearly related to the triplet $\{A_R, D_R, C_R\}$ by the similarity transformation $\left(U_1^T \mathscr{O}_{i_1}\right)$.

Remarks. (1) It turns out that the COVER algorithm is a generalization of the optimal, equation error-minimizing reduced models developed by Obinata and Inooka [25-27] and Eitelberg [28] for the case of impulse input. The generalization offered herein permits the construction of reduced models of order r_i for any i, whereas in [25-28] the reduced models are constrained to be of order k.

(2) Defining

$$\Psi_R \triangleq U_1^T \mathscr{O}_i \in \mathscr{R}^{r_i \times n} \tag{79a}$$

$$\Phi_R \triangleq X \mathscr{O}_i^T U_1 \left(U_1^T \mathscr{O}_i X \mathscr{O}_i^T U_1\right)^{-1} \in \mathscr{R}^{n \times r_i} \tag{79b}$$

the matrices $\{\mathscr{A}_R, \mathscr{D}_R, \mathscr{C}_R\}$ can be expressed compactly as

$$\mathscr{A}_R = \Psi_R A \Phi_R, \quad \mathscr{D}_R = \Psi_R D, \quad \mathscr{C}_R = C\Phi_R, \tag{80}$$

where the relationship $\mathscr{C}_R = C\Phi_R$ follows since

$$\begin{aligned}C\Phi_R &= [I_k \ 0]\mathscr{O}_i \Phi_R = [I_k \ 0]\left(U_1 U_1^T + U_2 U_2^T\right)\mathscr{O}_i \Phi_R \\ &= [I_k \ 0] U_1 U_1^T \mathscr{O}_i \Phi_R = [I_k \ 0] U_1 = \mathscr{C}_R,\end{aligned}$$

and where (73), (74a), (74c), and (79b) have been used. Note that $\Psi_R\Phi_R = I_{r_i}$.

The computational advantages of the COVER are obvious; it requires an SVD of an $ik \times r_i$ matrix and an inversion of an $r_i \times r_i$ matrix. Furthermore, if a reduced model of order $r \leq k$ is desired, then one may set $i = 1$ (i.e., $r_i = k$) in the COVER algorithm and obtain $\mathscr{S}(k)$ by simple calculations[11] and then transform $\mathscr{S}(k)$ to cost-decoupled coordinates to produce the desired reduced model of order $r \leq k$ by deleting the states associated with the smallest $(k - r)$ component costs.

The limitation of the COVER algorithm is the need to specify i a priori. On the other hand, in the CODH coordinates one may look at the ratio $\|A_{i,i+1}\|/\|A_i\|$ to determine i. Hence, with the gain of computational simplicity the power of determining r_i a priori is lost. Nevertheless, if the number of Markov parameters to be matched is specified a priori, then one may determine r_i from Lemma 6.

The COVER algorithm also offers an alternate view of constructing the COVERs. To explain this consider an augmented output

$$y^i(t) = \left[y^T(t),\ \eta_2^T(t),\ \eta_3^T(t),\ \ldots,\ \eta_i^T(t)\right]^T, \tag{81a}$$

where

$$\eta_j(t) \triangleq CA^{j-1}x(t), \qquad \eta_j \in \mathscr{R}^k,\ j = 2, 3, \ldots, i \tag{81b}$$

so that

$$y^i(t) = \mathscr{O}_i x(t),\ y^i \in \mathscr{R}^{ik}. \tag{81c}$$

[11] *Since (76) is similar to the reduced model produced from the CODH coordinates, $\mathscr{S}(k; \mathscr{A}_R, \mathscr{D}_R, \mathscr{C}_R)$ retains only the k states that have nonzero component costs.*

Note that the first k components of $y^i(t)$ constitute the actual output y(t), i.e.,

$$y(t) = [I_k \ \ 0]y^i(t), \qquad [I_k \ \ 0] \in \mathscr{R}^{k\times ik}. \tag{82}$$

Now, since $\mathrm{rank}[\mathscr{O}_i] = r_i \leq ik$, $y^i(t)$ does not contain a set of independent outputs. Furthermore, there exist matrices U_1 $\mathscr{R}^{ik\times r_i}$ and $U_2 \in \mathscr{R}^{ik-r_i}$ such that

$$\begin{bmatrix} U_1^T \\ U_2^T \end{bmatrix} [U_1 \ \ U_2] = I_{ik}, \tag{83a}$$

$$\mathrm{rank}[C^i] = r_i, \qquad C^i \triangleq U_1^T\mathscr{O}_i \in \mathscr{R}^{r_i\times n} \tag{83b}$$

and

$$U_2^T\mathscr{O}_i = 0.$$

Now consider the transformation

$$\xi(t) = \begin{bmatrix} \xi_1(t) \\ \xi_2(t) \end{bmatrix} = \begin{bmatrix} U_1^T \\ U_2^T \end{bmatrix} y^i(t) = \begin{bmatrix} C^i \\ 0 \end{bmatrix} x(t). \tag{84}$$

Thus,

$$y^i(t) = [U_1 \ \ U_2]\xi(t) = U_1\xi_1(t), \tag{85a}$$

and in particular,

$$\lim_{t\to\infty} \mathscr{E}\{y^i(t)y^{i^T}(t)\} = \lim_{t\to\infty} U_1\mathscr{E}\left\{\xi_1(t)\xi_1^T(t)\right\}U_1^T$$

$$= U_1C^iXC^{i^T}U_1^T. \tag{85b}$$

We therefore claim:

Corollary 5 (Minimal COVER of the augmented output). If $\mathscr{A}_R$ is asymptotically stable then $\mathscr{S}(r_i;\ \mathscr{A}_R,\ \mathscr{D}_R,\ U_1)$ is the minimal COVER of $y^i(t)$ where $y^i(t)$ is defined in (81).

Proof. With the definition of C^i in (83b), (76b) and (76c) become

$$\mathscr{A}_R = C^i A X C^{i^T} (C^i X C^{i^T})^{-1}, \quad \mathscr{D}_R = C^i D. \tag{86}$$

Now, pre- and postmultiply (75) by C^i and C^{i^T}, respectively, to get

$$C^i A X C^{i^T} + C^i X A^T C^{i^T} + C^i D W D^T C^{i^T} = 0 \tag{87a}$$

which in view of (86) can be written as

$$\mathscr{A}_R (C^i X C^{i^T}) + (C^i X C^{i^T}) \mathscr{A}_R^T + \mathscr{D}_R W \mathscr{D}_R^T = 0. \tag{87b}$$

The steady-state covariance of $\chi_R(t)$ denoted by $\mathscr{X}_R$ satisfies

$$\mathscr{X}_R \mathscr{A}_R^T + \mathscr{A}_R \mathscr{X}_R + \mathscr{D}_R W \mathscr{D}_R^T = 0. \tag{87c}$$

Since $\mathscr{A}_R$ is asymptotically stable, comparison of (87a) and (87b) yields

$$\mathscr{X}_R = C^i X C^{i^T}. \tag{88}$$

Thus, denoting the output of $\mathscr{S}(r_i; \mathscr{A}_R, \mathscr{D}_R, U_1)$ by $\hat{y}^i(t)$, we get

$$\lim_{t\to\infty} \mathscr{E}\{\hat{y}^i(t)\hat{y}^{i^T}(t)\} = U_1 \lim_{t\to\infty} \mathscr{E}\left\{\chi_R(t)\chi_R^T(t)\right\} U_1^T$$

$$= U_1 C^i X C^{i^T} U_1^T = \lim_{t\to\infty} \mathscr{E}\{y^i(t) y^{i^T}(t)\}.$$

Therefore the COVERs (76) satisfy not only (19) but also the following.

$$\lim_{t\to\infty} \mathscr{E}\ \hat{\eta}_j(t)\hat{\eta}_l^T(t) = \lim_{t\to\infty} \mathscr{E}\left\{\eta_j(t)\eta_l^T(t)\right\},$$

$$j, l = 2, 3, \ldots, i, \tag{89a}$$

where the $\hat{\eta}_j(t)$ are defined by

$$\left[\hat{y}^T(t), \hat{\eta}_2^T(t), \ldots, \hat{\eta}_i^T(t)\right]^T \triangleq \hat{y}^i(t) = U_1 \chi_R(t). \tag{89b}$$

It is interesting to observe that if

$$\mathscr{T}_l(n) = 0, \quad l = 1, 2, \ldots, i-1, \tag{90a}$$

then,

$$\frac{d^j}{dt^j}[y(t)] = CA^j x(t)$$
$$= \eta_{j+1}(t), \quad j = 1, 2, \ldots, i-1. \tag{90b}$$

It therefore follows from (89) and (90b) that

Corollary 6 (COVERs of higher order output derivatives). If (90a) holds then the COVER (76) of order r_i satisfies

$$\lim_{t\to\infty} \mathscr{E}\{\hat{y}^{(j)}(t)\hat{y}^{(l)^T}(t)\} = \lim_{t\to\infty} \mathscr{E}\{y^{(j)}(t)y^{(l)^T}(t)\},$$
$$j, l = 0, 1, \ldots, i-1, \tag{91a}$$

where

$$[\cdot]^{(j)} \triangleq \frac{d^j}{dt^j}[\cdot]. \tag{91b}$$

Consideration of the COVER algorithm from "the augmented output" point of view has an appealing relation to a common trick adopted by engineers: normally, one synthesizes a controller to minimize the cost function

$$\mathscr{V} = \lim_{t\to\infty} \frac{1}{T} \mathscr{E} \int_0^t \|y(\tau)\|_Q^2 \, d\tau \tag{92a}$$

with the allowable amount of control energy. However, to increase the damping in the closed-loop system one at times, augments the rates of the outputs in the cost function as

$$\mathscr{V}_a = \lim_{t\to\infty} \frac{1}{t} \mathscr{E} \int_0^t \left\{\|y(\tau)\|_Q^2 + \beta\|\dot{y}(\tau)\|_Q^2\right\} d\tau, \tag{92b}$$

where β is a design parameter, and designs a controller to minimize $\mathscr{V}_a$. Thus considering the augmented output (81) (which can be interpreted as including the information about the derivatives of the output y(t)) to extract a COVER permits the COVERs to include the output-rate information too.

Another practice adopted by engineers while synthesizing a controller based upon a reduced model is to obtain the reduced model by their favorite model reduction scheme and then improve the "quality" of the reduced model by "updating" a few or all of the parameters $\{A_R, D_R, C_R\}$; for example, see [19]. The following section offers such a "fine-tuning" technique pertaining to the COVERs.

D. GEOMETRIC INTERPRETATION AND "FINE TUNING"

The theory of covariance equivalent realizations yields a convenient geometric analysis of COVERs as reduced models. Using the notion of a generalized vector, the tracking error indices associated with these COVERs can be expressed in terms of the angle contained between these vectors. Furthermore, such an analysis naturally suggests a way of selecting certain parameters to reduce the tracking error index.

Using the notation

$$\mathscr{E}_\infty\{\eta, \mathscr{Q}\} = \lim_{t\to\infty} \frac{1}{t} \mathscr{E} \int_0^t \|\eta(\tau)\|^2_{\mathscr{Q}}\, d\tau \tag{93}$$

let the three vectors in Fig. 1 represent the following quantities:

$$|OA| = \mathscr{E}_\infty^{1/2}\{y, Q\} \tag{94a}$$

$$|OB| = \mathscr{E}_\infty^{1/2}\{\hat{y}, Q\} \tag{94b}$$

$$|BA| = \mathscr{E}_\infty^{1/2}\{\tilde{y}, Q\} \tag{94c}$$

where $|\cdot|$ denotes the length and

$$\tilde{y}(t) \triangleq y(t) - \hat{y}(t), \tag{94d}$$

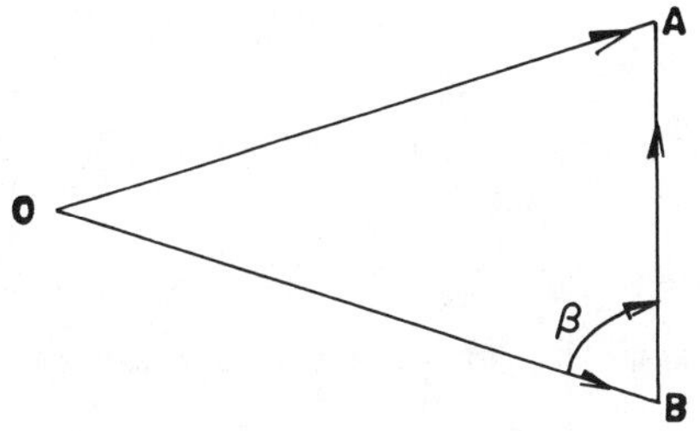

Fig. 1. Generalized vector representation of COVERs.

and where $\hat{y}(t)$ is the output from the COVER.[12]

Correspondingly define β, the angle contained between OB and BA as

$$\cos\beta \triangleq \frac{\mathrm{OB}\cdot\mathrm{BA}}{|\mathrm{OB}|\ |\mathrm{BA}|} = \frac{\lim_{t\to\infty}(1/t)\mathscr{E}\int_0^t \tilde{y}^T(\tau)Q\hat{y}(\tau)\ d\tau}{\mathscr{E}_\infty^{1/2}\{\hat{y},\ Q\}\mathscr{E}_\infty^{1/2}\{\tilde{y},\ Q\}}. \qquad (95)$$

To show that the definition of β in (95) does satisfy $-1 \leq \cos\beta \leq 1$ we will assume that the COVER has been obtained from CODH coordinates and consider the three terms involved in (95).

$$\mathscr{E}_\infty^{1/2}\{\hat{y},\ Q\} = \mathscr{V}_R^{1/2} = \mathscr{V}^{1/2}, \qquad (96a)$$

which follows since all COVERs are cost equivalent. From (51) and (60) we get

$$\mathscr{E}_\infty^{1/2}\{\tilde{y},\ Q\} = [\mu\mathscr{V}]^{1/2}$$
$$= \mathscr{V}^{1/2}\left[2\sum_{i=1}^{k}(1 - x_{ii})\hat{v}_i\right]^{1/2}. \qquad (96b)$$

The expression for the numerator is obtained as follows:

$$\tilde{y}^T(t)Q\hat{y}(t) = [y(t) - \hat{y}(t)]^T Q\hat{y}(t)$$
$$= x^T(t)C^T QC_R\hat{x}_R(t) - \|\hat{y}(t)\|_Q^2. \qquad (96c)$$

[12]*Since the COVERs are cost equivalent we have* $|OA| = \mathscr{V}^{1/2} = \mathscr{V}_R^{1/2} = |OB|$. *Thus the triangle in Fig. 1 is an isosceles triangle.*

Therefore,

$$\lim_{t\to\infty} \frac{1}{t} \mathscr{E} \int_0^t \tilde{y}^T(\tau) Q\hat{y}(\tau)\ d\tau = \mathrm{Tr}\left[C^T Q C_R X_{12}^T\right] - \mathscr{V}, \tag{96d}$$

where the definition of X_{12} in (52b) and (96a) have been used. Now it follows from the proof of Proposition 8 that

$$\mathrm{Tr}\left[C^T Q C_R X_{12}^T\right] = \mathscr{V} \sum_{i=1}^{k} x_{ii} \hat{\upsilon}_i, \tag{96e}$$

where $x_{ii} = [X_{12}]_{ii}$, $i = 1, 2, \ldots, k$. Thus

$$\lim_{t\to\infty} \frac{1}{t} \mathscr{E} \int_0^t \tilde{y}^T(\tau) Q\hat{y}(\tau)\ d\tau = -\mathscr{V} \sum_{i=1}^{k} \hat{\upsilon}_i (1 - x_{ii}), \tag{96f}$$

since from the definition (54d) of the normalized component costs $\Sigma_{i=1}^{k} \hat{\upsilon}_i = 1$. Substituting (96a), (96b), and (96f) in (95) yields

$$\cos \beta = -\frac{1}{\sqrt{2}} \left[\sum_{i=1}^{k} \hat{\upsilon}_i (1 - x_{ii})\right]^{1/2}. \tag{97}$$

The square roots in (96b) and (97) always exist since $|x_{ii}| \le 1$ from (58) which, also shows that $-1 \le \cos \beta \le 1$.

Proposition 12 (Relation between μ *and* β*).* The tracking error index μ is related to the generalized angle β by

$$\mu = 4 \cos^2 \beta. \tag{98}$$

Proof. From (96b) write

$$\mu = 2 \sum_{i=1}^{k} (1 - x_{ii}) \hat{\upsilon}_i, \tag{99a}$$

and from (97)

$$\sum_{i=1}^{k} (1 - x_{ii}) \hat{\upsilon}_i = 2 \cos^2 \beta. \tag{99b}$$

The proof then follows from substituting (99b) in (99a).

Alternatively one may use the following proof. Since OAB is an isosceles triangle (i.e., $|OA| = |OB|$),

$$\mu = \frac{1}{\mathscr{V}} |BA|^2 = \frac{1}{\mathscr{V}} \{2|OA| \cos \beta\}^2 = \frac{1}{\mathscr{V}} \{2\mathscr{V}^{1/2} \cos \beta\}^2 = 4 \cos^2 \beta.$$

Clearly, if $\beta = \pi/2$, i.e., if the error vector BA is orthogonal to the "approximate vector" OB, then $\mu = 0$. Of course, $\beta = \pi/2$ cannot be achieved if $\mathscr{S}(n)$ is observable and controllable since in this case $\mu = 0$ contradicts Kalman's minimal realization theory.

Recall that the relation (98) has been derived explicitly for the COVERs, and it will not hold for all arbitrary reduced models $\mathscr{S}(r)$. In particular, it will not hold for Wilson's [29] optimal reduced models which minimize μ. One of the necessary conditions for the optimality derived by Wilson is that the numerator of (95) be zero. Therefore if (98) holds, then these optimal reduced models will yield $\mu = 0$ contradicting the minimality (in the sense of Kalman) assumption of $\mathscr{S}(n)$. Thus (98) cannot hold for the optimal reduced models.

Conversely, the COVERs cannot be the optimal reduced models, since for COVERs $\beta \neq \pi/2$ which means that the numerator of (95) cannot be zero violating one of the necessary conditions [29] for optimality. However, if β is *close* to $\pi/2$ then the COVER would serve as a good reduced model. This then naturally suggests that by "rotating" the output vector $\hat{y}$ resulting from the COVERs one may reduce the tracking error index μ. Thus, the following problem is posed.

The Output Fine-Tuning Problem

Given $\mathscr{S}(n)$ and $\mathscr{S}(r)$

$$\min_{M_0} \mu^0 \triangleq \lim_{t\to\infty} \frac{1}{t} \mathscr{E} \int_0^t \|y(\tau) - y_R(\tau)\|_Q^2 \, d\tau \qquad (100a)$$

subject to

$$y_R(t) = M_0\hat{y}(t) \tag{100b}$$

where $M_0 \in \mathcal{R}^{k\times k}$ is the only parameter to be selected and $\hat{y}$ is the output of the $\mathcal{S}(r)$.

Remark. A similar problem has been posed as an "optimal aggregation model for stochastic inputs" by Siret *et al.* [30]. However, the results are different since in [30] it is assumed that $\mathcal{S}(r)$ is a *perfect* aggregation of $\mathcal{S}(n)$, i.e., the states $\hat{x}_R(t)$ of $\mathcal{S}(r)$ and $x(t)$ of $\mathcal{S}(n)$ are assumed to be related by [31]

$$\hat{x}_R(t) = \overline{\Psi}_R x(t), \quad t \in [0, \infty) \tag{101}$$

for some aggregation matrix $\overline{\Psi}_R$. This is equivalent to deleting only unobservable states.

Lemma 7 (Solution to the output fine-tuning problem). The solution to the output fine-tunging problem satisfies

$$M_0 C_R X_R C_R^T - C X_{12} C_R^T = 0 \tag{102a}$$

where X_R and X_{12} satisfy (11b) and (62a), respectively, and the corresponding tracking error index obeys

$$0 \leq \mu^0 = 1 - (1/\mathcal{V})\,\mathrm{Tr}\left[C_R^T M_0^T Q M_0 C_R X_R\right] \leq 1. \tag{102b}$$

Furthermore, the fine-tuned output $y_R(t)$ satisfies the inherent orthogonality condition

$$\lim_{t\to\infty} \frac{1}{t}\,\mathcal{E}\int_0^t [y(\tau) - y_R(\tau)]^T Q y_R(\tau)\, d\tau = 0. \tag{102c}$$

Proof. The proof of (102a) and (102c) is essentially similar to that used in [29], and, (102b) follows from the substitution of (102a) in (52a) with C_R replaced by M_0C_R.

Lemma 7 holds for any two models $\mathscr{S}(n)$ and $\mathscr{S}(r)$. A great simplification occurs when $\mathscr{S}(n)$ is in CODH coordinates and $\mathscr{S}(r)$ is its COVER with its parameters $\{A_R, D_R, C_R\}$ as given in (66).

Proposition 12 (Output fine-tuning of the COVERs). The M_0 which solves the output fine-tuning problem of a COVER is given by

$$M_0 = C_1 X_{11} C_1^{-1} \tag{103}$$

where X_{11} is the leading $k \times k$ submatrix of X_{12}.

Proof. Since the COVERs satisfy $C_R X_R C_R^T = CXC^T$, (102a) simplifies to

$$M_0 CXC^T = CX_{12} C_R^T. \tag{104a}$$

Substituting (12) and the structure of the matrices from (64) and (66) in (104a) yields

$$M_0 C_1 C_1^T = [C_1 \quad 0] X_{12} \begin{bmatrix} C_1^T \\ 0 \end{bmatrix} = C_1 X_{11} C_1^T. \tag{104b}$$

The proof now follows since $C_1 \in \mathscr{R}^{k \times k}$ is nonsingular.

Geometrically, the process of the solution to the output fine-tuning problem of the COVER is depicted in Fig. 2 where the lengths of the vectors OB' and B'A represent $\mathscr{E}_\infty^{1/2}\{y_R, Q\}$ and $\mathscr{E}_\infty^{1/2}\{y - y_R, Q\}$, respectively. It therefore follows from

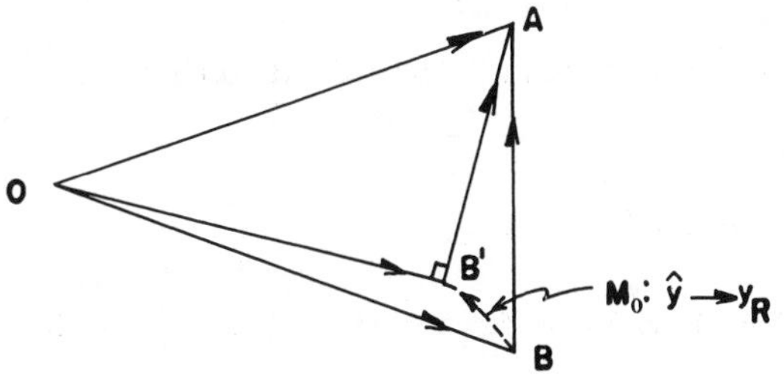

Fig. 2. Pictorial representation of the output fine-tuning process.

(102c) that OB' and B'A are orthogonal. Thus, the solution to the output fine-tuning problem yields an orthogonal projection of OA in the output space of the COVER.

Corollary 7 (The fine-tuning of the COVERs of MISO systems). The following simplifications result for the output fine-tuning of the COVERs of MISO systems.

(1) The tracking error index associated with the output fine-tuned COVER is

$$\mu^0 = 1 - x_{11}^2. \tag{105}$$

(2) The following relations hold

(a) $M_0 = x_{11} = -\cos 2\beta,$ (106a)

(b) $\mu^0 = \sin^2 2\beta,$ (106b)

(c) $\mathscr{I} = \cos^2 \beta = 0.25\mu,$ (106c)

where the fine-tuning *improvement index* $\mathscr{I}$ is defined by

$$\mathscr{I} \triangleq (\mu - \mu^0)/\mu. \tag{106d}$$

Proof. Since k = 1, from Proposition 3 and from the cost superposition property (5)

$$\mathscr{V} = \hat{\mathscr{V}}_1 = \alpha_1^2 = c_1^2 Q \quad \text{and} \quad \hat{\upsilon}_1 = 1. \tag{107a}$$

Now solve (103) for M_0 which is now a scalar to get $M_0 = x_{11} \in \mathscr{R}^1$ and substitute in (102b) to get

$$\mu^0 = 1 - \left(1/c_1^2 Q\right)\left\{c_1^2 x_{11}^2 Q\right\} = 1 - x_{11}^2,$$

by using (107a) and (41a). Substitution of $\hat{\upsilon}_1 = 1$ and (99a), (99b) in (98) gives

$$x_{11} = 1 - 2\cos^2 \beta = -\cos 2\beta.$$

(106b) and (106c) follow from using (105), (106a), and (106d) after some trigonometric manipulations.

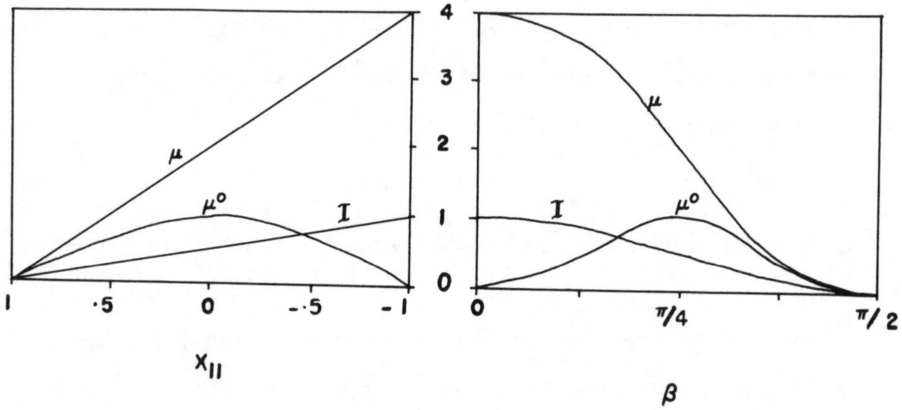

Fig. 3. Dependence of μ, μ^0 *and* $\mathscr{I}$ *on* x_{11} *and* β *for a COVER.*

From Corollary 7, Fig. 3 can be obtained to exhibit the dependence of μ, μ^0, and $\mathscr{I}$ on x_{11} $\left(=\lim_{t\to\infty} \mathscr{E}\left\{x_1(t)\hat{x}_1(t)\right\}\right)$ which measures the correlation between the actual state $x_1(t)$ and its approximation $\hat{x}_1(t)$. It also displays the effect of β on these indices. Clearly, for $x_{11} = -1$ (corresponding to $\beta = 0$ or π) maximum improvement can be achieved by fine-tuning the output of the COVER. However, for $x_{11} > 0.5$ $(3\pi/8 < \beta < 5\pi/8)$ fine-tuning does not offer a significant improvement. Figure 3 can therefore be used to determine whether the COVERs of a MISO system need to be fine tuned or not.

Quite often the purpose of a reduced model is to synthesize a controller based upon this model. This controller would then be used to drive the full-order model. The aim of the analyst is to design the controller so that (92a) is minimized, with the allowable control energy. However, the controller synthesis is based upon minimizing the approximate cost function

$$\mathscr{V}_R = \lim_{t\to\infty} \frac{1}{t} \mathscr{E} \int_0^t \|y_R(t)\|_Q^2 \, d\tau$$

$$= \lim_{t\to\infty} \frac{1}{t} \mathscr{E} \int_0^t \|\hat{y}(\tau)\|^2_{M_0^T Q M_0} \, d\tau, \qquad (108a)$$

where the relation $y_R(t) = M_0\hat{y}(t)$ has been used. Thus the output fine-tuning problem can be viewed as selecting an optimal output weighting matrix

$$Q_0 = M_0^T Q M_0 \tag{108b}$$

where M_0 is obtained from the solution to the output fine-tuning problem.

Now, it is only natural to expect that by duality, one can pose a similar problem to select an optimal input-intensity matrix W_0. It is also equally natural to expect that these two problems can be combined and posed as one problem.

The Fine-Tuning Problem

Given the model $\mathscr{S}(n)$ and its reduced model

$$\dot{\hat{x}}_R(t) = A_R\hat{x}_R(t) + D_R\hat{w}(t)$$

$$\hat{y}(t) = C_R\hat{x}_R(t), \tag{109}$$

find M_* and N_* to obtain

$$\min_{M_*, N_*} \mu^* = \lim_{t\to\infty} \frac{1}{t} \mathscr{E} \int_0^t \|y(\tau) - y_R(\tau)\|_Q^2 \, d\tau \tag{110a}$$

subject to

$$y_R(t) = M_*\hat{y}(t) \tag{110b}$$

$$\hat{w}(t) = N_* w(t). \tag{110c}$$

Remark. Note that since

$$\mathscr{E}\{\hat{w}(t)\hat{w}^T(\tau)\} = N_*\mathscr{E}\left\{w(t)w^T(\tau)\right\}N_*^T$$

$$= N_* W N_*^T \, \delta(t - \tau) \tag{111}$$

the choice of N_* can be interpreted as modifying the input intensity (in the reduced model) to minimize μ.

The solution to this problem is similar to that obtained by Wilson [29] hence we state the solution without the proof.

Proposition 13 (Solution to the fine-tuning problem). The solution to the fine-tuning problem satisfies

$$M_* C_R^T X_R C_R - C X_{12} C_R^T = 0, \tag{112a}$$

$$D_R^T K_R D_R N_* + D_R^T K_{12}^T D = 0, \tag{112b}$$

with X_R, X_{12}, K_R, and K_{12} satisfying the equations

$$X_R A_R^T + A_R X_R + D_R N_* W N_*^T D_R^T = 0, \tag{112c}$$

$$X_{12} A_R^T + A X_{12} + D W N_*^T D_R^T = 0, \tag{112d}$$

$$K_R A_R + A_R^T K_R + C_R^T M_*^T Q M_* C_R = 0, \tag{112e}$$

$$K_{12} A_R + A^T K_{12} - C^T Q M_* C_R = 0. \tag{112f}$$

Clearly this is not a closed form solution and an iterative scheme is required for the solution. This numerical scheme is presented in an algorithmic form in the Appendix where the convergence of the algorithm is also proved.

A comparison of this "restricted" parameter optimization approach with Mishra and Wilson's optimal algorithm [32] is in order. In [32] the three parameters $\{A_R, D_R, C_R\}$ are treated as variables whereas in the fine-tuning problem posed herein only $\{M_*, N_*\}$ are the variables and A_R is assumed *given* (by the COVER algorithm). Thus, loosely speaking, the fine-tuning problem can be viewed as fixing the eigenvalues and the eigenvectors of the reduced model and selecting the optimal input and output matrices by the method in [32]. The advantage of the present method is that it leads to a *convergent* algorithm and the computations are, naturally, greatly simplified. Even though the algorithm proposed in [32] does yield the optimal reduced model when a solution can be obtained, there is no guarantee that the algorithm will converge.

Often in many fields of engineering exact problems are posed, but only approximate solutions are computed since the exact solutions are difficult, if not impossible, to obtain. On the other hand, it is equally common for one to pose an approximate problem so that an exact solution to this approximate problem can be obtained. The fine-tuning problem posed herein falls in the latter category.

E. POSTAMBLE

The COVER theory which is developed from the concepts of component cost analysis [1-4] is geared toward obtaining partial realizations which maintain the RMS values of every component of the output. The intended applications of the COVER theory are the model reduction and the control reduction problems. In this section the model reduction problem has been treated in detail.

Since the subsequent controller design requires the reduced models to have a low tracking error index, the COVERs have been analyzed with respect to the tracking error index. Consequently, the flexibility available in the COVER-theory is used to reduce the tracking error index by, in general, increasing the order of the COVER. In the process a set of coordinates called cost-decoupled Hessenberg (CODH) coordinates have been presented, a special case of which has received the attention of many researchers. The CODH coordinates have primarily been used to derive the properties of the COVERs in the context of model reduction. A simple algorithm has been presented for the construction of the COVERs.

The COVERs thus generated yield a convenient geometric analysis which aids in "fine-tuning" the COVERs so that the tracking error index is minimized. A convergent algorithm is presented for this task.

V. EXAMPLES

In this section we will illustrate the application of the COVER theory for model reduction with the aid of a few numerical examples.

Example 1. Let $\mathscr{S}(2;\ A,\ D,\ C)$ be the given model with the parameters

$$A = \begin{bmatrix} -1 & 0 \\ 0 & -10 \end{bmatrix}, \quad D = \begin{bmatrix} 1 \\ 70 \end{bmatrix}, \quad C = [1 \quad -2], \quad W = Q = 1.$$

Since $n = 2$, the only conceivable reduced model is of order 1. The COVER for this example has the parameters

$$A_R = -10.897, \quad D_R = -4.668, \quad C_R = 2.7847.$$

In frequency domain this example can be stated as follows. The COVER of the transfer function

$$G(s) = \frac{-13s - 4}{s^2 + 11s + 10}$$

is given by

$$G_R(s) = \frac{-13}{s + 10.897}.$$

The COVER has an eigenvalue (-10.897) near the fast mode (-10) of $\mathscr{S}(2;\ A,\ D,\ C)$ as a consequence of the fact that this mode is highly controllable from $w(t)$.

Now, since $k = 1$, from Proposition 8, the bounds on the tracking error index are

$$0 \leq \mu \leq 4.$$

Table I. Comparison of Different Reduced Models of Example 1.

	COVER	Output fine-tuned COVER	Fine-tuned COVER	Optimal reduced model
A_R	-10.897	-10.897	-10.897	-12.220
D_R	-4.668	-4.668	-4.668	-4.668
C_R	2.7847	2.735	2.735	2.903
μ	0.03555	0.03528	0.03528	0.03128

The computed value of μ is 0.03555. Hence, for this example the upper bound "4" is very conservative. The evaluation of the generalized angle β and x_{11} yields $\beta = 84.59°$ and $x_{11} = 0.9822$. Since $\beta \approx \pi/2$, from Fig. 3 one does not expect a significant improvement by output fine tuning the COVER. Table I compares the output fine-tuned COVER, the fine-tuned COVER, and the optimal reduced model of [29].

As expected there is hardly any perceivable improvement offered by fine tuning the COVER. The fact that columns 2 and 3 of Table I are identical is not surprising. Since for SlSO systems with nonzero first Markov parameters it is a straightforward exercise[13] to show both the output fine tuning and the fine tuning of the minimal COVER yield the same results. Evidently, for this example, the COVER $\mathscr{S}(1; -10.897, -4.668, 2.7847)$ is fairly close to the optimal reduced model.

Example 2. Consider the following non-minimum-phase transfer function

$$G(s) = \frac{s - 10}{(s + 1)(s + 10)}$$

[13]*To show this substitute $M_* = x_{11}$ and $N_* = 1$ in (112a) to see that they are satisfied. Thus $M_* = x_{11}$ and $N_* = 1$ are the optimal matrices solving the fine-tuning problem. Furthermore, $M_0 = x_{11}$ $(=M_*)$ is the solution to the output fine-tuning problem.*

whose state-space representation $\mathscr{S}(2;\ A,\ D,\ C)$ in cost-decoupled coordinates has the form

$$\dot{x}(t) = \begin{bmatrix} -1.000 & 6.325 \\ 0 & -10.000 \end{bmatrix} x(t) + \begin{bmatrix} 1.414 \\ -4.472 \end{bmatrix} w(t)$$

$$y(t) = [0.707 \quad 0]\, x(t).$$

Note that A_{TR}, which is the (2, 1) entry of the plant matrix above, is zero thus identifying the "all-pass"network (s - 10)/(s + 10) in the transfer function G(s). The minimal COVER for this example is

$$\dot{\hat{x}}_R(t) = -1.0\ \hat{x}_R(t) + 1.414\ w(t)$$

$$\hat{y}(t) = 0.707\ \hat{x}_R(t).$$

Due to Proposition 7 this COVER is also stochastically equivalent [6]. Figure 4 offers the geometric representation of this COVER and the effect of output fine tuning it, where the notation used is consistant with that adopted in Section IV. Table II compares the COVER, the output fine-tuned COVER[14] and the optimal reduced model [29].

Note the significant improvement offered by output fine tuning the COVER. This improvement is reflected by the low value of β (see Fig. 4). Note that, as claimed in Lemma 6, the COVER matches the first Markov parameter of $\mathscr{S}(2)$. However, both

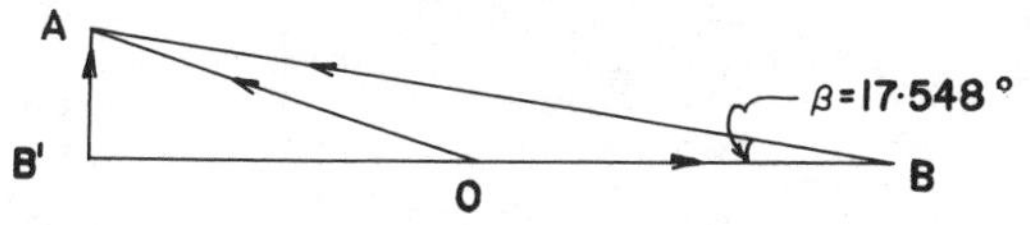

Fig. 4. Geometric representation of Example 2.

[14] *Since this example is a SISO system, the output fine-tuned COVER is also the fine-tuned COVER.*

Table II. Comparison of Different Reduced Models of Example 2

	COVER	Output fine-tuned COVER	Optimal reduced model
A_R	-1.0	-1.0	-0.6078
D_R	1.414	1.414	1.414
C_R	0.707	-0.5785	-0.4734
μ	3.6364	0.3305	0.2627

the fine-tuned COVER and the optimal reduced model do not, and in fact the first Markov parameters of these models have the opposite sign of that of $\mathscr{S}(n)$.

Example 3. The simply supported elastic beam shown in Fig. 5 is used as an illustrative example of a flexible structure. The beam has deflection u(x, t) only in the plane of the paper where x is the position from the left end of the beam. The beam parameters M (mass per unit length), I (moment of inertia), and E (modulus of elasticity) are assumed to be constant. The length of the beam is L.

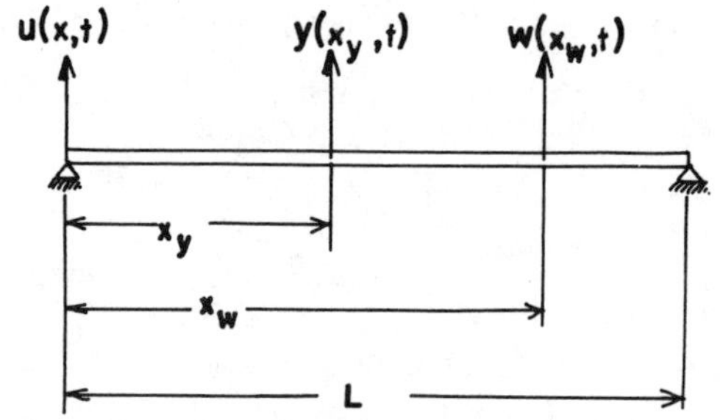

Fig. 5. Simply supported elastic beam.

The beam dynamics are modeled by the Euler-Bernoulli partial differential equation

$$M \frac{\partial^2}{\partial t^2} u(x, t) + EI \frac{\partial^4}{\partial x^4} u(x, t) = w(x_w, t), \tag{113}$$

where $w(x_w, t)$ is an input at $x = x_w$.

For convenience the properties of the beam are chosen as $L = \pi$, $M = EI = 2/\pi$. With these values the deflections are given by

$$u(x, t) = \sum_{i=1}^{\infty} \phi_i(x)\eta_i(t) \tag{113a}$$

where

$$\phi_i(x) = \alpha_i \sin(ix), \quad i = 1, 2, \ldots, \tag{113b}$$

are the mode shapes, and $\eta_i(t)$ satisfy

$$\ddot{\eta}_i(t) + i^4\eta_i(t) = d_i w(x_w t), \tag{113c}$$

and where $\omega_i \triangleq i^2$ is the modal frequency of the ith mode and $d_i = (1/\alpha_i) \sin(ix_w)$.

Now, using the following normalization,

$$\int_0^L M\phi_i^2(x)\, dx = \alpha_i^2 = 1, \quad i = 1, 2, \ldots, \tag{113d}$$

and by assuming a modal damping of $\zeta_i = 0.005$, the equation of motion (113d) can therefore be written as

$$\ddot{\eta}_i(t) + 2\zeta_i\omega_i\dot{\eta}_i(t) + \omega_i^2\eta_i(t) = d_i w(x_w, t). \tag{114}$$

The output of interest $y(x_y, t)$ is the deflection at $x = x_y$, and is given by

$$y(x_y, t) = \sum_{i=1}^{\infty} \phi_i(x_y)\eta_i(t). \tag{115}$$

For illustration we set $x_y = 0.45L$ and $x_w = 0.55L$, so that

$$d_i = \sin(0.55\pi), \quad y(t) = \sum_{i=1}^{\infty} \sin(0.45\pi)\eta_i(t). \tag{116}$$

By assuming that only five modes (i.e., i = 1, 2, 3, 4, 5) are sufficient to adequately model the beam, the parameters of the state space model $\mathscr{S}(10;\ A,\ D,\ C)$ of the Eqs. (114)-(116) take the following form.

$$\begin{aligned} A &= \text{diag}\{A_1, A_2, A_3, A_4, A_5\} \\ D^T &= \text{diag}\left[D_1^T, D_2^T, D_3^T, D_4^T, D_5^T\right] \\ C &= [C_1, C_2, C_3, C_4, C_5] \end{aligned} \tag{117a}$$

where

$$A_i = \begin{bmatrix} 0 & 1 \\ -\omega_i^2 & -2\zeta_i\omega_i \end{bmatrix}$$

$$D_i = \begin{bmatrix} 0 \\ d_i \end{bmatrix}, \tag{117b}$$

$$C_i = [c_i \quad 0].$$

The parameters ω_i, ζ_i, d_i, and c_i are given in Table III.

Table III. Modal Data for the Flexible Beam

i	*1*	*2*	*3*	*4*	*5*
ω_i	*1*	*4*	*9*	*16*	*25*
ζ_i	*0.005*	*0.005*	*0.005*	*0.005*	*0.005*
d_i	*0.9877*	*-0.3090*	*-0.8910*	*0.5878*	*0.7071*
c_i	*0.9877*	*0.3090*	*-0.8910*	*-0.5878*	*0.7071*

The model $\mathscr{S}(10; A, D, C)$ is observable and controllable. Since it is observable and has one output, it follows that $n_i = 1$, and $r_i = i$, for all $i = 1, 2, \ldots, 10$, where n_i is defined in (64) and r_i is the rank of the ith observability matrix, defined in (65b).

Now, since the first Markov parameter of $\mathscr{S}(10)$ is zero, the $\mathscr{S}(1)$ generated by the COVER algorithm is not asymptotically stable. However, for illustration purposes, three reduced models of orders 4, 6, and 8, respectively, are generated by the COVER algorithm and these are compared in the sequel

Table IV compares the eigenvalues of the four models of the beam. Note that r = 10 corresponds to the full model $\mathscr{S}(10)$. Figure 6 compares the time response of these models to (a) a unit impulse input and (b) to a step input of unit magnitude. In Fig. 6a there is almost no perceptable difference between the full model (r = 10) and the reduced model r = 8. Thus (from Table IV) the second mode ($i = 2$, $\omega_i = 4$) has the least influence on the output y(t). Note from Figs. 6a and 6b that the fourth order model (r = 4) has the maximum phase difference in the output and as a consequence yields the highest tracking error index; the tracking error indices associated with the reduced models of order r = 4, 6, 8 are, respectively, 1.733,

Table IV. Comparison of the Eigenvalues

Order of the model	*Eigenvalues*
10	$-0.005 \pm j1$, $-0.020 \pm j4$, $-0.045 \pm j9$, $-0.080 \pm j16$, $-0.125 \pm j25$
8	$-0.0042 \pm j1$, $-0.0425 \pm j8.95$, $-0.0776 \pm j15.95$, $-0.1248 \pm j25$
6	$-0.00008 \pm j10.2$, $-0.01 \pm j1.005$, $-0.1023 \pm j24.79$
4	$-0.0051 \pm j1.03$, $-0.0847 \pm j18.78$

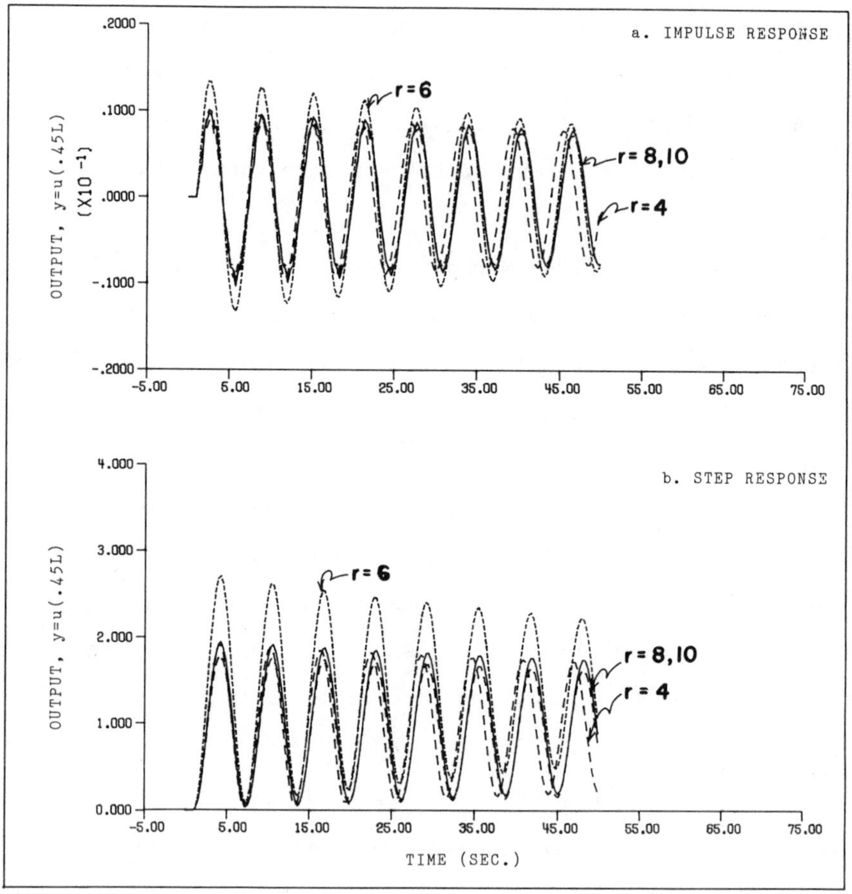

Fig. 6. Time response of COVERs of different orders. (a) Impulse response; (b) step response.

0.3075, and 0.01696. Even though the sixth-order model has a larger difference in the amplitude, it yields a smaller tracking error index than the fourth-order model due to smaller phase difference.

To display the effect of fine tuning the reduced model only the sixth-order model is considered. The results are shown in Fig. 7. The improvement offered by fine tuning[15] the COVER is

[15] *For this beam example, it turns out that the output fine-tuned COVER is also the solution to the fine-tuning problem.*

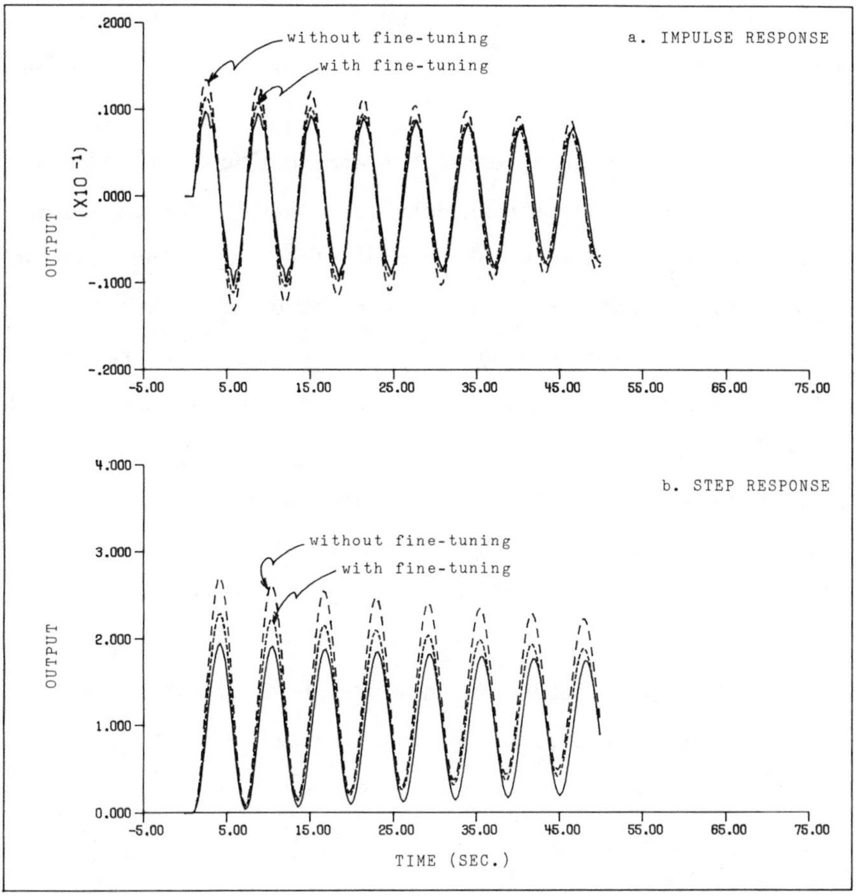

Fig. 7. Effect of fine-tuning the COVER of order 6. (a) Impulse response; (b) step response.

evident. The tracking error index associated with the fine-tuned COVER of order six is 0.2838, as compared with 0.3075 without fine tuning.

VI. CONCLUSIONS

A theory of covariance equivalent realizations has been presented as a candidate for a method which unifies both the model reduction and the control problems. The COVERs are defined as those realizations which maintain the steady state output covariance of the full model/realization. As a consequence, the COVERs maintain the RMS values of *every* component of the output vector.

This chapter has presented the application of the COVER theory to model reduction in detail. (See [7] for an adaptation of a similar theory to the controller reduction problem.) A convenient formula for the tracking error index associated with the COVERs has been specifically developed to present a set of coordinates called the cost-decoupled Hessenberg coordinates. These coordinates are a special case of the cost-decoupled coordinates. The CODH coordinates have been shown to determine the desirable order of the reduced model by considering the observability *and* the controllability of the states that are truncated. Since the computations involved in computing the CODH coordinates may, however, be formidable when the order of the model n is large, an alternative and simpler algorithm called *the COVER algorithm* has been presented.

The following properties for the COVERs thus generated have been derived:

The COVERs are observable, controllable and asymptotically stable.

Connections between the Markov parameters of the full model $\mathscr{S}(n)$, the controllability and the asymptotic stability of the reduced models are established.

When the order of the COVER equals r_i, where r_i is the rank of the ith observability matrix of $\mathscr{S}(n)$, the COVERs match the first r_i Markov parameters of $\mathscr{S}(n)$. Conversely, if a COVER is required by design to match i Markov parameters, then the order of the required COVER is r_i which can be determined a priori.

The COVER algorithm offers an interesting interpretation of the COVERs of order $r > k$, where k is the number of independent outputs: these COVERs are shown to be the *minimal* COVERs of the system with certain augmented outputs. This has an appealing connection to a common practice adopted by engineers in feedback loop designs.

Under certain conditions these augmented outputs can be viewed as the higher derivatives of the output. Thus the COVERs include the stochastic properties of the higher derivatives of the outputs.

The special properties of the CODH coordinates are shown to permit a convenient geometric analysis of the COVERs with respect to their tracking error index. Such an analysis has naturally led to an output fine tuning and a fine-tuning problem whereby the "quality" of these COVERs as reduced models is increased. A convergent, iterative algorithm has been presented to solve the fine-tuning problem, which is a generalization of the *output* fine-tuning problem.

APPENDIX. THE FINE-TUNING ALGORITHM

Step I

(a) Read the parameters $\{A, D, C, W, Q\}$ and $\{A_R, D_R, D_R\}$, and a "stopping index" ϵ, $0 < \epsilon \ll 1$.

(b) Compute X and $\mathcal{V}$ by solving

$$XA^T + AX + DWD^T = 0, \tag{A.1a}$$

$$\mathcal{V} = \mathrm{Tr}[C^TQCX]. \tag{A.1b}$$

(c) Set $M_* = I_k$, $N_* = I_q$, and $i = 0$.

Step II

(a) Compute X_{12} and X_R by solving

$$X_{12}A_R^T + AX_{12} + DWN_*^TD_R^T = 0, \tag{A.2a}$$

$$X_RA_R^T + A_RX_R + D_RN_*WN_*^TD_R^T = 0. \tag{A.2b}$$

(b) If $i \neq 0$, go to step IIc. Compute $\mu^*(i, i)$ from

$$\mu^*(i, i) = 1 + (1/\mathscr{V})\left\{\mathrm{Tr}\left[C_R^TM_*^TQM_*C_RX_R\right] - 2\,\mathrm{Tr}\left[C^TQM_*C_RX_{12}^T\right]\right\} \tag{A.3}$$

(c) Solve for M from

$$M \cdot M_*C_RX_RC_R^TM_*^T = CX_{12}C_R^TM_*^T \tag{A.4}$$

and set $M_* = MM_*$.

(d) Compute $\mu^*(i + 1, i)$ from

$$\mu^*(i + 1, i) = 1 + (1/\mathscr{V})\left\{\mathrm{Tr}\left[C_R^TM_*^TQM_*C_RX_R\right] - 2\,\mathrm{Tr}\left[C^TQM_*C_RX_{12}^T\right]\right\}. \tag{A.5}$$

(e) Compute $\mathscr{I}$ from

$$\mathscr{I} = [\mu^*(i, i) - \mu^*(i + 1, i)]/\mu^*(i, i). \tag{A.6}$$

If $\mathscr{I} \leq \epsilon$, STOP.

If not continue.

Step III

(a) Compute K_{12} and K_R by solving

$$K_{12}A_R + A^TK_{12} - C^TQM_*C_R = 0, \tag{A.7a}$$

$$K_RA_R + A_R^TK_R + C_R^TM_*^TQM_*C_R = 0. \tag{A.7b}$$

(b) Solve for N from

$$N_*^TD_R^TK_RN_*N = -N_*^TD_R^TK_{12}^TD \tag{A.8}$$

and set $N_* = N_*N$.

(c) Compute $\mu^*(i + 1, i + 1)$ from

$$\mu^*(i + 1, i + 1) = 1 + (1/\mathscr{V})\Big\{\mathrm{Tr}\Big[D_R N_* W N_*^T D_R^T K_R\Big] + 2\ \mathrm{Tr}\Big[D W N_*^T D_R^T K_{12}^T\Big]\Big\}. \tag{A.9}$$

(d) Compute $\mathscr{I}$ from

$$\mathscr{I} = [\mu^*(i + 1, i) - \mu^*(i + 1, i + 1)]/\mu^*(i + 1, i). \tag{A.10}$$

If $\mathscr{I} \leq \epsilon$, STOP.

If not set $i = i + 1$, and go to step II.

Proof of the convergence. Since $\mu^* \geq 0$, to prove the convergence of the algorithm it is sufficient to show that

$$\mu^*(i + 1, i) \leq \mu^*(i, i) \leq \mu^*(i, i - 1).$$

To show this consider step II. Since there is no updating from step IIIc to step IIb, $\mu^*(i, i)$ as computed from (A.3) must equal $\mu^*(i - 1, i - 1)$ as computed from (A.9). That is, (A.3) and (A.9) are alternative but equivalent statements. Now, since in step IIe only the M_* matrix is being updated (i.e., $MM_* \rightarrow M_*$), X_R and X_{12} remain unchanged. Hence, recognizing that $MM_* \rightarrow M_*$, (A.5) can be written as

$$\mu^*(i + 1, i) = 1 + (1/\mathscr{V})\Big\{\mathrm{Tr}\Big[C_R^T M_*^T M^T Q M M_* C_R X_R\Big] - 2\ \mathrm{Tr}\Big[C^T Q M M_* C_R X_{12}^T\Big]\Big\}. \tag{A.11a}$$

Making use of the trace identity $\mathrm{Tr}[AB] = \mathrm{Tr}[A^T B^T]$ and by using (A.4), from (A.3) and (A.11a) we get

$$\mu^*(i, i) - \mu^*(i + 1, i)$$
$$= 1/\mathscr{V}\ \mathrm{Tr}\Big[C_R^T M_*^T (I - M)^T Q (I - M) M_* C_R X_R\Big]. \tag{A.11b}$$

Now, if the controllable subspace of $\mathscr{S}(r)$ is asymptotically stable, then $X_R \geq 0$, [5]. Also since,

$$C_R^T M_*^T (I - M)^T Q(I - M) M_* C_R \geq 0,$$

it follows from (A.11b) that

$$\mu^*(i + 1, i) \leq \mu^*(i, i).$$

Proceeding similarly it can be shown that $\mu^*(i, i) \leq \mu^*(i, i - 1)$. Since at every iteration the upper bound of a lower-bound metric ($\mu^* \geq 0$) is being reduced, the iterative scheme must converge within a finite number of iterations.

REFERENCES

1. R. E. SKELTON, "Cost Sensitive Model Reduction for Control Design," in "Proc. AIAA Guid. and Control Conf., Palo Alto, CA, pp. 288-295, 1978.

2. R. E. SKELTON, "Cost Decomposition of Linear Systems with Application to Model Reduction," *Internat. J. Control 32 (6)*, 1031-1055 (1980).

3. R. E. SKELTON and A. YOUSUFF, "Component Cost Analysis of Large Scale Systems," in "Control and Dynamic Systems," Vol. 18, (C. T. Leondes, ed.), Academic Press, New York, 1982. Also see "Component Cost Analysis of Large Scale Systems," *Internat. J. Control 37 (2)*, 285-304 (1983).

4. R. E. SKELTON and C. Z. GREGORY, "Measurement Feedback and Model Reduction by Modal Cost Analysis," in "Proc. Joint Automatic Control Conf., Denver, Colorado, 1979.

5. H. KWAKERNAAK and R. SIVAN, "Linear Optimal Control Systems," Wiley, New York, 1972.

6. B. D. O. ANDERSON, "The Inverse Problem of Stationary Covariance Generation," *J. Statist. Phys. 1 (1)*, 133-141 (1969).

7. A. YOUSUFF and R. E. SKELTON, "Controller Reduction by Component Cost Analysis," *IEEE Trans. Automat. Control AC-29 (6)*, 520-530 (1984).

8. R. E. SKELTON and D. A. WAGIE, "Minimal Root-Sensitivity in Linear Systems," in "IFAC Workshop on Appl. of Nonlinear Prog. and Opt. Control," San Francisco, California, June 20-22, 1983. Also in J. Guid. Control 7 (6), 570-574 (1984).

10. W. M. WONHAM, "Linear Multivariable Control; A Geometric Approach," Springer-Verlag, New York, 1979.

11. M. F. HUTTON and B. FRIEDLAND, "Routh Approximations for Reducing Order of Linear, Time-Invariant Systems," *IEEE Trans. Automat. Control AC-20 (3)*, 329-337 (1975).

12. R. W. NEWCOMB, "Linear Multiport Synthesis," McGraw Hill, New York, 1966.

13. R. E. KALMAN, "Irreducible Realizations and the Degree of a Rational Matrix," *SIAM J. Appl. Math. 13 (2)*, 520-544 (1965).

14. B. NOBLE and J. W. DANIEL, "Applied Linear Algebra," Prentice-Hall, Englewood Cliffs, New Jersey, 1977.

15. T. KAILATH, "Linear Systems," Prentice-Hall, Englewood Cliffs, New Jersey, 1980.

16. R. V. PATEL, "Computation of Minimal-Order State-Space Realizations and Observability Indices using Orthogonal Transformations," *Internat. J. Control 33 (2)*, 227-246 (1981).

17. T. T. SOONG, "Random Differential Equations in Science and Engineering," Academic Press, New York, 1973.

18. R. V. PATEL, "Computation of Matrix Fraction Descriptions of Linear Time-Invariant Systems," *IEEE Trans. Automat. Control AC-26 (1)*, 148-161 (1981).

19. E. C. Y. TSE, J. V. MEDANIC, and W. R. PERKINS, "Generalized Hessenberg Transformations for Reduced-Order Modeling of Large Scale Systems," *Internat. J. Control 27 (4)*, 493-512 (1978).

20. W. R. PERKINS, E. C. Y. TSE, and J. V. MEDANIC, "Reduced Order Modeling Using the QL Algorithm," in Proc. 21st Mid-west Symp. Circuits and Syst.," 481-485, 1978.

21. C. P. Kwong, "Optimal Chained Aggregation for Reduced Order Modeling," *Internat. J. Control 35 (6)*, 965-982 (1982).

22. N. K. SINHA, I. EL-NAHAS, and R. T. H. ALDEN, "Routh-Hurwitz Approximation of Multivariable Systems," in "18th Allerton Conf. Comm. Contr. Comp.," Monticello, Illinois, 1980.

23. G. FORSYTHE, M. A. MALCOLM, and C. B. MOORE, "Computer Methods for Mathematical Computation," Prentice-Hall, Englewood Cliffs, New Jersey, 1977.

24. G. J. BIERMAN, "Factorization Methods for Discrete Sequential Estimation," p. 54, Academic Press. New York, 1977.

25. G. OBINATA and H. INOOKA, "A Method for Modeling Linear Time-Invariant Systems by Linear Systems of Low Order," *IEEE Trans. Automat. Control AC-21 (4)*, 602-603 (1976).

26. G. OBINATA and H. INOOKA, "A Method for Reducing the Order of Multivariable Stochastic Systems," *IEEE Trans. Automat. Control AC-22 (4)*, 676-677 (1977).

27. G. OBINATA and H. INOOKA, "Authors' Reply to 'Comments on Model Reduction by Minimizing the Equation Error,'" *IEEE Trans. Automat. Control AC-28 (1)*, 124-125 (1983).

28. E. EITELBERG, "Comments on Model Reduction by Minimizing the Equation Error," *IEEE Trans. Automat. Control AC-27 (4)*, 1000-1002 (1982).

29. D. A. WILSON, "Model Reduction for Multivariable Systems," *Internat. J. Control 20 (1)*, 57-64 (1974).

30. J. M. SIRET, G. MICHAILESCO, and P. BERTRAND, "Representation of Linear Dynamical Systems by Aggregated Models," *Internat. J. Control 26 (1)*, 121-128 (1977).

31. M. AOKI, "Control of Large-Scale Dynamic System by Aggregation," *IEEE Trans. Automat. Control AC-13 (3)*, 246-253 (1968).

32. R. N. MISHRA and D. A. WILSON, "A New Algorithm for Optimal Reduction of Multivariable Systems," *Internat. J. Control 31 (3)*, 443-466 (1980).

Decentralized Estimation and Control of One-Way Connected Subsystems

FARHAD KIANFAR

Industrial and Manufacturing Engineering Department
California State Polytechnic University
Pomona, California

I. INTRODUCTION

In the past few years, control engineers have considered many systems such as power networks, urban traffic networks, manufacturing processes, etc., which require a large number of variables to describe their dynamic behavior adequately. Such systems are called large-scale systems. The centralized control of these systems require many communication networks between the observation posts and the centralized controller as

ISBN 0-12-012722-9

well as a large computing facility, which may not be available. That is why most of these large-scale systems ought to be controlled in a decentralized manner; i.e., several controllers having different partial information on the system state are involved in controlling the same system.

In the standard theory of control and estimation of dynamic systems, there is one centralized controller and state estimator for the whole system regardless of its size. Let us consider a large-scale system which consists on interconnected subsystems. The main objective of this research is to decentralize the act of control and estimation to the level of each subsystem. i.e., to design separate but communicating controllers and state estimators, one in each subsystem, to make the closed-loop system asymptotically stable with minimum cost. Clearly, decentralized control and estimation are suboptimal with respect to centralized optimal control and estimation. So we define a measure of suboptimality to be the relative degradation in performance criterion defined by

$$\Delta J = \frac{J^0 - J^*}{J^*} \tag{1}$$

where J^o and J^* are the suboptimal and optimal values of the performance criterion, respectively.

The theory of this chapter is applied to a river pollution control and estimation problem. The river pollution model consists of two one-way connected subsystems; i.e., the state of the first subsystem affects the dynamics of the second one, but not vice versa. We solve this problem numerically in two stages. First, a crude stable suboptimal solution is found by ignoring the coupling between the two subsystems, and solving the matrix Riccati equation for each subsystem separately. Then in the second stage we consider this solution as the initial value of a parameter optimization algorithm, and improve it by optimizing the parameters in the control or filter gain matrix. We use the Fletcher-Powell method [1] as our parameter optimization algorithm. In each iteration of this method, we check the stability of the closed-loop system before taking a step to a new set of parameters. So the solution in each iteration is stable. We take the final solution as our best decentralized suboptimal solution.

The structure of this chapter will now be described. Decentralized control of one-way connected subsystems is discussed in Section II. In Section III, we introduce the dynamic model for the river pollution which is due to Beck [2], and state all the corresponding assumptions. Section IV presents a decentralized control scheme for the model, in which we first find a crude stabilizing suboptimal control for the system, and then improve it by doing parameter optimization on the decentralized gains. Section V is devoted to design decentralized Kalman filters for the two subsystems of the river pollution problem. Finally, conclusions of the research are presented in Section VI.

II. DECENTRALIZED CONTROL OF ONE-WAY CONNECTED SUBSYSTEMS

In general, a system consisting of two interconnected subsystems with two different controllers can be represented as

$$\dot{x}_1 = A_{11}x_1 + A_{12}x_2 + B_1u_1 \tag{2}$$

$$\dot{x}_2 = A_{21}x_1 + A_{22}x_2 + B_2u_2, \tag{3}$$

where x_1, x_2 are the states of dimension n_1, n_2 and u_1, u_2 are the controls of dimension m_1, m_2 of the corresponding systems, respectively; A_{11}, A_{12}, A_{21}, A_{22}, B_1, and B_2 are constant matrices of appropriate size.

The problem in this section is a special case of the above model with $A_{12} = 0$; i.e., the total system will be

$$\begin{bmatrix} \dot{x}_1 \\ \dot{x}_2 \end{bmatrix} = \begin{bmatrix} A_{11} & 0 \\ A_{21} & A_{22} \end{bmatrix} \begin{bmatrix} x_1 \\ x_2 \end{bmatrix} + \begin{bmatrix} B_1 & 0 \\ 0 & B_2 \end{bmatrix} \begin{bmatrix} u_1 \\ u_2 \end{bmatrix}, \tag{4}$$

and the performance criterion is

$$J = \int_0^\infty (x'Qx + u'Ru)\, dt, \tag{5}$$

where

$$Q = \begin{bmatrix} Q_{11} & Q_{12} \\ Q_{12}' & Q_{22} \end{bmatrix} \quad \text{and} \quad R = \begin{bmatrix} R_1 & 0 \\ 0 & R_2 \end{bmatrix},$$

and where Q and R are symmetric positive semidefinite and positive definite constant matrices, respectively.

We say that the system (4) consists of two one-way connected subsystems since the second subsystem does not affect the first. We assume that each subsystem is controllable, i.e., (A_{11}, B_1) and (A_{22}, B_2) are controllable, which implies that the whole system is controllable. We want to find a decentralized stabilizing control for the system (4).

The matrix Riccati equation for the system (4) given the performance index (5) is

$$A'P + PA - PBR^{-1}B'P + Q = 0 \tag{6}$$

where

$$P = \begin{bmatrix} P_{11} & P_{12} \\ P_{12}' & P_{22} \end{bmatrix}.$$

Assuming $P_{12} = 0$, (6) can be written in partitioned form as

$$A'_{11}P_{11} + P_{11}A_{11} - P_{11}B_1R_1^{-1}B_1'P_{11} + Q_{11} = 0$$

$$A'_{21}P_{22} + Q_{12} = 0 \qquad (7)$$

$$A'_{22}P_{22} + P_{22}A_{22} - P_{22}B_2R_2^{-1}B_2'P_{22} + Q_{22} = 0.$$

The first and third equations in (7) are the Riccati equations for the two subsystems, and from the second one we have $Q_{12} = -A'_{21}P_{22}$.

So Q will be

$$Q = \begin{bmatrix} Q_{11} & -A'_{21}P_{22} \\ -P_{22}A_{21} & Q_{22} \end{bmatrix}. \qquad (8)$$

Now, we should choose Q_{11} and Q_{22} in order to make Q at least positive semidifinite, i.e., $x'Qx \geq 0$, for all x, or

$$x_1'Q_{11}x_1 + x_2'Q_{22}x_2 \geq 2x_1'A'_{21}P_{22}x_2 \quad \text{for all } x_1 \text{ and } x_2. \qquad (9)$$

The right-hand side of the inequality (9) is independent of Q_{11}. So if the initial values of Q_{11} and Q_{22} do not satisfy (9), we can hold Q_{22} constant and multiply Q_{11} by a positive scalar to increase the left-hand side of this inequality. After finding those Q_{11} and Q_{22} that make Q positive (semi-) definite, the decentralized stabilizing controls can be determined as

$$u_1 = -K_1x_1$$

$$u_2 = -K_2x_2,$$

where K_1 and K_2 are given by

$$K_1 = R_1^{-1}B_1'P_{11}$$

$$K_2 = R_2^{-1}B_2'P_{22}. \qquad (10)$$

Using these gains, the closed-loop system matrix will be

$$A - BK = \begin{bmatrix} A_{11} - B_1K_1 & 0 \\ A_{21} & A_{22} - B_2K_2 \end{bmatrix}, \tag{11}$$

which is stable if the matrices $A_{11} - B_1K_1$ and $A_{22} - B_2K_2$ are stable. The stability of the matrices $A_{ii} - B_iK_i$ is guaranteed by the controllability assumption of subsystem i for i = 1, 2.

III. A DYNAMIC MODEL FOR RIVER POLLUTION

What is really required on a river is to maintain pollution levels within reasonable bounds consistent both with the needs of the community and the maintenance of a satisfactory ecological balance. A good measure of the quality of a stream can be obtained from two main factors:

(i) the instream biochemical oxygen demand (BOD), which is an aggregate measure of the level of oxygen absorbing material in the river; and

(ii) the amount of dissolved oxygen (DO) in the stream.

The control of these two state variables will be considered.

Let the reach of a river be defined as a stretch of the river of some convenient length receiving one major controlled effluent discharge from a sewage treatment facility. Then the dynamics of BOD-DO in a reach can be expressed by the equations

$$\text{BOD} \quad \dot{z}_i = -K_{1i}z_i + \frac{Q_{i-1}}{V_i} z_{i-1} - \frac{Q_i + Q_E}{V_i} z_i + \frac{Q_E}{V_i} mi$$

$$\text{DO} \quad \dot{q}_i = K_{2i}\, q_i^s - q_i + \frac{Q_{i-1}}{V_i} q_{i-1} - \frac{Q_i + Q_E}{V_i} q_i \tag{12}$$

$$- K_{1i}z_i - \frac{\eta_i}{V_i},$$

where

V_i is the volume of the water in reach i in millions of gallons;

Q_E is the flow rate of the effluent into reach i in 10^6 gal/day;

z_i and z_{i-1} are the concentrations of BOD in reaches i and i - 1 in mg/liter;

q_i and q_{i-1} are the concentrations of DO in reaches i and i - 1 in mg/liter;

K_{1i} is the BOD decay rate in reach i per day;

K_{2i} is the DO reaeration rate in reach i per day;

Q_i and Q_{i-1} are the stream flow rates in reaches i and i - 1 in 10^6 gal/day;

q_i^s is the DO saturation level for the reach i in mg/liter;

η_i/V_i is the removal of DO due to sludge requirements mg/liter/day;

m_i is the concentration of BOD in the effluent in mg/liter.

For a reach of the river Cam, near Cambridge in England, Beck has found the following values for the coefficients in (12):

$K_1 = 0.32$ per day, $K_2 = 0.2$ per day,

$\eta/V = 0.1$ mg/liter/day, $q^s = 10$ mg/liter,

$Q_E/V = 0.1$, and $Q/V = 0.9$.

Thus, for this reach, (12) becomes

$$\begin{bmatrix} \dot{z}_i \\ \dot{q}_i \end{bmatrix} = \begin{bmatrix} -1.32 & 0 \\ -0.32 & -1.2 \end{bmatrix} \begin{bmatrix} z_i \\ q_i \end{bmatrix} + \begin{bmatrix} 0.1 \\ 0 \end{bmatrix} m_i + \begin{bmatrix} 0.9z_{i-1} \\ 0.9q_{i-1} + 1.9 \end{bmatrix}. \quad (13)$$

We take the steady state values of the system (13) as the desired values of the state and control variables, which any controller should try to maintain. In the steady state, we have

$$-1.32\overset{*}{z}_i + 0.9\overset{*}{z}_{i-1} + 0.1\overset{*}{m}_i = 0$$
$$-0.32\overset{*}{z}_i - 1.2\overset{*}{q}_i + 0.9\overset{*}{q}_{i-1} + 1.9 = 0 \tag{14}$$

for i = 1, 2. Let it be assumed that in reach 0, $\overset{*}{z}_0 = 0$ mg/liter, and $\overset{*}{q}_0 = 10$ mg/liter; i.e., the reach 0 is very clean. Let the desired levels of DO in reaches 1 and 2 be 8 and 6 mg/liter, respectively. Then from Eqs. (14), we get $\overset{*}{z}_1 = 4.06$, $\overset{*}{z}_2 = 5.94$, $\overset{*}{m}_1 = 53.5$, and $\overset{*}{m}_2 = 41.9$. The results are summarized in Table I.

Now, let us consider a two-reach model of the Cam river, which is

$$\begin{bmatrix} \dot{z}_1 \\ \dot{q}_1 \\ \dot{z}_2 \\ \dot{q}_2 \end{bmatrix} = \begin{bmatrix} -1.32 & 0 & 0 & 0 \\ -0.32 & -1.2 & 0 & 0 \\ 0.9 & 0 & -1.32 & 0 \\ 0 & 0.9 & -0.32 & -1.2 \end{bmatrix} \begin{bmatrix} z_1 \\ q_1 \\ z_2 \\ q_2 \end{bmatrix} + \begin{bmatrix} 0.1 & 0 \\ 0 & 0 \\ 0 & 0.1 \\ 0 & 0 \end{bmatrix} \begin{bmatrix} u_1 \\ u_2 \end{bmatrix} + \begin{bmatrix} 0.9z_0 + 5.35 \\ 0.9q_0 + 1.9 \\ 4.19 \\ 1.9 \end{bmatrix}, \tag{15}$$

Table I. Desired Values of the State and Control Variables of the River Pollution Model

Reach	BOD	DO	Control
0	0	10	0
1	4.06	8	53.5
2	5.94	6	41.9

where the new control variables u_1 and u_2 denote the deviations of m_1 and m_2 from the desired control values, i.e.,

$$u_1 = m_1 - 53.5$$

$$u_2 = m_2 - 41.9$$

The system (15) can be divided into two second-order subsystems with (z_1, q_1) as the states of the first subsystem and (z_2, q_2) as the states of the second.

IV. DECENTRALIZED CONTROL OF RIVER POLLUTION

To set the steady state level of DO in reach i equal to its desired level, we introduce the state variable e_i [2], which is defined as the integral of the difference between the desired and actual levels of DO in reach i, for i = 1, 2, i.e.,

$$\dot{e}_1 = 8 - q_1, \quad \dot{e}_2 = 6 - q_2.$$

So the two-reach model (15) becomes

$$\begin{bmatrix} \dot{z}_1 \\ \dot{q}_1 \\ \dot{e}_1 \\ \dot{z}_2 \\ \dot{q}_2 \\ \dot{e}_2 \end{bmatrix} = \begin{bmatrix} -1.32 & 0 & 0 & 0 & 0 & 0 \\ -0.32 & -1.2 & 0 & 0 & 0 & 0 \\ 0 & -1 & 0 & 0 & 0 & 0 \\ 0.9 & 0 & 0 & -1.32 & 0 & 0 \\ 0 & 0.9 & 0 & -0.32 & -1.2 & 0 \\ 0 & 0 & 0 & 0 & -1 & 0 \end{bmatrix} \begin{bmatrix} z_1 \\ q_1 \\ e_1 \\ z_2 \\ q_2 \\ e_2 \end{bmatrix} + \begin{bmatrix} 0.1 & 0 \\ 0 & 0 \\ 0 & 0 \\ 0 & 0.1 \\ 0 & 0 \\ 0 & 0 \end{bmatrix} \begin{bmatrix} u_1 \\ u_2 \end{bmatrix} + \begin{bmatrix} 0.9z_0 + 5.35 \\ 0.9q_0 + 1.9 \\ 8 \\ 4.19 \\ 1.9 \\ 6 \end{bmatrix}. \tag{16}$$

with the initial conditions

$$x_1(0) = \begin{bmatrix} z_1(0) \\ q_1(0) \\ e_1(0) \end{bmatrix} = \begin{bmatrix} 10 \\ 7 \\ 0 \end{bmatrix},$$

$$x_2(0) = \begin{bmatrix} z_2(0) \\ q_2(0) \\ e_2(0) \end{bmatrix} = \begin{bmatrix} 5.94 \\ 6 \\ 0 \end{bmatrix}.$$

The performance index is taken to be

$$J = \int_0^\infty (x'Qx + u'Ru)\, dt \tag{17}$$

where $Q = I_6$ and $R = I_2$, i.e., Q and R are 6×6 and 2×2 identity matrices.

Now we are going to find a decentralized stabilizing control by ignoring the coupling between the two subsystems and solving the matrix Riccati equation for each subsystem separately. This suboptimal control is compared with the centralized optimal one. We shall improve the suboptimal control using a parameter optimization technique.

The centralized optimal control for the system (16) given the performance index (17) is

$$\overset{*}{u}_1 = -0.37z_1 + 1.04q_1 - 0.82e_1 - 0.13z_2 + 0.48q_2 - 0.57e_2$$

$$\overset{*}{u}_2 = -0.13z_1 + 0.03q_1 + 0.57e_1 - 0.2z_2 + 0.68q_2 - 0.82e_2. \tag{18}$$

The minimum value of the performance criterion is

$$J^* = 1329.22. \tag{19}$$

A. A CRUDE DECENTRALIZED STABILIZING SUBOPTIMAL CONTROL

By solving the matrix Riccati equation for each subsystem separately, we can get the following decentralized suboptimal control:

$$\begin{aligned} u_1 &= -0.24z_1 + 0.84q_1 - e_1 \\ u_2 &= -0.24z_2 + 0.84q_2 - e_2. \end{aligned} \tag{20}$$

Using these controls, the value of the performance index can be written as

$$\bar{J} = x'(0)Px(0) = 1604.07, \tag{21}$$

where P satisfies the Liapunov equation

$$(A - BK)'P + P(A - BK) + K'RK + Q = 0, \tag{22}$$

and where

$$K = \begin{bmatrix} K_1 & 0 \\ 0 & K_2 \end{bmatrix} = \begin{bmatrix} 0.24 & -0.84 & 1 & 0 & 0 & 0 \\ 0 & 0 & 0 & 0.24 & -0.84 & 1 \end{bmatrix};$$

A and B are the system and distribution matrices of model (16).

As a measure of suboptimality of the control (20), let us compute the relative degradation in performance criterion

$$\Delta\bar{J} = \frac{\bar{J} - J^*}{J^*} = \frac{1604.07 - 1329.22}{1329.22} = 0.2, \tag{23}$$

i.e., the cost of this control is 20% more than the minimum cost.

B. IMPROVED DECENTRALIZED SUBOPTIMAL CONTROL

There are some methods for finding an unrestricted local minimum of a function $f(x_1, x_2, \ldots, x_n)$ of several variables in the nonlinear programming literature. One of the most powerful of them is the Fletcher-Powell method [1]. Here, we want to use this method to improve the crude decentralized control

(20). The performance criterion is a scalar function of the six decentralized control gains. These gains are the parameters to be found in order to minimize the performance index.

Let us consider once more the two-reach river pollution model (16). One typical decentralized control for this system is

$$u = -K(\alpha)x \tag{24}$$

where

$$K(\alpha) = \begin{bmatrix} \alpha_1 & \alpha_2 & \alpha_3 & 0 & 0 & 0 \\ 0 & 0 & 0 & \alpha_4 & \alpha_5 & \alpha_6 \end{bmatrix},$$

and where $\alpha = (\alpha_1\ \alpha_2\ \alpha_3\ \alpha_4\ \alpha_5\ \alpha_6)'$ is the vector of the parameters to be optimized. Using this control, the closed-loop system will be

$$\dot{x} = A(\alpha)x \tag{25}$$

where

$$A(\alpha) = A - BK(\alpha)$$

$$= \begin{bmatrix} -1.32 - 0.1\alpha_1 & -0.1\alpha_2 & -0.1\alpha_3 & 0 & 0 & 0 \\ -0.32 & -1.2 & 0 & 0 & 0 & 0 \\ 0 & -1 & 0 & 0 & 0 & 0 \\ 0.9 & 0 & 0 & -1.32 - 0.1\alpha_4 & -0.1\alpha_5 & -0.1\alpha_6 \\ 0 & 0.9 & 0 & 0 & -1.2 & 0 \\ 0 & 0 & 0 & 0 & -1 & 0 \end{bmatrix}$$

and the performance criterion becomes

$$J(\alpha) = \int_0^\infty x\ Q(\alpha)x\ dt \tag{26}$$

where $Q(\alpha) = Q + K'(\alpha)RK(\alpha)$. Assuming $Q = I_6$ and $R = I_2$ as before, we have

$$Q(\alpha) = \begin{bmatrix} 1+\alpha_1^2 & \alpha_1\alpha_2 & \alpha_1\alpha_3 & 0 & 0 & 0 \\ \alpha_1\alpha_2 & 1+\alpha_2^2 & \alpha_2\alpha_3 & 0 & 0 & 0 \\ \alpha_1\alpha_3 & \alpha_2\alpha_3 & 1+\alpha_3^2 & 0 & 0 & 0 \\ 0 & 0 & & 1+\alpha_4^2 & \alpha_4\alpha_5 & \alpha_4\alpha_6 \\ 0 & 0 & & \alpha_4\alpha_5 & 1+\alpha_5^2 & \alpha_5\alpha_6 \\ 0 & 0 & & \alpha_4\alpha_6 & \alpha_5\alpha_6 & 1+\alpha_6^2 \end{bmatrix}.$$

Now, since the performance index (26) depends on the initial condition, we define for our parameter optimization problem a new performance criterion which is a scalar function of the parameter vector α and independent of the initial condition, i.e.,

$$\hat{J}(\alpha) = \mathrm{tr}(WP(\alpha)) \tag{27}$$

where W is a symmetric positive definite weighting matrix, and $P(\alpha)$ satisfies the following Liapunov equation:

$$A'(\alpha)P(\alpha) + P(\alpha)A(\alpha) = -Q(\alpha). \tag{28}$$

In each iteration of the Fletcher-Powell method, we need the value of the parameter vector α, the value of the function $\hat{J}(\alpha)$, and the value of the function first derivative, i.e., the gradient vector $\hat{J}_\alpha$. We may find each component of the gradient vector by solving a different Liapunov equation. Differentiating (28) with respect to α_i, we get

$$A'(\alpha)P_{\alpha_i} + P_{\alpha_i}A(\alpha) = -\left(Q_{\alpha_i} + A'_{\alpha_i}P(\alpha) + P(\alpha)A_{\alpha_i}\right) \tag{29}$$

where subscript α_i denotes the first derivative of the matrix respect to α_i. Equation (29) is itself a Liapunov equation for P_{α_i}. Then the ith component of the gradient vector is given by

$$\hat{J}_{\alpha_i} = \mathrm{tr}(WP_{\alpha_i}), \quad \text{for } i = 1, 2, \ldots, 6. \tag{30}$$

Table II. *Improved Decentralized Control Gains for the River Pollution Problem*

Iteration	α_1	α_2	α_3	α_4	α_5	α_6	$\hat{J}$	J
0	0.2383	-0.8356	1.0008	0.2383	-0.8356	1.0008	4555.213	1604.0690
1	0.2557	-0.8653	1.0559	0.2933	-0.8433	0.911	4538.644	1547.558
2	0.6811	-1.4908	1.3361	1.3763	-1.0041	1.1099	4535.886	1507.075
3	1.0587	-2.0178	1.1569	2.3132	-1.1278	1.0994	4507.074	1558.665
4	0.7074	-2.0547	1.1288	2.5755	-0.9605	1.111	4501.957	1576.666
5	0.7762	-1.9876	1.1342	2.5813	-0.6325	1.1113	4500.042	1611.016
6	0.607	-1.3465	1.0785	2.0396	-0.7695	1.0655	4482.019	1572.111
7	0.5044	-1.6205	1.0577	1.714	-0.7341	1.046	4478.906	1556.355
8	0.5037	-1.6224	1.0627	1.71	-0.74	1.0456	4478.707	1554.015
9	0.5036	-1.6229	1.063	1.7101	-0.7407	1.0456	4478.696	1553.864
10	0.5036	-1.6231	1.063	1.7101	-0.7409	1.0456	4478.55	1553.799

There is an easier way to find the gradient vector $\hat{J}_{\alpha}$, which requires the solution of only one Liapunov equation. Let $L(\alpha)$ satisfy

$$A(\alpha)L(\alpha) + L(\alpha)A'(\alpha) = -W, \tag{31}$$

then the ith component of the gradient vector can be written as

$$\hat{J}_{\alpha_i} = \mathrm{tr}\left[L(\alpha)\left(Q_{\alpha_i} + A'_{\alpha_i}P(\alpha) + P(\alpha)A_{\alpha_i}\right)\right]. \tag{32}$$

Obviously, we use the second method, i.e., Eqs. (31) and (32). for finding the gradient vector.

Thus in each iteration, we solve the Liapunov equations (28) and (31) using the Potter method. We know that the solution of a Liapunov equation by the Potter method will be correct if the closed-loop eigenvalues are stable. So in the line-search part of each iteration, we check the stability of the closed-loop eigenvalues before choosing the step size. If they are not stable, we shall make the step size smaller.

Table II contains the numerical results of the parameter optimization, where the initial values of the α_i, iteration 0, are taken to be the gains in the decentralized suboptimal control (20). To give the diagonal elements of the matrix $P(\alpha)$ in $\hat{J}(\alpha)$ the same weight as these elements in $J(\alpha)$, we choose the weighting matrix W as the following diagonal matrix:

$$W = \mathrm{diag}[100, 49, 1, 36, 36, 1].$$

As seen, the diagonal elements of the matrix W corresponding to nonzero initial conditions are taken to be the square of these initial conditions; and those corresponding to 0 initial conditions are 1.

As seen in Table II, $\hat{J}$ decreases monotonically but J does not. Our objective function to be minimized is $\hat{J}$, which is independent of x(0). But J depends on x(0), and it has its lowest value in the third iteration. The relative degradation of the final value of J from its central minimum is

$$\Delta J = \frac{1553.799 - 1329.217}{1329.217} = 0.16. \qquad (33)$$

Surprisingly, within the calculations of the first iteration, we find a set of parameters which has the lowest decentralized performance value among all we have found. These are

$$\begin{aligned} \alpha_1 &= 0.4064, \quad \alpha_2 = -1.1233, \quad \alpha_3 = 1.534, \\ \alpha_4 &= 0.7704, \quad \alpha_5 = -0.9105, \quad \alpha_6 = 0.1321, \end{aligned} \qquad (34)$$

with $\hat{J} = 11075.12$ and $J = 1396.223$.

The relative degradation of this J from its central minimum will be

$$\overline{\Delta J} = \frac{1396.223 - 1329.217}{1329.217} = 0.05. \qquad (35)$$

Since the initial conditions of the system (16) are practically important, the actual performance criterion is J, which depends on them. So the set of decentralized gains (34), which has a cost only 5% more than the centralized minimum cost, is of considerable importance.

C. BLOCK DIAGONALIZATION OF THE CENTRALIZED GAIN MATRIX

In this subsection, we want to verify the procedure in Section II by making the centralized gain matrix block diagonal. Let $Q_{22} = I_3$, $R_2 = 1$, and P_{22} be the solution of the matrix Riccati equation for the second subsystem. Then $\overline{Q}$ is taken to be

$$\bar{Q} = \begin{bmatrix} \bar{Q}_{11} & -A_{21}'P_{22} \\ -P_{22}A_{21} & Q_{22} \end{bmatrix}. \tag{36}$$

In order to make $\bar{Q}$ positive definite, we have to multiply the previous Q_{11} at least by 3000, i.e., $\bar{Q}_{11} = 3000I_3$. When we replace Q in the performance index (17) by $\bar{Q}$, the centralized optimal control for the system (16) will be

$$\begin{aligned} u_1^o &= -45.75z_1 + 47.11q_1 - 54.78e_1 \\ u_2^o &= -0.24z_2 + 0.83q_2 - e_2 \end{aligned} \tag{37}$$

or the centralized gain matrix is

$$K = \begin{bmatrix} 45.75 & -47.11 & 54.78 & 0 & 0 & 0 \\ 0 & 0 & 0 & 0.24 & -0.83 & 1 \end{bmatrix}, \tag{38}$$

which is block diagonal. The minimum value of the new performance index is

$$J^o = 408542.8 \tag{39}$$

As seen, the centralized control (37) is actually decentralized, i.e., the control of each subsystem is a function of only the states of that subsystem.

V. STOCHASTIC ESTIMATION OF THE RIVER POLLUTION PROBLEM

Let us consider the two-reach river pollution model (16) with additive system and measurement noises, i.e.,

$$\begin{aligned} \dot{x}_1 &= A_{11}x_1 + B_1u_1 + C_1w_1 \\ \dot{x}_2 &= A_{22}x_2 + A_{21}x_1 + B_2u_2 + C_2w_2, \end{aligned} \tag{40}$$

$$\begin{aligned} y_1 &= H_1x_1 + v_1 \\ y_2 &= H_2x_2 + v_2, \end{aligned} \tag{41}$$

where

$$x_1 = \begin{bmatrix} z_1 \\ q_1 \\ e_1 \end{bmatrix}, \quad x_2 = \begin{bmatrix} z_2 \\ q_2 \\ e_2 \end{bmatrix},$$

$$A_{11} = A_{22} = \begin{bmatrix} -1.32 & 0 & 0 \\ -0.32 & -1.2 & 0 \\ 0 & -1 & 0 \end{bmatrix}, \quad A_{21} = \begin{bmatrix} 0.9 & 0 & 0 \\ 0 & 0.9 & 0 \\ 0 & 0 & 0 \end{bmatrix},$$

$$B_1 = B_2 = \begin{bmatrix} 0.1 \\ 0 \\ 0 \end{bmatrix}, \quad C_1 = C_2 = I_3,$$

and

$$H_1 = H_2 = (0\ 1\ 1).$$

We assume that all random variables in the problem are Gaussian distributed with zero mean and unit variance. We also assume that they are independent of each other. Hence,

$$Q_1 = Q_2 = I_3 \quad \text{and} \quad R_1 = R_2 = 1,$$

where Q_1 and Q_2 are covariance matrices of w_1 and w_2, and R_1 and R_2 are variances of v_1 and v_2, respectively, and where I_3 is the 3×3 identity matrix. As seen, the pairs (H_1, A_{11}) and (H_2, A_{22}) are observable, which together imply the observability of (H, A).

The performance criterion for the quality of an estimate is taken to be the mean square error, i.e.,

$$J = E[\tilde{x}'\tilde{x}] = \text{tr}(P), \tag{42}$$

where P is the covariance matrix of the estimation error.

First, let us find the centralized optimal filter for the whole system, which will be used to measure suboptimality of the other filters later. The dynamic and measurement equations for the whole system are

$$\dot{x} = Ax + Bu + Cw$$
$$y = Hx + v. \tag{43}$$

The optimal filter gain is

$$K^* = P^*H'R^{-1} = \begin{bmatrix} -0.005634 & -0.003443 \\ 0.028193 & 0.006722 \\ 1.338496 & 0.101377 \\ 0.010308 & -0.000590 \\ -0.133716 & -0.011472 \\ 0.241815 & 1.443690 \end{bmatrix}, \tag{44}$$

where P^* satisfies the Riccati equation

$$AP^* + P^*A' - P^*H'R^{-1}HP^* + Q = 0, \tag{45}$$

and where $Q = I_6$, and $R = I_2$. The minimum value of the performance index is

$$J^* = \mathrm{tr}(P^*) = 5.589087. \tag{46}$$

The optimal filter equation will be

$$\dot{\hat{x}} = (A - K^*H)\hat{x} + K^*y + Bu. \tag{47}$$

As mentioned earlier, to find the best decentralized filter gains, we use a parameter optimization on the elements of these gains to minimize the performance index (42). We need a set of stabilizing initial gains to start this procedure. They can be found by ignoring the coupling between the two subsystems in (40), and solving the matrix Riccati equation for the error covariance matrix of each subsystem separately. We know that this set of gains makes the total closed-loop filter stable. Since the two subsystems have the same dynamics, their common initial gains are

$$K_1 = K_2 = P_1H_1'R_1^{-1} = \begin{bmatrix} -0.005771 \\ 0.028448 \\ 1.342146 \end{bmatrix}, \tag{48}$$

where P_1 satisfies

$$A_{11}P_1 + P_1A_{11}' - P_1H_1'R_1^{-1}H_1P_1 + Q_1 = 0. \tag{49}$$

Now, we are ready to start our parameter optimization method. Any decentralized filter gain for this system is of the following form:

$$K(\alpha) = \begin{bmatrix} \alpha_1 & 0 \\ \alpha_2 & 0 \\ \alpha_3 & 0 \\ 0 & \alpha_4 \\ 0 & \alpha_5 \\ 0 & \alpha_6 \end{bmatrix}, \tag{50}$$

where $\alpha = (\alpha_1\ \alpha_2\ \alpha_3\ \alpha_4\ \alpha_5\ \alpha_6)'$ is the vector of parameters to be optimized. Using this gain, the filter equation for the whole system will be

$$\dot{\hat{x}} = A(\alpha)\hat{x} + K(\alpha)y + Bu, \tag{51}$$

where

$$A(\alpha) = A - K(\alpha)H$$

$$= \begin{bmatrix} -1.32 & -\alpha_1 & -\alpha_1 & 0 & 0 & 0 \\ -0.32 & -1.2-\alpha_2 & -\alpha_2 & 0 & 0 & 0 \\ 0 & -1-\alpha_3 & -\alpha_3 & 0 & 0 & 0 \\ 0.9 & 0 & 0 & -1.32 & -\alpha_4 & -\alpha_4 \\ 0 & 0.9 & 0 & -0.32 & -1.2-\alpha_5 & -\alpha_5 \\ 0 & 0 & 0 & 0 & -1-\alpha_6 & -\alpha_6 \end{bmatrix}.$$

We want to minimize the performance criterion (42), which is now a scalar function of the parameters $\alpha_1, \alpha_2, \ldots, \alpha_6$, i.e.,

$$J(\alpha) = \mathrm{tr}(P(\alpha)), \tag{52}$$

where $P(\alpha)$ satisfies the following Liapunov equation:

$$A(\alpha)P(\alpha) + P(\alpha)A'(\alpha) = -Q(\alpha), \tag{53}$$

and where $Q(\alpha) = Q + K(\alpha)RK'(\alpha)$. Equation (53) is the steady state version of Eq. (8.50) in Meditch [3]. The definition of the performance index (52) implies that the weighting matrix W is taken to be the identity, i.e., $W = I_6$. Assuming $Q = I_6$ and $R = I_2$ as before, we have

$$Q(\alpha) = \begin{bmatrix} 1+\alpha_1^2 & \alpha_1\alpha_2 & \alpha_1\alpha_3 & 0 & & \\ \alpha_1\alpha_2 & 1+\alpha_2^2 & \alpha_2\alpha_3 & 0 & & \\ \alpha_1\alpha_3 & \alpha_2\alpha_3 & 1+\alpha_3^2 & 0 & & \\ 0 & 0 & 0 & 1+\alpha_4^2 & \alpha_4\alpha_5 & \alpha_4\alpha_6 \\ 0 & 0 & 0 & \alpha_4\alpha_5 & 1+\alpha_5^2 & \alpha_5\alpha_6 \\ 0 & 0 & 0 & \alpha_4\alpha_6 & \alpha_5\alpha_6 & 1+\alpha_6^2 \end{bmatrix}.$$

In each iteration of the Fletcher-Powell method, besides the value of the parameter vector α and the value of the function $J(\alpha)$, we need the value of the function first derivative, i.e., the gradient vector J_α. The ith component of J_α can be found as

$$J_{\alpha_i} = \mathrm{tr}\left[L(\alpha)\left(Q_{\alpha_i} + A_{\alpha_i}P(\alpha) + P(\alpha)A'_{\alpha_i}\right)\right], \tag{54}$$

where $L(\alpha)$ satisfies Liapunov equation

$$A'(\alpha)L(\alpha) + L(\alpha)A(\alpha) = -W, \tag{55}$$

and where W is the 6×6 identity matrix. Each subscript α_i represents the first derivative of the matrix respect to α_i for $i = 1, 2, \ldots, 6$.

Table III. Improved Decentralized Filter Gains for the River Pollution Problem

Iteration	α_1	α_2	α_3	α_4	α_5	α_6	J
0	-0.005771	0.028448	1.342146	-0.005771	0.028448	1.342146	6.159308
1	0.012113	-0.031085	1.342928	0.009331	-0.037488	1.384354	5.708549
2	0.005611	-0.032078	1.299099	-0.005698	-0.038105	1.438695	5.699641
3	0.005634	-0.033331	1.297604	-0.006218	-0.036889	1.440441	5.699451
4	0.005599	-0.033610	1.297183	-0.006228	-0.036508	1.440886	5.699437
5	0.004677	-0.036065	1.291673	-0.005890	-0.032486	1.447044	5.698421
6	0.004675	-0.036077	1.291650	-0.005888	-0.032466	1.447068	5.696749

Table III contains the numerical results of the parameter optimization, where the initial values of the α_i in iteration 0 are taken to be the decentralized filter gains in (48).

As seen in Table III, J decreases monotonically. We compute the relative degradations of the initial and the final values of J from its centralized minimum J^*. They are

$$\Delta J_0 = \frac{J_0 - J^*}{J^*} = 0.102, \tag{56}$$

$$\Delta J_6 = \frac{J_6 - J^*}{J^*} = 0.019. \tag{57}$$

The last row of the table shows the best decentralized filter gain; i.e.,

$$K^o = \begin{bmatrix} 0.004675 & 0 \\ -0.036077 & 0 \\ 1.291650 & 0 \\ 0 & -0.005888 \\ 0 & -0.032466 \\ 0 & 1.447068 \end{bmatrix} \tag{58}$$

Therefore, we have found a crude stabilizing decentralized filter gain in (48) with a 10.2% relative degradation in performance over the optimal one. Then we improve this gain by using a parameter optimization method to get the best decentralized filter gain in (58), whose performance is only 1.9% worse than the optimal one.

VI. CONCLUSIONS

This chapter presents some methods for decentralized estimation and control of dynamic systems consisting of one-way connected subsystems. Our main objective is to decentralize estimation and control to the level of each subsystem, while maintaining the stability of the closed-loop system and minimizing the total cost. The theory is developed in Section II and then it is applied to a river pollution problem to get a decentralized stabilizing suboptimal control (20). This control is crude in the sense that its corresponding cost is 20% more than the minimum cost. Then we improve this suboptimal control by using a parameter optimization on the decentralized control gains. Our best decentralized control in (34) has a cost only 5% more than the centralized minimum cost.

The estimation problem in Section V is the dual of the control problem in Section IV. This time we start from a decentralized filter that is 10.2% worse than the optimal filter, and end up with a decentralized optimal filter whose performance is only 1.9% worse than the centralized optimal filter.

The methods in this chapter are applicable to dynamic systems consisting of one-way connected subsystems. More general methods for decentralized estimation and control of large-scale systems can be found in [4].

REFERENCES

1. R. FLETCHER and M. J. D. POWELL, "A Rapidly Convergent Descent Method for Minimization," *Comput. J. 6*, 163-168 (1963).

2. B. BECK and P. YOUNG, "The Modeling and Control of Water Quality in a River System," *Automatica 10*, 455-468 (1974).

3. J. S. MEDITCH, "Stochastic Optimal Linear Estimation and Control," McGraw-Hill, New York (1969).

4. F. KIANFAR, "Estimation and Control of Large-Scale Systems," Ph.D. Dissertation, University of California, Los Angeles (1982).

Multivariable Feedback and Decentralized Control

G. ZAMES
D. BENSOUSSAN
Department of Electrical Engineering
McGill University
Montreal, Quebec, Canada

I. INTRODUCTION

An example might illustrate the class of problems that interest us. Imagine a house with many rooms in each of which a man tries to control room-temperature by watching a thermometer

ISBN 0-12-012722-9

and adjusting a heater. Each heater greatly affects the other rooms through highly conducting walls, except at high frequencies. There is uncertainty in the sense that no man knows what is happening in the others rooms. The question we would like to answer is, Under what conditions can each man control his own temperature without communicating with the others? The point is of course that in large systems a pricipal reason for decentralizing control is that communications are expensive.

A simple model of such a situation involves a multivariable plant P(s) (Fig. 1), with N input-output pairs (u_i, y_i), i = 1, ..., N, in which uncertainty occurs in the simple form of additive disturbances d_i. Each plant input u_i receives information about its own output y_i and command signal v_i, but not about the others; i.e., the feedback F(s) and filter G(s) are diagonal. It is desired that each command signal $v_i(s)$ control its own output $y_i(s)$ so as to achieve a nominal transmission $k_{ii}(s)$; i.e., the desired closed-loop matrix $[K_{ij}(s)]$ is diagonal. We would like to know under what conditions on the plant is it possible to find such a diagonal (F(s), G(s)) to achieve the closed-loop-decoupled result y(s) = K(s)v(s) for *all* inputs and disturbances that are likely to occur?

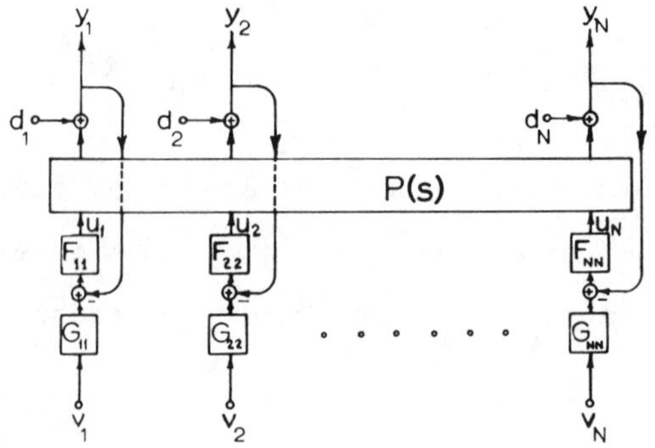

Fig. 1

If we insist on perfect decoupling, the conditions on P(s) are too restrictive to be of much practical value. However, if we settle for decoupling to an arbitrarily small tolerance they become more liberal and essentially the same as conditions for sensitivity reduction (see Section IV).

A. *SENSITIVITY REDUCTION BY FEEDBACK*

In an earlier paper [2] it was shown that feedback can reduce certain weighted measures of sensitivity whenever the plant has an "approximate inverse," and feedback can make weighted sensitivity arbitrarily small whenever $P^{-1}(s)$ is analytic in $Re(s) \geq 0$ and P(s) approaches 0 slowly enough as $s \to \infty$. The feedbacks in [2] were not diagonal.

Diagonal feedbacks are interesting because of their simplicity and their relevance to the above-mentioned problem of decentralized control. In comparison with [2], we shall achieve diagonal feedback at the cost of the restriction[1] that P(s) approach diagonal dominance as $s \to \infty$.

Diagonal dominance and weak-coupling conditions were introduced into feedback theory during the 1960s by Zames and Sandberg (see, e.g., [3-5]) in conjunction with the (incremental) small-gain and conic-sector theories for stability (sensitivity to perturbations). Rosenbrock has used Ostrowski's theorem to derive stability conditions for matrices of frequency responses that are diagonally dominant at *all* frequencies.

The requirement of diagonal dominance at all frequencies is quite restrictive and is satisfied by few multivariable systems in practice. On the other hand, many physical systems have

[1] *See Section V for nondiagonally dominant conditions.*

high-frequency attenuation rates that increase with distance. Such systems become diagonally dominant at high frequencies where, indeed, they approach diagonal.

Although the emphasis in this paper is on diagonal feedbacks, the methods are relevant to nondiagonal feedbacks too. If the requirement that feedbacks be diagonal is relaxed, then the diagonal dominance restriction on P(s) can be dispensed with.

II. TERMINOLOGY

A. *ALGEBRAS OF FREQUENCY RESPONSES*

We shall use the term "frequency-response" to denote a complex or matrix-valued function of the complex variable $s = \sigma + j\omega$.

If Ω is any region of the complex plane, let $\mathrm{Mer}^N(\Omega)$ denote the algebra of functions of a complex variable which assume values in the $N \times N$ matrices of complex numbers, and which are *meromorphic* in Ω, i.e., analytic except at (isolated) poles. Let $\mathrm{Anl}^N(\Omega)$ denote the subalgebra of functions *analytic* throughout Ω. Whenever $N = 1$, we shall suppress the superscript. A function $K(\cdot)$ in $\mathrm{Mer}^N(\Omega)$ will be called *strictly proper* iff the limit $\lim_{|s|\to\infty} K(s)$ is defined and equals zero.

$\mathbb{B}^\infty$ is the normed algebra over the real field of complex-valued functions of a complex variable, which have the conjugate symmetry $K(\bar{s}) = \bar{K}(s)$, and are analytic and bounded in the closed right half-plane $\mathrm{Re}(s) \geq 0$, under the norm

$$\|K(\cdot)\|_\infty \triangleq \sup_{\mathrm{Re}(s)\geq 0} |K(s)|.$$

This norm can be evaluated on the imaginary axis, $\|K(\cdot)\|_\infty = \sup_\omega |K(j\omega)|$.

$\mathbb{B}^{\infty}$ is a subalgebra of the Hardy space $\mathbb{H}^{\infty}$ (whose region of assured bounded analyticity is restricted to the interior of the half-plane $\text{Re}(s) \geq 0$).

If A is any matrix of complex numbers, we shall denote its largest and smallest singular values (i.e., square-roots of the eigenvalues of A^*A) by the notations $\overline{\sigma}[A]$ and $\underline{\sigma}[A]$ respectively. The norm of A is $||A|| = \overline{\sigma}(A)$.

Let $\mathbb{B}^{\infty N}$ denote the algebra of $N \times N$ matrices of functions in $\mathbb{B}^{\infty}$ under the (singular value) norm

$$||K(\cdot)||_{\infty} = \sup_{\text{Re}(s)\geq 0} ||K(s)||.$$

That supremum too can be evaluated along the imaginary axis.

B. INVERTIBLE AND ULTIMATELY DIAGONALLY DOMINANT FUNCTIONS

Let $K(\cdot)$ be any function in $\text{Mer}^N[\text{Re}(s) \geq 0]$. Then $K(\cdot)$ is *analytically invertible* in $\text{Re}(s) \geq 0$ if there is a function $K^{-1}(\cdot)$ in $\text{Anl}^N[\text{Re}(s) \geq 0]$ which inverts $K(\cdot)$, i.e., $K(s)K^{-1}(s) = K^{-1}(s)K(s) = I$ for all $\text{Re}(s) \geq 0$. (For example, if $K(\cdot)$ is a ratio of coprime rational factors in $\text{Anl}^N[\text{Re}(s) \geq 0]$, $K(s) = K_n(s)K_d^{-1}(s)$, then $K(s)$ is analytically invertible in $\text{Re}(s) \geq 0$ iff $\det K_n(s) \neq 0$.)

$K(\cdot)$ will be called *ultimately diagonally dominant* iff there can be found a diagonal function $D(\cdot)$ in $\text{Mer}^N[\text{Re}(s) \geq 0]$ and a constant α $(0 \leq \alpha < 1)$ such that

$$\sup_{|s|\geq R, \text{Re}(s)\geq 0} ||\{K(s) - D(s)\}D^{-1}(s)|| \to \alpha \quad \text{as} \quad R \to \infty. \quad (1)$$

α will be called the coupling constant of $K(\cdot)$ at ∞, and $K(\cdot)$ will be called *ultimately diagonal* when $\alpha = 0$.

III. RESULTS ON SENSITIVITY REDUCTION

A. *EXISTENCE OF A DESENSITIZING FEEDBACK*

Let $P(\cdot)$ be a strictly proper plant in $\mathrm{Mer}^N[\mathrm{Re}(s) \geq 0]$. For any feedback $F(\cdot)$ in $\mathbb{B}^{\infty N}$, the closed-loop frequency responses are represented by the matrix (see Fig. 2)

$$\begin{bmatrix} (I + FP)^{-1} & P(I + FP)^{-1} \\ F(I + PF)^{-1} & (I + PF)^{-1} \end{bmatrix}. \tag{2}$$

We shall call (2) stable iff all its elements belong to $\mathbb{B}^{\infty N}$. We would like to find a feedback F to make the sensitivity function $(I + PF)^{-1}$ small over some specified frequency interval, without causing $(I + PF)^{-1}$ to become too large at other frequencies, or creating instabilities in (2). We shall derive such an F in a theorem divided into three parts, the first part dealing with the existence of F, and the other parts dealing with methods of constructing F.

Theorem 1A. If

(H1) $P(s)$ is analytically invertible in $\mathrm{Re}(s) \geq 0$, and ultimately diagonally dominant with coupling constant α at $s = \infty$ $(0 \leq \alpha < 1)$; and

(H2) $P(s)$ satisfies the following restriction on attenuation near $s = \infty$:

$$\underline{\sigma}[P(s)] \geq \eta|s|^{-k} \quad \text{for} \quad |s| \geq R \tag{3}$$

where $\eta > 0$, $R > 0$, and $k > 0$ are some constants,

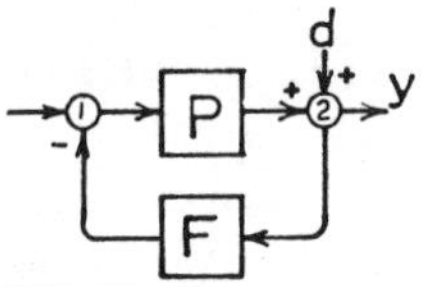

Fig. 2

then given any constants $\epsilon > 0$, $\omega_0 > 0$, and $M > (1 - \alpha)^{-1}$, there exists a diagonal, strictly proper feedback F in $\mathbb{B}^{\infty N}$ (described by (5) below) for which the frequency response matrix (2) is stable, and for which the sensitivity function satisfies the inequalities

$$\|\{I + P(s)F(s)\}^{-1}\| \leq \begin{cases} \epsilon & \text{for} \quad s \in [-j\omega_0, j\omega_0] \\ M & \text{for} \quad \mathrm{Re}(s) \geq 0 \end{cases} \tag{4}$$

Sets of disturbance or input power spectra can conveniently be described by a weighting [2] or envelope function. Let $W(\cdot)$ be any weighting function in $\mathbb{B}^{\infty N}$, and

$$w_\infty \triangleq \lim_{|s|\to\infty, \mathrm{Re}(s)\geq 0} \|W(s)\|.$$

Corollary. Under the hypotheses (H1)-(H2), if ϵ is any constant satisfying $\epsilon > (1 - \alpha)^{-1}w_\infty$, then there exists a strictly proper feedback F in $\mathbb{B}^{\infty N}$ whose sensitivity function satisfies $\|W(I + PF)^{-1}\|_\infty \leq \epsilon$, and for which the matrix (2) is stable.

B. CONSTRUCTION OF THE FEEDBACK F

Our feedback F will consist of a high gain in conjunction with a frequency function that approximately inverts F at high frequencies. Let us introduce some concepts useful in describing such a function.

Let $K(\cdot)$ be any frequency-response in $\mathrm{Mer}^N[\mathrm{Re}(s) \geq 0]$. An ultimate approximate right inverse of K of radius $\alpha_1 \geq 0$, abbreviated to *ultimate right* α_1*-inverse*, is any function $V(\cdot)$ in $\mathrm{Anl}^N[\mathrm{Re}(s) \geq 0]$ such that

$$\lim_{R\to\infty} \sup_{|s|>R, \mathrm{Re}(s)\geq 0} \|K(s)V(s) - I\| \leq \alpha_1$$

and is an *ultimate right inverse* iff $\alpha_1 = 0$.

There are many possible ultimate α-inverses. The following theorem shows that any one of them can be used to define a sensitivity reducing feedback. In Theorem 1C a particular α-inverse will be constructed.

Theorem 1B. Under the hypotheses of Theorem 1A, the specified sensitivity (4) can be achieved by a strictly proper feedback F defined by the formula

$$F(s) = \gamma V(s)\left(\frac{m}{s+m}\right)\left(\frac{n}{s+n}\right)^k \tag{5}$$

in which $V(\cdot) \in \text{Anl}^N[\text{Re}(s) \geq 0]$ is any (not necessarily diagonal) ultimate right α-inverse of $P(s)$ analytically invertible in $\text{Re}(s) \geq 0$, and the gain $\gamma > 0$ and integers $m > 0$, $n > 0$ are large enough.

C. *CONSTRUCTION OF AN ULTIMATE INVERSE*

Let us construct such an ultimate α-inverse, and use it to complete the definition of F by (5).

Suppose the hypotheses of Theorem 1A to be true. Let $D(\cdot) \in \text{Mer}^N[\text{Re}(s) \geq 0]$ be the diagonal frequency response for which the dominance condition (1) is satisfied, and suppose the functions $D_{ii}(s)$ have no pole-zero cancellations.

Lemma. There exists $R > 0$ with the property that for all s in the region $|s| \geq R$, $\text{Re}(s) \geq 0$, $D(s)$ is analytic, strictly proper, $\det D(s) \neq 0$, and the smallest singular value of $D(s)$ has the lower bound

$$\underline{\sigma}[D(s)] \geq c_1|s|^{-k} \tag{6}$$

where $c_1 > 0$ is a constant.

It follows from the lemma that all the poles and zeros of the functions $D_{ii}(s)$, $i = 1, \ldots, N$, are confined to the region $|s| < R$, $\mathrm{Re}(s) \geq 0$, and are therefore finite in number. Let $D_{ii}^{+}(s)$ be the rational function whose poles and zeros are precisely the poles and zeros respectively of $D_{ii}(s)$ in $\mathrm{Re}(s) \geq 0$. As $s \to \infty$, $D_{ii}^{+}(s)$ approaches a function of the form $c_i s^{-q_i}$. Let the diagonal function $Z \in \mathrm{Mer}[\mathrm{Re}(s) \geq 0]$ be defined by the expression

$$Z(s) = \mathrm{diag}\left[c_i(s + s_0)^{-q_i}\left(D_{ii}^{+}\right)^{-1}(s)\right]$$

for some constants $s_0 > 0$, and let[2]

$$D_v(s) = Z(s)D(s). \tag{7}$$

$D_v(s)$ is diagonal, has no poles or zeros in $\mathrm{Re}(s) \geq 0$, approaches $D(s)$ as $s \to \infty$ (since $Z(s) \to 1$), and is therefore strictly proper.

Theorem 1C. The function $D_v(s)$ defined by (7) is in $\mathrm{Anl}^N[\mathrm{Re}(s) \geq 0]$, is analytically invertible in $\mathrm{Re}(s) \geq 0$, and is a diagonal ultimate right α-inverse of P.

Remark. It follows from Theorems 1A-1C that a *diagonal* feedback F which produces the low sensitivity specified in Theorem 1A is given by (5) if we set $V(s) = D_v^{-1}(s)$.

D. EXAMPLE

The plant

$$P(s) = \frac{1}{(s + 2)^2(s - 2)}\begin{bmatrix} s - 1 & -7 \\ 1 & s + 3 \end{bmatrix}$$

is meromorphic in $\mathrm{Re}(s) \geq 0$, unstable, and strictly proper. $P(s)$ is not diagonally dominant, as the largest element at

[2] *The point of this construction is to remove the RHP singularities of D(s) but to preserve its high-frequency behavior*

$s = 0$ is P_{12}. However, the off-diagonal transmissions attenuate faster than the diagonal ones as $s \to \infty$. Therefore, $P(s)$ is ultimately diagonal, approaching $s^{-2}I$. Also $P(s)$ is analytically invertible and

$$P^{-1}(s) = (s - 2)\begin{bmatrix} s + 3 & 7 \\ -1 & s - 1 \end{bmatrix}$$

$P(s)$ satisfies the attenuation condition $P(s) \geq \text{const } |s|^{-2}$ for large s. The hypotheses of Theorem 1A are therefore fulfilled with $k = 2$ and $\alpha = 0$.

Any ultimate inverse will do in (5), and in this rational example the diagonal $V(s) = s^2 I$ would be suitable. The more complicated construction of Theorem 1C, aimed at irrational plants, would yield in this case

$$D(s) = (s - 2)^{-1}(s + 2)^{-2} \operatorname{diag}[s - 1, s + 3]$$
$$D_V(s) = (s + s_0)^{-1}(s + 2)^{-2} \operatorname{diag}[s + s_0, s + 3], \tag{8}$$

and $F(s)$ would be defined by (5) with $V(s) = D_V^{-1}(s)$.

IV. REMARKS ON DECENTRALIZED CONTROL

Suppose that the inputs and disturbances drop off at high frequencies and are bounded by a diagonal strictly proper weighting function $W(s)$ in $\mathbb{B}^{\infty N}$, i.e.,

$$|d_i(j\omega)| \leq |W_i(j\omega)| \quad \text{and} \quad |u_i(j\omega)| \leq |W_i(j\omega)|$$

for $i = 1, \ldots, N$. The problem of decentralized control introduced in Section I,A is to realize some desired matrix $\operatorname{diag}[K_{ii}(s)]$ by means of a feedback $\operatorname{diag}[F_{ii}(s)]$ and prefilter $\operatorname{diag}[G_{ii}(s)]$ with arbitrarily good precision.

Let $F_{m,n}$ be the diagonal feedbacks (5) constructed in Theorems 1B-1C (see proofs), and let the prefilter $[G_{ii}(s)]$ coincide with $[K_{ii}(s)]$. Since $\|W(I + PF_{m,n})^{-1}\|_\infty \to 0$ as m, n $\to \infty$, by Corollary 1, it follows that the transmissions from v to y approach diag$[K_{ii}(s)]$ in the sense that

$$\|WPF_{m,n}(I + PF_{m,n})^{-1}K - WK\| = \|W(I + PF_{m,n})^{-1}K\| \to 0$$

(i.e., in the auxiliary norm $\|\cdot\|_W \triangleq \|W(\cdot)\|_\infty$). In other words, the system approaches diagonal for all possible inputs and disturbances bounded by $|W(j\omega)|$.

V. RELAXATION OF ULTIMATE DIAGONAL DOMINANCE

If we dispense with the requirement of diagonality, then we can also dispense with the assumption of ultimate diagonal dominance of P(s), and still achieve the low sensitivity stipulated in Theorem 1. For stable plants, this was in an earlier paper [2, Corollary 6.2] in which the stabilizing feedback were parametrized. The present derivation suggest an obvious alternative way of achieving the same result.

Theorem 2. If P(s) is not necessarily ultimately diagonally dominant but satisfies the other hypotheses of Theorems 1A-1B, then there exists a not necessarily diagonal feedback F(s) that satisfies the remaining conclusions of those theorems for any $M > 1$.

Theorem 2 is established by constructing the ultimate right α-inverse,

$$V(s) \triangleq P^{-1}(s + s_0),$$

valid for every $\alpha > 0$, with s_0 such that $V(s)$ has no $Re(s) \geq 0$ singularities (as in Section III,C). The rest of the proof of Theorem 2 is completely similar to that of Theorem 1.

VI. PROOFS

For any $R > 0$, let Ω_R denote the set $\{s : Re(s) \geq 0, |s| \geq R\}$. Therefore, Ω_0 denotes the closed RHP.

A. *PROOF OF THE LEMMA*

The hypotheses of Theorem 1A are assumed to hold. Let us first show that there are constants $R > 0$ and α_1 $(0 < \alpha_1 < 1)$ for which the inequalities

$$\bar{\sigma}[D(s)] \leq (1 - \alpha_1)^{-1}\bar{\sigma}[P(s)] \tag{9}$$

$$\underline{\sigma}[D(s)] \geq (1 + \alpha_1)^{-1}\underline{\sigma}[P(s)] \tag{10}$$

are true for all $s \in \Omega_R$.

From the ultimate diagonal dominance assumption on P, there are constants $R_0 > 0$ and α_1 $(\alpha < \alpha_1 < 1)$ for which

$$||P(s)D^{-1}(s) - I|| \leq \alpha_1, \quad \text{for} \quad s \in \Omega_{R_0}. \tag{11}$$

Since $P(s)$ is strictly proper, there exists R $(R \geq R_0)$ with the property that $P(s)$ is analytic in Ω_R. Also, $P^{-1}(s)$ is analytic in $Re(s) \geq 0$, and a fortiori in Ω_R. For any point s of Ω_R which is not a pole of $D(s)$, we have the inequalities

$$\begin{aligned} ||D(s)|| &= ||D(s)P^{-1}(s)P(s)|| \leq ||D(s)P^{-1}(s)|| \; ||P(s)|| \\ &= ||[I + P(s)D^{-1}(s) - I]^{-1}|| \; ||P(s)|| \\ &\leq \frac{||P(s)||}{1 - ||P(s)D^{-1}(s) - I||} \leq \frac{||P(s)||}{1 - \alpha_1}, \end{aligned} \tag{12}$$

where (11) has been used. Since (12) holds in some δ-neighborhood $0 < ||s - s_0|| < \delta$ of every point s_0 in Ω_R and $P(s)$ is analytic in Ω_R, s_0 cannot be a pole of D(s). It follows that D(s) is analytic in Ω_R and that (9) is true. From (9) and the strict propriety of P(s), D(s) must be strictly proper. Similarly, for any point $s \in \Omega_R$ which is not a pole of $D^{-1}(s)$, we have

$$\begin{aligned} \|D^{-1}(s)\| &= \|P^{-1}(s)P(s)D^{-1}(s)\| \\ &\leq \|P^{-1}(s)\| \; \|P(s)D^{-1}(s)\| \\ &\leq \|P^{-1}(s)\| \; (1 + \alpha_1) \end{aligned} \tag{13}$$

from which it follows that since $P^{-1}(s)$ is analytic in Ω_R, $D^{-1}(s)$ must also be analytic there, so that det $D(s) \neq 0$ and (13) holds for all $s \in \Omega_R$. Furthermore, since for any invertible matrix A, $\underline{\sigma}(A) = \|A^{-1}\|^{-1}$, (10) is true. (6) now follows from (10) and hypothesis (3) on $P(\cdot)$. Q.E.D.

B. PROOF OF THEOREM 1C

By construction, $D_V(s)$ is diagonal, analytic, and det $D_V(s)$ has no zeros in $\mathrm{Re}(s) \geq 0$. To prove the theorem we shall show that

$$\lim_{R\to\infty} \sup_{s\in\Omega_R} \|P(s)D_V^{-1}(s) - I\| = \alpha \tag{14}$$

Let all "lim sups" be defined as in (14). We obtain

$$\begin{aligned} &\lim\sup \|\{P(s) - D_V(s)\}D_V^{-1}(s)\| \\ &\quad = \lim\sup \|\{P(s) - D_V(s)\}D^{-1}(s)Z^{-1}(s)\| \\ &\quad = \lim\sup \|\{P(s) - D_V(s)\}D^{-1}(s)\| \\ &\qquad\qquad (\text{since} \quad Z^{-1}(s) \to I \quad \text{as} \quad s \to \infty) \\ &\quad = \lim\sup \|P(s)D^{-1}(s) - I + Z(s) - I\| \end{aligned}$$

$$= \lim \sup \|P(s)D^{-1}(s) - I\|$$

(since $[Z(s) - I] \to 0$ as $s \to \infty$)

$$= \alpha$$ Q.E.D.

C. *PROOF OF THEOREMS 1B AND 1A*

Suppose that the hypotheses of Theorem 1A are fulfilled, and constants $\epsilon > 0$, $\omega_0 > 0$, and $M > (1 - \alpha)^{-1}$ are given. Let $F(s)$ and $V(s)$ be defined as in Theorem 1B.

Step 1. Let us show that $F(\cdot)$ is strictly proper. Since $V(\cdot)$ is an ultimate α-inverse of $P(\cdot)$, we have

$$\lim \sup \|P(s)V(s)\| \leq 1 + \lim \sup \|P(s)V(s) - I\| = (1 + \alpha) \tag{15}$$

where lim sup denotes $\lim_{R\to\infty} \sup \Omega_R$. Now

$$\overline{\sigma}[V(s)] \leq \overline{\sigma}[P(s)V(s)]\overline{\sigma}[P^{-1}(s)] = \overline{\sigma}[P(s)V(s)]\{\underline{\sigma}[P(s)]\}^{-1} \tag{16}$$

and on applying (15) and (3) to (16) we conclude that

$$\overline{\sigma}[V(s)] \leq \text{const}|s|^k \tag{17}$$

for $s \in \Omega_{R_0}$, R_0 being large enough. On applying the bound (17) to Eq. (5) which defines $F(\cdot)$, we conclude that $F(s) \leq$ const $|s|^{-1}$ for $s \in \Omega_{R_0}$, and therefore that $F(\cdot)$ is strictly proper.

Step 2. Restrictions on m and n. Let $J_n(s)$ denote the $\mathbb{B}^\infty$ function

$$J_n(s) \triangleq n(s + n)^{-1}, \tag{18}$$

n being a positive integer. The feedback (5) can be expressed in the form

$$F(s) = \gamma V(s) J_m(s) J_n^k(s). \tag{19}$$

Without loss of generality we can restrict m and n to satisfy the inequalities

$$|J_m(j\omega)| > 2^{-1/2} \quad \text{for} \quad |\omega| \le \omega_0 \tag{20}$$

$$|J_n^k(j\omega)| > 2^{-1/2} \quad \text{for} \quad |s| \le \omega_0. \tag{21}$$

(20)-(21) will be true provided $m \ge \omega_0$, $n \ge [2^{k^{-1}} - 1]^{-1/2} \omega_0$. We also restrict m to be large enough so that P(s)V(s) is analytic in Ω_m; this is possible since P(s) is strictly proper and V(s) is analytic in $\text{Re}(s) \ge 0$.

Step 3. Let $\xi \triangleq \inf_{\text{Re}(s)\ge 0} \underline{\sigma}[P(s)V(s)]$, and let us show that $\xi \ne 0$. Since P(s) is analytically invertible in $\text{Re}(s) \ge 0$, and $\underline{\sigma}[P(s)] = ||P^{-1}(s)||^{-1}$, $\underline{\sigma}[P(s)]$ is a nonvanishing function of s in $\text{Re}(s) \ge 0$. A similar conclusion holds for V(s), which is analytically invertible by the hypotheses of Theorem 1B. It follows that $\underline{\sigma}[P(s)V(s)]$ is nonvanishing in $\text{Re}(s) \ge 0$. Also,

$$\begin{aligned} \lim\inf \underline{\sigma}[P(s)V(s)] &\ge 1 - \lim\sup \overline{\sigma}[P(s)V(s) - I] \\ &\ge (1 - \alpha) > 0 \end{aligned}$$

Therefore, $\underline{\sigma}[P(s)V(s)]$ is a continuous nonvanishing function of s in $\text{Re}(s) \ge 0$, which is bounded from below by a positive constant at infinity and must have a nonzero infimum, i.e., $\xi \ne 0$.

A fortiori, if we let

$$\xi_1 \triangleq \inf_{|\omega|\le\omega_0} \underline{\sigma}[P(j\omega)V(j\omega)],$$

then $\xi_1 > 0$.

$$\gamma \ge 2 \max\left[\xi_1^{-1}\left(1 + \frac{1}{\epsilon}\right),\ \xi^{-1}\left(1 + \frac{1}{M}\right)\right] \tag{22}$$

Let us show that this choice of γ ensures the following.

Step 4. Validity of (4) for $|s| \le m$. For any $|\omega| \le \omega_0$, the sensitivity function satisfies the following inequalities

$$\begin{aligned} ||(I + PF)^{-1}(j\omega)|| &\le |1 - \underline{\sigma}[P(j\omega)F(j\omega)]|^{-1} \\ &= \left\{\gamma\underline{\sigma}P(j\omega)V(j\omega)J_m(j\omega)J_n^k(j\omega) - 1\right\}^{-1} \end{aligned}$$

whenever γ is large enough to make the last expression positive. Now

$$\underline{\sigma}\left[J_m(j\omega)J_n^k(j\omega)\right] \geq \frac{1}{2} \quad \text{for} \quad |\omega| \leq \omega_0$$

by (20)-(21). Therefore, for γ large enough, we have

$$\|(I + PF)^{-1}(j\omega)\| \leq \left(\frac{1}{2}\gamma\underline{\sigma}[P(j\omega)V(j\omega)] - 1\right)^{-1}$$

$$\leq \left(\frac{1}{2}\gamma\xi_1 - 1\right)^{-1} = \epsilon \quad \text{(by (22))}$$

Similarly, it can be shown by (22) that

$$\|(I + PF)^{-1}(s)\| \leq M \quad \text{for} \quad |s| \leq m, \quad \text{Re}(s) \geq 0.$$

Therefore, our choice of γ ensures that $(I + PF)^{-1}(s)$ is analytic and that the inequalities (4) are satisfied for $\text{Re}(s) \geq 0$, $|s| \leq m$.

Step 5. Verification of (4) for $|s| \geq m$. We shall use the fact that $\gamma J_m(s)$ is positivie-real, i.e., that $\text{Re}[\gamma J_m(s)] \geq 0$. It follows from standard arguments about positivity and contractiveness [4] that the function $(1 + \gamma J_m)(s)$ is analytically invertible in $\text{Re}(s) \geq 0$ and satisfies the inequalities

$$\|(I + \gamma J_m)^{-1}(s)\| \leq 1 \tag{23}$$

$$\|\gamma J_m(1 + \gamma J_m)^{-1}(s)\| \leq 1 \tag{24}$$

(whose validity is also clear from the explicit formulas for the frequency responses involved).

The "return difference" [I + PF] is now expressed in terms of $\gamma J_m(s)$ as follows. For any $s \in \Omega_m$,

$$(I + PF)(s)$$

$$= \left(I + \gamma PVJ_mJ_n^k\right)(s)$$

$$= \left\{I + \gamma J_m + (PV - I)\gamma J_m + PV\gamma J_m\left(J_n^k - I\right)\right\}(s)$$

$$= \left\{I + \left[(PV - I)\gamma J_m + PV\gamma J_m\left(J_n^k - I\right)\right](I + \gamma J_m)^{-1}\right\}(I + \gamma J_m)(s)$$

$$\underline{\sigma}[(I + PF)(s)]$$

$$\geq \underline{\sigma}\left[\left\{I + \left[(PV - I)\gamma J_m + PV\gamma J_m\left(J_n^k - I\right)\right](I + \gamma J_m)^{-1}\right\}(s)\right]$$

(by (23))

$$\geq 1 - \underbrace{\left\|\left\{(PV - I)\gamma J_m(I + \gamma J_m)^{-1} + PV\gamma J_m\left(J_n^k - I\right)(I + \gamma J_m)^{-1}\right\}(s)\right\|}_{\theta(s)} \tag{25}$$

provided $\|\theta(s)\| \leq 1$. Now, $P(s)V(s)$ is analytic for $s \in \Omega_m$ (by choice of m) and we have

$$\|\theta(s)\| \leq \|(PV - I)(s)\| \; \|\gamma J_m(I + \gamma J_m)^{-1}(s)\|$$
$$+ \|P(s)V(s)\| \; \left\|\left\{\gamma J_m(I + \gamma J_m)^{-1}\left(J_n^k - I\right)\right\}(s)\right\|. \tag{26}$$

Now since V is an ultimate right α-inverse of P, there is an integer m_0 such that for any $m \geq m_0$, $\|(PV - I)(s)\| \leq \alpha_1$. Henceforth, suppose that $m \geq m_0$. We apply this result, (24), and the identity

$$\gamma J_m(I + \gamma J_m)^{-1} = \gamma(1 + \gamma)^{-1}J_{m(1+\gamma)}$$

to (26) to obtain

$$\|\theta(s)\| \leq \alpha_1 + \left\{\gamma(1 + \gamma)^{-1}\|P(s)V(s)\| \times \|J_{m(1+\gamma)}(s)\| \; \left\|\left(J_n^k - I\right)(s)\right\|\right\}. \tag{27}$$

Now as $J_{m(1+\gamma)}(s)$ and $J_n^k(s)$ are strictly proper, whenever m is fixed and $n \to \infty$, $\|J_{m(1+\gamma)}(s)\|$ approaches 0 uniformly in Ω_n, and $\left\|\left(J_n^k - I\right)(s)\right\|$ approaches zero uniformly in the region $\{s \in \Omega_m : s \notin \Omega_n\}$. Therefore

$$\sup_{s\in\Omega_m} \|J_{m(1+\gamma)}(s)\| \; \left\|\left(J_n^k - I\right)(s)\right\| \to 0 \quad \text{as} \quad n \to \infty.$$

Consequently, for n large enough, the { }-bracketed term on the right-hand side of (27) is less than $(1 - \alpha_1) - M^{-1}$, and then

$$\|\theta(s)\| \leq 1 - M^{-1} < 1. \tag{28}$$

From (28) and (25) it follows that $\underline{\sigma}[(I - PF)(s)] \geq M^{-1}$ for $s \in \Omega_m$, and therefore $(I + PF)^{-1}(s)$ is analytic and (4) holds for $s \in \Omega_m$.

Step 6. We have now shown that $(I + PF)^{-1}(s)$ is analytic and (4) holds for all $\mathrm{Re}(s) \geq 0$. It follows that $(I + PF)^{-1} \in \mathbb{B}^{\infty N}$. Also $F(I + PF)^{-1}$ is in $\mathbb{B}^{\infty N}$ since $F \in \mathbb{B}^{\infty N}$. It remains to be shown that the other closed-loop responses in the matrix (2) are in $\mathbb{B}^{\infty N}$.

Now, in Ω_m, both P and F are analytic and bounded, and therefore all the responses in (2) are analytic and bounded in Ω_m. (The boundedness of $(I + FP)^{-1}$ follows from the identity $(I + FP)^{-1} = I - F(I + PF)^{-1}P$.) Let us show analyticity for $|s| \leq m$, $\mathrm{Re}(s) \geq 0$.

Observe that $P(I + FP)^{-1} = (P^{-1} + F)^{-1}$. By choice of γ, for any $|s| \leq m$, $\mathrm{Re}(s) \geq 0$, we have $\underline{\sigma}[F(s)] > \overline{\sigma}[P^{-1}(s)]$. It follows that $\underline{\sigma}[P^{-1}(s) + F(s)] > 0$ there, so $P(I + FP)^{-1}$ is analytic and consequently also bounded in the compact region $|s| \leq m$, $\mathrm{Re}(s) \geq 0$. Also $(I + FP)^{-1}$ is bounded-analytic in that region since $(I + FP)^{-1} = P^{-1}P(I + FP)^{-1}$ and P^{-1} is analytic and bounded in that region. Consequently, $P(I + FP)^{-1}$ and $(I + FP)^{-1}$ are both in $\mathbb{B}^{\infty N}$, and the matrix (2) is stable. Q.E.D.

D. *PROOF OF THE COROLLARY*

Let M be any number satisfying

$$(1 - \alpha)^{-1} < M < \epsilon w_\infty^{-1} \tag{29}$$

since $w_\infty < M^{-1}\epsilon$ by (29), there exists $R > 0$ such that $\|W(s)\| < M^{-1}\epsilon$ for $|s| \geq R$, $\mathrm{Re}(s) \geq 0$. By Theorem 1A, there exists a feedback F such that

$$\|(I + PF)^{-1}(j\omega)\| < \epsilon[\sup_{|\omega_1|\leq R} \|W(j\omega_1)\|]^{-1}$$

for $|\omega| \leq R$ and $\|(I + PF)^{-1}(s)\| \leq M$ in $\mathrm{Re}(s) \geq 0$. We now have

$$\|W(I + PF)^{-1}(j\omega)\| \leq \|W(j\omega)\| \; \|(I + PF)^{-1}(j\omega)\|$$

which gives

$$\|W(I + PF)^{-1}(j\omega)\| \leq \epsilon\|W(j\omega)\| \; [\sup_{|\omega_1|\leq R} \|W(j\omega_1)\|]^{-1} \leq \epsilon$$

for $|\omega| \leq R$;

$$\|W(I + PF)^{-1}(j\omega)\| \leq \|W(j\omega)\|M \leq \epsilon \quad \text{for} \quad |\omega| \geq R$$

Consequently, $\|W(I + PF)^{-1}(j\omega)\| \leq \epsilon$ for all ω, and the corollary is true. Q.E.D.

REFERENCES

1. D. BENSOUSSAN, "Sensitivity Reduction in Multivariable Systems, " Ph.D. Thesis, McGill University, 1981.

2. G. ZAMES, "Feedback and optimal sensitivity: Model reference transformations, multiplicative seminorms, and approximate inverses," Proc. 17th Allerton Conf., Oct. 1979, pp. 744-752; also, in *IEEE Trans. Automat. Control AC-26* (2), 301-320 (1981).

3. G. ZAMES, "Contracting transformations — A theory of stability and iteration for nonlinear, time-varying systems," pp. 121-122, in 1964 Internat. Conf. on Microwaves, Circuit Theory and Information Theory.

4. G. ZAMES, "On the input-output stability of time-varying nonlinear feedback systems," Parts I and II, *IEEE Trans. Automat. Control AC-11*, 465-476 (1966).

5. M. I. FREEDMAN, P. L. FALB, and G. ZAMES, "A Hilbert Space Stability Theory over Locally Compact Abelian Groups," *SIAM J. Control 7* (3), 479-495 (1969).

INDEX

D

E

U

W